THE PURSUIT OF HERESY

Rabbi Moses Hagiz and the
Sabbatian Controversies

THE
PURSUIT
OF
HERESY
Rabbi Moses Hagiz and the
Sabbatian Controversies

ELISHEVA CARLEBACH

Columbia University Press
New York

Columbia University Press
New York   Chichester, West Sussex
Copyright © 1990 Columbia University Press

All rights reserved
Library of Congress Cataloging-in-Publication Data

Carlebach, Elisheva.
    The pursuit of heresy : Rabbi Moses Hagiz and the Sabbatian
controversies / Elisheva Carlebach.
    p. cm.
    "Winner of the Salo Baron Dissertation Prize in Jewish Studies"–
–P.
    Includes bibliographical references and index.
    ISBN 0-231-07190-6
    ISBN 0-231-07191-4 (pbk.)
    1. Hagiz, Moses, 1671–ca. 1750.   2. Rabbis—Biography.
3. Sabbathaians.   I. Title.
BM755.H19C37   1990
296'.092—dc20
[B]   90-41380
                                                                 CIP

Casebound editions of Columbia University Press books are printed
on permanent and durable acid-free paper.

⊗

Printed in the United States of America

c 10 9 8 7 6 5 4 3 2 1
p 10 9 8 7 6 5 4 3 2 1

משה, אברהם, ושרה
ילדים יקירים
אשר חנן אלקים אותי

Contents

Foreword

HISTORICAL SCHOLARSHIP often progresses dialectically. In nineteenth century Jewish historical writing an ingrained rationalist bias and
a need for apologetics combined to suppress or to vilify kabbalistic mysticism and the eruption of mystical messianic heresies from Sabbatai Zevi
to Jakob Frank. It was only in our century that Gershom Scholem, at
first singlehandedly and later with the aid of his disciples, restored Jewish mysticism and the kabbalah to a central place in Jewish historiography, and reconstructed the history of the Sabbatian movement and its
offshoots in a manner that rendered their ideologies intelligible and revealed their historical fates in their full tragic pathos.

The achievement of Scholem and his school is one of the most remarkable in modern Jewish scholarship and much of it will surely endure. We can now recognize, however, that their pioneering passion to
understand the heretics was so consuming that, perhaps inevitably, there
was little energy or desire left to understand the opponents and pursuers
of those very heretics. The result is that although a historical injustice
had been redressed, we still do not have a balanced picture of the phenomenon of heresy and counter-heresy as a whole. Yesterday's villains
have become today's heroes, while the former heroes, the guardians of
tradition, have been cast as villains or largely ignored. Clearly the time
is ripe for yet further reevaluation. We must begin to approach the opponents of Sabbatianism and its subsequent incarnations, not with the
schematic prejudice that they were Jewish inquisitors, but with the same

leap of empathy that has made possible such a rich understanding of the heretics themselves.

Such an approach may now be said to have begun with Elisheva Carlebach's path-breaking study of Moses Hagiz, one of the seminal figures in the post-Sabbatian heresies. With a broad background in Jewish history and an easy fluency in classical and medieval Hebrew texts, she has brought to this task a meticulous attention to detail that never loses sight of the larger trajectories. Above all, she has demonstrated a willingness and ability to approach her subject inductively and without bias. Her Hagiz is neither hero nor villain, his flaws are not glossed over even as his virtues are recognized. Without invoking "psycho-history" or any other methodological fashion, she has managed to understand at least some of his motivations and the factors, familial and external, that made him what he was.

At the same time, she has given us more than Hagiz himself. Like all true biographers, she has captured, through her protagonist, much of the texture of the age in which he lived and the world in which he moved. Thus her book illuminates such vital aspects of late seventeenth- and eighteenth-century Jewish history as the dynamics of the young or reconstituted communities of Northern Europe, the phenomenon of the itinerant rabbi so characteristic of the period, the links between leading anti-Sabbatians in several lands, and the erosion of the authority of the rabbinate in Western and Central Europe prior to the Haskalah. As such, her first book is already a major contribution to Jewish historiography.

It remains for me to close on a personal note. The fact is that this book requires no prefatory word from me or anyone else; it speaks for itself with sufficient force and eloquence. I regard my foreword simply as a symbolic opportunity to link my name to it and so close an arc that began to be drawn more than a decade ago with a tentative conversation in Cambridge, Massachusetts. Since that meeting I have witnessed her achievement of her doctorate, her appointment to the faculty of Queens College, and, most recently and appropriately, her receipt of the Salo and Jeanette Baron Award for the best dissertation written on a Jewish subject in any department of Columbia University during the past five years. I take this opportunity to thank her publicly for the sheer pleasure of working with her and knowing her over the years. It is from such as she that I remind myself, in faltering moments, that teaching in the academy is not a chore but a privilege.

Yosef Hayim Yerushalmi
Columbia University

Acknowledgements

THE COMPLETION of my book allows me to express my gratitude to the many who have had a share in it. I begin with the greatest debt of all, to my parents, who were my first and best teachers in life and in learning. To describe even a small amount of the nurturing and encouragement that they have provided would be impossible in this limited space. Dr. Jean Jofen has been a special source of inspiration to me.

I have been blessed with many wonderful teachers over the years. In Brooklyn College, Professor Teo Ruiz introduced me to the drama of history; Professor Elizabeth A.R. (Peggy) Brown to the importance of writing it well; and Professor David Berger, to the study of Jewish History. His rare combination of deep scholarship and humility remain an ideal for me. My students and colleagues at Touro College, and more recently at Queens College, CUNY, have taught me much and have always supported my work.

Professors Isaac Barzilai, Eugene Rice, Ismar Schorsch, and Michael Stanislawski were the first critics of my dissertation. All or portions of the manuscript were read by Professors David Berger, Sid Z. Leiman, David Ruderman, Teo Ruiz, and Rabbi Jacob J. Schachter. Their constructive comments saved me from many errors and helped to clarify many points.

The choice of Moses Hagiz as the ideal vehicle for the study of the eighteenth-century rabbinate grew out of a suggestion by Professor Yosef Hayim Yerushalmi. His careful reading and wise criticism inform every aspect of this book. His example as teacher and historian, and the warm friendship he continues to extend have immeasurably enriched my work and my life. His gracious acquiescence to my request for a Foreword is the least of the many ways he has encouraged the most tentative of students, and for his constant support I will always remain deeply thankful.

I gratefully acknowledge the financial support I have received for various stages of this work. I thank Columbia University for the President's Fellowship; the Memorial Foundation for Jewish Culture and Columbia's Center for Israel and Jewish Studies, for graduate fellowships; Queens College for a Faculty-in-Residence Award and a PSC-CUNY Research Award. The National Foundation for Jewish Culture provided generous grants for several years of graduate study, and the Lucius N. Littauer Foundation made it possible for me to complete the final stages of this book.

I thank the committee of the Faculty of Columbia's Graduate School of Arts and Sciences that chose this work for the first Salo and Jeanette Baron Prize in Jewish Studies. I was privileged to receive the prize from Professor Baron himself several months before his passing. It was his wish to have it published by Columbia University Press that brought book and publisher together.

The staffs of the Columbia University Library, the Jewish Theological Seminary Library, The Jewish Division of the New York Public Library, the Jewish National and University Library of Jerusalem, and the Central Archives for the History of the Jewish People have been extremely helpful. I owe a special debt of gratitude to the staff of Hebrew Union College's Klau Library where I spent many pleasant hours on the research and writing of this book. Head Librarian Dr. Phillip Miller, and his erudite assistant, my friend Mr. Henry Resnick, graciously accomodated my every request, and spared no effort to procure the materials I needed. On my recent visit to Jerusalem, Mrs. Etty Liebes and the staff at the Scholem Library were exceedingly gracious.

I thank the American Academy for Jewish Research for permission to publish portions of my article "Redemption and Persecution in the Eyes of Moses Hayim Luzzatto and his Circle," *PAAJR*, (1987) 54:1–29.

Malka Gold maintained her good cheer through innumerable drafts of this manuscript. Her sound advice and eye for fine detail were indispensable. My editors at Columbia University Press, Kate Wittenberg and Leslie Bialler, and my friend Saralie Faivelson contributed their editorial expertise.

Despite so many excellent contributors to the final shape of this book, errors, omissions, and perversities remain. For these, I bear full responsibility.

Elisheva Carlebach
New York, 1990

THE PURSUIT OF HERESY

Rabbi Moses Hagiz and the
Sabbatian Controversies

Introduction

 THE LIFE of Rabbi Moses Hagiz [1671–1751] spanned a period of turmoil and uncertainty in the Jewish communities of Western Europe.[1] In an era of expulsion and resettlement, as old communities were dissolved and new ones established, the most venerable institutions within the Jewish community were challenged to their core. The rabbinate, never a monolithic establishment in the medieval period, suffered a great erosion of its powers. Newly constituted Jewish communities unrestrained by the trammels of traditional political configurations kept the reins of power firmly in the hands of the founding lay elite. A tradition of hostility toward religious authority accompanied some Iberian Jewish exiles, or their Marrano successors, and it flourished in their new abodes. Lurianic Kabbalah in its various permutations profoundly altered the spiritual landscape, while the Renaissance ideals of humanism and historicism influenced intellectual discourse. Conflicting forces of martyrdom and apostasy, science and mysticism, rational skepticism and messianic activism tore at the fabric of Jewish communal life. It is against this background that we must seek to understand the rabbinic quest for a center that would hold.

(1)

THE QUEST FOR CENTER

The most celebrated attempt to create a center in Jewish life in the early modern period was the sixteenth-century Safed attempt to revive *semik-hah*, ordination. The revival of this ancient means of transmitting apostolic authority would be the first step toward the creation of the Sanhedrin, the highest Jewish court and ancient center of supreme judicial authority. It was one of the most powerful expressions of the passionate yearning for a tangible core of unity and authority in Jewish life which surfaced in centers of Sephardic Jewry, sometimes generations after the expulsions which had led to the formation of the Sephardic Diaspora. The various messianic, mystical, and psychological dimensions that converged in the attempt to revive semikhah, and its importance as an expression of profound weariness with the exile should not obscure the central fact that the entire drama was enacted squarely within the rabbinic ambit.

In the seventeenth century, there was another rabbinic initiative to create an authoritative center, this time in Jerusalem. The author of that attempt was Jacob Hagiz, father of the subject of this book. His approach differed in many respects from that of the Safed group. He set out to accomplish de facto what the Safed rabbis had failed to do de jure: to make Jerusalem a center of authority for all Jewry, primarily rabbinic in nature. For a brief time in the mid-seventeenth century the experiment was a remarkable success. A rabbinic circle of international stature gathered around Jacob Hagiz. The works that were produced by members of the circle remain halakhic classics. Jacob Hagiz' effort to establish a new Jerusalem was derailed by an event that turned attention away from his austere circle of scholars. The eyes of all Jews were trained on a new center stage occupied by a spectacular messiah and his retinue. The messianic movement led by Sabbatai Zebi can be seen as the culmination of a different path in the quest for center. It emphasized the redemptive power of revelatory and ecstatic religious expression, in contrast to the traditional rabbinic stress on scholarship and piety. Jacob Hagiz died before he could formulate an effective response to Sabbatianism, and his dream of a central rabbinic authority in Jerusalem did not materialize.

These events form the background and genesis of Moses Hagiz' construction of an ideal typology for the rabbinate. He translated his father's dream of a center into a lifelong mission to fortify and rebuild rabbinic authority. Hagiz' career embodied the will to mold a community unified in belief and practice, to impose a consensus, and to eliminate dissent.

Given the strife and uncertainty that already marked Jewish communal life, the foundations were laid for a period of unprecedented controversy and communal conflict.

THE CHRONOLOGICAL and geographical range of Hagiz' career, as well as his varied interests and wide circle of contacts, make Hagiz an ideal vehicle by which to portray the vicissitudes of his age. As is the case with every biography, the illumination shed by the life depends on the position of the subject. In the case of Hagiz, we are seeing history from the perspective of an elite within the Jewish community. Hagiz had a very distinctive sense of his leadership role, and his concerns were directed primarily toward leaders, not the masses.

Hagiz wrote original works in the fields of halakha, Biblical exegesis, ethics, and social criticism. As a result of his prodigious activities in the world of Hebrew publishing, he saw scores of his own and other's works to print. Some of his writings have survived in manuscript, while other products of his prolific pen were lost. For the biographer of Hagiz, the biggest loss is his autobiography, *Hayyei Moshe*, [The Life of Moses], which apparently did not survive, along with half of his opus, *Mishnat Hakhamim*. While Hagiz' social criticism and his polemics dominate his historical profile and emerge as the most fruitful subjects in this study, the multifaceted character of his career and achievements should not be obscured. If Hagiz' attainments in the field of Halakha, ethics, or exegesis did not endure as works of the very first rank, they were nevertheless respected and substantial and must be counted in the overall measure of his career.[2]

PARALLEL CAREERS

For Hagiz, the move from the Jerusalem of his youth, from circles of idealists steeped in the sanctity of the Holy Land, to the secularized, lay dominated communities in Western Europe, produced a profound sense of rupture. Hagiz first came to prominence in Western Europe in his role as critic of Jewish society. The main theme of his outspoken criticism of religious and moral lapses, real and perceived, was the failure to accord proper honor to the authority of the rabbinate. Hagiz' role in confronting challenges to rabbinic authority and tradition has long been noted by historians, from Azriel Shohat's *Im Hilufei Tekufot* to the recent study by Shalom Rosenberg, "Emunat Hakhamim." His passionate call for a return to an idealized past, in which rabbinic sages exercised absolute authority over every aspect of Jewish religious life, reached its fullest expression in his most significant work, *Mishnat Hakhamim* [*The Lore of the Sages*].

Hagiz judged the Jewish communities of Western Europe against this ideal and found them lacking. His sharp strictures, often directed at powerful figures, pitted him against vested interests in the community. In this respect, Hagiz' career can be considered a prototype of other rabbinic careers in the seventeenth and eighteenth centuries. Many rabbis who had emigrated from the Levant to Western Europe, as Hagiz had, felt similarly alienated from the lay dominated and sometimes hostile communities. In some cases, this sense of alienation was reinforced by their inability to secure appropriate rabbinic positions. Hagiz was one of a cadre of itinerant rabbis of the highest caliber and ability relegated to the periphery of the communal structure. Their status as outsiders freed them to be more acutely critical than their counterparts who were caught up in mundane administrative duties. Their pronouncements contributed to the very atmosphere of crisis that they decried.

Many of these prominent rabbinic careers contained striking parallels to Hagiz' and were shaped by a similar constellation of influences. One of the earliest exemplars of this pattern was R. Isaac Uziel of Fez. A scholar of prodigious interests and abilities, Uziel fled from North Africa in the early seventeenth century to the fledgling community of Amsterdam, where he languished for several years without a position. When he was later appointed rabbi of the Neveh Shalom congregation in Amsterdam, his tenure was fraught with controversy. In his sermons, he ceaselessly inveighed against laxity in ritual observance, and he singled out "Marranos who had not completely abandoned Christian views." Perhaps he felt especially constrained to establish a strict code of "normative" conduct and beliefs in a community too young to be bound by precedents. As a result of the friction he caused, many individuals left Uziel's congregation to form their own. Such division as a result of communal friction had already become a standard response in the sixteenth century. Although we do not have Uziel's own account of these events, the transition from the idealized society of his youth to the new mercantile colony of Amsterdam was decisive for Uziel.[3]

The pattern of a traumatic dislocation and acute alienation in a new society, followed by an attempt to re-create the new society in the image of the idealized one, is repeated in the career of Jacob Sasportas. Born in Oran, Algeria (1610) to a rabbinic family descended from Spanish exiles, Sasportas' rise in the rabbinic ranks was meteoric. At age 18, he was appointed a member of the rabbinic court at Tlemçen, where he subsequently became chief rabbi. In 1647, when his political activities turned into a dangerous liability, Sasportas was forced to flee for his life. After his arrival in Amsterdam his position altered greatly. Unable to secure a rabbinic position, he earned a pittance as an editor and proofreader for the press of Menasseh ben Israel. Sasportas expressed the anguish and estrangement he felt during this period, a fall "from the heights to the depths of a deep well." He felt like a "young fly whose wings had been clipped." Despite Amsterdam's "renown as a city of scholars and a generous haven for refugees," Sasportas felt "like a stranger in the land, a guest who had come to spend the night."

Sasportas traveled to major Sephardic capitals in Western Europe, and held brief appointments as rabbi in London, Hamburg, and Livorno. Although he had taken positions on social issues before his departure from North Africa, the role of critic now became the preeminent one. Throughout his peregrinations, Sasportas conducted a campaign to restore rabbinic authority and prestige. Marranism as a matrix of Jewish heterodoxy was one of his key themes. "They ridiculed the words of our Sages . . . and are to be judged as heretics." Conversos who chose not to reintegrate into the Jewish community posed a further threat. By remaining on the periphery of the community, they reminded rejudaized Marranos of the voluntary nature of their commitment, further eroding the tenuous hold of Jewish religious authority over them. Sasportas' campaign against the Sabbatian messianic movement must be seen in the context of his career as a social critic. The predominant theme in his anti-Sabbatian chronicle Zizat Nobel Zebi is that a Messiah who did not conform to rabbinic predictions, and whose antinomian tendencies were manifest, would undermine Jewish tradition.

In 1680, Sasportas mounted a vituperative and sustained campaign against the lay leaders of Livorno who had passed an ordinance that would wrest the litigation of torts from rabbinic courts. The lay leaders were ultimately forced to retract the ordinance; the rabbinate won a fleeting victory. Like Hagiz, Sasportas considered himself to be a representative of the "old order" and respect was due to his position rather than his person. He claimed that his sensitivity to slights against his honor went beyond personal egotism. When Sasportas was censured for violating the jurisdiction of other rabbis, he replied that the issues involved transcended the domain of individual rabbis. Sasportas died shortly after his appointment to the rabbinate of Amsterdam, after a lifetime pursuing controversy.[4]

R. Hayim Yosef David Azulai [HID″A] was another eminent rabbi whose career contained striking resemblances to that of Hagiz. Born in Jerusalem in 1724 to an eminent rabbinic family, Azulai traveled through Europe and the Ottoman Empire as an emissary of a yeshiva in Hebron. A scholar of the first rank, he soon developed a reputation as an intercessor. In disputes between scholars and laymen, Azulai would champion the cause of the scholars, although he prided himself on using skillful diplomacy rather than confrontation.[5]

All these figures created a typology of the rabbinate and its position within the Jewish community based on nostalgia for an idealized past. They pronounced their disappointment and frustration with the decline of rabbinic authority and other Jewish traditional values in Western European Jewish communities. The historian Jacob Katz has commented that the role of figures such as Jacob Sasportas, Moses Hagiz, Jacob Emden, and Elijah, Gaon of Vilna, was necessarily limited because they stood outside the communal organization and their authority was based on voluntary supracommunal recognition. However, from the case of Hagiz, we can argue that their power derived precisely from their freedom from communal constraints. Their function was not to wield authority but to influence and activate those in positions of power, to use it in the direction which they urged.

Ezekiel Katzenellenbogen argued that he was a professional rabbi, while Hagiz was the professional zealot who occupied a special role outside the parameters of the institutional rabbinate.

> I am a very busy man, I have no leisure whatsoever, I am engaged in the study of the Torah and burdened by public affairs while your honor [Hagiz] is free from one of these obligations, for you do not bear the burden of the public. Therefore it is incumbent upon you to investigate thoroughly."

In the career of Hagiz we have an opportunity to examine in detail the causes and nature of individual religious zealotry. No evaluation of his role would be complete without consideration of his personal proclivity for zealotry. His polemics were suffused with a conviction that he was destined for historic achievement. "I have zealously pursued the cause of God, at the imperative of my father and grandfathers, for the Crown of the Torah and of the Good Name have never ceased from our illustrious family, of the sages and scholars of Castile." The bleak prospect of remaining a childless last link to this great chain may have contributed to his need to seal it with a shining moment of glory.[6] Hagiz' analysis of contemporary events, and his role within them, was influenced by a heroic self image: "It is a special kindness of the Lord's that these heretics have arisen first in our generation, so that we can be the first to stand in the breach and refute them." The title page of one of his polemical works queried dramatically whether such wickedness had ever existed among Jews since the exodus from Egypt. Obscuring the closer historical antecedents of the controversy served to amplify and emphasize the importance of events of his own day. Hagiz pledged his steadfast commitment to the thankless role: "I will persist in being a rod of chastisement to them all my days on this earth."

As the particulars of Hagiz' career unfold, there is ample opportunity to compare and contrast his responses to those of his rabbinic colleagues. The correspondence of Hagiz (who advocated zealous extirpation of all deviance) with Samson Morpurgo (who championed individual imperative above external conformity) is a wonderful example of the conflict between these two voices within the rabbinate. Some rabbis rejected Hagiz' confrontational tactics while others avidly adopted heresiology and polemic as a primary preoccupation. This exclusive focus on combating heresy as a mainstay of a rabbinic career is a virtual novum in early modern Jewish history. While we seek answers to account for zealotry in the seventeenth and eighteenth centuries, the contemporary resonances of these concerns are apparent.

HAGIZ AND THE SABBATIAN CONTROVERSIES

Although Hagiz built upon and shared the legacy of his rabbinic iconoclastic predecessors, in some respects, particularly with regard to his polemics, he was unique. He surpassed the others in his elevation of controversy to pride of place, and in his rejection of the value of the individual rabbinic voice in favor of a rabbinate unified through polemical campaign. Hagiz is the central figure in an entire chapter in the history of internal Jewish polemic that has hitherto remained unwritten. Unlike his social criticism, whose ultimate effect is blunted because it was directed at many different elements, his polemical attacks always featured Sabbatians as their sole target.

Who were the Sabbatians? Sabbatai Zebi led a popular messianic movement that reached its apogee in 1666. He later converted to Islam under duress; he died in 1676. Many of his adherents refused to relinquish their faith even in the face of his apostasy and death. Their inner experience of a new era had been so profound that even historical events could not sway their beliefs. For a brief period after these stunning developments, the term Sabbatian simply implied an obstinate belief in the messianic mission of Sabbatai, despite everything.

This overt messianism had long been repudiated by the time of Moses Hagiz. His generation was confronted with a more complex legacy, of a spiritual movement that had developed far beyond its point of origin, in many different directions. The complexion of Sabbatianism manifested itself in two interrelated but not identical ways: Sectarianism and heretical theology. The sectarian aspects included the closely ordered circles of social contacts, and deviations in calendrical observances, prayers and rituals among circles of the "believers." These circles varied widely with regard to the degree of deviance from normative practice. Some, performing only occasional symbolic violations, were barely distinguishable from the many circles of pietists and spiritual seekers that proliferated in the Jewish world, while others practiced extreme antinomian rituals and bizarre acts. Regardless of where an individual group stood along the spectrum, this network of clandestine contacts, with its own charismatic and authoritative figures, provided many Jews with an alternative source of social consensus which circumvented and weakened conventional rabbinic authority.

The second aspect of Sabbatianism provided the intellectual underpinnings of the sectarian developments. Sabbatian theology is rooted in Lurianic Kabbalah. Its key elements were transfigured into a distinctive doctrine, formulated initially by Nathan of Gaza to justify Sabbatai's strange acts, and subsequently expanded to justify the apostasy. It was a doctrine rooted in paradox, in which conditions of exile still existed after the redemption had begun; in which the redeemer had to plumb the depths of evil and darkness before the era of light could begin. This theology developed in two different directions. In the first instance, it remained the central unifying doctrine for committed believers in their various incarnations, from Nathan of Gaza to Barukhya Russo to Jacob Frank. The figure of Sabbatai was central to this strain of Sabbatian theology, which retained a strong, open relationship to its Sabbatian roots. Its followers tended to practice the most radical deviations.

Sabbatian kabbalah also developed in a second direction. Retaining some of the elements that Nathan had introduced, such as the centrality of a messiah figure for the final act of cosmic restoration (tikkun), and the multiple nature of the Godhead, it became increasingly distanced from its historical Sabbatian roots. Kabbalah had absorbed stronger and stranger heretical influences in the past. There remains the tantalizing possibility that these ideas would have been absorbed as a legitimate branch of kabbalah if they had not been tainted by these historical roots. Many who were branded Sabbatians did not necessarily accept all the assumptions and conclusions of the most committed Sabbatian believers, yet they were attracted to the theosophical issues raised by this line of Kabbalistic inquiry. Most moderate Sabbatians continued to conduct their lives as before, with a more heightened awareness of an imminent messianic denouement. These moderate Sabbatians were the target of Hagiz' campaigns.

Hagiz was the chief architect of three major anti-Sabbatian controversies in the early eighteenth century. In order to highlight the variations and progressions in Hagiz' polemical discourse, I shall structure the account of the controversies in broadly chronological order. Hagiz initiated the Hayon controversy of 1713; the Sabbatian controversy in Eastern and Central Europe of 1725–26; and the Luzzatto controversy of 1730–36. The target of the first polemical war was an itinerant Kabbalist, Nehemiah Hiya Hayon, originally from Sarajevo. Although he published his first "heretical" book in Venice, and another in Berlin, it was in Amsterdam, where Hagiz then resided, that rabbinic zealots began their first efforts to pursue and persecute Hayon. Hundreds of rabbis from dozens of Jewish communities in Europe and the Levant participated at Hagiz' urging.

The polemic against the Sabbatians was renewed several years later. Its primary target in this instance was a group of wandering students and preachers. They were accused of being Sabbatian emissaries, distributing Sabbatian documents, and disseminating Sabbatian lore in the course of their travels. In some towns of Central Europe and Poland, the inns frequented by these suspected emissaries were subject to surprise raids by rabbinic pursuivants, who opened the luggage of the travelers to check for tainted manuscripts. The manuscript mentioned most frequently in the sources was *ve-Abo ha-Yom el ha-'Ayin* [*And I Came This Day upon the Fountain*], a kabbalistic treatise betraying definite Sabbatian influence, attributed to R. Jonathan Eybeschutz. The emissaries were also accused of deviant sexual practices. Although only the most extreme Sabbatians engaged in ritual antinomian acts, it was common for their opponents to portray the entire sect with the most unflattering aspects of its most extreme members.

The Luzzatto controversy of the following decade provoked impassioned debate on a broader spectrum of substantive issues than any of its predecessors. A young Italian literary genius, Moses Hayim Luzzatto of Padua, and the members of his circle, were the focus of this six year controversy. Luzzatto, a highly gifted Hebrew poet, kabbalist, and essayist, was a visionary who claimed to have received revelations of mystical lore through angelic visitations. Although Luzzatto was accused of being a Sabbatian, the controversy ultimately shifted to a larger question: the possibility of the renewal of divine revelation. Hagiz contended that the consequences would be unthinkable; Luzzatto's supporters argued that the possibility always existed and the door to divine illumination must always remain open. A result of the protracted controversy over Luzzatto was the severe persecution of this promising figure, resulting ultimately in his flight from his hometown, and his premature demise on the road.

In addition to his deliberate orchestration of the controversies, Hagiz modernized the techniques of controversy, refining the old standbys and implementing new and effective methods. Hagiz recast the dissenting Jewish past to provide the ideological underpinning for his career as a professional rabbinic zealot. His polemical interpretation of Sabbatianism tended to conflate Sabbatianism with other well-known Jewish sects of the past. At various times he likened Sabbatians to Samaritans, Saducees and Boethusians, and Karaites. Hagiz' goal was to force Sabbatianism into the same byways of Jewish history as other ancient sects. His polemical merging of Sabbatian sectarianism with other sectarian movements of the past is paralleled by a similar purposeful obfuscation of divisions within the Sabbatian camp. Complex distinctions between Sabbatian subgroups were deliberately obscured in the course of the polemic, although Hagiz was thoroughly acquainted with the spectrum of ideologies which made up eighteenth century Sabbatianism. It was easier and more dramatic to simplify the welter of different voices into one starkly drawn adversary. This was Hagiz' definition of the sect to be ostracized: "The villains are . . . all those . . . , from the upheaval of Sabbatai Zebi until today . . . and anyone following any of their wickedness, or nuance thereof." Generalization in this manner enabled the polemicist to project the most aberrant characteristics of some individuals in the group onto the entire group.

Nowhere in his works did Hagiz admit to the existence of Sabbatian believers who were devout and scrupulously observant. The entire rabbinic polemical oeuvre could not comprehend, or more likely, could not admit to, a Sabbatianism which did not possess all the extreme tenets of the more radical segments. This ideological casting of Sabbatianism as a perverse, heretical ideology and its adherents as depraved deviants provided the framework for the next logical step in the campaign, the attempt to isolate the Sabbatians into a sectarian existence. Once he established that Sabbatians were dangerous sectarians, Hagiz demanded that they should be segregated from the Jewish community.

THE CONFLICT BETWEEN RABBINIC AUTHORITY
AND LAY LEADERSHIP

The age-old tension between rabbinic and lay leadership was a subtext of Hagiz' career and a source of considerable conflict in the Sabbatian controversies. Hagiz identified three instruments of communal authority and consensus which he wanted to bring under sole rabbinic control: *herem*, *haskamah*, and *hebrah*. Herem, the ban of excommunication, along with its less potent variants, *niddui* and *shamta*, had been one of the most powerful weapons of social control available to communal leaders. From an expression of censure to total ostracism, the mere threat of herem generally kept deviance well checked. The power of herem underlay the constitution of every Jewish community, and it was invoked for many infractions. Essentially Talmudic in origin, the use of herem was adopted and greatly expanded by medieval Jewish communities. Herem could be leveled against individuals or groups, by rabbis or lay leaders.

In the early modern period herem became one of the pawns in the struggle between lay and rabbinic leaders. Hagiz and many colleagues resorted ever more frequently to the pronunciation of bans as a means of asserting their right to exercise this important power. Invoking their traditional right to excommunicate heretics, some rabbis used herem whenever the opportunity presented itself. Slighting a rabbi or deviating in minor custom could be construed as heresy, and the rabbis often used these grounds to excommunicate lay leaders or even other rabbis. As a result the force of herem diminished with frequent use, and the image of rabbinic contentiousness was heightened. The indiscriminate use of bans in the Sabbatian controversies had the opposite effect of the one intended by Hagiz. Instead of becoming a new source of power for the rabbinate, the effectiveness of bans was further diluted, so that by the late eighteenth century, their use—by any authority—was a formality with very little real impact.[7]

A second medium of communal power which Hagiz tried to reclaim for the rabbinate throughout the controversies was the haskamah, approbation of books. From the time of the earliest Hebrew books printed during their author's lifetime, rabbinic haskamot were de rigueur, placed first at the end of books and later after the title page. They served many purposes. Ostensibly, they were letters of recommendation to rabbinic colleagues. In addition, they often served the purpose of copyright, protecting an author's exclusive right to reprint his work within a specified time. Haskamot became a means of exercising Jewish self-censorship, as well as intracommunal censorship. In 1554, a rabbinical synod in Ferrara passed an ordinance that required the haskamot of three rabbis before the first edition of any book could be printed. Many communal ordinances passed in Eastern Europe similarly required rabbinic pre-publication approval.

As Hebrew printing flourished, rabbinic scholars, especially those in cities with Hebrew presses, were inundated with requests for haskamot. Rabbis could not always find the time to read all the manuscripts that were sent to them for approbation, while authors found it impractical and costly to send entire bulky manuscripts over long distances in order to procure a prestigious haskamah. A practice developed of sending only sample leaves, often preprinted especially for that purpose. Moses Hagiz had engaged in this practice when he sought to publish his own works. An author could finance his work more easily once the haskamot had been obtained. The writing of rabbinic haskamot began to deteriorate into an empty formality. Any approbation given under such circumscribed circumstances could not really comment on the contents of the book. Proper editorial "censorship" of books occurred only after a book was published. Then, it could be banned or confiscated if the contents proved to be objectionable. This power resided mainly in the hands of the lay leadership. Hagiz believed that rabbinic scholars had relinquished an important prerogative when they relaxed their pre-publication censorship. In order to recover this power for the rabbinate, he urged a renewed emphasis on the aspect of consent and approval in haskamot.

ANOTHER CHALLENGE to rabbinic authority in early modern Jewish society was posed by the proliferation of hebrot, voluntary fraternities. These associations had religious or social goals, such as study of holy texts or social welfare and charity. The hebrot formed a social infrastructure parallel to the communal hierarchy—often cooperating with it, sometimes overlapping it, but completely independent of it. The founding charters of many societies often expressed dissatisfaction with the conditions existing in the community.

The small size of the fraternities, twenty members on average, meant that every member played an important role in them. The number of hebrot, often twenty or thirty in a large city, meant that a significant proportion of the Jewish population looked to these fraternities for their primary social identity. Since admittance to a hebrah was often restricted on the basis of wealth, family, and scholarship, membership was a coveted privilege. For some, expulsion from a hebrah was sometimes the equivalent of excommunication. According to the historian Jacob Katz, the associations often served as an alternative for those who could not attain leadership positions within the communal structure. The elite of wealth and scholarship were rabbis and *parnassim* of the community, while the next tier would assume leadership of the hebrot. Communal leaders were often forbidden to fill similar positions in a hebrah, which maintained their own prayer groups or were allocated special opportunities to lead the services in the main synagogue. Some study societies had their own scholarly leaders, *Marbizei Torah*, who functioned as the rabbi or Hakham of the group. The tensions with the rabbinate provoked by the solidarity of a hebrah can be seen from the following responsum:

> "May the rabbis excommunicate those who strut through the city streets with false pretensions to scholarship? There is a hebrah of undertakers, consisting of 150 members, all loyal to one another. Some have joined forces against a local scholar and the rest avert their eyes. They strut about the city pretending to be scholars. So the scholars put them under ban, not to strut about this way, as it would be an embarrassment for the Torah. The members of the hebrah refused to obey the scholars. They added to their original offense by gathering their members from all other synagogues and making their own synagogue, and they have refused to appoint a hakham over themselves."

From this responsum we can see how a hebrah came into direct conflict with rabbinic authority and how its members flaunted their independence of it. This particular hebrah was blamed for fostering an anti-rabbinic atmosphere, caricaturing rabbinic posture, and refusing to permit any rabbinic authority to prevail over their circle. This hebrah had become a sufficient source of social consensus for its members, another symbol of the forces that diminished the authority of the traditional rabbinate. The same can be said for the circles that nurtured Sabbatianism, and later, Hasidism as well. Although Hagiz did not argue for the elimination of hebrot, two of the three campaigns he conducted were against members of these circles.[8]

Although the rabbinate and lay leadership did contend for the right to be the arbiters of Jewish thought and social control, we should not conclude that the rabbinate wished to suppress dissent while lay leaders championed tolerance. To the contrary: the lay leaders used their power to stifle any discordant notes sounded within the Jewish community. The founding fathers of the Jewish communities in which the Sabbatian controversies erupted—London, Amsterdam, and Hamburg—were all too

aware of the tenuous, and very recent nature of their foothold. Many
were themselves victims or refugees from persecution. Numerous parallels can be found to demonstrate that refugees from intolerance are not
necessarily willing to extend the rights they have painfully gained to others. The rigid standards of conformity and limits of toleration demanded
by the Jewish lay communal authorities of the seventeenth and eighteenth centuries were conditioned by their own experience of persecution. Those who had developed successful polemical mechanisms to parry
the thrusts of their mortal religious foes easily adapted them to internal
polemical battles. The issue of security also played a role. Jewish communal leaders believed that the newly granted toleration by Christian
society extended only to those who shared the belief system of normative
(rabbinic) Judaism. They felt a civic duty to suppress any deviance that
might reflect negatively on the ideological wholesomeness of the Jewish
community.

HISTORIOGRAPHICAL CONSIDERATIONS

Two areas of Jewish historiography converge in a study of Hagiz' career:
rabbinic biography and Sabbatian studies, the latter having burgeoned
into a very substantial subdiscipline of Kabbalah studies. These two fields
have had a dramatic and problematic confrontation in the work of Gershom Scholem, which, needless to say, has provided the essential background and stimulus for the present work. While doing more than any
contemporary historian of the Jews to assail the idea of a monolithic Judaism, Scholem has transferred this concept to the rabbinate, where it
is equally unsuitable.

The rabbinic perspective has shaped the Jewish historical imagination
through the medieval period. In mapping out its geography the sects
were always relegated to byways. Rabbinic historiography was based on
a particular view of the ideal Jewish society, which was symbiotically
bound to halakhah, and to rabbinic leadership; everything else was ancillary. Sects were projected as anti-rabbinic, and therefore outside mainstream Judaism; Sabbatianism was no exception. Rabbinic opponents
preserved the records of the movement and its sectarian offshoots as a
warning to posterity of the dangers of premature messianism. Jacob Sasportas, Moses Hagiz, and Jacob Emden preserved unique records and
presented Sabbatianism as an exemplar of the most vile and subversive
Jewish messianism and heresy since the birth of Christianity. A close

reading of Sasportas and Emden show that they were remarkably aware of the power of controlling the historical record. Their attempts to conflate Sabbatianism with other ancient heresies, although they clearly had no historical link, is typical of rabbinic historiography.

The practitioners of Wissenschaft des Judentums sensed the continuity between the development of Kabbalah and Sabbatianism, and condemned both, in the most colorful terms, as alien to the essence of Judaism. Some, such as Heinrich Graetz, David Kahana, and Sha"i Hurewitz, made significant contributions to the knowledge of Sabbatianism long before the work of Scholem. Nevertheless, as was the case with other Jewish sects, all the records of this movement had been preserved by those who regarded it with the greatest contempt. Jewish memory of these events was molded by a succession of interests bent on preserving the memory in the most negative light, and as outside of, or at best peripheral to, mainstream Jewish history.

The recent maturation of Karaite studies, with its new evaluation of the dynamic relationship of Karaism with the Geonic establishment, contains implications for the new more pluralistic way in which historians have begun to view Judaism and its sects in the past century. Scholem's analogous transvaluation of Sabbatianism can best be described in his own words: "Eben ma'asu ha-bonim, hayta le-rosh pina. [The stone rejected by the masons became the cornerstone"] Scholem's description is perfectly accurate. He took a despised and repudiated sect and transformed it into a cornerstone for a new "pluralistic hermeneutic" of Judaism. Scholem's words contain the explanation for both the celebration of his work, as well as the impassioned criticism which followed its publication. In the words of the literary critic Barukh Kurzweil, "*Sabbatai Zebi* was not a new historiography of Sabbatianism, it was a new historiography of Judaism." As was the case with other Jewish sects and movements, its elevation to a legitimate branch of historical inquiry was long overdue. More scholarly work and popular attention have been focused on this aspect of Scholem's work than perhaps on any other.

The Sabbatian movement is the line of demarcation for Scholem's periodization of Jewish History: its nihilistic forces shattered medieval ghetto existence and by hastening the breakdown of traditional Jewish society, ushered in the modern era. Sabbatianism, for Scholem, is the matrix of every significant movement to have emerged in the eighteenth and nineteenth century, from Hasidism, to Reform Judaism, to the earliest masonic circles and revolutionary idealism.

For Scholem, halakhic, or rabbinic Judaism was an inhibiting force, developed by the exigencies of the dialectical process which had lost its capacity for renewal because it had no central myth. Scholem's interpretation of kabbalah as counter-force perpetuated the construct of an oppressive conservative rabbinic Judaism, incapable of inner renewal. He revived an old caricature of the rabbinic establishment out to perpetuate itself and suppress all affirmations of renewal and redemption. This is one of the harshest evaluations of rabbinic or traditional Judaism in the present century, not unlike the programmatic attacks in the nineteenth century of the very circles he set out to replace.[9]

When Raphael Mahler published his socio-economic, Marxist analysis of Karaism, *Kara'imer*, Gerson Cohen criticised, "The time had passed for students of Judaism to entertain the stock cliches of rabbinic authoritarianism, oppressiveness, insensitivity to mass Jewish needs and aspirations, and smug propagation of passive acceptance of subjection and exploitation in the Diaspora." Mahler saw Geonic culture as a web of doctrines and institutions deliberately calculated to nourish the interests of the establishment. Mahler's biases were strenuously rejected by one historian after another, although his positive contributions were appreciated.[10] In Sabbatian scholarship, Scholem revived precisely this caricature of a rabbinic establishment, out to perpetuate itself and suppress all affirmations of redemption.

It is the greatest irony that rabbinic historiography has lent support to this construct, for its own reasons. Rabbinic controversialists sought to impose a one-dimensional view on the past, to legitimize their claim to sole authority. In the case of Sabbatianism, rabbinic polemicists supported the notion of an unbridgeable abyss between Sabbatianism and rabbinism—as forces in Jewish history, they were diametrically opposed to one another. This is Jacob Emden's view of Sabbatianism and rabbinic Judaism just as surely as it is Scholem's.

This refusal to allow for the possibility that the two tendencies could reside in a more integrated picture of Judaism—already appears in the conceptions of the earliest anti-Sabbatians. There are numerous examples of how Sasportas, and Hagiz, refused to accept the evidence that many rabbinic colleagues were Sabbatians. Only when the evidence was overwhelming did they make a complete reversal, and deny the man's stature as a rabbinic scholar. In the heat of controversy, they refused to entertain the possibility that open contradictions, as well as more subtle tensions and doubts could reside in the souls of the greatest of men. This rigid preconception has continued to dominate the field of rabbinic biography.

Scholem's characterizations of Sabbatians as warm imaginative spiritual seekers, and their opponents as cold rigid inquisitorial zealots is simply a myth. It cannot explain why decades after the apostasy, some of the greatest rabbinic figures were Sabbatians, and some of the most avid Sabbatian ideologues and Kabbalists were learned rabbis. It cannot explain why there were lay leaders who vehemently opposed Sabbatianism, or why outspoken opponents were among the foremost popularizers of Kabbalah in their generations. Nor can it account for those who harbored messianic aspirations of their own. Scholem's version obscures the development of the branch of Sabbatian kabbalah which negated or totally ignored Sabbatai's role as an instrument of redemption, although a messiah continued to play a strong role. This non-Sabbatian Sabbatianism may explain some of the instances of rabbi-Sabbatians.

This false polarity between the two has kept us as historians from seeing what other phenomenological purposes Sabbatianism served aside from an anti-rabbinic-establishment one. Placing the blame for the failure of Jews to rise up against the exile on the shoulders of the traditional rabbinate is a dramatic technique (indeed it is used by noted Israeli playwrights) but in the case of Sabbatianism it is poor history. Jacob Sasportas, Jacob Hagiz, Moses Hagiz, and Jacob Emden are interesting not because they confirm Scholem's picture, but because of the many ways they don't. Their own profound yearning for redemption and spiritual center was no less powerful than the impulses of those who stood at the other side of the polemical barricades. By refining the art and science of rabbinic biography and reappraising the figures whose historical profiles have been distorted, we can begin to redress some of the imbalances imposed by the prevailing conception. I hope that this life of Hagiz will contribute in some small way and more importantly, stimulate further study.

CHAPTER I

Antecedents

 IF CERTAIN historical figures loom in retrospect as particularly representative of their age and culture, Moses Hagiz may well serve as an exemplar within the eighteenth-century Sephardic rabbinate. Even his family history is somehow paradigmatic. Both his Hagiz and Galante ancestry linked him directly to the flower of Spanish Jewry expelled in 1492. Their settlement and subsequent destinies in their respective places of exile reflect typical patterns of the Sephardic diaspora.

THE HAGIZ FAMILY

Moses' father, Jacob Hagiz, traced his descent to "royal lineage, of the nobility, the exiles of Jerusalem in Spain who were expelled from there. . . . They went forth first to the city of Fez, . . . the father of my grandmother Paloma, R. Judah HaKohen of the Elders of Castile and her Sages."[1] The arrival of the Spanish exiles in Fez revitalized the Jewish community there, and Fez became known in the sixteenth century among Iberian conversos as an ideal place to revert to Judaism. Many Marranos sent their children to Fez for a Jewish education, and some remained and prospered there. But the Sephardim achieved dominance at the expense of considerable friction with the native Jews. They formed a "community of Exiles" [Kehillat Megorashim], and promulgated ordinances based on Judeo-Spanish custom rather than local custom.[2] Jacob's great-grandfather, *Hakham* Samuel Hagiz, signed the ordinances of the "Community of Exiles" in 1543, 1568, and 1575. The signature of Jacob Hagiz' grandfather and namesake, Hakham and Dayyan in Fez, appears on many ordinances at the turn of the sixteenth century. In 1605 he signed on sumptuary laws to discourage flaunting of costly garments and jewelry, and, of greater portent, a law granting the support of his community to the Jews of Jerusalem. He preached a sermon to a special prayer gathering of all the Jews of the mellah in the synagogue of the "Natives" in 1621. Upon his death in Fez he was honored with an unusually large funeral, indication that he had earned the respect of all segments of the Jewish community.[3]

Israel Zafrani, writing in 1596 of Samuel b. Jacob Hagiz, referred to Fez as "the place in which he and his forebears are renowned."[4] The family had become firmly ensconced at the helm of the Jewish community of Fez, and Samuel Hagiz became the head of the Yeshiva there, together with his prominent rabbinic contemporaries, members of the Uziel and ibn Danan families. While in Venice to publish his own books, *Debar Shemuel*, a commentary on the midrash *Debarim Rabbah*, and *Mebakesh HaShem*, a commentary on the Pentateuch, he served as proofreader in another press, perhaps to defray some of the expenses of his journey.[5] His participation in the life of the presses inaugurated an involvement in Hebrew printing that was to last through the generation of Moses Hagiz. The length of his stay in Italy is not known. A letter of Leone Modena, one of the most colorful and intriguing Italian rabbinic figures, written in Florence in 1609, refers to a Hakham Hagiz as "one of the Torah scholars of this place," which may imply a period of settlement. Samuel Hagiz died in 1633.[6]

Jacob Hagiz, only child of Samuel and Sarah Hagiz, was born on January 31, (26 Shevat), 1620.[7] His life and achievements still await comprehensive biographical treatment, but the outlines are important because they held great meaning for Moses.[8] Although his literary output was prodigious, Jacob Hagiz was very reticent in personal matters. He did not record the place of his birth, which is presumed to be Fez. From childhood on his parents trained him vigorously for his future calling. "My father preferred learning with me for an hour—he could not spend the entire day with me because of his public duties—to my loitering with many friends." When he was thirteen years old, his father died and his mother continued to supervise his training: "Although father had provided abundantly so that she could sustain me like a prince, my mother Sarah . . . fed me sparingly, so I would not become accustomed to greed like other children."⁹ Jacob received a thorough Jewish education, and at least a rudimentary introduction to secular lore. In an epilogue to one of his books, Jacob wrote, "Investigate the sciences with all your strength, and above all, the knowledge of Torah."¹⁰

Jacob does not specify when he arrived in Italy; in 1645 at the age of twenty-five, he was in Verona. There, he forged a lasting friendship with Samuel Aboab, who served as rabbi of Verona until 1650. He taught in the *Bet Midrash* of Aboab during these years. His earliest works, *Sefer Dinim* and *Orah Mishor*, are written in the style of student manuals. In Italy, Jacob's mother Sarah befriended the wife of Samuel Aboab. They continued to correspond even after Sarah accompanied Jacob's household to Jerusalem.¹¹

Jacob's greatest success in Verona was in the field of publishing. He was solely responsible for the establishment of a printing press in Verona, having bought and transported the type himself. During the years of his sojourn in Verona, 1645–52, the press published his works as well as those of others. The first fruit of his labor was *Ein Yisrael*, Leone Modena's adaptation of Jacob ibn Habib's popular *Ein Ya'akob*. The distinctive style of his press was a small, pocket size format, to make the works widely affordable and less cumbersome to carry. The manuscript which Jacob prized the most, however, his opus on the Mishnah, was not successfully brought to press.¹²

Although we hear nothing of Jacob Hagiz' first marriage to the daughter of R. David Karigal until he mourns her passing in a letter, it is quite possible that he married her at the beginning of his sojourn in Italy. Upon her death, she bequeathed him property in Venice. His daughter from that marriage married R. Moses ibn Habib of Jerusalem shortly after their arrival there, but she died while still young. A son, Samuel, also died in his youth.¹³

In 1652, Jacob left Verona for Venice. There he published *Petil Tkhelet*, his commentary on the *Azharot* of Solomon ibn Gabirol. The *Azharot* enumerate the 613 precepts in liturgical verse. Jacob's didactic work is partly his own commentary, in his characteristic terse and lucid style, and part explication of divergent opinions.¹⁴ Jacob's epilogue to the *Petil Tkhelet* comes as close to a personal statement from an author who shied away from self revelation as anything he wrote. In it, Jacob wrote that he took as his model the great scholar, R. Simon ben Zemah Duran, and that he aspired to write an infinite number of books. The epilogue also contains Jacob's first words of social criticism, reproof of the lifestyle of Sephardic and Italian Jews with whom he came into contact in Western Europe. He warned them to refrain from using the name of God for profane purposes; from idle preoccupations; from fashioning garments of wool and linen together; and above all, from ridiculing rabbinic teachings. The latter was to become a leitmotif in the campaigns of Moses and his contemporaries.[15]

Jacob remained in Venice for a very brief time, when he heard of the "magnificent press that had emerged in Livorno," the printing press established by Yedidiah Gabai in 1650.[16] Jacob was drawn by the hope that he could succesfully publish his treatise on the Mishnah there, and he was not disappointed. The publication of the *Ez ha-Hayim,* a commentary on the entire Mishnah, brought Jacob Hagiz the greatest renown in his lifetime (the *Halakhot Ketanot* was published posthumously). Within the past century, there had been a renewed emphasis on study of the Mishnah in some circles, as the maggid of R. Joseph Karo attests, and Jacob Hagiz' work can be seen as part of this revival. Many years of toil and much intellectual energy were invested in the Mishnah commentary, which reveals Jacob Hagiz to be a masterful pedagogue, a teacher of Torah *par excellence.* Jacob used the commentary of Rashi on the Talmud as a touchstone to create a work which is lucid, concise, and intimately familiar with the entire range of pertinent scholarship.[17] From the carefully structured introduction to the methodology and hermeneutic rules which apply to the study of the Mishnah, to the diagrams that graphically explicated difficult concepts, the work quickly became so popular that, together with Jacob's *Tekhillat Hokhma,* it formed part of the fixed program of daily study for many of Constantinople's great rabbis.[18]

Livorno exerted a hold over Jacob Hagiz far beyond its initial attraction as a place for printing. In 1652, the very year of Jacob's arrival, a French priest passing through the city described the Jewish community as a very prosperous one, of about four thousand souls, with a grand synagogue and freedom from any marks of religious degradation such as the yellow Jew's cap.[19] The "livornina," the Charter of 1593, had established Livorno as a free port for men of all Nations, with the specific proviso that, "none shall be able to make you any inquisition, inquiry, examination or accusal against you or your families, although living in the past outside our Dominion in the guise of Christians." This freedom beckoned invitingly to many Marranos, who accepted the offer with alacrity. At first the newcomers were dominated by the Jewish community of Pisa, but that relationship was soon reversed, and Jewish merchants played a substantial role in developing its commerce.[20]

Since the founding fathers of the Livorno Jewish community were former Marranos, Jacob felt a special responsibility to ease their integration into the traditional Jewish community. He sought a suitable introduction to Jewish Law and lore for them and found it in the *Menorat ha-Maor* [*Shining Candelabrum*] of Isaac Aboab (I). It forms part of a corpus of literature directed at former Marranos which was not polemical but pedagogic, intended to supplement their fragmentary Jewish knowledge. The *Menorat ha-Maor* is neither ethical treatise nor halakhic code, but a combination of the two. Although it had previously gone through numerous Hebrew editions, Jacob Hagiz abridged and translated the work into fluent Spanish, its first translation into the vernacular, "por benefisio comun." The targeted readers were those who, "no son muy corientes en declaros de nuestros Sabios, y en lenguage vulgar por lo poco corientes en el Ebraico." Hagiz wrote that these former Marranos were living blindly until they learned the basics of religious thought and praxis. Unlike his other books, which were generally pocket-sized, the *Almenara de la Luz* was produced in a large, handsome, beautifully bound format, intended as a reference work and adornment for the libraries of prosperous ex-Marranos. Unlike other works of this genre whose sources are the *Zohar* and other Kabbalistic works, the primary source of *Menorat Ha-Maor* is the rabbinic Aggadah.[21]

Jacob Hagiz' splendid edition of the *Almenara*, with its evident concern for re-integrating Marranos into all spheres of Jewish life, contrasted sharply with his harsh stance *vis à vis* the legal status of the Marrano who did not revert to Judaism. "That which is said of an apostate, 'Although he sinned, he still remains an Israelite,' was said only to be stringent . . . the marriages he may contract are valid . . . *not for his benefit*." His rationale for this can be learned from another responsum related to the Marrano issue. An inquirer asked whether donations made by Anglicans to the Holy Land could be accepted for sacred Jewish purposes. The inquirer reasoned that there might be grounds for permitting these Gentile donations because Anglicans are not considered idol-worshipers (unlike Catholics?). Moreover, there had been forced baptisms in that country, and some Jews had become "like children in captivity among the Gentiles"—the donors might technically be considered Israelites. Hagiz responded that an evaluation of the status of forced converts must be made on the basis of their original motivation. If their conversion was motivated by fear for their lives, they were to be accepted; if it was prompted by concern for their fortunes, they were to be spurned.[22]

Jacob found many supporters for his projects among the Livornese Jews. His work on the Mishnah was sponsored by Abraham Israel Amnon. The *Alemenara de la Luz* was published at the "cost of David de Iahacob Valensi," member of a well-known family originally from Valencia, who had traveled the same route as the Hagiz family—first to

Fez, and then to several Italian cities. The greatest tribute to the esteem in which Jacob came to be held was the major endowment provided by members of the Vega-Passarigno family for the realization of Jacob's fondest wish—the establishment of an institution of higher learning in Jerusalem with himself at its helm.[23]

The Vega were the most affluent family in the Jewish community of seventeenth-century Verona. A quarter of its entire tax revenue in the years 1640–1660 was collected from the Vega family. In 1660, when crisis overtook the "ghetto nuevo" of the Sephardim in Verona, David, son of Isaac Vega, bought up all the houses in the ghetto.[24]

A former disciple of Jacob Hagiz', R. Samuel de Pas of Livorno, writing in 1703, shed some additional light on Jacob's influence and activities: "From my youth he raised me as a father, here in Livorno, while he was occupied with publishing his treatise on the Mishnah . . . He toiled all his days to enrich the public with knowledge . . . And he continued to do so even after he went to the Land of Israel . . . he became a *Resh Metivta* [head of the Academy] there." His words affirm that Jacob played an active role in public Jewish life, especially in education, although not necessarily in any official capacity.[25]

One other important activity of Jacob's during his Italian years comes to our attention through a responsum of R. Raphael Meldola. The writer challenged the validity of a Pisan tradition that there were arrangements in effect to permit carrying certain things on the Sabbath. Meldola replied that there "was no trace in the *Sefer Takkanot* [Book of Ordinances] that their Hakhamim [rabbinic leaders] ever made them renew the arrangement, even though at their helm, on the rabbinical seat they had formidable rabbis: the author of the *Gidulei Terumah* [Azariah Figo] and R. Jacob Hagiz, author of the *Ez ha-Hayim*."[26] Thus, he probably served as rabbi on the Bet Din in Pisa for some time before leaving to Jerusalem in 1658. There is no other information that can determine precisely the duration of that tenure. Given the close relationship between Pisa and Livorno, it was probably contemporaneous with his year of publishing at Livorno.

In the years before he immigrated to Jerusalem, Jacob remained in close contact with R. Samuel Aboab in Venice, and occasionally visited him. Moses Hagiz wrote that Jacob had written a book, now lost, of social criticism of Italian Jewry very similar in nature to Aboab's *Sefer ha-Zikhronot*. If the similarity between the two works was as striking as Moses Hagiz claims, it is possible that they had jointly discussed these issues. The harsh criticisms apparently prevented Hagiz from finding a publisher for his work—even Aboab had to publish anonymously.[27] The special ties that had developed between the Jewish communities in Italy and those in the Holy Land (Jerusalem, Safed, Hebron) were largely due to the efforts of Aboab. Under his guidance, the Italian Jewish communities, especially Venice, became the West European entrepot for donations to the Holy Land.[28] His contacts and encouragement may have been helpful to Hagiz who had been planning to immigrate there at least since 1655. Aboab had been instrumental in advising other scholars who planned to establish yeshivot in Erez Israel. In his own *Debar Shemuel*, Aboab included a "traveler's manual" for those contemplating a pilgrimage. He advised R. Joseph Alkalai to stop in Livorno before embarking on his journey, "Because it is customary for the wealthy of this city to establish yeshivot in Erez Israel." He advised Joseph Hamiz, a disciple of Leone Modena, never to rely on the mails for fund-raising. To be effective, he should send emissaries from Erez Israel. Aboab recommended the yeshiva of his father, Abraham Aboab, as a paradigm to be emulated as closely as possible. Not all the signals that came from Erez Israel were encouraging. In 1649, Aboab wrote a letter to Moses Zacut on behalf of some young men (one of whom may have been Joseph Richetti) who had left Erez Israel for lack of funds.[29]

By 1658 Jacob Hagiz had left Italy for Jerusalem. The first year was filled with personal vicissitudes. His only daughter was betrothed and married to R. Moses ibn Habib, an eminent scholar in Jerusalem, but she was to die shortly thereafter. Jacob's wife died shortly after their arrival, leaving him with an investment in Venice which had to be liquidated. Apparently, this did nothing to ameliorate the poverty in the Hagiz home in Jerusalem. In his introduction to *Halakhot Ketanot*, he wrote, "In my home there is neither food nor clothing."[30]

We do not have a clear picture of the Jewish community in Jerusalem at the time of Jacob Hagiz' arrival. The community had grown slowly, in the face of many difficulties. Jews were subject to cruel and capricious persecution that sometimes resulted in forced flight from the city. Intermittent plagues and drought also prompted occasional exodus to other cities. Nevertheless, Jacob Hagiz was determined to build Jerusalem into a spiritual center, one which would have the same stature throughout the seventeenth century Jewish world as Safed had enjoyed in the sixteenth. We know that several eminent figures lived in Jerusalem at the time of Jacob Hagiz' arrival. R. Jacob Zemah, the physician and kabbalist was one of the most renowned. Zemah was a Marrano physician, born in Viano da Caminha, Portugal c. 1584. He emerged as a Jew in Salonika and later made his way to Jerusalem, c. 1640. His Kabbalistic writings follow those of R. Hayim Vital, with no trace of the influence of the

Italian Lurianic kabbalists, Israel Sarug and Menahem Azariah Fano. His son, Abraham Zemah, was also prominent figure in Jerusalem. R. Abraham Gediliah, author of a commentary to the *Yalkut Shim'oni* (whom Jacob had met in Livorno); Moses ibn Habib; and Moses Galante were some of the other rabbinic figures in Jerusalem before Jacob Hagiz' arrival.

Jacob established the academy "Beth Jacob" (Vega) soon after he arrived. It immediately became the spiritual and scholarly center of Jerusalem, providing a forum for the scholars already there, while attracting other noted figures. R. Abraham Hanania came to Jerusalem from Safed, and R. Samuel Garmizan, a native of Salonika, came to Jerusalem from a difficult position as rabbi in Malta. Others who came to study with Hagiz included R. Solomon Alghazi and R. Abraham Amigo.[31] These were not disciples, but members of the Hesger (cloister), the elite inner circle who shared policy-making responsibilities with the head of the Yeshiva, and like him received a stipend. Sephardic yeshivot were unlike the East European model. The latter were devoted mainly to education of the young, while the former primarily supported established scholars, on the model of the Babylonian Yeshivot. According to Moses Hagiz, "They instituted a *Hesger*, a gathering place for scholars, and provided for all the needs of the scholars and students so that they would not be distracted by the search for a livelihood." Although the Hesger was the crown of the institution, Jacob Hagiz also established an educational system which included elementary and intermediate grades.[32]

The most unusual aspect of Jacob Hagiz' yeshiva was not its structure, but its curriculum. Other small, tightly knit study groups formed by scholars who emigrated to the Holy Land were motivated by an overtly messianic purpose. This was reflected in their commitment to the study of Kabbalah; its dissemination was believed to be a prerequisite for the coming of the messiah. Jacob Hagiz' yeshiva deviated from this tradition by eschewing the study of Kabbalah in favor of the traditional rabbinic texts of Talmud and Codes, a surprising departure. Jacob Zemah, the Kabbalist, was deeply disappointed that the revitalized Jerusalem failed to resemble Safed of the previous century as a center for Kabbalistic studies:

> Although the coming of the messiah depends upon repentance, study of the *Zohar*, and the wisdom of Kabbalah, her sons [Jerusalem's] do not take up this study. . . . Because there is no house of study devoted to it in every city as there is for Talmud, he [the messiah] has not come. . . . There is no one to establish study halls devoted

to its [the Kabbalah's] wisdom. Everyone seeks their bread through study of the Law.

The Beth Jacob yeshiva served many functions other than education. It was the judicial, legislative and economic center of Jerusalem as well. It appears that the rabbinical court of Jerusalem consisted of members of the Beth Jacob Hesger, and was not a separate, independent entity. Jacob Hagiz, for example, served as the divorce registrar, responsible for the text of every Jewish writ of divorce granted in Jerusalem. His treatise on divorce law, "Kuntres le-Gittin," undoubtedly emerged from the period during which he served in this capacity.[33]

The Vega family took a close interest in matters pertaining to the yeshiva. When Samuel Aboab wished to secure admittance to Hagiz' yeshiva for the sons of a deceased friend, R. Joseph Alkalai, he advised the youths to apply directly to the Vega brothers. When one of the youths turned out to be extremely unsuited for Hagiz' yeshiva, Hagiz wrote Aboab that he intended to expel him. Aboab warned Hagiz of the possible damage that could result if the young man were to return to Italy bearing unhappy reports of the yeshiva. He suggested that Hagiz find him another occupation. The correspondence demonstrates that Hagiz could be pressured by the Vegas regarding internal affairs of the yeshiva. He had to be concerned lest funds be curtailed because of a negative report from a disgruntled student. In addition to the regular funds, Hagiz persuaded Abraham Israel Vega to set aside sums of money as prizes to motivate the poor to continue their studies, and to pay for their clothes once a year.[34]

The work which yields the most insight into the life of Jacob Hagiz in the setting of the Hesger is his only published work of responsa, *Halakhot Ketanot*. From its pages one can catch glimpses into his personality, his relationships with his disciples, and the scope of the activities of the yeshiva. The responsa are based on actual repartee that took place in special weekly sessions of the yeshiva under Jacob's tenure. "I have seen fit to record some of the questions that were posed in our study hall, Beth Jacob, each week." Many identical questions appear in the responsa of other members of the hesger, such as Samuel Garmizan and Moses ibn Habib, indicating that the queries were posed to all the members of the hesger. If the *Halakhot Ketanot* contains minor errors because of its spontaneous air, it compensates for them by recording Jacob's reactions to many issues that may never have found their way into a more rigorously edited responsa volume. Jacob even allowed a rare glint of his wry humor to remain. When asked whether a man who marries may recite the blessing "*Shehekheyanu*" (the blessing for partaking of something new), Hagiz replied, "The questioner should have asked whether he is permitted to bless "*Dayyan Emet,*" (the blessing said upon hearing of a death).[35]

In *Halakhot Ketanot* we learn that Jacob regarded custom as so crucial that it often overrode new, more accurate findings in Law, and he went to great lengths to preserve it. When asked whether the Ashkenazic custom of two blessings on the phylacteries was not preferable, he responded, "What a great joy it would have been to be born into an Ashkenazic family and perforce bless twice, for that seems more correct. But, alas, I cannot change the custom of my fathers." Jacob went to great lengths to preserve customs that were observed in Jerusalem in unique ways, and he does not even adopt the pretense of a responsa format; he records them simply to preserve them.[36]

Because *Halakhot Ketanot* records decisions as they were reached, they are often rendered without the customary legalistic debate of responsa literature. Critics argued that Jacob's terse style did not provide the halakhic researcher with sufficient material to form his own opinion. Jacob gave ample justification for his style. He cited his love of succinctness, as well as a practical reason: the questions were debated in weekly sessions on Fridays, a day too short to conduct adequate research. But the pedagogic impulse was paramount to Jacob, and he felt that "even if my work is useless for Halakha, it will sharpen the minds of my students." His brevity would force the students to exercise their memory by recalling the sources on their own.[37]

The laconic style and clarity of line in *Halakhot Ketanot* is not just a matter of stylistic affectation. The work is almost devoid of pilpulistic argumentation, and in this it paves the way for the work of others in Hagiz' circle. Moses ibn Habib's *Get Pashut* and Hezekiah da Silva's *Peri Hadash* are models of a fresh approach in Halakha. This represents a reversal of the trend of pilpul [dialectic] that had originated in Eastern Europe and influenced the work of Sephardic scholars as well. While it did not begin with Jacob Hagiz, the return to a more direct approach found powerful exponents in Hagiz' circle.[38] The circle of Jacob Hagiz sparked a revival of the beleaguered Jerusalem community not only by introducing fresh approaches to Halakha but also by reinforcing its ranks.[39] According to the admiring assessment of his son Moses: "Among the achievements [of Jacob Hagiz] from the day he arrived in Jerusalem— its population swelled and the city flourished, and the great Sages of

Israel flocked to it." Moses Hagiz later echoed the cries of educational critics of his father's generation to call for a halt to *pilpul* in Ashkenazic yeshivot. "Their shortcomings are due to the fact that they do not learn the root of the matter to comprehend it, but they are satisfied with memorizing dialectics . . . and superficial knowledge. After this training, they lack understanding of the direct sense of the law and they go astray."

THE LIFE of Jacob Hagiz, with its manifold successes and setbacks, serves not merely as a perfunctory preface to that of Moses, but rather as the perfect foil. Where Jacob succeeded in returning from the dispersion to build up a center, Moses would be forced to leave the center and become an exile. Jacob used his energies and his ancestral legacy to pioneer a creative renewal; Moses would transform his own frustrated energies into zeal for persecution, conflict, and criticism—the suppression of all that was new.

The very special filial bonds that united Moses with the memory of Jacob served to heighten this contrast on a profound psychological level. Moses was deeply involved in efforts to reconstruct, and follow, the model of his father's life. By devoting a substantial portion of his publishing career to his father's works, he became intimately familiar with every word and nuance. This meshing of identities on a psychological level, which was not fulfilled on the historical plane, contributed to the feeling of frustration and rage that pervades the body of Moses' polemical works.

MOSES GALANTE

Moses Galante, maternal grandfather of Moses Hagiz, was no less crucial to his formative years. Sometime between the years 1659–1667, Jacob Hagiz married Miriam, the daughter of Moses Galante, in Jerusalem. Galante had been very desirous of this match for his daughter; he took great pride in the stature of his son-in-law, and even distributed Jacob Hagiz' books when he traveled.[40]

Like the Hagiz family, the Galantes were among the exiles from Spain in 1492, and their collective ancestral profile in dispersion reflects a similar pattern. Mordecai (Angello) Galante left Spain in 1492, and settled in Rome, where he died sometime after 1541. Mordecai's sons, Abraham and Moses (I) both migrated to Safed. Abraham "the Holy" was distinguished as a pious disciple of Cordovero. Moses, also a student of Cordovero, was among those chosen for ordination in the historic revival of the ancient *Semikhah* [ordination] in sixteenth century Safed. He succeeded Moses de Trani as chief of the Safed rabbinical court. One of the first products of the printing press in Safed was his commentary to Ecclesiastes, the *Kehillat Ya'akob*.

Moses b. Jonathan Galante, grandfather of Moses Hagiz, was born in Safed in 1621, where he studied Torah with R. Barukh Barzilai.[41] The family moved from Safed to Jerusalem, where Jonathan occupied a rabbinical position. Moses Galante was regarded by his contemporaries as a scholar of first rank, and upon his father's death, he succeeded him. An eschatological zeal and idealistic vision remained with him from his Safed heritage, and he participated in the attempt to foster a renaissance of Jerusalem modeled after that of sixteenth century Safed.

In 1674, upon the death of his son-in-law Jacob Hagiz, Moses Galante succeeded him as head of the Yeshiva Beth Jacob. He also undertook the responsibility of raising and educating his grandson, Moses Hagiz, becoming his foster father. Moses Hagiz always spoke of him with great affection and admiration, though his deceased father remained the preeminent influence.

During his years at the helm of Beth Jacob, Galante tried to maintain the original spirit of Jacob Hagiz' enterprise. There is evidence that he was the first to use the title of chief rabbi of Jerusalem. By a twist of fate, the work for which he gained the most renown among his contemporaries, his responsa *Elef ha-Magen*, (MaGen is an acronym for Moses Galante) never reached the printing press.[42] Two of his works were published posthumously by Moses Hagiz; they were prepared by Galante for publication during his years at the helm of Beth Jacob. *Korban Hagigah*, a collection of homilies, was prepared in 1686, and *Zebah ha-Shelamim*, novellae on the Talmud, in 1687. Like the *Halakhot Ketanot* of Jacob Hagiz, these works emerge from the daily discourse of the yeshiva, and, like Jacob Hagiz, Galante set Fridays aside to write.[43] He requested that Moses Hagiz publish them if the opportunity arose, a request Hagiz fulfilled. He not only published them, but lovingly edited them, sporadically injecting his own comments.[44]

Like Jacob Hagiz, Galante was active in instituting "customs of Jerusalem," and he too wrote of them wherever he found an appropriate place in his writings, so that their memory would be perpetuated. From one of Galante's comments, we learn the procedure for establishing a custom: "They testified that this has been the custom [of Jerusalem] during the time of the greatest sages, and a decision was reached to follow that custom." From this we can see that there was a conscious effort on the part of the Jerusalem circle to establish its own customs. Their historical point of reference was ancient Jerusalemite custom, and their defiance in resurrecting it in face of opposition from Karo's Shulkhan Arukh and the Tur testifies to the renaissance of Jerusalem they dreamed of effecting. While some customs were instituted on the basis of historical precedent, others were clearly established because of their significance for the future redemption.[45] Galante passed away on 21 Shebat, 1689. While his circle never exerted the same profound influence on the diaspora as his namesake, the 'Rav ha-Musmakh' [ordained rabbi] of Safed, his students included all the rabbinic luminaries to emerge from Jerusalem in that period, including Hezekiah da Silva, Abraham Yizhaki, Moses ibn Habib, and Joseph HaKohen.[46]

JACOB HAGIZ AND THE SABBATIAN MESSIANIC MOVEMENT IN JERUSALEM

The Sabbatian messianic movement of 1665 caught both Jacob Hagiz and Moses Galante in its vortex. The rabbinate of Jerusalem was regarded as an important authority on matters of spiritual renewal, especially at the height of Jacob Hagiz' efforts to build an authoritative center. Followers of Sabbatai were anxious for Jerusalem's rabbinate to legitimate his messianic mission. Its failure to authenticate the movement could prove to be a severe setback. As the preeminent figure of the Jerusalem rabbinate in 1665, Jacob Hagiz was catapulted to the center of the messianic drama. Yet this period of his life remains a tantalizing and mysterious void in his biography. We shall try to reconstruct his role from the material available to us. It is important not only because of Jacob's profound influence on his son Moses Hagiz but also as a contribution to an analysis of the opposition to Sabbatianism while the movement was at its height. The motives and methods of Jacob Hagiz and his contemporaries were free of the complex psychological baggage which burdened the second generation, that of Moses Hagiz.[47]

Jacob Hagiz and his circle were staunchly opposed to Sabbatai's messianic claims. In mid-summer of 1665, they issued a ban of excommunication against Sabbatai signed by Abraham Amigo, Samuel Garmizan, Jacob Zemah, and Jacob Hagiz. Together with Abraham Yizhaki, then a disciple of the Hesger, these rabbis formed the nexus of opposition to Sabbatai in Jerusalem. Samuel Garmizan preached an anti-Sabbatian sermon before a great multitude, and an Armenian source described "a Sage and elderly physician who preached sermons in Jerusalem against Sabbatai," who may have been Jacob Zemah.[48] They sent a full report of their decision to the rabbis of Constantinople, capital of the Ottoman Empire. Jacob Sasportas emphasized repeatedly that only word from Jerusalem could certify the new messiah. In the absence of any further pronouncements, rumors arose that the Jerusalem rabbinate had reversed itself. These initial bold steps against Sabbatai in Jerusalem were followed, however, by total silence. This lack of any further action on the part of the Jerusalem rabbinate—its failure to continue its initiative and galvanize an opposition movement contributed to the disunity and discord within rabbinic ranks during the height of the movement.

The motivations for rabbinic opposition to Sabbatai were varied and complex. Sabbatai Zebi did not conform to most traditional rabbinic criteria for the Messiah; moreover, his flagrant antinomian violations clearly rendered him objectionable. This was coupled with the traditional conservatism of rabbinic leadership *vis-à-vis* messianic movements, a result of harsh political reality reinforced by many bitter experiences. The rabbis in Ottoman lands feared the wrath of Turkish authorities; those in Christian countries feared the ridicule of their neighbors and increased vulnerability in future theological polemics. They were concerned that tenuous Jewish footholds in newly established communities would be endangered.[49]

The Sabbatian movement divided the rabbinate in many ways. Of course the most basic division is between those who believed in Sabbatai's messianic claims and those who did not. The faith of the believers has been extensively explored by historians; the opponents, however have been neglected. Scholem and others utilized the writing of opponents solely to glean information about the movement itself. We shall focus on the opposition. The rabbinate faced the task of formulating the ideology to oppose Sabbatianism as well as choosing a strategy to combat it. The voluble Jacob Sasportas, who relentlessly gathered damaging information and inundated his fellow rabbis with a barrage of missives concerning the movement, was but one end of the spectrum. The middle is represented by Samuel Aboab of Venice who adopted an agnostic stance at first, awaiting further developments. He later abandoned his hesitancy and denounced Sabbatai.[50] There were many who followed this path for a number of reasons. Some rabbis doubted Sabbatai's messianic claims, but felt that the waves of penitence, prayer, and widespread religious revival inspired by the messianic movement were more beneficial than harmful. It was neither credulity nor weakness that made them suspend their judgment, but rather lack of historical perspective and practical foresight. Some rabbis held their peace for fear of losing the public favor, others actually feared the physical violence of frenzied mobs.

Rabbis Aaron Lapapa and Joseph Halevi of Smyrna, opponents of the Sabbatian movement at its height, are examples of rabbis who felt the public displeasure for their lack of faith in the messiah. Aaron Lapapa lost his position after a bitter struggle to R. Hayim Benveniste because of his unpopular views. A similar incident occured in a small village in Turkey, about six months after the Lapapa incident, to an unknown rabbi. When a Sabbatian loyalist heard that the rabbi had blasphemed against the messiah, he informed on him and his followers to the authorities who inflicted murderous lashings on them, jailed them and caused them grave financial losses. He coerced the townsfolk to remove him from his position and made them swear that they would not permit him to teach there for three years.[51]

Others believed that the less public debate about the matter, the more quickly it was likely to subside of its own accord. Their refusal to make public pronouncements over any aspect of the Sabbatian movement denied it legitimacy; acknowledgment in rabbinic discourse would lend it respectability. This seems to be the rationale of those who immured themselves behind a thick wall of silence.

Was "conspiracy of silence" the official policy of the Jerusalem rabbinate? A distinction must be drawn between the Bet Din, the official judicial arm of the rabbinate, and individual rabbis in a less formal capacity. After the Bet Din's initial expulsion and excommunication of Sabbatai, denunciations by individual rabbis did not cease during the height of the movement. If anything, they were characterized by extraordinary virulence and asperity. Sabbatai had spent time in Jerusalem and may have been known to these rabbis for his odd habits. Nathan Ashkenazi of Gaza, the messiah's prophet, had been a student of Jacob Hagiz' in Yeshiva Bet Jacob, a bright and accomplished pupil. Jacob Hagiz even arranged the marriage of Nathan to the daughter of the wealthy Samuel Lissabona, who resided in Gaza.[52] The notion of this pair parading around with messianic pretensions must have struck their former teachers and cynical acquaintances as especially absurd. Prophets are often rejected by those who know them best, and the contempt bred by familiarity surely operated in this case. The argument that even the most perspicacious rabbi must have regarded initial reports of the Messiah with some measure of credence, or agnosticism at the least, would not be relevant to the case of Jacob Hagiz or Joseph Eskapha of Smyrna. Those who were familiar with Sabbatai and Nathan from the vantage of having been their teachers never viewed their claims with anything but skepticism. As early as 1649, Eskapha, who was Sabbatai's principal teacher rebuked and outlawed him, announcing that "whoever strikes him down deserves a reward, for he [Sabbatai] will lead Israel into sin and make a new religion."[53]

The evidence indicates, however, that the rabbinical court of Jerusalem, and Jacob Hagiz within its ranks, refused to conduct further deliberations on the legitimacy of Sabbatai after the first formal excommunication. Documents prove that a conspiracy of silence had indeed been adopted, and enforced, for a somewhat later period.[54] Jacob Hagiz never openly referred to the Sabbatian movement in any of his extant writings. (Most of his works were written before the advent of Sabbatianism; the one large work prepared for publication at a later date was lost.) In his only volume published after 1666, *Korban Minhah*, there is one line which may be relevant. Jacob wrote of his gratitude to the Lord for enabling him to survive a severe illness, and for protecting him from death by "the dangers of the paths I have chosen to walk. If not for the assistance of God, my mortal enemies would have destroyed me."[55] Is it possible that Jacob was referring here to the implacable enmity of Sabbatian adherents? We know of no other enemies.

If Jacob Hagiz opposed Sabbatai because of his personal experience with him, myriad social, intellectual, and historical forces shaped the other opposition to Sabbatai. Jacob Zemah believed that Sabbatian teachings were a perversion of Lurianic Kabbalah. Even in the instance of Jacob Sasportas, intellectual grounds may have contributed to his continued opposition in later stages of the movement. Sasportas believed that Cordovero's Kabbalah was superior to Luria's and he rejected the Sabbatian ideology that was rooted in Lurianic teachings.[56] The caustic works of the brothers Immanuel and Jacob Frances provide another instance of intellectual opposition. Jacob was a rationalist who objected to the indiscriminate dissemination of Kabbalah, Sabbatianism being a perfect example of the danger of allowing esoteric teachings to fall into the hands of the masses. He was also a critic of rabbinic leadership, and he regarded Sabbatianism as an additional instance of the rabbinate betraying its responsibility.[57]

Familiarity with Christian polemics was another matrix of anti-Sabbatianism. From the inception of the Sabbatian movement, and particularly after the apostasy, the parallels between Sabbatianism and Christianity were apparent to Christian polemists. Their Jewish counterparts were haunted by the spectre of opening a new window of Jewish vulnerability to the Christian polemical arsenal. This argument is a central theme in Sasportas' anti Sabbatian work, *Zizat Nobel Zebi*. It became the basis of a confluence of Jewish anti-Christian and anti-Sabbatian polemics. That the anti-Christian animus in the thinking of former Marranos became a cornerstone in their development as anti-Sabbatians is demonstrated by the biographies of Isaac Cardoso and Isaac Orobio de Castro. As Marranos, these figures had wrestled with, and rejected, elements of Christian theology such as denial of the validity of the Law, interpretation of prophetic passages concerning the fate of the Messiah, and criteria for true prophecy. When parallel elements were cited in support of Sabbatai's claims, learned Marrano spokesman were ready with rebuttals.[58]

The developments in the movement after Sabbatai's apostasy must have been a source of great chagrin to Jacob Hagiz with his former disciple at the fore of the movement, and many former pupils still within its ranks. In the years between 1666 and 1670, Jacob was stricken by an illness from which he despaired of recovering. In 1674, while in Constantinople to oversee the publication of his work *Lehem ha-Panim*, Jacob died. The book was never published. Upon his death, leadership of the Jerusalem hesger passed to his father-in-law, Moses Galante.

Unlike Jacob Hagiz, Galante apparently welcomed the messianic tidings and played a role as a prophet in the movement. There is a detailed description of an outbreak of prophecy in Aleppo when Sabbatai Zebi visited there: "We have today in this city twenty prophets . . . two of them are from among the rabbis, the distinguished R. Moses Galante . . . who left Palestine as an emissary only a short time ago." We know from other sources that Moses Galante did indeed travel as an emissary at about this time.[59]

After the Sabbatian frenzy had abated with the apostasy of Sabbatai Zebi in 1666, Galante left Jerusalem for an extended tour as an emissary. His journey may have been part of an effort sponsored by the Jerusalem rabbinate to bolster the shattered morale of a disillusioned Jewry.[60] Of Galante's feelings toward the apostate messiah we have no clue. In 1667 he went to Turkey, and his path can be traced through Constantinople, Salonika, Belgrade, and Ofen-Buda. In Turkey, Galante could have ascertained the circumstances of the apostasy for himself. In Salonika, he corresponded with Abraham di Boton; in Belgrade with R. Joseph Almosnino; and in Buda with R. Ephraim HaKohen of Vilna, with whom he maintained friendly contact after he returned to Jerusalem. Was it sheer coincidence that each of these figures remained Sabbatians after the apostasy? Joseph Almosnino was originally a disciple of Jacob Hagiz', a friend and colleague of Nathan of Gaza from their student days, and he remained a Sabbatian believer after the apostasy. His public sermons containing Sabbatian allusions aroused controversy. Di Boton remained a Sabbatian, and there is evidence that Ephraim HaKohen [great grandfather of Jacob Emden] may have harbored a tolerance for Sabbatianism as well.[61] Galante referred to these years as a period of exile, and by 1673, he had returned to Jerusalem. While we have no hard evidence of his joining the ranks of crypto-Sabbatian rabbis, his contacts with Almosnino and di Boton may have shown him the possibility of this option.

The years between Jacob Hagiz' death and that of Moses Galante were years of decline for the Bet Midrash Beth Jacob. Whether due to secret sympathies that Galante may have harbored, indifference, or impotence, crypto-Sabbatian strength grew in Jerusalem. Sabbatian elements that dared not surface in Jacob Hagiz' presence attained positions of eminence during Galante's interregnum.[62]

The lack of rabbinic unity was most harmful to the interests of the rabbinate. The division between rabbinic adherents and opponents, and the many factions into which each of these groups were splintered, left the credibility of the rabbinate badly shaken. A leadership which could neither come to any consensus, nor marshal effective means to deal with a great crisis, could not lay claim to the unquestioning loyalty of those they had failed. Many of the forces that had long begun to erode rabbinic authority crystalized around this failure. This conjuncture of embattled rabbinic authority and heretical messianism were to define the parameters of Moses Hagiz' career as polemicist.

CHAPTER 2

Youth in Jerusalem

 THE BRUTAL conditions of Jewish existence in the Jerusalem of his youth remained with Moses Hagiz all his life. At the time of his birth in 1671, the Jewish community of Jerusalem was in desperate straits.[1] The small enclave lived on the brink of extinction, in constant and unremitting misery. The conditions in the Ottoman Empire that had caused the decline of Safed in the sixteenth century were exacerbated in the seventeenth and eighteenth centuries.

SEVENTEENTH-CENTURY JERUSALEM

A pattern of weak central government and erratic local leadership left petty potentates free to terrorize unprotected inhabitants. Jerusalem had few natural resources, fewer opportunities for employment, and had suffered more than its share of natural disasters. Both Jews and Christians were subjected to ruinous taxation. The Jewish community depended completely on the generosity of contributions from the Diaspora for its financial sustenance.[2]

A foreign traveler to Jerusalem close to the year of Moses Hagiz' birth accurately portrayed the circumstances of this embattled community:

> The State of the Jews at Jerusalem was such they would not live and subsist there without some yearly supply and contribution from

their Brethren abroad, because the place doth yield them little or
no trading whereby to maintain themselves; but their love to the
place doth oblige them to remain there, although with great poverty
and want; and their Brethren abroad among the Nations, have been
willing to uphold them there at Jerusalem that the place should not
be left destitute of some considerable number of their nation, . . .
to show their hopes, till a full restitution come. . . . Since the
desolation brought by the war upon Poland . . . their widows fam-
ished to death, and the taxes laid upon them by the Turks being
rigorously enacted, they were haled into prison, their synagogues
were shut, their rabbis and elders beaten and cruelly used . . .
finding at Amsterdam little relief from the Portugal Jews, . . . they
have bound themselves over unto the Bassa, . . . and engaged their
lives, Court, School, Wives and Children to him.[3]

Long after he departed, Hagiz continued to identify himself as a son of
Jerusalem; he kept abreast of its development all his life. These conditions were to become the basis for his *Sefat Emet*, an enduring classic of
emissary literature.

We can glean some information on Hagiz' early development from
scattered remarks in his writing. Upon his father's death at a tender age,
he was raised by his mother, Miriam, and her father, Moses Galante.
Galante held up Jacob Hagiz as a model for Moses to emulate—a goal
Moses labored all his life to attain. "Although I was not able to serve
him much in his lifetime, the day is still long; all the days of my life I
will remember his deeds . . . and slake my thirst from the waters of his
books." The natural desire of a son to follow in the footsteps of his famous father, was intensified for Moses, who did not have the living reality to temper the ideal. He strove to heighten the parallels between his
life and Jacob's: "What occurred to the fathers, occurred to their sons."[4]

Moses' educational paideia was a combination of several influences.
He spoke of, "My masters, and the rabbis of Jerusalem." Foremost in
both of these categories was Moses Galante, responsible for Moses Hagiz'
education from his earliest youth. Through Galante, he gained entry to
the inner chambers of the Jerusalem rabbinate as Galante enjoyed the
status of *primus inter pares* in a rabbinate which traditionally eschewed
such elevations.[5] "I recall that as a tot, I sat astride the shoulders of my
revered teacher and grandfather, Moses Galante, and the great Sages of
our generation . . . and they exchanged views for many long hours."[6]
Moses Hagiz was privy to their deliberations, sessions which made a
lasting impression on him. He often cited the rabbis of Jerusalem, par-

ticularly Alghazi, Amigo, and Garmizan, as authoritative sources, especially on matters of custom. These Sages were among his earliest models, and their causes became his own. His positions on such issues as tax exemptions for scholars, relations between rabbis and lay leaders, and the honor of the rabbinate grew from this early identification.

Of his all his mentors, Hagiz referred only to Abraham Yizhaki as his *Rab Mubhak*, the rabbi to whom he had formed the closest attachment.[7] Hagiz studied in the Yeshiva Beth Jacob as soon as he became of age, and it is likely that his first contacts with Yizhaki occurred there. We can construct the broad outlines of his education from our information on the curriculum at similar yeshivot.[8]

The extent of Galante's Sabbatian entanglement must have posed a severe conflict for Moses Hagiz. Like many others of his generation, he was forced to face the fact that his revered forebear had fallen into the "snare" of Sabbatianism, if even for a brief, intense interlude. In the case of a rabbinic forebear, this was especially troubling. How could a great rabbinic sage have lacked the prescience to repudiate the movement from the start? In his biography of the anti-Sabbatian rabbi Jacob Emden, Jacob J. Schachter has suggested that the paradox presented by rabbi-Sabbatians was worked out by their descendents who fought zealously to extirpate remaining vestiges of Sabbatianism and compensate for the error of their fathers. This explanation provides a plausible, if partial, working hypothesis, since autobiographical formulations are difficult to locate.[9] Another clue to Moses Hagiz' approach can be found in his introduction to Galante's *Korban Hagigah*. In it, he stated his belief that Galante had truly attained the holiness for prophetic powers—but he was careful to stipulate that it was the prophecy of rabbinic knowledge rather than ecstatic state of mind. (*ma'alat nebu'at RaZa"L*) If the Sabbatian prophet in Aleppo was "our" Moses Galante, then this is a very interesting formulation. It is unlike the rueful attitude of the eighteenth century rabbi Hayim Yoseph David Azulai, who could deal with the paradox at a greater historical remove. He acknowledged the phenomenon of Sabbatian rabbis as a lapse that did not negate their rabbinic stature, but did taint it. Moses Hagiz, to whom the conflict was painfully immediate, transfigured the lapse into a positive attribute.[10]

Thus, Moses Hagiz' anti-Sabbatianism was a compound of several influences. Most conspicuous is the example set by his father Jacob. The desire to expiate for Galante's involvement and to avenge him against the forces that had misled him was another important psychological factor. The most important direct influence on Hagiz' anti-Sabbatian activism was Abraham Yizhaki. Yizhaki may have been similarly motivated to stifle vestiges of a movement that had led his own father astray, and he was undoubtedly one of those who implanted an early antipathy to Sabbatianism within Moses Hagiz. With the exception of Galante, the circle of rabbis from Moses' earliest memories was virulently anti-Sabbatian, and it is probable that he had overheard hostile deliberations on the subject. This foundation of hostility to Sabbatianism lay dormant, until it erupted violently in 1713.

In 1687, at the age of sixteen, Moses married the daughter of Raphael Mordecai Malkhi, a wealthy physician originally from Livorno who rose to become lay leader of the Jewish community in Jerusalem. Because of his medical expertise, Malkhi was consulted not only by the rabbis of Jerusalem, but by Muslims and Christians as well.[11] Hagiz' nuptials assumed an incidental place in his memory in contrast to the startling revelation made to him in that year, "I had heard in 1687, when I was entering under the wedding canopy in the home of my grandfather . . . M. Galante, of the apostasy that occurred in the great Jewish city at the behest of Joseph Filosof and his cohort, Florentin. Then I saw that this false faith was still leading wise men astray."[12] The realization that Sabbatianism still retained a malevolent potency, was intertwined in Hagiz' recollection with his passage into manhood and responsibility. The Sabbatian apostasy was to assume central importance in his polemic against the movement; it constituted irrefragable evidence of the evil roots and consequences of Sabbatian belief.[13]

The foundations of the Yeshiva Beth Jacob had already begun to erode during the tenure of Moses Galante. According to one report, "At last, the little sanctuary was destroyed because the bountiful generosity that was there at the beginning was withdrawn. Despite this, the rabbi [Galante] tried to sustain the Hesger. After the death of Moses [Galante], it was completely destroyed."[14] Galante's death in 1689 marked the start of a chain of events in which natural calamities and human factors conspired to close it permanently. Moses Hagiz recalled that, "In 1689, after the death of my revered grandfather . . . there was no wheat." Within a short span of time numerous scholars died, among them many senior members of the yeshiva, perhaps as a result of the famine or a plague. Raphael Mordechai Malkhi wrote, "Now in 1689 the land is almost comletely barren. . . . Within two years, thirty six scholars have died." Almost a decade later, he lamented the absence of rabbis qualified to issue a writ of divorce "because all the earlier sages have passed away."[15]

The atmosphere of crisis and instability was exacerbated by the appointment in 1689, of Cuprilizada Mustafa Pasha, a new Vizier, who was determined to overhaul the chaotic state of affairs of the Ottoman

Empire. Among the reforms he instituted was a new system of taxation that directly affected the Jewish inhabitants of Jerusalem. Under the new rules, even the most indigent were to pay a substantial head tax. The funds that had sustained the Yeshiva Beth Jacob were cut off and the beleaguered citadel of learning that had survived so much hardship, was forced to close its doors. "The Holy City was destroyed, the lights were extinguished, the channels were plugged and turned into useless wells that could not contain water." Hagiz mourned his loss: "This distress has penetrated the inner recesses of my heart—it alone has thrown my spirit into turmoil."[16]

For a short time after his grandfather's death in 1689, Moses Hagiz struggled to maintain the fragments of the Yeshiva Beth Jacob. Without the support of its patrons, this proved impossible. Then in 1693, another series of personal misfortunes struck. His wife, the daughter of Raphael Mordechai Malkhi, died, and Malkhi ceased providing him with personal income. Moreover, the rabbinate of Jerusalem had long discouraged bachelors and widowers from remaining in Jerusalem where the sparse population diminished the opportunities for (re-)marriage. According to one source, "After he [Hagiz] was smitten with his wife's death, he was unable to find a mate, and was banished from here.[17] When, in addition to these problems, his mother's source of income suddenly dried up, Hagiz decided to leave Erez Israel. He hoped to regain support for Yeshiva Beth Jacob, and to settle the financial affairs of his mother.[18]

RAPHAEL MORDECAI MALKHI: THE SABBATIAN CONNECTION

The demise of the Yeshiva Beth Jacob was not due to natural disaster alone. Why were funds from the Vega trust cut off from Hagiz when they were most needed? Close examination of the sources reveals that Hagiz had found himself at the heart of a fierce internecine struggle for control of Jerusalem's Jewish community.

In his pioneering essay on the Yeshiva Beth Jacob and the attempted renaissance of seventeenth-century Jerusalem, Meir Benayahu suggested that the real issue behind the struggle was the penetration of crypto-Sabbatian elements into the yeshiva, the seat of power in Jerusalem. Shlomo Zalman Havlin reevaluated the sources, including certain documents unavailable to Benayahu and concluded that there was no proof of Benayahu's hypothesis. He maintained that because there were no overt references to Sabbatian motives in the public documents, none existed. Upon closer examination, all the new material seems to suggest, to the contrary, a strong Sabbatian strand running through the entire affair, which would confirm Benayahu's original intuition.[19]

Raphael Mordecai Malkhi was a crypto-Sabbatian who dedicated his career to remaking Jerusalem into a Sabbatian stronghold. When the charismatic Sabbatian leader R. Judah Hasid fell ill several days after his arrival in Jerusalem, only Malkhi was permitted to visit him. Jerusalem figured prominently in Malkhi's eschatological schemes: "I say that the true sign of the redemption will come when we see Jerusalem inhabited and restored, its settlement peaceful; then we should surely anticipate immediate redemption."[20] Malkhi recorded the state of the Jewish community in Jerusalem in lavish detail because of his belief that its restoration was a precondition for the redemption.[21] At the heart of Malkhi's vision of a rebuilt Jerusalem was a yeshiva (*midrash*):

> At the end of days the Semites [Israelites] will seek Jerusalem . . . and *from their lands they will establish a "midrash"* in Jerusalem of seventy scholars over them. Out of oppression the Lord will bring many settlers who will cultivate the land, and remain free of taxation, because their brethren in the Diaspora will accept their tax burden. And [the representative of Diaspora Jewry in Jerusalem], will be empowered to . . . defray most of the expenses—either for taxes, or for sitting in the *Armon*. This *Armon* is the *establishment of a headquarters for scholars* (Beit Va'ad la-Hakhamim) *as I have proposed.* The era of this *takkanah* is the time of the approach of the redemption. . . . The King Messiah will emerge from among them.[22]

Malkhi attributed the imperative to establish this yeshiva to a divine message. He said it came to him via the Armenian Patriarch of Jerusalem, who claimed to have found the message inscribed on a large leaden tablet in a cave near a convent on Mount Sinai. Later, Malkhi claimed that "a great and important person told me of this." Malkhi's "prophecy" explains his elaborate record-keeping concerning the population and finances of Jerusalem. Although his interest was more eschatological than statistical, his precise records are a primary source of great importance. The prophecy also explains his eagerness to have his daughter marry Moses Hagiz. The Sabbatians in Jerusalem must have sighed in relief when control of Yeshiva Beth Jacob passed from their foe, Jacob Hagiz, to a supporter, Moses Galante. Moses Hagiz, the heir apparent, was an infant at the time. Malkhi coveted a liaison with Galante's young grandson as a means of securing a foothold in Beth Jacob. It was not until after the wedding that Moses Hagiz asserted his allegiance to his father's anti-Sabbatianism rather than to his grandfather's tolerance. This caused a serious rift between young Hagiz and his father-in-law. Malkhi tried to persuade Hagiz of the error of his ways, to no avail. The example of his father, and the influence of his teacher, Abraham Yizhaki, prevailed. According to Hayon's account in *Moda'a Rabbah:* "After the marriage [Malkhi] supported him [Hagiz] from his pocket all the days that Hagiz was his son-in-law. He bore his burden, his youth and his folly, as is well known in the city. [Malkhi] would reprove him, and [Hagiz] would respond impertinently, and he came to hate him." When his daughter died, Malkhi was determined to wrest control of Beth Jacob away from his former son-in-law.[23]

Malkhi's "prophecy" for the midrash of messianic times stipulated that it should be constituted of scholars from the diaspora, and headed by a leader who had emigrated from the diaspora. This leader would control all revenue coming to Jerusalem from the diaspora, and he could use it to pay the debt of the entire community as well as to finance the yeshiva. If adopted, the proposal would bar Moses Hagiz, a native Jerusalemite, from heading Beth Jacob, while Malkhi would remain qualified.

Furthermore, Malkhi argued that the control of the yeshiva of Jerusalem should not remain in the hands of individuals. He urged the communities that supported yeshivot to establish a rule "that no individual may organize a yeshiva for himself, under his own control." Instead Malkhi urged that control be assigned to the *parnassim*, the lay leaders, of the community. Again, this stipulation would disqualify Hagiz, while Malkhi, a *parnass* of the community, would remain eminently eligible. Malkhi complained of scholars "who arrogated the power and reign to themselves and barred others from participating." Since the yeshiva played an important role in the administration of all communal affairs, Malkhi argued, it should remain in the public domain.[24] Hagiz and his supporters maintained that these institutions, created by the initiative of one individual, and maintained by dint of his efforts, should remain under the control of that individual. When Moses Galante died, "malevolent people halted the financial support which had been sent to the yeshiva every year."

As soon as Hagiz left Jerusalem, Malkhi took further steps to displace him. Unbeknownst to Hagiz, Malkhi requested of the lay leaders of Livorno's Jewish community that they move a different yeshiva into the quarters that had been occupied by Beth Jacob Vega, the school founded by Jacob Hagiz. In its stead he proposed the Yeshiva Beth Jacob Pereira, under the leadership of Malkhi's other son-in-law, Hezekiah da Silva.

This yeshiva had been established by da Silva in 1691, just as Hagiz' yeshiva was at its nadir. Perhaps Malkhi favored the Pereira yeshiva because it had already been penetrated by Sabbatian elements and would have been more sympathetic to his aspirations. Da Silva himself had studied under R. Judah Sharaf, a known Sabbatian, while he was in Livorno. Furthermore, the patrons of the Yeshiva were members of a most prominent Sabbatian family.[25]

We must bear in mind that when Moses Hagiz left Jerusalem in 1693–94 he was unaware of these connections. He left for Egypt with two goals: the settlement of his mother's finances, and the reestablishment of a solid fiscal basis for his Yeshiva. He carried with him a number of manuscripts to publish, ultimately the most successful project on his itinerary. He began his odyssey through the diaspora in high spirits, unaware of the efforts being made to frustrate his mission.

CHAPTER 3

Beginning of an Odyssey

 MOSES HAGIZ set out for Egypt in 1693, on the first leg of a journey that would take him, in several stages, ever farther from the Jerusalem of his youth. The odyssey was fraught with difficulties from the beginning. Travel on the route from Jerusalem to Egypt was extremely hazardous, as one contemporary related:

> It is impossible to traverse that road except by caravan, many together, due to fear of brigands. It is a thirteen or fourteen day journey through the desert to Egypt, and even on the Sabbath, Jews must travel with the caravan for it will not wait for the Israelites. . . . Because their lives would be endangered, the Sabbath is superseded. Therefore, it was not often that Jews travelled from Jerusalem to Egypt, except if there was an urgent need.

The responsa literature contains many references to people who lost their lives on this route. R. Jacob Halevi Berukhim, a disciple of Moses Galante, was killed in the Sinai desert when raiders attacked his caravan as he traveled from Egypt to Jerusalem. Hagiz completed the perilous journey without incident.[1]

IN EGYPT: THE MAECENAS OF ROSETTA

Hagiz' destination was the city of Rosetta, a commercial center on the western mouth of the Nile, which had a considerable Jewish merchant population in the seventeenth century. His mother had invested her inheritance with a certain wealthy Isaac Coutinho of Rosetta, who had withheld her income for the past two years. In 1694, Hagiz presented his mother's case to the rabbinical court of R. David Gershon (HaRav DaGa"N). The rabbinical court found for Miriam Hagiz and ruled that the investor should return the principal investment over a period of three years. Notwithstanding the ruling, "Isaac, may his bones be ground . . . violated his oath, and though he is financially able to repay, he has not done so despite the passage of ten years. This entire matter is well known to the public.".[2]

The frustrating outcome of his mother's affairs was compensated for Moses by his deepening friendship with David Gershon. "He was like a father to me all the days I remained there. He never desisted in his affection for me, and sustained me daily with his bread, the bread of Torah." Gershon's lasting influence can be seen from the many references to his teachings in Hagiz' subsequent work. Hagiz was invited to sit with Gershon and R. Jacob Faraji on a rabbinical court, a token of their esteem for him.[3]

Gershon's influence brought Hagiz into the good graces of Abraham Nathan, a native of Salonika who had prospered mightily in Rosetta. He was renowned as a philanthropist who supported Torah institutions, and he had endowed a fund to publish scholarly works.[4] Hagiz was successful in persuading Nathan to allocate the stunning sum of 30,000 rials to establish a yeshiva in Nathan's name, to be headed by Hagiz in Jerusalem. The money was to be invested in Livorno, Amsterdam, or Venice (or all three), and the income would go exclusively to support this new hesger. Nathan retained discretionary powers over the fund in his lifetime; upon his death, his entire legacy would revert to Hagiz' yeshiva. At the end of the document, signed in the fall of 1695, Gershon appended a clause to insure its permanence: "I decree with the authority of Torah that this will cannot be annulled, neither in its entirety, nor any part thereof; whoever shall effect changes . . . may the curse and ban fall upon him.[5]

The funds were to be released from Nathan's bank in Livorno. Nathan empowered Hagiz, R. Samuel Costa of Livorno and the merchant A. Attias to arrange for the transfer. Nathan's agents there were the bankers

Abraham Suleima and sons. With the proliferation of documents necessitated by a mortmain transaction of this scope, technical difficulties arose.
One of Nathan's brokers had discovered minor discrepancies between the
numerous documents, and threatened to invalidate the entire will. Moreover, certain stipulations made by Nathan conflicted with Livornese legal
requirements. To resolve the snags that had developed, Moses set his
sights toward the Italian city.[6]

LIVORNO: DISAPPOINTMENTS

In 1696, Hagiz left Egypt for Livorno. He hoped to settle matters there
as quickly as possible, and to return to Jerusalem. "All my compatriots
know that when I left Jerusalem to go down to Egypt, I was compelled
by circumstance. It never dawned on me that my exile . . . would last
even one year, and it has persisted, because of my sins, for many years.[7]

The journey must have been planned even before his departure to
Egypt, for Hagiz had other business to pursue there. Jacob Alvarez, son-
in-law of Raphael Vega, who now controlled the Vega fortune, resided
in Livorno. Only successful intercession by Hagiz could restore the flow
of funds from the Vega estate to the Yeshiva Beth Jacob, the cause that
lay closest to his heart. Nathan's bequest was clearly intended to establish a different institution.

Hagiz had made many favorable contacts during his stay in Egypt.
Before his departure from Egypt, he procured letters of reference from
the rabbinates of Rosetta, Cairo, and Alexandria. All the letters supported his claims on the Vega estate, by virtue of his being sole heir to
Jacob Hagiz and Moses Galante. The letter from Alexandria contained
the signatures "of the merchants and powerful men of the land," in Latin
characters following the Hebrew signatures of the rabbis. The letters
urged the influential men of Livorno—Emanuel Ergas, Raphael de Medina, and Abraham del Rio, to assist Moses in any way possible.[8]

Upon his arrival in Livorno, Hagiz was befriended by R. Samuel Costa,
apparently on the recommendation of David Gershon. In 1697 Costa wrote
a detailed letter to Gershon, outlining Hagiz' progress with Nathan's endowment, and requesting Gershon's intercession with Nathan himself.
The resolution of technical discrepancies, and conformity to Livornese
legal requirements were the only impediments. "It seems clear to us that
R. Abraham Nathan has not acted with malice, but out of ignorance of
our legal tradition. We have decided that the aforementioned rabbi [Moses

Hagiz] will remain here until the matter is resolved." No answer to this query was forthcoming, but by 1700, funds had already been transferred to Abraham Suleima, Nathan's designated agent. As Nathan had stipulated, "The plot of land that the Grand Duke has sold to [A. Suleima & Sons] in the name of the Nathan endowment is an exceedingly beautiful site, better than the land of the wealthiest people, for it faces the main thoroughfare of the city." The homes that were to be erected there would provide the income to sustain the yeshiva. It is unclear whether these initial difficulties that Hagiz encountered were in fact the products of Nathan's ignorance, as Costa supposed, or whether they were deliberate obstacles placed by his enemies.[9]

In the spring of 1698 four Jerusalem rabbis, Joseph Hazzan, Siman-Tob Obadiah, Judah Ergas and Joseph ben Joseph, sent a letter to the lay officials of Livorno. All were relative newcomers to Jerusalem; none had participated in Yeshiva Beth Jacob. Ergas was a lay leader of Jerusalem, the others were respected members of the rabbinic community. They encouraged the lay leaders of Livorno to maintain Nathan's endowment for Jerusalem, but under penalty of ban "no appointment or responsibility [should be permitted to Hagiz], neither of the old *midrash* of Vega, nor any other new *midrash*—for we have been informed of the bequest of Nathan that [Moses Hagiz] was involved with it." They also requested regarding Hagiz that "no confidential affairs of our community should be revealed to him, as it would be against our honor."[10]

What motivated these Jerusalemite rabbis to intervene just when Hagiz appeared to be succeeding in his efforts to establish a new yeshiva? The instigator behind the attempt to frustrate Hagiz' efforts appears to have been none other than his former father-in-law, Raphael Mordechai Malkhi. Malkhi had lived in Livorno until 1672, and he had many contacts there who shared his Sabbatian aspirations for Jerusalem. When Malkhi attempted to displace Hagiz by alloting the premises of his yeshiva to da Silva's, Hagiz responded by publicizing Malkhi's proposal in a manner which impugned Malkhi's motives. Stung by this open challenge to his authority, Malkhi marshalled the aid of these four members of the Jerusalem community. Their letter to the lay leaders of Livorno defamed Hagiz, claiming he had acted irresponsibly. This was no mere disagreement with Hagiz over petty matters of policy; their plan was to discredit Hagiz utterly and sever all his links to Jerusalem's affairs.[11]

Their letter bore immediate fruit. Why was the lay leadership of Livorno's Jewish community so amenable to Malkhi's machinations against Hagiz? The Jewish community in Livorno was a center for crypto-Sabbatian activity. A full history of this important Jewish community has yet to be written; when it is, the struggle for power by Sabbatian elements is certain to emerge as a principal theme. Jacob Sasportas, the father of anti-Sabbatian polemicists, chose Livorno for a showdown with lay leaders. Sabbatianism in this context was more than an esoteric ideology shared by men who found it to be a source of spiritual sustenance. Networks of Sabbatians concerned themselves with much more than the circulation of Sabbatian manuscripts. As this episode with Hagiz and Malkhi indicates, the real goal was to infiltrate the loci of power in the Jewish community. The Sabbatians in Jerusalem worked in concert with those of Livorno, and it need not concern us that the Sabbatian motivation does not surface more openly in the documents. Crypto-Sabbatians took elaborate precautions to conceal their true concerns from the uninitiated.[12]

During Hagiz' absence from Jerusalem, the struggle for power over Jerusalem's institutions continued. Abraham Yizhaki, Hagiz' mentor, was leader of the anti-Sabbatians, while Raphael Malkhi led the forces who wished to empower Sabbatian sympathizers. Malkhi had the support of a powerful Livornese *parnas*, Raphael di Medina, who had been appointed to oversee the affairs of Hezekia da Silva's yeshiva, [Hagiz' competition], in Jerusalem. These hostilities were echoed in Livorno, and Hagiz protested in his *Leket* the humiliation that was perpetrated on R. Samuel Costa by the sextons of the *Yeshiva Ba'alei Teshuba*. "They sought groundless excuses to persecute him. . . . The Lord will not absolve them, and will hold them accountable for the blood of the persecuted."[13] The principal instigator of this persecution of Costa, Hagiz' ally in the Nathan affair, was none other than the Livornese lay leader, Raphael de Medina, whom Hagiz had accused of preventing the restitution of the Vega funds to him. The Livornese *Parnassim* protested bitterly to their counterparts in Amsterdam for permitting the incident to be published.

When the defamatory letter from Jerusalem reached Livorno, Hagiz' allies there immediately rallied to his defense. They addressed an open letter of protest to the leadership of Jerusalem, indicating that the four dignitaries who had signed the letter may have been misled into doing so by the powerful Malkhi. They argued that regardless of the circumstances, it was unconscionable to sully the name of Hagiz because his motives—to rebuild the ruins of Jerusalem—were unquestionably pure. Moreover, they hinted, any public squabbling would ultimately be to the detriment of Jerusalem's welfare. The letter was signed by Costa, along with Jacob Jeshurun Lopez and Gershon Tilki.[14]

The initiative against Hagiz had been unknown to the anti-Sabbatian rabbis in Jerusalem until they received the protest of Costa. In early 1700, they responded, admonishing the Livornese leaders for permitting malicious slander to fall on willing ears, and upholding Hagiz' integrity with the loftiest praises. The letter was signed by rabbis Hiyya di Boton, Judah HaKohen, Moses Ibn Habib, Hanun Navon, and Samuel HaKohen. Most had been associated with Yeshiva Beth Jacob. In 1700, Hagiz received another letter of support against "the sect of slanderers and purveyors of falsehood" from a venerable anti-Sabbatian—none other than the aged rabbi, poet, and social critic, Immanuel Frances, who had apparently continued to play a role in Livornese Jewish communal politics. His defense and friendship provided Hagiz with a link to the previous generation of anti-Sabbatians, the peers of his father Jacob.[15]

In early 1700, an extremely nasty and insulting letter was written by an anonymous "rabbi of Jerusalem" sojourning then in Livorno. The letter was forwarded from Livorno to the wealthy Abraham Rosano in Rosetta, to convince him to influence Nathan to remove the trust fund from the hands of Hagiz. Apparently a copy was retained by the lay leaders of Livorno, who later used it against Hagiz in a dispute of 1707 when they forwarded it to Amsterdam.[16]

As a result of the conspiracy of Hagiz' enemies, all further development of his yeshivot ceased. In 1700 he rushed back to Rosetta to quell the assaults on his integrity. Despite recommendations to Nathan from powerful allies, and the continued interest of R. David Gershon, Hagiz' efforts failed.[17] The gist of the campaign against him had reached Nathan's ears. After spending a month in Rosetta, Hagiz was forced to agree to a second recension of Nathan's testament in which many of the original provisions were rescinded, so that the funds were no longer accessible to him. "The mediation of evil men has caused the *hekdesh* to be withdrawn."[18] Hagiz blamed R. Shabbatai Nawi, successor of Gershon as head of Rosetta's rabbinical court, who did not uphold the validity of the original bequest; he believed that the rabbinical courts were intimidated by his powerful opponents. Seven years later, Hagiz complained, "I have remained silent because one cannot get a fair judgment against one who is more powerful." Only after the passage of seven years without satisfaction did he decide to publish the names of the witnesses to his original document in the hope that they could be moved to issue a vindication. He returned to Livorno chagrined by the turn of events, to face a mounting campaign to impede his efforts.[19]

Just as the promising Nathan endowment ended in a futile entanglement, Hagiz' efforts to release the Vega funds were similarly marked by a succession of hopes and disappointments which terminated in failure.

A letter from Hagiz' supporters in Jerusalem to the leadership of Livorno in 1702 stated categorically that while general bequests to Jerusalem could be controlled by Livorno, the Vega fund was emphatically not a general bequest; it was the private province of Moses Hagiz. Their designated agent—the same Abraham Suleima who had been chosen by Nathan—was welcome to appoint other partners along with Hagiz. Under no circumstances could Hagiz be shunted aside. Their directive went unheeded. As Hagiz later mourned, "I have toiled over this [with all my strength] but I have not profited. I spent my days and years trying in vain to restore the crown of Torah."[20]

HOPE AND DESPAIR

The cumulative effect of the repeated rebuffs became manifest during the latter part of Hagiz' sojourn in Livorno (1701–2). Hagiz felt that he had reached an impasse in his career. He was approaching his thirtieth birthday, which brought with it the realization that he had spent nearly a decade of his life in a fruitless endeavor. The major projects he had undertaken had been consistently frustrated, and the future seemed bleak, with no prospects on the horizon. A sense of personal failure, compounded by a growing feeling of alienation assailed his spirit. He wrote a vivid account of his plunge into utter despair and his unexpected recovery; it forms part of his introduction to his father's *Halakhot Ketanot*. "I mourned over the past, was dismayed by the present, and felt apprehensive of the future. I did not know how to proceed, where to turn for relief to lift me out of the morass, to rescue me from the many perplexities that raged within me like a fire consuming my innards." Melancholy thoughts of self-reproach tormented him. He wondered whether God had ever supported his mission, indeed, whether Divine Providence still guided his destiny at all. "On my bed in the nights, when my mind was emptied of ideas . . . sleep wandered and a thought kept me awake, saying, 'When, O Lord, will come the end of my travails?' "[21]

Hagiz' account of how he was elevated from his despondency is extraordinary:

And He [the Lord] sent a *benevolent guardian angel* to instruct and chastise me . . . and he taught me and spoke to me both *in script* and orally. "How long, indolent one, will you remain lying inert on your side? You have turned your heart from Me. . . . It is true that you have been exiled from the Holy Land for ten years, and your enterprise in its behalf has been thwarted. Follow my advice diligently: Gain mastery over those things that are within your grasp . . . the constellations will not fail you—only sloth and weak resolve can hold you back. Know that the Lord will cause you to prevail. . . . If you choose the good, you will receive good from the Lord and He will illuminate your night as day in this world."[22]

This remarkable episode, unique in Hagiz' biography, illuminates the spiritual and psychological world which he inhabited. The contents of the message highlighted the most important transition point in his career. Was Hagiz' emphasis that the angelic words came "*in script* and orally" simply a strong metaphor for an inspirational moment or was he describing something he experienced as externalized from his psyche, perhaps implying automatic writing? If the latter, it would be a most striking occurrence, in which a well known medium of mystical revelations was used to convey a purely psychological message.[23] Regardless of whether Hagiz is to be taken literally, it is clear that a one-time intervention during a spiritual crisis provided him with psychological motivation and concrete suggestions. The revelation served to remind him that he carried with him the means to achieve some notice, not to mention income, which he had hitherto neglected. The "angel" had artfully woven into the message the titles of numerous works by Jacob Hagiz and Moses Galante that Moses Hagiz carried with him in manuscript. By publishing them, he could achieve some measure of acclaim and possibly earn a profit, in addition to providing a forum for his own scholarship. In fact, shortly after this visitation Hagiz moved to Venice where he began publishing these works with alacrity. Hagiz was to participate in publishing ventures throughout his career, and they remained his most prodigious accomplishments. His subsequent success undoubtedly lent the visitation retroactive validity.[24]

The revelation held yet another message for Hagiz, no less important, though more subtly stated:

While your strength is fresh, hasten to the battlefield. Arise and act swiftly to attain and preserve the Divine spirit that hovers. . . . Know that many have succumbed to despair and inertia—the Lord tests his faithful. Embrace and emulate the paths that your father Jacob Israel has trodden with zeal, and Moses [Galante] the faithful shepherd.[25]

It directed Hagiz to emulate his father's zealous ways, to unbridle all his powers in the pursuit of good and the rejection of evil. These lines constitute a brief but apt characterization of a zealot. The divine assurance of success and victory in his zealotry provides a key to understanding the fearlessness, indefatigability, and ferocity of his polemics. Hagiz now *knew* that any issue on which his father had taken a stand—social criticism and Sabbatianism come first to mind—he was divinely ordained to pursue until he should prevail. Here we see the process by which the great energy and talent which he had intended to use for creative purposes were rechannelled by Hagiz into more bitter pursuits. This spiritual crisis sealed a chapter in Hagiz' past, and adumbrated the dimensions of his future career. Significantly, a similar sense of extreme alienation was the cynosure of the careers of many rabbis whose peripatetic lives closely paralleled that of Hagiz.

Transformed and revitalized, Hagiz made preparations to leave Livorno in 1702. He had completed the preparation of several manuscripts for publication. He decided to travel to Venice, renowned for its Hebrew presses and where his father Jacob had printed *Petil Tekhelet*. Before his departure, Hagiz obtained letters of recommendation from Livornese rabbis Samuel Costa, Samuel de Pas, and Eliezer Kohen. The letter from Immanuel Frances dated Fall of 1702 is the last document concerning his activities in Livorno. Shortly thereafter, manuscripts in hand, Hagiz wended his way to Venice. The period of crisis and depression had passed; he was ready to lay the foundations for a new life.[26]

VENICE: AUSPICIOUS BEGINNINGS

From the time of his arrival, in Spring 1703, Hagiz' activities in Venice were off to an auspicious start. His parallel careers as publisher and social critic were launched with vigor. The first project he attempted was grandly conceived: he would publish his father's halakhic opus, *Halakhot Ketanot*, together with Moses Galante's *Korban Hagigah*, and a "small work" of his own, an early draft of *Leket HaKeMaH*. The entire volume was tentatively entitled *Magen Abot* [*Shield of Patriarchs*]. The size of the project required a considerable financial outlay; this proved to be a substantial impediment which forced him to reduce the original scope of the volume and lay aside his own work. Fortunately for the destiny of the *Leket Ha-*

KeMaH, the events which followed were to induce a further change of heart.

> Now that the Lord has begun to ease my sorrows . . . He has brought me from the distant corners of the earth to meet a desirable match . . . and being that this is the request of her relatives . . . I will set aside these days of betrothal for sacred work, and in place of gifts I will adorn her with the twenty-four bridal ornaments, the completion of my "*Likutim*" [digest] in the aforesaid manner.[27]

In Fall 1703, Moses was betrothed to Venturina, daughter of a wealthy businessman, the deceased Asher Hefez-Gentile, and they were married shortly thereafter in Verona. The Hefez family was an eminent Italian Jewish family. Menashe Hefez, son of Jacob Hefez, a renowned scholar and rabbi of Gorizia, became Moses' brother-in-law. He was appointed rabbi in Verona in 1705. Together with another relative, Gabriel Padovano, Menashe encouraged Hagiz to resume and expand his abandoned work, the halakhic digest *Leket HaKeMaH*. The marriage provided Hagiz with an entree into the Italian rabbinic community; it generated friendships and solidified bonds of support which would be crucial to his future enterprises.[28]

One of the most enduring bonds which Moses forged in Venice was the friendship with Rabbi Samson Morpurgo, who had been a disciple of Jacob Hefez. From their initial meeting, the relationship between Morpurgo and Hagiz was one of mutual admiration and affection, tempered by the younger Morpurgo's respect for Hagiz. This was reflected in their sustained correspondence, which lasted over a quarter of a century from their first exchange.[29] Through Morpurgo, he came to know R. Samuel David Ottolenghi, a senior rabbinical colleague of Morpurgo's in Padua. Ottolenghi had requested an approbation for his forthcoming work *Me'il Shemuel*, [*Cloak of Samuel*], an abridged version of Isaiah Horowitz' classical *Shenei Luhot ha-Berit* [*Two Tablets of the Covenant*]. Hagiz complied with a reply that was deemed too lengthy by the printer, Aaron Volterra. Ottolenghi requested that Hagiz abridge his reply to comply with Volterra's limit. Apparently, Hagiz did not feel constrained to abbreviate his words, as his letter of approbation did not appear.[30]

Hagiz' publishing career actually began in Venice, in September 1703, with the publication of David Ibn Abi Zimra's *Or Kadmon* [*Primordial Light*]. This was a wise choice, as the reclamation of Zimra's manuscript was a project that readily found financial backers. Hagiz took advantage of this first appearance in print by appending a short treatise of his own "to fill the blank pages."[31] After the brief hiatus, during which Hagiz published *Or Kadmon*, he returned to his original project. In the spring of 1704, shortly before Passover, his annotated edition of Jacob Hagiz' *Halakhot Ketanot* appeared in print, bound together with Moses Galante's *Korban Hagigah*. In order to obtain the funds and the letters of approbation needed to raise them, Hagiz enlisted the aid of Menahem Krakovia, an influential resident of Venice with strong ties to Central and Eastern Europe. Krakovia sent several sample pages [*alim le-terufah*], which Hagiz had preprinted, as was customary. Hagiz received responses from several rabbis of Central Europe, most notably, David Oppenheim.[32] The rabbis of the *"Yeshiva Klalit"* of Venice gave Hagiz a 'copyright' letter on 23 Adar (I), 1704; shortly thereafter he got a response from R. Hananiah Kazis of Florence. Although he was able to put his stamp on the volume in the form of comments and several sections of his own responsa, his own work, *Leket HaKeMaH*, which was to have been the third segment of the volume, was not included. Perhaps lack of sufficient funds or obstruction by the Italian rabbinate caused the delay.[33]

JERUSALEM AND PRAGUE

At this time, Hagiz received desperate news from his mother. Widowed for the second time, she lived alone, and her financial arrangements had once again fallen into disarray. He dropped all his activities to hasten to her aid. There is no trace of this visit in any of Hagiz' extant works; perhaps there were sound reasons for discretion. That Hagiz deliberately concealed this trip seems clear from his correspondence with Morpurgo. In Fall 1704 Hagiz wrote to Samson Morpurgo that he was hesitant to remain in Venice for the winter. He had intended to travel to Germany directly, but 'the pestilence had begun,' in Poland, and he was concerned that it might reach the cities he planned to visit. The next letter of Hagiz is dated Winter 1704/5, several months later. In his response Morpurgo wondered why "Moses had tarried so long in replying" and speculated that Hagiz may have been ill, as he had previously mentioned that he was recuperating from a fever. In fact, Hagiz had traveled to Jerusalem first.

Our information regarding this secretive excursion comes from a detailed responsum written by David Oppenheim concerning a visit Hagiz paid to Jerusalem on behalf of his mother in 1705. The details of his mother's predicament are of intrinsic interest, and they shed light on Jerusalem ten years after Hagiz' departure. Despite all Hagiz' efforts on her behalf in Egypt and Italy, and her marriage to a man of means, Miriam's fortunes had not improved. Her second husband lost his money. She told Moses that she had lived in poverty and distress during the past decade, "and in order to survive, I was forced to sell all the valuables of our home, yours and mine." Miriam's second husband, Ezra, had left her a courtyard in which she could dwell until her death, when all his property would revert to the community. A wall of this courtyard crumbled into a public thoroughfare. Miriam requested that it be mended at the community's expense since the property would ultimately belong to them and she did not have the means to make the urgently needed repair. The officials of the court countered that they had no responsibility to the property until it came into their possession. They offered to take immediate possession of the property in exchange for an annual stipend, an offer which Miriam was forced to accept as the property was uninhabitable in its condition. In the interim, she sent for Moses. Upon his arrival, she argued that her claims should not have been litigated in Jerusalem since all members of the community stood to profit from a decision against her. The Jerusalem court acquiesced to this argument and consented to let Moses present the entire case before an impartial arbiter. Hagiz' choice was David Oppenheim, then rabbi of Prague, and he set off for central Europe.[34]

Although Hagiz had not yet become personally acquainted with Oppenheim, their paths had crossed earlier. Oppenheim had provided enthusiastic support for Hagiz' publications, and Hagiz was deeply grateful. Their relationship may have extended even further back. In 1701, three months after the arrival of R. Judah Hasid and his adherents in Jerusalem, the Ashkenazic Community of Jerusalem offered David Oppenheim the honorary appointment as "Prince of Israel." The community of Jerusalem was alarmed by the influx of a large population whose members included numerous Sabbatian sympathizers. The appointment of a renowned anti-Sabbatian rabbi would reaffirm Jerusalem's identity as an anti-Sabbatian center and provide an antidote to the recent arrivals. Hagiz, who had maintained close contact with his confreres in Jerusalem, undoubtedly had been apprised of these developments.[35]

Concern over the growing influence of Sabbatians in Jerusalem did not abate with the appointment of Oppenheim. In 1705, the *Kehilla* sent a document to the Council of Four Lands in Poland, entreating the Council to use its influence against Jerusalem's Sabbatians. The signatories pleaded that their identity be concealed, for fear of reprisals. In the same year the anti-Sabbatian rabbis of Constantinople wrote an epistle against the renewed Sabbatian activity emanating from Jerusalem. It is possible that parallel efforts by Jerusalem's Sephardic anti-Sabbatians beckoned to Hagiz to return to Jerusalem in 1705. His choice of David Oppenheim to adjudicate his mother's case may have been motivated by this common interest.[36]

Oppenheim was not eager to become involved in the dispute, but he consented to take the case on account of Hagiz' "daily entreaties." His decision, rendered in 1706, vindicated the officials of Jerusalem. They were not technically responsible to repair property then in Miriam Galante's possession, but Oppenheim urged them to make strenuous efforts to help her recover her earlier investments, so that she could afford to cover the expenses.

During his stay in Prague, which lasted at least six months, Hagiz received encouragement to continue his own work. Oppenheim was instrumental in helping Hagiz obtain funds to complete his *Leket Ha-KeMaH*. Hagiz received enthusiastic encouragement from many others, most notably from Oppenheim's brother-in-law Jacob Reischer, a great scholar in his own right. The encounter between Reischer and Hagiz subsequently blossomed into a warm friendship.[37]

IN AMSTERDAM: THE LANGUAGE OF TRUTH

When Hagiz concluded his business in Central Europe, he headed for Amsterdam, arriving in early 1707. His emotional return to Jerusalem and warm reception in Prague contrasted dramatically with the atmosphere that greeted him in Amsterdam, whose Jewish community was the shining exemplar of Jewish resettlement in Western Europe in the post expulsion era. It was founded as a merchant colony toward the end of the sixteenth century by Marranos seeking religious freedom. The great prosperity and relative religious liberty overwhelmed Hagiz: "Surely there are no more than two or three communities in all the Dispersion which sit as confidently and securely, enjoying wealth and honor, as those of London and Holland, may the Lord perpetuate their well-being." These communities were justly fabled among emissaries for their Jewish nobility and wealthy merchants. But the wealth he encountered in Amsterdam merely confirmed for Hagiz the uneasy perceptions he had voiced after his stay in Livorno. Beneath the glittering surface, he detected rot gnawing at the very foundations of the community: "The communities were blessed with Divine abundance . . . but due to a diminution of Divine Providence, they are being turned into dry wells. . . . Their money is disbursed for sinful pursuits—consorting with women, riding magnificent carriages, consuming rich food, and building homes and courtyards."[38] Hagiz attributed this hedonism to the combination of unprecedented freedom and wealth. The disdain with which he was treated by some of the prosperous Jewish citizens of Amsterdam rankled deeply. These factors combined to bring forth the full force of Hagiz' power as a social critic.

With the publication of *Sefat Emet* (*The Language of Truth*) Hagiz entered the ranks of the important social critics of his generation. His earlier works, such as *Leket HaKeMaH*, had contained scattered words of criticism; their impact diluted within the context of the whole work. *Sefat Emet* is the first full-length publication devoted solely to the goal of criticism. Hagiz' criticism was rooted in an idealized conception of Jewish society in his birthplace: "It is said, 'The Land is good, but it is a golden dish brimming with scorpions'—*these are the scholars dwelling there who compel, . . . smite, and punish* in accordance with the Law."[39]

On the surface, *Sefat Emet* is a defense of Erez Israel, the land of Moses' provenance. Hagiz' defense of the sanctity of the Holy Land stands by itself; but the book must also be interpreted as an expression of his vision of the restoration of central religious authority in Jewish life. Hagiz believed that the shift of the locus of power within the communities to the lay leadership was the root of all the malaise plaguing the Jewish communities of Western Europe, a theme he expanded on later in his *Mishnat Hakhamim*.

Hagiz employed two literary artifices to soften his attack on the powerful lay leaders of Amsterdam. The introduction contains an apology which lavishes praise on Amsterdam Jewry, and directs words of criticism only at "those who are empowered to prevent this behaviour, but have neglected to do so." This might have been intended to neutralize pre-publication objections to the work by the *ma'amad* [the lay council]. Hagiz had been supporting himself during this period by tutoring the children of wealthy merchants and this apology would provide recourse were he accused of ingratitude to his patrons.[40] In addition, Hagiz presented *Sefat Emet* as a response to a query posed by a sincere questioner, an anonymous "gevir" [wealthy Jew] of Amsterdam.[41] These devices notwithstanding, both the overall content, as well as explicit statements in the work, show that Hagiz intended to assail the entire Sephardic community of Amsterdam, both its institutions and individual members: "These words are addressed to her leaders and functionaries, her masses and scholars." The Hebrew body of the work is preceeded by a summary of the most trenchant arguments in Portuguese, so that the casual reader who could not peruse it easily in Hebrew would immediately become informed of the most salient points in the book. With this reproach directed to an entire community, Hagiz consigned himself to the lonely position of critic and perenniel outsider. "Hagiz knew the pride of the Parnassim, and their power to persecute him, yet he did not have mercy on himself."[42]

Sefat Emet is a work with many levels of meaning that contain distinct messages for each segment of the audience. The issues Hagiz raised ranged from those of an immediate or transitory nature, to profound questions that have been part of the vocabulary of the Jewish Diaspora from its earliest existence. On one level, *Sefat Emet* can be comfortably enshrined as a classic of emissary literature. Every emissary sent from Israel to the Diaspora was equipped with individual letters of recommendation to every community on his circuit, attesting to his character and integrity. In addition they often carried a general epistle, available to all emissaries, which detailed the travails of the Jewish community in the Holy Land. The common formulaic descriptions in several of these works demonstrates that some achieved the status of classics and were widely emulated. The early seventeenth century work *Horebot Yerushalaim* [*Ruins of Jerusalem*], published in Venice, is an example of a very widely circulated emissary tract. Hagiz' *Sefat Emet* attained similar fame in the eighteenth century; it was still used by emissaries through the nineteenth century.[43] Within this genre, Hagiz' work serves both as a chronicle of early eighteenth century Israel as well as an advocate for its emissaries. He devoted an entire section, "Table of Expenses and Explanation of the [Growing] Debt," to respond to the charge that the constant flow of money to the coffers of Eretz Israel from all corners of the Diaspora never seemed to suffice. Its detailed analysis of the income and expenditures of the community in Jerusalem make it a particularly valuable source.[44]

After he demonstrated the financial need of the community, and the worthiness of the charitable institutions to be recipients of philanthropical largesse, Hagiz proceeded to a more sensitive and personal issue— the treatment accorded the emissaries who represented those institutions. Hagiz defended the personal integrity of emissaries, and assailed the shabby treatment they were accorded. Contemporary sources support Hagiz' claim that emissaries were regarded with disdain in parts of Western Europe. Some Italian *Kehillot* had requested that emissaries not visit their town because the income they collected would be consumed by their travel expenses. A letter of recommendation for the emissary G. Cordovero stressed that his services were voluntary and he would be paid no commission. Emissaries were barred completely from entering certain communities. A letter given to emissary Moses Sasportas in 1695 states that Sasportas is being sent as an emissary against the specific wishes of the local rabbi because of the community found itself in unusually difficult straits. A French community requested in 1699 that Safed cease sending emissaries. Some communities put a ceiling on the amounts that could be donated by any individual. Hagiz, in an unrelated responsum, referred to an Italian community which fixed the maximum at seven scudi. Communal concerns that charity begin at home were mirrored in the treatment accorded to emissaries.[45]

Although Hagiz was not an official emissary for any institution, he had undoubtedly experienced the scorn heaped upon emissaries when he sought funds for his yeshiva and his publishing ventures. In a letter supporting Hagiz, R. Abraham Broda of Prague wrote, "I beseech my brethren in the Diaspora not to regard him [Hagiz] as just another passerby; . . . it is too shameful for him. . . . Wherever he goes, he should be accorded cordiality and hospitality." Though he was not an emissary, Hagiz considered himself on a par with them. "The emissaries are greeted with hostility in many communities and are considered to be nuisances. . . . Some say, what a joy the Messiah will bring—for he will bring relief to the poor and we will no longer be obliged to dole out charity to them!" Wealthy householders complained that the entire phenomenon of emissaries was "one large conspiracy to empty their pockets."[46] Other sources indicate that Hagiz' criticisms were somewhat exaggerated.[47]

Although the precept of giving charity was deeply ingrained in Jewish tradition, Hagiz reiterated the basic moral arguments for philanthropy. He evoked the perpetually spinning wheel of fortune, and characterized the emissaries as divine agents who could enable the prosperous Jews of the Diaspora to share in the merit of their impoverished brethren in Palestine at relatively little sacrifice on their part. Ultimately, Hagiz reasoned, the callous West European Jews betrayed their own interests with their insensitive behavior. Emissaries of the highest caliber refused to render themselves vulnerable to this abuse: "They [the Europeans] say to the emissaries, 'why are you soliciting funds? So that scholars can drink coffee and chew tobacco, and scribble whatever comes to mind so they can publish it?' My own ears have heard emissaries being mocked and taunted . . . by the citizens of these provinces . . . It is no wonder that some emissaries give just cause for grumbling—the Jews of these provinces have themselves to blame. For when it became known in Erez Israel that Western European Jews treat the emissaries with scorn, there wasn't a single bona-fide scholar who would willingly come here."[48] Hagiz resorted to a stab of irony in his final appeal to the wealthy Jews of Amsterdam—he accused them of seeking the welfare of the Gentile indigent 'to maintain peaceful relations,' with greater ardor than they applied to their private charity lists for the needy of Erez Israel. He assailed these private lists, which circulated in Amsterdam, Venice, and Livorno as inappropriate and insufficient. He opposed the private lists on the grounds that they favored well-connected individuals, and undermined communal efforts to divide the proceeds of charity fairly.[49]

Having excoriated the wealthy West European Jews, Hagiz turned to the emissaries themselves. They were not exculpated either, for they had permitted themselves to fall victim to this abuse without vigorous protest. He urged an intensive effort to burnish their collective image. By accepting paltry sums which fell far below their needs as well as below the capacities of the givers, they permitted the wealthy to claim, "Surely the emissaries speak nothing but falsehoods . . . they do not suffer, nor do they have debts. For if all their stories were true, they could never be mollified by the pittances we toss them!" "The gentle and soft-spoken among them commit a serious miscalculation. He who requests his portions with humility and deference will end up with nothing." Hagiz deplored the practice of sending important emissaries upon the heels of one another; yet, he noted, even when an adequate interval had elapsed, the yield was often meager. No emissary should promise that a specific sum would dissolve the debt when large donations were proferred, giving rise to the expectation that the *Kehillot* in Erez Israel would be permanently free of debt. The credibility of all emissaries was shaken when that did not turn out to be the case. No needy group should be given preference over another: "The Lord knows the love that binds me to all the indigent of Israel . . . but I love the truth even more." Truth dictated that only the local authorities had the right to determine the precise allocation of funds.[50]

In earlier times, Hagiz argued, the primary task of the emissaries had been to admonish and criticize, to teach and offer moral guidance. They had become expert at offering tactful reproof, and they had achieved close rapport with their audience. Hagiz mourned that emissaries had now turned their energies solely to the collection of funds, and had neglected their former role. As a result, people had grown distant from them. He conceded that in order to remedy the problem at its roots, they would have to cease collecting all monies for a time, "and rouse the hearts of every person in these communities to renew their faith and their commitment to observe the Torah—then, tiresome efforts on behalf of Jerusalem will become superfluous."[51]

Of greater moment than the relationship between the source of philanthropy and the emissaries who channeled it was the fundamental question of the merit of the recipients. In addition to the classical formulation, "that they perpetuate the Jewish settlement in Erez Israel, and stand guard over its ruins," Hagiz felt compelled to answer more profound challenges to the legitimacy of Jewish residence in Israel. Some claimed that the current inhabitants were dwelling there contrary to the will of God. "The Lord has evicted us from there, to lands where we dwell in peace. Despite this, some Jews have decided to live there. Then, they wish to take our money to redeem themselves!"[52] The suffering visited upon these obdurate inhabitants was God's way of showing his displeasure. To this, Hagiz replied that the abject state of these Jews was not a punishment for their own misdeeds, but a vicarious atonement for the sins of their pleasure-pursuing brethren in Western Europe. It was incomprehensible that all the Jews of Palestine, the other Ottoman lands, Germany, and Poland were suffering for their own sins while the West-European minority, consuming the fat of the land in the freedom of their surroundings, had achieved atonement. The argument of abject status as evidence of guilt, was a standard Christian triumphalist polemic against Jews. Hagiz' response that suffering is not indicative of inherent guilt could have been borrowed from the Jewish-Christian polemical context. His reworking of these themes could be especially effective on Marranos in his audience.

Beyond the issue of individual settlers in Erez Israel, Hagiz probed the more basic question of the inherent sanctity of the land in contemporary times. "I have heard from many quarters the argument that there is no hallowed status for Erez Israel—in the era of exile all Jewries are equally close (or equidistant) from God. The Divine Presence [*shekhina*] has withdrawn from there, and the whole world is the same."[53] Hagiz' reply to this challenge is a virtual catalogue of the special spiritual qualities of the Holy Land, an eloquent restatement of the classical answers: "The vestiges [*reshimu*] of sanctity that have remained, elevate the land and its inhabitants above all others. It still remains the portal of entry for all Jewish prayer and divine blessings." Hagiz' arguments were not original here, which has masked the timeliness of the debate that had been revived when Ottoman rule fostered significant Jewish settlement in Palestine.[54]

Echoes of this debate reverberated in scholarly writings throughout the early modern period. Samuel de Medina, one of the earliest champions of diaspora independence, repeatedly stressed, contrary to the prevailing view, that charitable institutions in Salonika were *equal in sanctity* to those in Israel, and that halakhic decisions rendered by rabbis of Israel were invested with no greater sanctity than those of Diaspora leaders. Hagiz' contemporary, Mordecai Halevi, voiced a similar opinion:

They have written that scholars of Erez Israel must be given preference, as there is no Torah like that of Erez Israel. My heart shuddered upon hearing this, . . . for while I do not deny that the atmosphere of Erez Israel is conducive to acquiring wisdom . . . Nevertheless the Lord has not abandoned his people and when the Israelites were exiled from their land, the *Shekhina* followed. It hovers over us in our exile, to illuminate our paths in the farthest reaches of the Dispersion. Enlightenment can radiate from our exile to all the world.[55]

While Hagiz did not advocate special status for the halakhic decisions of emissaries, he argued that those who negated the special spiritual status of Israel were subverting the meaning of the Torah and misleading the ignorant.[56]

Ultimately, *Sefat Emet* transcended specific issues to become a metaphor for the problems of the Jewish Diaspora. If Erez Israel possessed no special sanctity, "then every city and province is as hallowed as the cities of Judah and Israel." "Each one in his city says, I am at peace, for this is Jerusalem to me!" Hagiz developed this line into one of the earliest modern polemics against assimilation of Jews to the larger society. "They become complacent with the children of Gentiles—they adopt the values of the culture of their host country. One result of this is the dissolution of bonds with other Jews. They develop the sense that Jews in other lands are foreigners to them, as is common among former-Marrano *Parnassim* and their mentors."[57]

Hagiz even argued that callousness toward the reality and ideal of Erez Israel was conducive to other heresies. Those who denied its present sanctity implicitly repudiate its past sanctity as well, and thereby divest even the Bible of its status. They extend this negation to the future and negate Jewish messianism. "They rebel against the Lord and his Messiah. I myself have heard some of them say, out of the boorishness and complacence bred by wealth: 'If the Messiah should arrive, and equate rich and poor, what need have we of him?' " Hagiz equated an irreverent attitude to Erez Israel and its representatives with a compromised Jewish identity. He related a small blemish on the complexion of the community to issues which were central to its identity. *Sefat Emet* was the first full flowering of Hagiz' powers as social and religious critic and in it he came to terms with this aspect of his identity. He defended the lonely role to which he would be relegated: "If his [the critic's] protests are not inspired

by ulterior motives, but solely for the honor of God and his Torah, I
am certain that no harm will befall him, and God Himself would support
him."[58]

LEKET HAKEMA"H: HAGIZ AS HALAKHIST

Another vehicle for many of Hagiz' animadversions was his *Leket Ha-
KeMa"H*, a digest of recent halakhic responsa. Ironically, this work, initially undertaken as a purely private and utilitarian effort, gained him
more enduring renown in rabbinic literature than any other. As is often
the case with works of this genre, the genesis of the *Leket* was in private
notes jotted down, "as the need arose, whenever I had to turn to the
laws that were relevant when the masses directed queries to a Hakham."
The transformation from private notebook to a work of universal appeal
in the field of practical Halakhah was accomplished in several stages.[59]
The first phase was a "digest of selections I have collected and edited in
my youth, from my living and deceased Masters." The first effort was
strictly limited to halakhic developments that emerged in the most recent
responsa literature. "Whenever I come across any new valuable ruling
which had practical application, I would underline it and write it in my
book in the most concise manner possible, to serve me as a reminder."
Hagiz appended two small portions of this work—on Nazirite laws and
writs of divorce, to his father's *Halakhot Ketanot*, which he published in
1704. When the funds to publish his own work failed to materialize,
Hagiz decided to shelve it, "like a stillborn creature who will never see
light . . . it will languish in a drawer with my other digests." He com-
forted himself with the thought that "even if I were to publish, not even
one scholar in each city would hurry to buy it and learn something new."[60]
    When Hagiz' Italian relatives-by-marriage, Menashe Hefez and Ga-
briel Padovano, prevailed upon him to resume work on the abandoned
Leket, they advised him to expand and revise it by systematically reviewing all recent halakhic material, not just that which he happened upon,
on the model of Isaac Jeshurun's *Panim Hadashot*.[61] From the first four
pages of the Venice 1704 edition, which was never completed, we can
piece together the structure of the *Leket* as it would have appeared in
1704, and contrast it to the edition subsequently published in Amsterdam in 1707. There are several substantive changes in the Amsterdam
edition in addition to the correction of errors. Responsa volumes that
become known to Hagiz after 1704 were incorporated, as well as several

manuscript collections of responsa. He broadened the scope to include not only responsa but also practical halakhic decisions which were embedded in works of Talmudic novellae. He also went back chronologically to include works which had been available to Jeshurun but were omitted by him. Thus, he fashioned his work to be a complement to Jeshurun's, both horizontally and vertically. The addition which most enhanced the value of Hagiz' volume was the decision to print Jeshurun's entire *Panim Hadashot*, section by section, together with the *Leket*. Together, they would constitute the most comprehensive compendium of practical halakhah in the post-*Shulkhan Arukh* period. (Joseph Karo's sixteenth century code, the *Shulkhan Arukh*, was universally accepted as the most authoritative code of Jewish law.) In fact, Hagiz scaled the edition to the exact same size as the popular Amsterdam edition of the *Shulkhan Arukh* (with *Be'er Hagolah*) of 1662–66, evidence that he intended it to stand side by side as a companion to the *Shulkhan Arukh*. Beginning with the *Shulkhan Arukh* published in Durenfurth, 1743, the *Leket* was published at the back of most standard editions, and Hagiz' work was integrated into the development of subsequent halakhah.

In some ways, the *Leket* is characteristic of all of Hagiz' halakhic works. Its primary contribution lies not in profound, novel thought, but in its successful system of organization, "both a labor and an art." Hagiz tried to impart his messages by reworking existing classics rather than writing more innovative works. This was due not necessarily to intellectual limitations, but rather to his special circumstances. Hagiz felt the need to apologize for leaving the more abstract and profound areas of study. "It is already several years that I have left the Holy Land, and because of the burdensome nature of my exile I have thrown off the weight of Talmud study. Responsa literature has served me as a Divine consolation wherein my soul can take pleasure and my spirit be restored." Hagiz' *Leket* must also be viewed in relationship to the halakhic activity of his contemporaries. Joseph, youngest son of Samuel Aboab, had written a similar work, *Hidushei Soferim*, which Hagiz saw in manuscript. Hagiz criticized the work for being excessively abbreviated—Aboab never cited the actual decisions as they were rendered, and the work would not be useful to very many students.[62]

As is often the case with literature that codifies and condenses from original sources, criticism was leveled against the *Leket*.[63] Hagiz anticipated this and in his introduction he stated emphatically that he intended the work to be used as a reference and guide to the original sources, not as a replacement for them. "And he who relies on this digest will not remain blameless." To ward off potential critics, and to prevent abuse by pseudoscholars who had no scruples about relying on convenient abbreviations to render decisions, Hagiz built a safeguard into the *Leket*. In the weighty and complex areas of divorce and *agunah*, Hagiz abandoned his usual custom of bringing the final ruling of the source he cited. He gave only the reference to the location of the ruling, "so that the pseudoscholars will not be able to commit a misdeed by relying on these brief notes, heaven forbid." Even after the success of the *Leket* was secure, criticism and misgivings lingered: "I suspect I have done wrong with my *Leket*, a small index of the later *poskim*, for reasons I had stated there."[64]

Hagiz saved most of his own responsa to be published separately; very few were included in the *Leket*. As a very small portion of his total output was ultimately published, any attempt to construct a halakhic profile of Hagiz rests on a limited basis. Hagiz' rulings are varied, and there is a fair balance between leniency and stringency. His rulings are conspicuous mainly in that they often come to overturn an accepted ruling or custom. In one instance, Hagiz declared that a practice widely believed to be forbidden [inhaling snuff on the Day of Atonement] was perfectly permissible. Those who wished to be strict with themselves were welcome to refrain, but the public should be aware that this restriction was not authored by God! At the end of the volume, Hagiz justified this dethroning of an entrenched custom: "It was my intent to show the masses that the purpose of the rabbis is to restrict only when the prohibition is mandated, but if there is room for leniency, they will be lenient."[65]

It is one of the paradoxes of Hagiz' position that while he devoted a great deal of energy to a campaign that called for submission to rabbinic authority, he himself often dissented from accepted rabbinic rulings. Perhaps this can be explained by his continual differentiation between the role of the masses and their leaders. Like his greatly admired brother-in-law, Hezekiah da Silva, he did not hesitate to oppose the rulings of Joseph Karo: "God forbid, we cannot accept that these words in Our Holy Master [Karo]'s work were in fact his opinion; if that were so, the halakhah has vanished from him. *We must conclude that a misguided disciple appended these words.* Therefore, one should follow this true ruling of mine, which I have rendered in public, and which was well accepted. . . . Even if the greatest sages in Israel had issued opposite rulings, what of that? Even an orphaned generation such as ours is divinely inspired just as they were, and they have left us room to speak our minds."[66] The much admired da Silva did not command Hagiz' adherence either: "Although he is great and mighty, an erudite expert to the multitudes, sharp and penetrating, nevertheless, in some places in his work [*Peri Hadash*] he was not careful, and ruled stringently when he should have been lenient, and vice versa, on the basis of a minority opinion . . . All this I have written at length, as is not my wont, to erase the error from the hearts of those who have followed the stringent ruling of my brother-in-law, who had no basis for this prohibition."[67]

Only the first half of the *Leket* was published in 1707, volumes *Orah Hayim* and *Yoreh De'ah*. Hagiz planned to publish the other half as soon as the sale of these volumes realized enough income to finance the remainder of the project. While Hagiz castigated those who published for sheer profit, he urged rabbis who received his book to respond in currency and not in kind with their own books, so that he could complete publication. In fact, only one other volume, part of *Eben ha-Ezer*, was published in 1719. *Hoshen Mishpat*, which would have been the largest volume, was never published, probably because of the prohibitive expense.[68]

CENTRALITY OF KABBALAH

If his published works can be said to serve as a window into the inner world of Moses Hagiz, then it is apparent that Kabbalah was a major force in that world. In the decade between his first publication in 1703 until the eruption of the Hayon controversy in 1713, Hagiz was instrumental in the publication of no fewer than five Kabbalistic works. The first book he ever published, *Or Kadmon* (*The Primordial Light*) was an anthology of Kabbalistic liturgical poetry to be recited on the Day of Atonement. The crowning jewel of the small anthology was the "Keter Malkhut" (Royal Crown) of David Ibn Abi Zimra, a liturgical poem about the attributes of God, patterned on Solomon Ibn Gabirol's famous poem of the same name. The manuscript was one of several that Hagiz had brought with him 'in his satchel' from Jerusalem, and his edition was the first publication of this work.[69]

> We feel compelled to proclaim that anyone who separates himself from this sublime lore [kabbalah] has renounced eternal life. In it, one can apprehend and know God . . . in His Unity and Providence. The *Tikkunim*, the *Zohar* and *Tikkunei Zohar* teach us which *Tikkun* (Divine Restoration) is performed with each *mitzvah*.
>
> The sacred worship of the children of Israel is requisite for the Almighty, especially from the period of the Destruction of the Temple, when the four uppermost *sefirot* departed . . . As the AR"I

[Luria] has stated . . . "and the righteous men, with their Torah activities at midnight . . . restore it little by little."

Hagiz accepted Kabbalistic teachings as the central religious truth in Judaism. He upheld even doctrines which were widely disputed: "Belief in transmigration has been verified, and transmitted from the earliest generation . . . Therefore, anyone who questions it, is, in my eyes, as one who denies the existence of God and His judgment." He advocated acceptance of elaborate penances as the most efficacious means of repentance.[70]

Despite the primacy of Kabbalistic doctrines in Hagiz's thought, he cannot be characterized as a mystic. Other than the "apparition" that appeared at a time of grave personal crisis, Hagiz did not record experiences which might be termed mystical, nor did he attempt to induce them. The most extreme statement of spiritual aspiration is found in the preface to the *Idrot:* "Fortunate is the man who is patient and attains the level wherein a fraction of the mystery shall be revealed through him. . . . I speak these words with a saddened heart, for I know myself to be ignorant in the ways of the Lord." Hagiz refrained from writing Kabbalistic works himself, "for it is impossible to render on parchment and explain that which only a true Kabbalist can teach."[71]

In 1708, Hagiz published his second Kabbalistic book, *Sefer ha-Idrot ha-Kedoshot (Book of the Holy Assemblies).* Because Hagiz had published works critical of the lay leadership of Livorno and Amsterdam in the five-year hiatus before the publication of the *Idrot,* Hagiz was put under a ban which prohibited him, "to sell, distribute, or export any book in any language," and he was warned "not to publish, from this day forward any book or sheet of paper without the prior consent of the *Mahamad."* Hagiz disobeyed the ban, and continued to publish without submitting his work to prior examination. To accomplish this, he was forced to conceal his true role in publishing ventures after this date. A prologue or epilogue by Hagiz, or identification of him as proofreader, is often sufficient evidence to indicate that he was primarily responsible for the appearance of a work. In the *Idrot,* the only name to appear on the title page is Joseph HaKohen, a former disciple of Galante's from Jerusalem, who is named as underwriter. Hagiz' role is limited to a lengthy introduction in which he appears only under the acronym HaMaNiaH (Moses Ibn Jacob Hagiz).

The *Idra Rabbah* (Great Assembly), is a segment of the *Zohar* describing the convocation of the Tanna R. Simon b. Yohai and his companions in which he expounded to them mysteries concerning the Primordial Man. *Idra Zuta* (Small Assembly), the concluding portion of the *Zohar*, depicts the scene at the deathbed of R. Simon bar Yohai, at which more mysteries were revealed.[72] In his preface, Hagiz described the practice of reciting the *Idrot* on certain dates. It had originated with a circle of Jerusalem rabbis who went to pray at the tombs of Rachel and Samuel the Prophet. At the appointed times, they would remain at the sites all night and recite the *Idrot*. "At midnight, they would wail and mourn over the Exile of Israel. After that, they would extinguish the candles and commence the *Tikkun Rahel*, with great enthusiasm. Then they would study Torah until daybreak, and recite one more prayer upon leaving the grave." Hagiz added a plea for contributions toward the sustenance of the Torah scholars of Jerusalem, and to members of this sacred circle in particular. Contributions were to be channeled through the head of the circle, 'presently head of the Jerusalem Kehilla, the son of holy fathers, Abraham Yizhaki.' It is likely that Yizhaki had brought this project to Hagiz' notice, and he was influential in facilitating at least one other Kabbalistic publication of Hagiz'.[73]

Hagiz stated that he had proofread and corrected the *Idrot* from a copy of the *Zohar* which had once belonged to the great Kabbalist R. Nathan Shapiro, which he had found in the home of Joseph Zarfati. Zarfati, a brother-in-law of the distinguished Amsterdam publishers, the Foa brothers, was renowned for maintaining an open house for passers-by, particularly emissaries. Zarfati encouraged the Foas to specialize in publishing the work of emissaries and this may partly explain Hagiz' switch, in 1710, from the publishing house of Proops, eminent Jewish publisher in Amsterdam, to the house of Foa. Hagiz may even have been a partner in their publishing ventures during the years 1710–1713.[74] He believed that the Foa press was superior to that of Proops and this new alliance seemed auspicious at the outset. However, Nathanel Foa was the son-in-law of Solomon Ayllon, rabbi of Amsterdam. When the Hayon controversy erupted in 1713, Foa was forced to terminate his relationship with Hagiz, who had become an adversary of Ayllon.

In 1710, Hagiz published *Mafteah ha-Zohar* (*Index to the Zohar*), at the Foa press. The first edition of a work by this title had been made by Hagiz' ancestor, Moses Galante of Safed, in Venice, 1566. That first edition had been indexed according to Biblical passages. Hagiz published an eminently more useful manuscript, reorganized according to topic. The manuscript was of very recent Jerusalem provenance—it had been brought to Hagiz by Abraham Rovigo. The book lacks all the customary appurtances such as approbations or the identity of individuals who prepared the work for the press. On the final page there is a paragraph by Hagiz' calling for wider dissemination of Kabbalistic classics.[75]

In 1711–12, a now-rare edition of the early Kabbalistic work *Sefer Yetzirah* (*Book of Creation*) was published. The *Sifra de-Zeni'uta* as amended by Moses Zacuto, a prayer of Elijah the prophet, and Masekhet Tamid was appended to it, but the collection did not reveal the name of its compiler. Only the familiar acronym of Hagiz in the Introduction revealed his participation.[76]

The last Kabbalistic work Hagiz brought to press, in 1713, was David Ibn Abi Zimra's *Magen David* [*Shield of David*]. It is a treatise on the Kabbalistic significance of every aspect of every letter of the Hebrew alphabet—pronunciation, form and shape, numerical value, and combination values. The science of letters was especially important for the theurgical, semi-magical school of Kabbalah: "Their combinations and reversals, particularly of the Ineffable Name, can create new beings."[77] Of all the Kabbalistic works Hagiz brought to press, the publication of this one involved the greatest intrigue. While Hagiz himself later stated that he had published the book, his role in the work was concealed, and credit for bringing the work to press is given to R. Yohanan of Helischau. In the "Apology" following the preface, R. Yohanan stated that Hagiz' redaction of the text was crucial to its publication. Apparently, the Hayon controversy erupted when the work was nearly completed and since Hagiz found himself on the opposite side of Foa he was forced to have the first signature (four pages) printed elsewhere.[78]

Hagiz gathered an extensive collection of Kabbalistic manuscripts. He hoped to publish and disseminate as many of these manuscripts as possible, and saw in the popularization of Kabbalah the antidote to many of the deficiencies for which he castigated Jewish society.[79] *Magen David* contains clear evidence that the published books represent only a fraction of the total Hagiz had prepared for publication. Preceeding Hagiz' Introduction to *Magen David* is another introduction titled "Introduction by the one who has brought *Tikkunei Zohar* to press." The content and style, as well as continuity with the second introduction, all point to Hagiz as the author. He had apparently prepared an edition of *Tikkunei Zohar* for publication, and when prevented at the last minute from bringing it to press, he inserted the introduction into *Magen David*. Hagiz alluded to plans for a reprinting of the *Zohar* itself. These projects never materialized.Hagiz credited two mentors from his youthful days for his love of Kabbalistic lore. The first was his revered teacher, Abraham Yizhaki, who had taught him during Galante's tenure at the helm of the Yeshiva

Beth Jacob. It was Yizhaki who had interested Hagiz in publishing the *Idrot*. The second was his grandfather, Moses Galante. In his introduction to the *Idrot*, Hagiz cited an excerpt from a Kabbalistic work of Galante's which was never published. In the excerpt, Galante quotes the work of Jacob Zemah, the leading Kabbalist in Jerusalem, and in all likelihood Galante's teacher of Kabbalah. In addition to composing many important Kabbalistic works, Zemah was one of the primary disseminators of the writings of Hayim Vital, disciple of Isaac Luria. Thus, Hagiz had an impeccable chain of Kabbalistic tradition reaching back to Luria. Nevertheless, Hagiz was not a proponent of exclusively Lurianic Kabbalah. David Ibn Abi Zimra, who represented the culmination of pre-Lurianic school of Kabbalah, also figured prominently in Hagiz' works.

The tensions between Kabbalah and halakhah are almost nonexistent in Hagiz thought. Each served a distinct function, and they could coexist harmoniously so long as the boundaries between them were not erased. Halakhah was the unshakable superstructure that shaped every aspect of Jewish life, but for Hagiz it did not constitute the sum total of Jewish spirituality. The true core of Jewish spiritual vitality was Kabbalah. The two were inseparably conjoined and Hagiz stated that his goal was "To study and to teach, the exoteric and the esoteric . . . so that they may be united by me."[80] For Hagiz this relationship was Sanaitic in origin, and 'even the Talmud contained many cryptic references to the True Lore' [Kabbalah]. Only in the sphere of action did halakhah reign as the final arbiter. In support of this position Hagiz adduced the statement of David Ibn Zimra, who ruled that any place where Kabbalistic teachings conflict with the Talmud, the Talmud and Codes are to be followed."[81] Hagiz exhorted his rabbinic contemporaries to refrain from making their own deviant legal decisions, "with the excuse that they have a reliable source for their rulings—the *Zohar*." In Hagiz' only volume of halakhic responsa, *Shetei ha-Lehem*, Kabbalah is rarely invoked; responses were based solely on halakhic precedent.[82]

The relationship between these two axial elements of Hagiz' thought is most evident in his work on the 613 precepts, *Eleh ha-Mizvot* [*These are the Commandments*] (Amsterdam, 1713). Hagiz wrote it to defend the traditional rabbinic interpretive structure of Jewish law, "to muzzle the mouths of those who deny the truth, to admonish them, . . . for if any of them denies even one rabbinic teaching, he is considered by us, the faithful, to have strayed from the truth." To those who demanded proof that the Oral Torah was also given at Sinai, the proof lay in the esoteric infrastructure, the Kabbalah." [Rabbinic] Teachings, which are perceived anew each day, were already enunciated by the Almighty to Moses, none are truly novel. No creature can challenge even the tiniest minutiae, for every letter contains the secrets of the celestial light, as is known to all who are privy to their hidden meaning."[83]

Hagiz' defense of the rabbinic, nonliteral interpretation of the *lex-talionis* provides a good illustration of his method: "They say, if [the rabbinic interpretation] is so, why has the Torah not specified "financial compensation?" The audacity of the heretics, may their memory rot, is motivated by their desire to add or detract from the Torah. The true reason, known to all Kabbalists, is that the Torah letters form names of God, and *the literal text had to conform to this inner meaning."* The true meaning of many laws is known only by those who have been initiated into "the secret of God to those who love Him." As a proper introduction to study of the precepts, Hagiz recommended a portion of the *Zohar*, and Isaiah Horowitz's *Shnei Luhot ha-Berit*, a guide to halakhah in which Kabbalah has pride of place. Hagiz' *Eleh ha-Mizvot* was divided into seven daily portions of study, and it proved very popular.[84]

KABBALAH—FOR THE MASSES?

The first publication of the *Zohar*, the canonical text of Kabbalah, in 1588, had provoked a storm of controversy over the popularization of a heretofore esoteric knowledge. By the first half of the seventeenth century, Lurianic Kabbalah had percolated down and in various forms permeated every corner of Jewish life. The question of whether, and to what extent, to disseminate Kabbalistic works was revived after the collapse of the Sabbatian messianic movement in the mid seventeenth century. As we have seen, Hagiz' stance was positive, although he harbored some reservations.[85]

Of all the Kabbalistic works Hagiz published, none were original treatises. They were all classics intended for a wide general audience, even if offered ostensibly as *Tikkunim* for recitation rather than as mystical texts for contemplation or scholarly study. The *Or Kadmon* anthology was meant to be recited on the Day of Atonement. The title page of the *Idrot* proclaims that the work was published "pocket size, so that *everyone* could *conveniently* carry it on them wherever they went," and it was bound with other *Tikkunim*. The *Mafteah ha-Zohar* was a technical aid that opened the *Zohar* by its topical index, "so that every individual could easily find the object of his search in it." Hagiz chafed at the customary copyright/approbation generally required of those who republished classics. "They lock the doors in the face of those who come to publish." The ideal situation would be that all "the Jewish classics, *the Zohar among them*, would be printed annually until every Jew owned a copy—even those who don't even know how to 'open' them." In contrast to the edition of 1568, Hagiz' *Sefer Yezirah* was published without scholarly commentaries.

Had pecuniary considerations been paramount, Hagiz could just as easily have chosen to publish non-Kabbalistic books that guaranteed wide circulation. His decision to publish Kabbalistic works was motivated by his genuine belief that Kabbalah was an antidote to the pervasive spiritual malaise he encountered among Jews in Western Europe. His works are replete with excerpts from confrontations he had with Jews who were apathetic, dissaffected, or who harbored a rationalist skepticism which threatened the core of Jewish tradition. Hagiz believed that Kabbalah, with its elemental style and profound consideration of the nature of God, the human soul, and exile and redemption, was the best means of stimulating a renewed quest for meaning which would result in a reaffirmation of hallowed traditions and beliefs.

From the outset Hagiz recognized that in the very beauty and boldness of the Kabbalah lay its danger to the uninitiated. The stark symbolism, particularly the "Shiur Komah" in the *Idrot*, measurements of the 'body' of God which are analogous to the human body, could be interpreted as the grossest anthropomorphism. True, a profusion of Kabbalistic works was readily available, and the barrier of secrecy had long been breached. Nevertheless, Hagiz seized every opportunity to warn the novice. His Introduction to the *Idrot* is preceeded by a bold *WARNING: A Note to the Reader*. "An explicit warning to anyone who reads of these divine subjects in the *Zohar*, let him not commit the mortal sin of taking these words literally . . . To remove obstacles from the path of the tyro . . . understand that all terms employed in the *Zohar*, such as forehead, eyes, nose, and other physical limbs, particularly in the *Idrot*, in which these phrases abound, represent attributes and *sefirot* which are purely metaphysical. There is no affinity between them and God." An identical warning is issued in the Introduction to *Magen David*.[86]

With the eruption of the Hayon affair late in 1713, the synapsis between Kabbalah and persistent crypto-Sabbatianism became an urgent problem for Hagiz. Sabbatians had developed a ramified Kabbalistic system based on ingenious extrapolation from Lurianic doctrine and radical reinterpretation. It is significant that after the dramatic watershed of the Hayon controversy, Hagiz ceased to publish Kabbalistic works. After the controversy he reversed his earlier position, and advocated that Kabbalah be restored to its status of esoteric lore to prevent its further subversion in the wrong hands. The Hayon controversy opened Hagiz' eyes to the fact that Kabbalah was being used to provide the intellectual underpinnings for a movement subversive of the values he sought to safeguard, on a much larger scale than he had dreamed. When the dust of the Sabbatian controversies settled, Hagiz would seek another doctrine to replace Kabbalah as the spiritual fare of the Jewish masses. Before we reach that point in the development of Hagiz' thought, we must follow the course of the controversies that occupied the next two decades of his life.

CHAPTER 4

Eruption of the Hayon Controversy

MOSES HAGIZ was the catalytic force behind a series of controversies that took place in the early eighteenth century. The first of these was the Hayon controversy. It began on 9 Tamuz (July 3), 1713, when Nehemiah Hiya Hayon, an itinerant Kabbalist, arrived in Amsterdam. An investigation into the character of his recently published works swiftly assumed larger dimensions. Hayon's opponents accused him of concealing Sabbatian and heretical tendencies. The controversy which ensued engulfed the most prominent Jewish communities, spread quickly from West to East, and shattered half a century of silence by Jewish leaders on crypto-Sabbatianism, the sectarian outgrowth of the Sabbatian messianic movement. It became the prototype for a series of similar eruptions which occurred with rhythmic regularity through the first half of the eighteenth century. The drama was reenacted in 1725–26 with the young R. Jonathan Eybeschutz, among others, as target; and in the 1730s with Moses Hayim Luzzatto. The impulse finally spent itself in the climactic, convulsive controversy between Emden and Eybeschutz in mid-century. These controversies aroused many latent passions and spawned a vast polemical literature which reveals a complex interplay of motivations. By carefully unraveling some of the tangled lines, we may recover some of the realities and inner forces which shaped Jewish life in a period of great ferment.

A CONSPIRACY OF SILENCE?

Why did Hagiz not open his campaign against crypto-Sabbatianism long before 1713? In his entire oeuvre of Kabbalistic, Halakhic, and homiletic works to that date there is scarcely a trace of Hagiz' awareness of, and antipathy toward, crypto-Sabbatianism. One of the rare fleeting references, made in the course of a disquisition on the study of Kabbalah, is an instructive example: "We were told by our forebears of a *small fraction* of a *tiny number* of people who abandoned our covenant and converted on the basis of interpretations extrapolated from the text of the *Zohar*."[1] Hagiz' clearly intended to minimize the scope of the movement in this reference to the apostasy of hundreds of Sabbatians in Salonika to Islam. It does not even reveal that he was referring to crypto-Sabbatianism, or that the sect was still pervasive and vital at the time he wrote.

Given Hagiz' previous entanglements with Sabbatian sympathizers in Jerusalem, his history as an outspoken social critic, and his volatile temperament, the omission is striking. The puzzlement can be extended to many of his rabbinic contemporaries who joined him in the campaign against Hayon but had never before spoken publicly on the subject. An inquiry into the particular combination of timing and events that prompted them to polemicize publicly against Hayon and crypto-Sabbatianism in 1713 must be preceded by the question of why they did not do so earlier.

Was the silence a result of the secrecy that enveloped the sect and kept opponents ignorant of the identities of adherents? There are many remarkable examples of virulent opponents of Sabbatianism who remained unaware of the Sabbatian beliefs of some of their associates. Ber Perlhefter, a relative of R. Jonathan Eybeschutz and an active crypto-Sabbatian in Prague recalled, "I had been asked by R. Jacob Sasportas . . . for my commentary to *Sifra de-Zeniuta*. . . . We knew each other from Hamburg, where he served as *Dayyan* of the Sephardim, and I, of the Ashkenazim." Had he known of Perlhefter's Sabbatian inclination, Sasportas, an inveterate opponent of Sabbatianism from its inception, would never have made this gesture of respect. Sasportas also lauded R. Judah Sharaf, a radical crypto-Sabbatian.[2] Abraham Rovigo was a Sabbatian whose early fervor endured after the apostasy: "I can scarcely permit slumber to conquer my eyes [from great excitement] over this faith which is engraved in my heart, which entertains no doubts, for I am one of the true believers." After he weathered the crisis of Sabbatai Zebi's death, Rovigo remained a Sabbatian activist of the first rank, his home a nerve center for Sabbatian activities.[3] Yet Moses Hagiz reserved the loftiest encomia for Abraham Rovigo in his scathing work of criticism, *Sefat Emet.* He was oblivious to Rovigo's enthusiasm for the Sabbatian movement. The ignorance of anti-Sabbatians can be attributed partly to the elaborate efforts of crypto-Sabbatians to conceal their true beliefs, sometimes under the guise of rabbinic pietism.

Discovery of Sabbatian sympathies where none were presumed caused great consternation, as in the following responsum. "A wealthy philanthropist had pledged an annual stipend to a circle of scholars who were renowned as men of pious activities [*Hasidim ve-Anshei Ma'aseh*] . . . but only the Lord can see to man's heart . . . after a year or two it was revealed that beneath the facade, most of them had followed the path of ill repute."[4]

The internecine strife among the various schools of Sabbatian believers also generated great confusion. In their drive for preeminence within the sect, subsects would denounce and persecute one another, leading the uninitiated to believe that they were anti-Sabbatians. Samuel Primo ("Scribe to the Messiah") waged a campaign against the Sabbatian theologian Abraham Miguel Cardoso, because Cardoso opposed the deification of Sabbatai Zebi. This led to the anomalous situation of Primo reaping praise in a violently anti-Sabbatian, anti-Cardoso tract, Elijah Kohen's *Sefer Meribat Kadesh:* "Samuel Primo, disseminator of Torah and rabbi, whose precious esteem is unsullied, from whom no secret is concealed sent for [Cardoso] in order to dispute his faith . . . and eventually had Cardoso expelled." Primo's own congregation in Adrianople was apparently unaware of his beliefs until Cardoso declared that he would "bring convincing proof from Istanbul that [Primo] believed in the divinity of the Messiah."[5] R. Hayim Alfandari, a disciple of Cardoso until he joined the more radical school of Primo, joined the campaign against Hayon in 1714 because Hayon followed Cardoso's more moderate Sabbatianism.[6] Some adherents of Sabbatianism were so repulsed by Hayon's grandiloquent claims and odd mannerisms that they repudiated him without ever having read his books. Elijah Mujajon, a rabbi of Ancona on the same Bet Din as Samson Morpurgo, and a Sabbatian, "was infuriated by his [Hayon's] follies and his words, and ejected him from his presence." Hayon would later seize upon this confusing state of affairs to conceal his own loyalties.[7]

While these instances prove that confusion was rampant, they do not yet constitute a satisfactory answer to our question. The overwhelming testimony of Hagiz and his rabbinic colleagues demonstrates that there was a high degree of awareness of the pervasiveness of Sabbatianism as well as particularized knowledge of the activities of certain individuals.

In 1714, R. Benjamin Halevi of Smyrna recounted, "It was approximately six years ago that the enemy of Israel [Hayon] visited here. I heard that he had written a book, *Kodesh ha-Kodashim*, and when it passed my way, I read it from beginning to end. I recognized his hallucinations and heresies . . . but I refrained from taking action, for it would have been a waste of my Torah-study time." R. Netanel Halevi of Pesaro, recalled in 1714, "Approximately two years ago, [Hayon] had passed through Lugo where I was serving as rabbi. . . . He showed me his manuscript which included the *Mehemnuta de-Khola* [attributed to Sabbatai Zebi]. . . . I rejected it . . . but I did not speak of this to anyone because it was the way of that generation to sit in the study halls and suppress such matters, in fulfillment of the verse, 'and he who is wise at that time, will remain silent.' I had known of these matters since my youth, but I had kept the words guarded in my heart."[8] Joseph Ergas related that he had been fully aware of Hayon's beliefs years before the controversy erupted.

> In 1710, the serpent [Hayon] arrived here [Livorno], and we went to discern his nature, I and another local scholar. Hayon presented his manuscript for us to read . . . and I realized that the core of the work was a homily by Sabbatai Zebi himself. When I confronted Hayon, he lowered his eyes to the ground and did not respond; we argued over the contents of the first page until dusk. A few days later, while passing his hostel, I again engaged him in debate until he shouted that he could not bear this wearisome quarreling any longer, but he would continue the debate in writing. . . . His words revealed his profound and zealous cleavage to the faith of Sabbatai Zebi (for there are many among them who abominate the evil act [of apostasy] yet cling to his faith.)[9]

At the time, Ergas took no further action against Hayon. R. Abraham Segre received a letter from a friend in Livorno at the height of the controversy: "Three years ago, Hayon passed through our city, and I rebuked him saying that his exposition was contrary to tradition and his proofs were unconvincing. He replied that I was correct, but the source of his work was angelic revelation. I pressed him . . . but he evaded me. . . . In the end, he went and published it."[10]

The torrent of anti-Sabbatian polemics in 1713–15 released a spate of recollections of a stifling consensus of silence that had prevailed until then. Hagiz claimed to have known of R. Solomon Ayllon's Sabbatianism since 1698, but he did not say a word when Ayllon was appointed rabbi of the Sephardic Kehilla in London or in Amsterdam. "When the news [of Ayllon's appointment] was received by the rabbinic leaders, they averted their eyes as if they were unaware of it [of Ayllon's Sabbatianism]. The Lord God knows that when I was questioned by the community in 1698, *I withheld my testimony* in order not to weaken the resolve of the penitents (*Ba'alei Teshuba*), and I thought, since he has already ascended, let him remain, out of respect for the community that had innocently erred."[11] There is no evidence to support or gainsay Hagiz' claim, but since the admission does not redound to his credit, there is no reason to reject it. Hagiz implied that especially in communities of "penitents," former Marranos, the rabbinate deliberately concealed instances of Sabbatianism within its own ranks from the public, in order to maintain its credibility. Even at the outset of the Hayon controversy, Hagiz recalled that his first instinct was to preserve the silence: "Our entire goal in the early days [of the controversy] was to render a verdict on Hayon in order to oppose and stifle his illusory beliefs . . . but not to publicize any of his doctrines. . . . When the aura of secrecy vanishes, calamity ensues . . . so I had intended to let the matter remain shrouded in silence." The controversy spurred Hagiz to reevaluate this policy, and he concluded with regret that the silence had been too costly. "Indeed, withholding our testimony was the cause of much inadvertent wrongdoing, particularly in this case." In a letter to Morpurgo, Hagiz exulted over his pioneering decision "not to follow the pattern of concealment that many had considered to be the proper course of action." A decade after the Hayon controversy, in 1726, Hagiz recalled that even at the height of the controversy, Solomon Ayllon, supporter of Hayon, had been treated with extra courtesy by rabbinic polemicists because of his rabbinic position. "Our task cannot be completed as long as protection remains. . . . If Ayllon was treated with partiality in the battle of the serpent (Hayon) . . . look at the abominations that have resulted. . . . The Jewish public is crying fraud . . . accusing the Sages of our generation of covering for those who have protectors, and hounding only those that are defenseless."[12]

Years after his monumental controversy with Jonathan Eybeschutz, Jacob Emden recalled his initial reaction to the discovery of Sabbatian manuscripts in Prague: "I did not see publicity as a remedy for the matter, and I thought, 'Silence is fitting.' Therefore, I instructed that the 'leaven' be destroyed so that the contamination should not spread." R. Ezekiel Landau, contemporary of Emden, advised that the most expeditious way to bury Sabbatianism was concealment, in this instance, of Sabbatian artifacts. "The rabbinic court that encounters Sabbatian amulets may not open or read them at all. They should bury them in clay

vessels, so that the excitement will subside."[13] R. Leib b. Ozer wrote in
1717: "Whoever is a good Jew would not dare mention him [Sabbatai],
for who would wish *to violate such a great ban?*" There is some evidence
that bans that had been pronounced against mentioning Sabbatai Zebi
or his adherents were still considered to be in effect in the eighteenth
century, and this contributed to the atmosphere of taboo that surrounded
the subject.[14]

Some rabbis refrained from publicizing their knowledge of Sabbatian
activity, not out of fear that knowledge of Sabbatian doctrines would
spread among Jews, but that it would reach the ears of Gentiles. Others
were afraid to oppose Sabbatians because of the positions of power that
they held within the community. "Many important, affluent members
of our community had been swayed [by Hayon]. . . . My whispered
admonitions during his sojourn were later justified." An eighteenth century Christian missionary noted with amusement that the fast of the Ninth
of Ab was widely violated in one city: "*Haben . . . gefressen, gesoffen, und
gesagt messias sei schon gekommen.*" But the offenders could not be reproved
"because a wealthy and influential court Jew inclined toward them."
Samson Morpurgo warned Hagiz to exercise caution in his selection of
targets for his polemic, "for the sinners are always able to find a sturdy
mountain, bedecked in gold . . . to protect them."[15] Some rabbis remained silent although they disagreed with Sabbatian interpretations, because they saw no need to extirpate the exponents of these doctrines.
Others felt remote from the Kabbalistic subject matter that was under
dispute, and regarded the whole issue with aloofness or apathy. The silence became a polemical weapon in the hands of Hayon's adherents: "If
you were aware all along, why did you not notify the public long ago?
Why did you wait for the biased judgment of Hagiz and Zebi?[16]

The only important exception to the picture we have drawn was the
single-minded, single-handed pursuit of Sabbatian theologian Abraham
Cardoso, his writings, and his disciples by Abraham Yizhaki. Yizhaki's
activities were largely confined to the East, and his early pronouncements against Hayon caused no tremors at the time. Yizhaki excepted,
the prevailing rabbinic posture toward Sabbatianism in the early eighteenth century was a resigned, passive, albeit regretful silence. The
transfiguration of the rabbinate to a vigorous, aggressive force in the pursuit of Sabbatianism was due largely to the efforts of Moses Hagiz.

PRECEDENTS AND INFLUENCES:
ABRAHAM YIZHAKI

Hagiz' central role in the Hayon controversy tends to obscure the relatively temperate and deliberate pace with which he entered the controversy in its very early stages. Hagiz had not invented this opportunity for protracted exchange of hostilities. Abraham Yizhaki, mentor and teacher of his youth, led the earliest opposition to Hayon; yet, it was not personal fealty to Yizhaki which motivated Hagiz to follow suit. Hagiz had at first deliberately eschewed the open pursuit of Sabbatians that Yizhaki had advocated for many years. As we shall see, Hagiz expressed great dismay when his colleague Hakham Zebi published an antagonistic document that would thrust them headlong into public confrontation with Hayon. And yet, shortly thereafter Hagiz overcame his initial reluctance when he saw his own interests mesh with the campaign against Hayon. From that point it was to become his own cause, transformed into something of far far greater magnitude than Yizhaki had envisioned.

In the two decades that passed since Hagiz left Jerusalem in 1694, the internecine squabbling over limited resources and political control continued unabated within the Jewish community of Jerusalem. The struggle centered on the efforts of various crypto-Sabbatian elements to establish themselves in Jerusalem, and build it into a Sabbatian stronghold. After the departure of Hagiz, Abraham Yizhaki remained the most influential monitor and opponent of these efforts. The activity of Sabbatian groups intensified at the turn of the century, and many Sabbatians successfully implanted themselves there. Abraham Cardoso, one of the most important Sabbatian theologians, had maintained close ties to Sabbatians in Jerusalem since 1680. The years from the immigration of Judah Hasid, Hayim Malakh, and their followers in 1700, through that of Abraham Rovigo and his circle in 1706, were years of mounting messianic excitement. Cardoso intensified his activities in Jerusalem. He polemicized against followers of other schools of Sabbatian thought, particularly that of Samuel Primo which Hayim Malakh disseminated. Cardoso bemoaned "that there are at present, several [Sabbatian] scholars who follow the 'faith of Samuel Primo,' *even in Jerusalem*," and he assigned his copyists to disseminate his own treatises there to counter the influence of Malakh. "Malakh tried to distance people from me *even in Jerusalem*, just as others had tried in Smyrna. . . . The Ashkenazi Judah Hasid, who perished upon his arrival in Jerusalem, had also received teachings of the Divine Mystery from [Hayim Malakh] . . . This faith is false . . . it is nonsense which will contribute nothing toward our redemption. To prevent further error, I have hastily prepared the treatise which follows."[17]

In addition to the polemical motive, Jerusalem played an important role in Cardoso's own eschatological scheme. Not surprisingly, the first priority on his agenda was to establish a yeshiva once he got there: "He said to his adherents, 'In the academy on High there are two yeshivot, one for Elijah, the other for R. Simon Bar Yohai. And I will establish a third one . . . for I possess a veritable treasury of esoteric lore. . . . I will bestow upon every member [of my yeshiva] an angel or a *maggid* . . . and the news will spread: Whoever wishes to prophesy, shall find his way to me."[18] In 1703, Cardoso arrived in Jaffa, on his way to implement his plans in Jerusalem. The vigilant Yizhaki persuaded the rabbinate of Jerusalem to bar Cardoso from entering. According to Yizhaki, it was at this juncture that Cardoso met with, and influenced, Nehemiah Hayon, who was in Safed at the time. Yizhaki later testifed that Hayon had been engaged in spreading his "heresies," and upon hearing of Hayon's activity, "I became possessed with zealotry for the Lord, and I issued a permanent injunction that all the people whom he had gathered to study with him should separate themselves from him and disperse immediately, to remove the unclean spirit from the land." Thus Yizhaki had pursued Hayon as early as 1703, yet so long as Cardoso was alive, Hayon remained an ancillary target. Yizhaki rebuffed Cardoso successfully, and Cardoso eventually left Erez Israel without having gained access to Jerusalem. Cardoso's death in 1706 inspired his disciples to increase their efforts to disseminate his works. Yizhaki believed, correctly, that Hayon led this effort among Cardoso's disciples.[19]

In 1708, Hayon succeeded in securing generous financial backing in Smyrna to establish a yeshiva in Erez Israel. Coincidentally, Yizhaki ascended to the position of chief rabbi of Jerusalem in the same year. Yizhaki immediately employed the prestige of his new position (often greater in the Diaspora than in Jerusalem itself) to thwart the plans of Hayon. In late spring of 1708, scarcely a month after Hayon had obtained a commitment from his supporters, Yizhaki fired off a letter in the name of the rabbinate of Jerusalem to the rabbinate of Smyrna:

> We have heard . . . that the debased and repulsive Hayon arrived in your city . . . and has established a good reputation for himself. . . . He is a master of the lore of the unclean, deceitful and licentious . . . He is a fortune teller, sorcerer and heretic in his own right . . . who practiced sorcery while in Egypt. . . . Our hearts shuddered at the news that he has beguiled people into com-

mitting their funds to him. . . . He has written a book that deserves to be burned. . . . We have come to give notification that since he is a heretic and a sorcerer, it is forbidden to support him.[20]

As chief rabbi, Yizhaki shouldered the burden of Jerusalem's troubled finances, and he soon took up the wandering staff of the emissary to raise funds. Far from abandoning his campaign, he incorporated it into his itinerary. Crypto-Sabbatians in Jerusalem had long utilized their assignments as emissaries as pretexts for Sabbatian proselytization and propaganda.[21] Yizhaki was determined to use his travels to further his anti-Sabbatian endeavors. In Constantinople in 1709, Yizhaki had another confrontation with Hayon. Together with two other emissaries, he issued a general ban against Hayon and his works: "We declare with the full force of malediction, with the power of the sanctity of Erez Israel and the spirit of the Lord that hovers over it, that no Jew should read the works of that serpent, and whoever possesses copies of it should burn them. . . . The author is immersed in evil, . . . He is hereby banned and excommunicated. . . . The gates of repentance are barred against him." The ban repeated Yizhaki's earlier charges against Hayon and stressed his relationship to Cardoso.[22]

Yizhaki traveled through Italy in 1711–12. In Livorno, he made the acquaintance of R. Joseph Ergas; in Ferrara, he was warmly welcomed by R. Isaac Lampronte, who presented his three most promising disciples to Yizhaki. In Verona, his arrival was duly noted in the communal archives; in Padua he added his name to a communal tax ordinance that was not being properly observed; in Venice, he joined Jacob Aboab in a similar undertaking.[23] Although we have no references to anti-Sabbatian agitation in Italy, Samson Morpurgo reminisced in 1712, "I recalled the quarrels and divisiveness which rent the city of Jerusalem asunder . . . Abraham Yizhaki opposed them and reviled them and pursued them. . . ." Long after Hagiz assumed leadership of the campaign against Hayon, Hayon fulminated against "that man," Yizhaki, the root of all his troubles. Benjamin HaKohen of Reggio wrote in a private letter at the height of the controversy that it was "an ancient cavil and suppressed hatred that was born in Turkey between R. Yizhaki and Hayon. . . . Upon the arrival of Yizhaki in Amsterdam as an emissary, he notifed Hakham Hagiz, and he, together with R. Zebi, sparked the conflagration when Hayon arrived there."[24]

Later that year, Yizhaki traveled through Amsterdam. During this sojourn he conveyed the details of his pursuit of Cardoso and Hayon to Hagiz. He warned Hagiz that a disciple of Cardoso's would try to publish Cardoso's work *Boker Abraham* in Amsterdam. Within months, Elijah Tarragon, a disciple of Cardoso and friend of Hayon, arrived in Amsterdam with Cardoso's manuscript and R. Solomon Ayllon, Sephardic chief rabbi of Amsterdam, approved it for publication. However, the *Ma'amad*, the lay council, forewarned by Yizhaki, condemned it to the flames. This occurred scarcely a month before the arrival of Hayon.[25] Hagiz' meeting with Yizhaki helped shape his position in the controversy. A formal request to participate came somewhat later, from the rabbinate of Smyrna, in a letter of February 1713.

> Steadfast warrior of Torah battles, Moses Hagiz: We have long been distressed over anonymous writings circulating among the *Yehidim* of our city. We were unable to determine their nature . . . until the arrival of the great emissary, R. Abraham Yizhaki. He unmasked their shame in public as the work of Abraham Cardoso. . . . We took counsel with the *Ma'amad*, and ordered that the treatise be brought before us. We immediately sentenced it to be confiscated and burned . . . and we celebrated the day as a victory for the rabbinate.
>
> We have heard rumors that they [Cardoso's disciples] have sent [an agent] from here to publish these writings [in Amsterdam] . . . Warn the publishers, in unequivocal terms . . . that if these manuscripts come their way, they must be rejected. . . . If they have already been brought to press, surreptitiously or openly, confiscate them so they do not circulate. . . . Publicize our actions, with pronouncement of bans and curses, to caution the public against this vile work.
>
> Notify the Italian cities and their environs of our admonitions regarding public proclamation and publication. . . . Although we have also written to the *Ma'amad* [of Amsterdam], following proper procedure, we direct our plea especially to you, to be particularly diligent."
>
> [signed] Israel Benveniste, Benjamin Halevi, Jacob ibn Na'im[26]

While this letter preceded the eruption of the controversy by several months, it already contained many portents of its character. The letter appealed to Hagiz as a zealot of long standing, with influential ties to the publishing houses of Amsterdam, as well as to the rabbinate of Italy. In addressing its counsel to Hagiz, the rabbinate of Smyrna was aware that it risked offending Solomon Ayllon, Sephardic rabbi of Amsterdam, as well as the lay ma'amad. The duplication of this letter to the ma'amad was an acknowledgement of the tension between Hagiz, who had no official standing in the community, and the official leaders of the Jewish community in Amsterdam.

In the course of the controversy, Hagiz would receive confirmation that the fusion of his interests with those of Yizhaki was warranted for personal reasons, in addition to ideological ones. During the height of the controversy, Yizhaki wrote to the ma'amad of Amsterdam, urging them to repudiate Hayon. They replied: "We could not have hoped for clearer evidence of a conspiracy to discredit Hayon . . . His comportment has been exemplary, corresponding to the testimony received by our ma'amad from certain gentlemen of Livorno, *among them Mssrs. Suleima*, who commended Hayon for his great sagacity and piety."[27] These were the same Suleimas who had been appointed agents of Abraham Nathan in Rosetta to transfer funds to the control of Moses Hagiz. The funds were frozen under their ostensibly neutral management, and the delay cost Hagiz his only opportunity to establish a yeshiva in Jerusalem. Their attempt to destroy the credibility of Yizhaki was apparently due to the same impulses that moved them to harm the interests of Hagiz.

On the day that Hayon arrived in Amsterdam, Hagiz met with Dr. Zemah Aboab, a prominent lay leader. Hagiz informed Aboab of Hayon's arrival, and of Yizhaki's suspicions concerning Hayon's Sabbatian activities as a disciple of Cardoso. This information prompted the Parnassim to dispatch the physician Dr. Solomon de Mesa to inquire into the matter by asking his celebrated patient, Hakham Zebi. Hakham Zebi corroborated Hagiz' report, and Dr. de Mesa relayed this to the ma'amad. On this basis, the parnassim overruled the lone dissenting voice of their rabbi, Solomon Ayllon, and ordered Hayon to remain under a house arrest pending a plenary session of the council. Before rendering a final decision, the parnassim appointed an ad-hoc Bet Din to examine Hayon's books thoroughly. The court consisted of R. Solomon Ayllon and six prominent lay leaders; Hayon provided each with a copy of his work. Hayon went to great lengths to withhold his books from potential detractors. A dauntless layman spirited a copy out of Ayllon's home and made it available to Hagiz and Hakham Zebi for a brief period. Their hasty perusal confirmed their original suspicions of Hayon, and added new charges as well. Despite this, Hagiz warned Hakham Zebi to act cautiously and hold his counsel until the ad-hoc court reached a conclusion. When the latter disregarded Hagiz' recommendations and published *le-Einei Kol Yisrael*, a denunciation of Hayon, Hagiz felt that Hakham Zebi had acted imprudently. He expressed fears that Zebi's haste would "engulf the community in tumult." Nevertheless, he could not withdraw his support from Zebi, and together they frantically searched for a copy of Hayon's book in order to issue a proper, chapter and verse, polemical refutation. When they finally obtained a copy at an outrageously inflated price, they both subjected it to thorough scrutiny. At this point, their focus shifted from consideration of Hayon's character to the issues and ideas contained in his books.

NEHEMIAH HAYON

At the epicenter of the violent polemical storm that erupted in 1713 and shattered the uneasy silence stood the figure of Nehemiah Hiya b. Moses Hayon. What was Hayon's role in the controversy? Was he merely a minor picaresque figure swept up by overwhelming historical forces, or did he and his works truly embody the heresy and subversion that the opposition claimed? While certain questions regarding Hayon's innermost beliefs must remain unanswered, his articulate defense of his cause leaves no doubt that he was an active and central figure, not a hapless victim.

Hayon was born about 1655, and his place of birth is uncertain. He claimed to be "from Safed in the upper Galilee," and when pressed, he said that his true birthplace was Alexandria. His early rabbinic adversaries in Smyrna claimed that he was born and raised in Sarajevo.[28] As a child he was taken to Jerusalem and Nablus; there he studied under R. Hayim Abulafia and R. Judah de Leon, among others. At age nineteen, he returned to Sarajevo where he married Mazal Tov, daughter of Samuel Almoli. He spent several years in Belgrade, until its occupation by Austria in 1688.[29]

Since many Sabbatians who had converted to Islam in Salonika passed through Belgrade at the same time as Hayon, it is possible that Hayon learned about the radical Sabbatians at this time. After that he may have joined his father as an emissary to Italy for the ransoming of captives from Belgrade. If his father, Moses Hayon, was a Sabbatian emissary, as Scholem asserts, it is during these years that Hayon probably made contacts with Sabbatians in Italy.[30] He later obtained a rabbinical position in Uskup with the support of R. Aaron HaKohen Perahia, an acquaintance of his father's. According to his detractors, his departure from there and his subsequent travels were laced with scandalous adventure.[31]

Hayon returned to Erez Israel in 1695, where he remained for some time. In 1702, after the death of his first wife, he married the daughter of Joseph Bizas in Safed, where a son was born to him. In 1702, he left

Safed for Egypt, where he immersed himself in the study of Kabbalah, acquired a reputation for practicing strange mystical acts, and probably wrote his dual commentary, *Oz le-Elohim* and *Bet Kodesh ha-Kodashim*. A gap in his biography ends in 1708, when Hayon appeared in Smyrna to seek funding to publish his works and to establish a yeshiva in Erez Israel, with himself at the helm "for the duration of his life." His first efforts met with great success. Pillars of the Jewish community of Smyrna united to support Hayon's venture:

> We all obliged ourselves to enable him to complete his works . . . in the Holy Land, and to bring them to press. We also undertook to establish from our personal funds a yeshiva of ten scholars of which he would be dean. He would be permitted to establish it in the city of his choice, Safed, Tiberias or Jerusalem, as he saw fit, and he should decide who to admit. The stipend shall be as he stipulates. . . . We are prepared to supply them with all their needs, year after year.
> [signed Elijah Caldiron, Elijah de Cordova, Joshua Cardoso, Salomon Arditi, Benjamin Isaac Zebi, Jacob Salinas Enriques, Hananel Esporno, and Abraham Arditi].[32]

This show of support for Hayon was marred by the growing number of enemies who recalled his "bizarre activities" in Egypt. While his supporters sent him off to Sidon with a lavish farewell, Hayon complained that his detractors, prominent rabbis in Smyrna, had sent a messenger, Absalom Halevi, on the very same ship, to convey a defamatory letter to Abraham Yizhaki in Jerusalem. Yizhaki, who was then chief rabbi of the Sephardic community in Jerusalem, undoubtedly perceived Hayon's plans as another attempt by Sabbatian sympathizers to wrest control of the important institutions in Jerusalem. From this point, Yizhaki was to become an implacable foe of Hayon's, following his every step, and pursuing him relentlessly with bans and public defamations. Hayon in turn was to become secretive and suspicious, worrying that every bystander could be an agent of Yizhaki's.

Upon hearing of Hayon's ambitions, Yizhaki immediately relayed negative reports to Hayon's supporters in Smyrna, urging them to retract their pledges. Only the Arditi brothers remained loyal to Hayon for some time. Hayon labored vainly to salvage the remainder of his endowment, but the core of his support dissipated, and his plans for a yeshiva in Erez Israel remained unfulfilled.

The similarity between the tribulations of Hayon and Hagiz' earlier frustrated endeavors are striking. There is some evidence that Hayon directly contributed to the collapse of Hagiz' projects. Abraham Suleima, who had been appointed conservator of Abraham Nathan's bequest to Moses Hagiz, turned out to be a supporter of Hayon. Perhaps it was this connection that caused the Nathan funds to be diverted from the control of Hagiz.[33] But whether or not this was actually so, the parallel effort by Hayon to establish a yeshiva to be run completely in accordance with his spirit and supported by the largesse of generous Diaspora donors was close enough to Hagiz' life-long, unrealized goal to exacerbate his sense of Hayon as his elusive nemesis. Hayon was, like himself, an itinerant scholar and an outsider to the pale of the institutional rabbinate, which could only have heightened the pangs that assailed Hagiz upon realizing that Hayon's career, outwardly so similar, was dedicated to ideals that subverted his own. The undercurrent of personal animosity generated additional poisonous darts in a polemic already replete with bitter ad hominem invective.

Like Hagiz, Hayon tried to recover his good name, claiming that he had been maligned. He requested that the rabbinate of Smyrna convoke a special committee to determine whether Yizhaki's charges were justified, but they refused to do so. Hayon complained bitterly that he was refused a fair hearing because of the perception that "If R. Yizhaki would be proven wrong, Jerusalem would be humiliated. . . . So the honor of Jerusalem was spared, and I was denied justice." Hayon then tried to salvage his reputation by arranging an open written polemical confrontation with Yizhaki. He turned to a former disciple and sympathizer, Isaac HaKohen of Jerusalem, asking him to publish a response which Hayon would prepare, refuting Yizhaki "letter for letter, word for word." But the conspiracy of silence which muffled the voices of non-Sabbatians, bound many sympathizers as well. However uneasy the regnant status quo, Isaac HaKohen did not care to change it. "While your anguish distresses me, I am unable to do your bidding. One who conceals contumely is wise. What benefit can I derive from initiating hostilities? Silence is a wiser policy . . . for I have seen battles. Each side amasses replies to every epistle. There will be no relief for you through them. It is unfitting to publicize this issue. My advice is, bide your time, and in the end, the honor due to you will surely arrive . . . Of course, wherever I go, I shall spread your good name and deny the slander."[34]

Hayon traveled to Italy, in 1710, when he met R. Joseph Ergas, the eminent kabbalist. By 1711, he had published in Venice the first work to adumbrate his controversial views, *Raza de-Yihuda* [*The Mystery of Unity*]. In 1712, he sojourned in Prague, where he impressed many as an "eminent Sephardic *Hakham*," including the son and son-in-law of Chief Rabbi

David Oppenheim, who accorded him the warmest hospitality. He was able to collect a substantial sum of money in Prague. He then made his way, through Nicholsburg, Prosnitz, and Vienna to Berlin. There, in 1713, he published *Dibrei Nehemiah*, a book of homilies, and his commentaries *Oz le-Elohim* and *Bet Kodesh ha-Kodashim*, to a manuscript he titled *Mehemnuta de-Kola*. The latter was to become the central focus of the controversy which erupted when he arrived in Amsterdam later that year.

Beyond the skeletal outline of Hayon's biography (for which he is the chief source), and apart from his usual public demeanor as an 'esteemed Sephardic Hakham,' there is another aspect of Hayon which was occasionally exposed to his admirers and detractors alike. We can detect certain traits in Hayon which he shared with other early modern "Enthusiasts," a term applied to individuals and groups whose claims of direct communication or contact with the Divine (illuminism) usually set them apart from the prevailing institutional religion until they eventually formed a separate sect. Fruitful parallels can be drawn from the development of these Christian sects and their relationship with the Church, to the relationship between crypto-Sabbatians and others who maintained the revelatory aspect of kabbalah, and the rabbinate.[35]

R. Naphtali Kohen of Frankfurt, who was so taken by Hayon's scholarly mien that he thought himself in the presence of a man of God upon first meeting him, later claimed that he was horrified to hear Hayon boast in public that he had "sat in communion with Metatron, guardian angel of the inner heavenly chambers, and that he had succeeded in bringing down from the celestial realms the chariot, and all became slaves bound to serve him." Another testimony recalled that "wherever he stayed, they said a prophet of the Holy Land has passed through the community. He boasted that he could perform any magical act in the world, without limitation." Joseph Fiametta, in a private correspondence with Solomon Ayllon, described Hayon's passing through Ancona. "He likened himself to a heavenly creature, claimed that he had ascended above all, like the Most High, that he had seen Ezekiel's Chariot, and God's servant Metatron, and could evoke Samael." Elijah Mujajon, although a Sabbatian, wrote that he was repulsed by Hayon's "hallucinatory rantings"; Benjamin Halevi by his "heretical phantasms."[36] An anonymous source recalled that during Hayon's stay in Rosetta . . . "he ordered that he be given a solitary room to meditate . . . with a ritual bath . . . a distance of six hours from the city. He ordered that once every twenty-four hours, food be brought to him . . . and he occupied himself during that time with administering oaths to Metatron, the heavenly guard. . . . After much

time had elapsed, . . . thunder and lightening appeared, and an angel
came to him, I don't recall if it was in human form . . . [Hayon] began
praying to God, 'Please reveal to me the true Mystery of the Godhead
[*Sod ha-Elohut*] . . . for there are so many different versions.' " All the
denunciations of Hayon that appeared between 1708 and 1712 do not
charge Hayon with any specific heresy. They focused exclusively on his
"practice of sorcery," his issuing "demoniacal amulets," and his licentious
and eccentric behavior.[37]

Hayon's pecularities were fully exploited by his enemies from the beginning of their campaign. They expected him to be vulnerable prey.
This expectation did not materialize. Hayon proved to be an exception-
ally resourceful and resilient opponent, who drew on his vast store of
knowledge, mastery of intricate casuistry, and a steady sense of self assurance to parry the many assaults on his integrity. He was adept at
marshalling support, and he singlehandedly kept the European rabbinic
establishment at bay for many years. Hayon's strengths, not his flaws,
lent the controversy its drama, its vitality, and its long duration.

SABBATIAN MESSIANISM AND HAYON'S SABBATIANISM

Do not consider the calculators of the End to be rebels. . . . If
they err . . . and he should tarry, wait on . . . for myriad thoughts
assail hopeful hearts when they are aching.[38]

The intensity of the original Sabbatian messianic hope persisted in
some circles well into the eighteenth century. The apostasy and death
of Sabbatai Zebi were explained by dedicated adherents as necessary acts
of temporary disappearance and concealment, a deliberate descent into
the depths of darkness from which Sabbatai would presently emerge.
Those who tenaciously persevered in this faith formed the core of the
various crypto-Sabbatian sects. One of their first tasks was to fix a date
for the reemergence of the Messiah. A period of forty years from the
first revelation of Sabbatai soon crystalized in their thought as the requisite waiting time: "Just as the first redeemer [Moses] was hidden for
forty [years] and then was revealed, so too the ultimate redeemer [Sab-
batai]."[39] This calculation, which designated 1706 as the year of the redemption, was endorsed by many prominent Sabbatian leaders. It nourished much of the messianic agitation of the late seventeenth century.

"R. Leibele of Prosnitz and his 'miracles,' R. Mordekhai of Eisenstadt and his 'prophecies,' R. Judah Hasid and the call for an immediate migration to Erez Israel filled the spiritual void of the faithful during those forty years."[40]

Many of those who continued to cultivate the most intense messianism were rabbinic scholars of some repute. "The strangest wonder, in my opinion, is that many great, established sages still persist in their naivete and believe in him [Sabbatai Zebi] even after his death. They claim that he is still alive, but concealed from all living beings, secreted among the Sons of Moses until the appointed time." R. Leib b. Ozer Rosenkrantz, the Yiddish chronicler of the Sabbatian movement, described the followers of R. Leibele of Prosnitz as 'the scholars' (*lomdim*). A rabbinic query from R. Meshullam Zalman Pincherle in Rovigo, addressed to R. Benjamin HaKohen of Reggio in 1706, pleaded, "If there be any great news in the world, please inform me . . . for I was told that you had written to Casale to urge them to repent, as the day of the Lord is near . . . 1706."[41]

A great deal of the messianic activism during this period was directed at Jerusalem. Abraham Cardoso enjoined his followers: " 'Let us arise and go to Zion.' . . . Then they rented a ship . . . and set their sights toward Jerusalem." In 1694–5, R. Zadok of Horodna traversed Lithuania and Poland, an apostle for the imminent arrival of Sabbatai Zebi, eventually leading a group to settle in Jerusalem. "He announced that the End was near, that all should repent, and that the redeemer was Sabbatai Zebi and none other. . . . He said that Sabbatai had not died, but had been concealed." He was influential in persuading Abraham Rovigo to settle in Erez Israel as well. Rovigo, whose impeccable piety and righteousness disarmed even Moses Hagiz, was a model of the "moderate Sabbatian," whose chief activity was the intense preparation for the imminent revelation of the messiah. Rovigo nursed ambitions that his faith would be rewarded by his designation as viceroy to the messiah.[42]

The disappointment of the hopes for 1706 precipitated a renewed crisis within the ranks of the faithful, followed immediately by another spate of calculations. Various dates were bandied about, especially 1714, but the most popular calculations pushed the onset of the wondrous age to 1740.[43] Isaac Cantarini's lyrical speculation on the year of the redemption, *Et Kez*, was written in 1707, the crucial year following the crisis of 1706.

Excitement mounted as the designated year 1740 drew closer. Some rabbis saw in the maintenance of a feverish pitch of messianic hope a means of confuting the claims of Christianity, of asserting that "He has not exchanged our homage for that of another." It is no surprise that

Christian missionaries closely monitored every development in the years right before 1740. One Christian met a rabbi in Holland in 1734 "who anticipated that in five years the Great Sabbath will commence and the messiah will arrive. When I proved to him the absence of any basis for his hope, he began to speak of the profundity of the prophets." In another testimony of 1734, the same Christian spoke to a rabbi who had rejected the opinion of many Jews that the messiah was to arrive in six years. Five years after the 'new' appointed time, Moses David, a Bohemian Jew, reminisced to the missionary: "When the Emperor Charles VI lay on his deathbed [in 1740], with no male heirs, he invited the grand rabbi of Prague [Jonathan Eybeschutz] and other rabbis and Jews of Bohemia, Moravia, and Hungary. He explained to them that the redemption would occur immediately without a doubt. For just as the Emperors ascended to their position when the Jews were first exiled, now that the root has withered, [with the last Habsburg] their messiah must arrive. . . . After many trials and tribulations, the French army came in stead of the messiah."[44]

At the same time, even during the first forty year waiting period, the primary concern of some Sabbatians began to shift, especially in the area of Kabbalistic theosophy. By the time of the second phase, the cultivation of intense messianic expectation branched off more markedly from mainstream Sabbatian thought. Cantarini conceded that Sabbatai may have ushered in the era of the Restoration, but he utterly rejected the claim that Sabbatai would be the future Redeemer. "The Zebi has fled without bringing any good." The appointed time would be 1740, with a messiah who had yet to be born.

Many rabbis who did not favor the nihilistic, antinomian, radical wing of Sabbatianism were nevertheless attracted to Sabbatianism as an opportunity for inner spirtual renewal promoted by the heightened, intense anticipation. This remained their link to Sabbatianism. R. Jacob Culi, author of the Judeo-Spanish biblical commentary *Me'am Loez*, R. Hayim Abulafia, and the circle around Moses Hayim Luzzatto exemplify approach in which the connection between their messianism and its original Sabbatian impulse has become attenuated.[45] Intense messianic expectation did not necessarily lead to Sabbatianism; once they were no longer conjoined, messianism was able to return to its independent position within the tradition. Perhaps the provocative thesis regarding the messianic aspirations of R. Jacob Emden, the most renowned anti-Sabbatian controversialist, can be understood in this light. I have found no parallel motive in the anti-Sabbatianism of Moses Hagiz.[46]

Messianic activism is completely absent in the published works of

Nehemiah Hayon. The one overt reference is in *Diberei Nehemiah*. It is a unique instance, and peripheral to the main interests of his work:

> Thus we have found with the incident of R. Joseph della Reina in Safed: he would have brought the redeemer had he not erred but in one thing. . . . Any person who dedicates his whole soul can attain the power to redeem Israel, and in that type of redemption, the messiah will be King David himself. But in the ultimate redemption, it will be messiah of the seed of David . . . And if you should object: 'Son of Man, how dare you preach this homily that any man can arouse the redemption when all the Sages have explained the verse [Song of Songs, 3:5] 'Lest you stir or arouse my love until it desires to awake,' that the Almighty coerced mankind to take an oath that they would not arouse the redemption until He indicated;' I would reply that indeed, just the opposite is apparent from the verse. The intent of scriptures is: The Almighty adjured Israel that if they begin to arouse, there will be a great arousal without end, until the *Shekhina* is appeased. . . . Nor will the redemption aroused through repentance come to naught . . . for that would be akin to telling a bride to ornament herself for a wedding, and then breaking off the betrothal . . . She was better off before the bitter disappointment. . . .
>
> Know what the Sages have said: . . . the exile will last through the fifth millenium; and in the sixth, the first five hundred years are called night, and the last five hundred are day. [The Jewish date 5500 A.M. is equivalent to 1740 C.E.].[47]

Hayon, therefore, did devote some thought to the problems of the imminence of the redemption—and he mentions the year 1740—but this paragraph constitutes his entire commentary on the subject in his published works.

In the polemics of Hagiz against Hayon, the messianic element is mentioned, but it occupies a negligible place. It was an easy target for mockery, but Hagiz did not seriously address Sabbatian messianism as an independent issue: "They deny the coming of the saviour, for in their opinion he has already appeared, and he is Sabbatai Zebi."[48] In part this may have been due to the acute tension in the post-Sabbatian era between the rabbinic obligation to subdue subversive messianism while maintaining the vitality of classical messianic hopes in the Jewish tradition. The vestigial role of messianism in Hayon's thought simply did not warrant greater emphasis. It was not Hayon's messianism, but his theological heresies rooted in Sabbatian kabbalah which aroused the greatest opposition. A telling transformation occurs in the anti-Sabbatian polemics of David Nieto, *Esh Dat* and *Reflexiones*. In all the references to Sabbatai Zebi, Nieto designated him as "heresiarch" rather than "false messiah," which would have been more appropriate to Sabbatai himself. Nieto implied that drained of its potency as a messianic movement, Sabbatianism's only significant legacy was its heretical theosophy.

The doctrines formulated in Hayon's printed works formed the single most important component of the controversy. They were endlessly cited and explicated in the polemical writings against Hayon, as they provided more substantive proofs of his "subversive" and "heretical" inclinations than the unconventional episodes in his personal life.[49]

Hayon's first published work, *Raza de-Yihuda* (*The Mystery of Unity*), appeared in Venice, 1711. It contains an approbation from the rabbinate of Venice. Although published first, it was written after Hayon's opus was already complete in manuscript form. The title page advises that the book contains Kabbalistic devotions that should accompany the verse of unity, "Hear O Israel"; its actual purpose was to summarize and advertise the contents of Hayon's larger forthcoming work in the hope of attracting financial support: "In its merit I hope to publish the rest of my books. . . . I beseech the receiver of this book . . . to extend a generous hand." The brief book contained many of the ideas for which Hayon was attacked after the publication of his major work in 1713. These included the tripartite nature of the Godhead, and a very literal interpretation of anthropomorphic functions ascribed to it.

In addition to the central doctrine, the work contained several other peculiarities which his vigilant opponents seized upon in 1713. At the very end of the work, Hayon appended a "poem which is befitting for recital after reading the Idra of the *Zohar*." His foes contended that the poem contained subversive ideas: that Israel had worshipped false gods after the era of R. Simon bar Yohai. Hayon denied this. They also charged that the opening words of the Aramaic verse cleverly corresponded, in pronunciation and meter, to a popular bawdy ditty, "La Bella Margarita." Hayon did not deny this, but later justified it: "Most authors of sacred poetry in the Turkish provinces match the opening line of sacred works to a popular profane tune, so that the public can intone the words melodiously."[50] Hayon imputed grand powers to his small book: "Anyone who studies this work diligently is promised a share in the world to come." Whoever reads his liturgical poem *Keter Elyon* (*The Supernal Crown*) which he appended to the book, "It is as though he has read the entire *Zohar*." If it contained such subversive material, why was the book not condemned until after the controversy erupted two years later? The rabbis who signed the approbation, [Solomon b. Isaiah Nizza, David b. Solomon Altaras, and Raphael b. Salomon da Silva] later claimed that they had seen only part of the work. Hayon wrote that he was offering the work to "selected individuals," presumably as a gift to potential supporters. Apparently, he exercised extreme caution in the distribution of the miniature sized book, so that it should not fall into unfriendly hands. Even during the controversy, Hayon's books were difficult to obtain.[51]

The first book Hayon published in Berlin was *Diberei Nehemiah*, a book of homilies on the weekly portions of the Bible, which he claimed to have written during a three-month sojourn in Prague. It carried the approbations of rabbis David Oppenheim, Gabriel of Nicholsburg, Aaron of Berlin, and Judah Leib of Glogau. Oppenheim's approbation contained the caveat that he had seen only one sample page "and should have refrained from approving it on that slender basis." Most of the material in the book is standard for the homiletic genre; only a few instances are conspicuous for their allusions to Sabbatian themes.

In the first selection, Hayon considers the Midrashic statement:

> *The earth was empty and void*, these are the deeds of the wicked. . . .
> *Let there be light*, these are the deeds of the righteous. I don't know
> which deeds He prefers until the verse concludes, "And the Lord
> saw the light and it was good'. . . . He desires the deeds of the
> Righteous." [*Genesis Rabbah*, 2, 7] How can the deeds of the wicked
> be equated with the deeds of the righteous? Is it possible that He
> could prefer the former to the latter?. . . . We must concede that
> we are speaking of a *sin committed with holy intent*, or a good deed
> devoid of intent . . . even the holy sin of a righteous person is
> preferable to a holy good deed of a wicked person. . . . When the
> righteous man commits the redemptive sin . . . only the Lord can
> perceive *"that it is good,"* and holy.[52]

One other homily deals with the concept of an evil deed performed with the holy intent of redeeming the cosmos, but Hayon emphatically rejected conversion to another faith as the ultimate fulfillment of this concept:

> Know the principle among masters of esoteric knowledge: The re-
> demption cannot come . . . unless Israel can extract all the Holy
> Sparks from the husks [*kelipot*]. . . . In this principle, some have
> erred and said, let us go and worship alien gods in order to over-
> come the husks. . . . Although their intention is good, . . . they
> sin greatly by worshipping idolatry. . . . There is no forgiveness

for them despite their good intentions . . . for this is not akin to the concept of "holy sin." The concept of holy sin refers to an isolated transgression such as that of Ya'el . . . who knew that the precept of taking revenge against the nations took precedence over "Thou shalt not commit adultery." But if an individual, a family or a tribe commits idolatry . . . this will not defeat the husk but add strength to it.[53]

Hayon rejected outright the extreme interpretations of the Turkish Donmeh sect, who converted to Islam in 1683, but he vindicated other antinomian acts undertaken for redemptive purposes, and emphasized the example of Ya'el who suspended the prohibition against adultery. Additional citations from *Diberei Nehemiah* were occasionally used against Hayon, but overall, this book played a marginal role in the polemics.

Hayon's magnum opus, the centerpiece of the controversy, was his work *Oz le-Elohim/Bet Kodesh Ha-Kodashim* also published in Berlin, 1713. It consisted of three parts. The core of the work was a Kabbalistic treatise which Hayon called *Mehemnuta de-Kola*. While Hayon did not claim to be the author of this treatise he did not refer to a source or an author in the *Oz le-Elohim*. On other occasions he gave conflicting accounts of its origin. In one later work, Hayon swore that he had received the work "neither from Sabbatai Zebi, nor from his disciples, but I copied it in fragmented condition from an old volume of the Zohar in Safed . . . and I did not attribute it to myself because while I am the first to have edited it, I did not supply the raw material." On another occasion he said that the treatise had been dictated to him by a *maggid* while he was in Rosetta.[54]

What was the true provenance of the manuscript which formed the core of Hayon's major work? It was commonly believed, by faithful Sabbatians and their opponents alike, that the author was Sabbatai Zebi himself. Hakham Zebi Ashkenazi wrote shortly after it was published that the author was "the notorious apostate, Sabbatai Zebi," and that "the other Sabbatians knew full well that the tract contained the *Sod ha-Elohut* (the Mystery of the Godhead) which he [Sabbatai] had invented." Joseph Ergas stated repeatedly in his polemics that the tract was known to have been composed [by Sabbatai] in Alqum. Yet, all the evidence indicates that the original source was not Sabbatai himself, but Abraham Cardoso. In his tract *Raza de-Razin*, Cardoso stated, "When I was in Rodosto in 1697, a tract came into my hands entitled 'The Mystery of the Faith,' (*Raza de-Mehemnuta*), written by a rabbi in Alqum at the instructions of Sabbatai Zebi." Cardoso explicitly denied that the tract was written by

Sabbatai himself. In another reference, Cardoso presented a more elaborate version of how he obtained the manuscript: A rabbi who claimed he had traveled to Alqum disguised as a Turk stayed with Sabbatai for four months, and wrote down the "mystery" as he heard it from Sabbatai. This rabbi transmitted the "mystery" to Cardoso's students. This subterfuge justified Cardoso's efforts to divulge this secret "mystery" which all other Sabbatians had sworn never to reveal. Recent scholarship has pointed to Cardoso as the sole author of the *Raza de-Mehemnuta*. He attributed it to Sabbatai so that his version should be accepted as the authentic teaching of Sabbatai. Hayon inherited from Cardoso both this version of the Mystery of the Godhead, as well as the freedom from constraint to publish it.[55]

The first task faced by Hayon's opponents was to persuade the uninitiated that Hayon's work proved him to be a crypto-Sabbatian and a heretic. Hayon's writing is completely devoid of reference to Sabbatai Zebi, to Sabbatai's messianic mission, or to any other authors of Sabbatian Kabbalistic theosophy.[56] Hayon was sufficiently confident that his works did not overtly betray a Sabbatian inclination to respond indignantly to the accusation of Hakham Zebi and Hagiz, "that Nehemiah Hayon has published *Oz le-Elohim* to maintain the false faith of Sabbatai Zebi and Cardoso . . . to lead Israel astray. . . . I swear by God, that I am innocent."[57]

It is precisely over the place of Sabbatai Zebi within the school of Sabbatian Kabbalah that Hayon differed from his predecessors. Hayon wished to purge it completely from that system of thought. Joseph Fiametta pondered the possibility that the school of Kabbalistic thought which traced its genesis to the Sabbatian movement might have eventually severed all links to its matrix in the course of time "were it not for its adversaries," who insisted that the two were inseparable. Hayon complained that his enemies found him guilty by the most slender threads of association. First, he complained, they established his alleged Sabbatianism. Then, with a small leap of the imagination "they accused me of having been an apostate."[58] However, whether Hayon wished to sever or merely to conceal links to the figure of Sabbatai, his opponents correctly discerned that he was working within a Sabbatian framework. He adopted its fundamental assumptions, theosophical problems, and vocabulary.

The theosophy of the Sabbatian messianic movement was developed first by Sabbatai's prophet, Nathan of Gaza. He developed an entirely original theosophy in which all the cosmic problems considered by Kabbalists, particularly Lurianic Kabbalists, were considered in light of Sabbatian thought. When the abrupt apostasy of Sabbatai transformed the movement into a clandestine sect, Nathan intensified his labors, and directed his efforts to the ingenious integration of that ultimate betrayal into an article of the Sabbatian faith. Nathan's theology differentiated between a totally transcendent First Cause, and the immanent God of Israel, creator of the world, which had emanated from the First Cause and was the real object of religious worship. His development of the cosmic function of the messiah, and the resultant similarity between the roles of messiah and God of Israel, evolved into the apotheosis of the messiah himself. Some of the most radical elements in Sabbatian antinomianism, nihilism and mass apostasy, were rooted in the doctrines of evil and cosmic redemption first formulated by Nathan.[59]

The foundations laid by Nathan were developed in several different directions. One of the most influential and widely read Sabbatian authors after the death of Nathan was Abraham Miguel Cardoso (1626–1706), former Marrano and physician. Cardoso identified Sabbatai's apostasy with the travails of his own crypto-Jewish background, and concluded that apostasy was the inevitable destiny of the Messiah. But while Cardoso upheld Nathan's dualistic conception of God, he sharply attacked the deification of the messiah. He supported the antinomian conclusions derived from the concept of a new Torah in the messianic age, although he shrank from publicly practicing antinomian acts.[60]

Of all the Sabbatian kabbalists, Hayon's shows the closest filiation to that of Cardoso. Hayon's principal opponents charged that he was a disciple of Cardoso. According to Yizhaki, they had met while both were in Safed. One of the major premises of Moses Hagiz' *Sheber Posh'im* was the close relationship between Cardoso and Hayon. Hagiz charged that Hayon belonged to a circle of Cardoso's disciples who had tried earlier to publish Cardoso's works in Smyrna, without success. They then sent an agent, Elijah Tarragon, to Amsterdam on the same mission. Hagiz charged that Tarragon, arriving scarcely a month before Hayon, also served as a "spy" to clear the way for Hayon's arrival by procuring R. Solomon Ayllon's assurance of help in publishing the material. He charged that Ayllon had upheld Tarragon's right to publish Cardoso's work *in the vernacular* in the face of opposition from the lay leadership.[61] David Nieto, in his Spanish introduction to *Esh Dat* repeatedly emphasized the relationship between the thought of Hayon and Cardoso's treatise, *Boker Abraham*. The minor differences with Cardoso, which Hayon pointed out in self defense, did not obscure the fundamental bonds between their work. Yet, the polemic of 1713 concentrated almost exclusively on the writings of Hayon. It is within the parameters of Hayon's work that we must search for the reason why he merited a more violent reaction than Cardoso or any of his predecessors.

The death of Cardoso in 1706 coincided with the great disappointment of unrealized messianic hopes in some Sabbatian circles, as it marked the end of the forty-year waiting period that had begun in 1666. For those who hoped to see the movement breathe its last, it seemed to mark the beginning of the end. Hayon's activity proved the heralds of the demise of crypto-Sabbatianism to be false prophets. Rather than flickering out with the passage of time, crypto-Sabbatianism in the eighteenth century continued to flourish as the old structure was infused with new meaning. Hayon's Sabbatianism was not messianic in the expectant, eschatological sense. Instead, it was focused on the historical present and its energies directed to this world. Hayon borrowed the language of Lurianic Kabbalah to articulate solutions to new realities of early modern Jewish life. In doing so, he implicitly attacked the fundamentals of rabbinic Judaism. Hayon's open advocacy of individual inquiry into the most secret and sacred questions of religion, untrammeled by the bonds of tradition, obviated the obligations of submission to rabbinic authority and interpretation. Hagiz' response to Hayon—consolidation of rabbinic powers, along with banishment of crypto-Sabbatians from the communal polity—must be understood in light of this challenge. Hayon's deviations from classical Kabbalah were a secondary issue.

Nowhere in Hayon's writing were his ideas expressed more brazenly than in his introductory "investigations" to *Oz le-Elohim*. Their effect was to throw the doors of Kabbalistic inquiry open to all comers, to remove utterly every last vestige of esotericism that still accompanied study of the Kabbalah. Hayon recalled that the impulse to lay bare the truth came to him with "the earliest blush of youth . . . when I saw that even within the 'lore of truth,' so many versions abounded, no mind could tolerate them all. . . . I decided to seek out His true essence and unity."[62] Hayon believed that this personal inquisitive imperative was incumbent upon all thinking men. From the author's verse at the very opening of *Oz le-Elohim*, which guaranteed "that he who will investigate every approach diligently . . . will be rewarded by recognition of the true essence of God, with no dilutions," and the subtitle to his preface: "A decision by the rabbi-author which directs and encourages penetrating investigation into the realm of esoteric lore," Hayon's entire introductory essay is informed by the consciousness that he is advocating something bold and momentous. The lengthy prolegomenon, which stands independent of the main body of his work, is devoted solely to a passionate argument for dissolution of the constraints imposed by tradition to ensure prudent transmission of the esoteric lore. To soften the impression that he was flatly contradicting tradition, Hayon cited the standard rabbinic dicta against popularization of the Kabbalah, then radically reinterpreted them to suit his argument.

Hayon's flagrant and deliberate disregard for time-hallowed interpretations infuriated his opponents. He proleptically dismissed the fulminations of "those who sit on sage councils and say we have no business in the celestial abode . . . Do not pay heed to the nonsense of those who gainsay the intellectual investigation of mysteries—they are blind."[63]

Hayon first considered the Mishnaic dictum:

> One may not expound on [the subject of] forbidden relations in the presence of three, nor the Work of Creation in the presence of two, nor the Work of the Chariot in the presence of one, unless one is a sage and understands by himself. Whoever speculates upon four things, a pity on him! He is as though he had not come into the world.[64]

He turned the traditional understanding on its ear. According to Hayon, the only valid way to transmit esoteric lore and remain faithful to this principle in the Mishnah would be to print and distribute the work! Reading does not involve the interaction of even two people; "There is no whisper lower than the printing of a book, to be read by a person in solitude." As to the injunction against speculation on cosmic mysteries, Hayon's reversal of accepted interpretation was no less radical. In his opinion the phrase "as though he had not come into the world," must be taken as a positive injunction, for the soul is clean before it enters the world. If the Sages had intended to prohibit the activity, they would have used the phrase "he will have no share in the world to come." Their choice of words indicated that whoever would delve into these hidden realms was promised an absolution of all his sins, as though he had just come into the world.[65]

Hayon's second "investigation," sharply attacked the notion of a hierarchy of transmission from a qualified authority. "There are false and contemptible opinions which declare that it is not desirable to learn Kabbalah except from a master who is like an angel of God." "Who is wise? He who learns from all people. From this we learn that anyone who refuses to learn from *all* people is not wise, but foolish." Hayon's argument was calculated to challenge the position of the established rabbinate as sole conservator of divine lore. Those "persons of repute" who prevent the public from hearing the Torah of outsiders are guilty of "preventing Israel from knowing its Creator." God prefers those who, like

Job, come to know Him from independent examination, *not through words of scribes.* Hayon castigated those who read the Kabbalah by rote without independent questioning or investigation. "The words of the prophet have come to pass: Israel has gone many days with no Torah, and without the true God." Although Hayon opposed classical philosophical speculation, the free inquiry which he postulated emptied the Kabbalah of its most basic and literal sense as a "transmitted lore." He argued that even if solitary contemplation led to heresy, the process was dear to God. Hayon derided the cautious Kabbalists who enumerated the attributes of each successive emanation, but never penetrated to the essence of God, source of all life, toward which the soul naturally strives. Hayon called for the elimination of the role of master in the elemental search for knowledge of God. In his own way, Hayon was inching closer to the opinions of heretical former Marranos, such as Uriel d'Acosta, who first questioned and then flatly denied the authority of the rabbinate, and the of the Oral Torah in Jewish life. Almost identical ideas were being expressed at the same time by contemporary religious figures far beyond Hayon's world. John Wesley, founder of Methodism, wrote: "I must still insist on the right of private judgment. I dare call no man rabbi. I cannot yield either implicit faith or obedience to any man or number of men under heaven."[66]

The boldest stroke in Hayon's work is to be found beyond the prefatory essay in the body of the text. The unprecedented publication of the tract *Raza de-Mehemnuta* [Mystery of the Faith], appearing unchanged in Hayon's *Oz le-Elohim* under the title *Mehemnuta de-Kola* [Faith of All] was a culmination of all the arguments advanced by Hayon. As we have seen, it was widely regarded in many circles (although not by Hayon) as the only authentic Kabbalistic treatise by Sabbatai himself. It remains the only classical Sabbatian text to have been printed before modern times. By its publication Hayon brought to fruition all the ideas he advocated in the introduction to his volume.

The text of the *Mehemnuta* was framed by Hayon's two commentaries on each page. The first commentary, *Oz le-Elohim*, was primarily intended to polemicize against differing interpretations, "to investigate, to establish fundamentals, and refute every teaching which was inconsistent." The second, *Bet Kodesh ha-Kodashim* [House of the Holy of Holies], "trod mightily, accompanied by hundreds of dicta of the Zohar for support." Its primary purpose was to prove through his exegetical acumen the harmony and close relationship between the *Zohar* and the *Mehemnuta.* Hayon's commentaries did not purport to be a creative innovation. He imprinted his stamp on the material by his bold and unhedging restatement of perennial Kabbalistic problems and their solutions, in a manner similar to his Sabbatian predecessors, and in particular to Cardoso, his mentor.

Hayon's treatise opened by questioning the possibility of a simple, uncompounded, absolutely pure deity. How could an impulse for creation, an act of self-limitation, arise within such pure simplicity? The Kabbalistic notion of *zimzum*, the withdrawal of God into Himself to leave a void in which to create the world, Hayon imagined as a literal process. It had to have occurred in time. There must have been a motivating, willful, and self-limiting force within the simple Divine Essence which acted at a certain time. The amorphous primordial Divine material, (*Atika Kadisha de-Khol Kadishin* = The Holy Ancient of Days) was activated by a Spirit that permeated it and coexisted with it, (*Nishmata de-Kol Hayei* = The Spirit of all Life). This spirit is identified with the infinite *Ein Sof* of classical Kabbalah. At its hidden root, (*shoresh ne'elam*), this Spirit has a Will, and a definite structure (*shi'ur komah*), which are finite and distinct from the infinitely extending radiance of the Divine illumination. Only the infinite aspect of God is beyond the apprehension of man. For all the rest, Hayon held an anthropomorphic conception. "We must ask why the Bible is riddled with anthropomorphisms. If we say that the Bible is speaking allegorically, Heaven forfend, this would make the Bible meaningless, a series of parables and allegories."

The first phase of creation, according to Hayon, occurred when the Ancient of Days became manifest in the cosmos as Primordial Man. He contained the roots of Emanation, the "Sefirot." When the Primordial Vessels shattered the finite roots of 'Din' [Judgment], were extended into the Ancient of Days. Then, the infinite rays had to be contained so that they would not overwhelm the Primordial Space again. Hayon depicted the mythical battle in which seven kings, hidden roots of the emanations before they crystallized, battled to contain the Light by controlling the Line of Justice (*Kav ha-Yosher*). None could control it except the Eighth King. He became the ruler, and he is identical with the original Ancient of Days, who had now proved his hegemony. The text of the *Mehemnuta* recounts that after the victory, the two elements within the Ancient of Days coupled and produce a "son," an epicene offspring containing both *Malka Kadisha* [the Holy King, male attributes] and *Shekhinah* [the Divine Presence, female attributes], justice and mercy. This is the God of Israel, King of the world, the god who acts in history and to whom human beings pray. For Hayon, anyone who identified this God of Israel with the transcendent Ein Sof, was a fool and a heretic. This "God of Israel" appeared within time, and immediately began the process of creation, because that was his purpose.

From this account, Hayon derived a trinitarian configuration of the Godhead: "The secret of Unity is the Triple Bond of Faith, the 1. Ancient of Days, [Hayon's 'First Cause'], 2. The *Malka Kadisha* [the male element], and 3. The *Shekhinah* [the female element]." The latter two elements, which rule the world in tandem, appear from the human perspective to be differentiated aspects. This is the background for the *Raza de-Yihuda* [Secret of Unity], Hayon's work on man's obligation to unite the three in his devotions. The goal of these devotions is to stimulate the consummation of the union between the two latter elements. The souls conceived from that union contain the seeds of the new era, and this is the secret of Hayon's inner devotions of Unity. Hayon's illustration of this concept is a good e...mple of his bold style:

> What distinguishes external from inner devotions? All the external attributes are like the limbs; the inner unity is like the soul to the body. Today, because of our sins, we are in exile, and the two elements, *Kudsha Berikh Hu* [= *Malka Kadisha*] and the Shekhinah are asleep. . . . If a man and his wife were asleep, and it would be necessary to couple them while they slept, although one could unite them by putting limb to corresponding limb . . . the coupling will be unsuccessful, for there is no desire in sleep. But if they are aroused and their inner spirit awakens, why, they will unite of their own volition.

The transcendent Ein Sof is not included in this trinity because it is remote and unreachable; and it has no relationship to the creation, to Divine Providence, and to revelation. This dualistic separation is rooted in the thought of Cardoso.

Hayon's trinitarian configuration of the immanent God stands in opposition to the conception of the school of Sabbatian leader Samuel Primo, which elevated Sabbatai, the Messiah, into the trinity. Hayon concluded that his exposition on the trinitarian bond "is the true faith of Israel. All the precepts one fulfills are as naught if one denies this basis of Jewish faith. He is like a gentile who rested on the Sabbath—he deserves the death penalty . . . for whoever denies this faith is not of the community of Israel."[67]

Hayon's treatise was subjected to extraordinary scrutiny, because opponents of Sabbatianism had never before been granted the opportunity to study a printed Sabbatian work. Every element of Hayon's thought—

his literalism, dualism, trinitarian conception, was attacked ferociously, including elements which had always existed in classical Kabbalah. The brazen, aggressive style in which Hayon exposed his teachings mattered more than their content. "All the Kabbalists, *even those who agree with his* [*Hayon's*] *teachings* should pursue him, and destroy his book, because this author has vulgarized in the streets matters which they whispered from one ear to another in awe and trembling."[68] A staunch supporter of Hayon admonished him: "You yourself are the cause of all this agitation, for you have spoken in such direct language, accessible to the masses. . . . Most people understand absolutely nothing of Kabbalah, and they are unaccustomed to this, particularly your introduction."[69] Because Hayon breached every last sanction against mass popularization and broke down all constraints of self-censorship, both within classical and Sabbatian Kabbalah, his opponents felt that the time was ripe to put an end to their own long, self-imposed silence.

HAGIZ AND THE LAY COMMUNAL LEADERSHIP

The perennial and ubiquitous tensions between rabbinate and lay leadership were raised to a dramatic pitch in the Hayon controversy. The lay leadership of Amsterdam repeatedly affirmed its resolve not to yield one iota of its power and autonomy to any other body, for any reason. Its animus was directed particularly against rabbinic encroachment. Impervious to the opinions of its most outstanding rabbinic contemporaries, the ma'amad [lay council] proudly and self-consciously defended its sovereignty. In its rejection of individual and collective rabbinic claims to authority within the larger Jewish community, the pronouncements of the ma'amad were sharp and unequivocal, classical articulations of the lay position. To R. Judah Briel, the ma'amad replied disdainfully, "Surely you are aware that our city has a noble and ancient . . . Kehillah which is subservient to none, nor obligated to follow the opinions of any other." Hagiz was acutely aware of their image of themselves: "They audaciously pronounced in their declaration that their Kehillah was free and independent . . . subject to no other Kehillah. . . . No one can influence them to reverse their opinion. . . . It is as though they say, 'who can be a master over us?'. . . . They are challenging all the sages of Israel."[70]

Hagiz stood poised in an adversary relationship with lay communal leadership long before the Hayon controversy erupted. He had provoked resentment and outrage among the lay leaders of Livorno and Amsterdam, duly recorded in the archives of Amsterdam a scant five years earlier. One document of 1708 recorded a resolution adopted by the ma'amad of Amsterdam to ban and suppress Hagiz' *Sefat Emet* because it contained "inaccuracies, and was written in a shocking, scandalous" tone. Another document of March 8, 1709, upheld the judgment of the Amsterdam ma'amad to permit Hagiz to publish his *Leket HaKeMaH*, in response to a complaint from the ma'amad of Livorno. The Livornese leaders felt sorely slighted by certain passages in Hagiz' book [*Sefat Emet*], and threatened drastic measures against the Amsterdam ma'amad which had permitted its publication.

In fact, the Amsterdam ma'amad appeared more eager to defend itself than the work of Hagiz. "We cannot help but wonder how you had the audacity to slander *us* by saying *we* had acted improperly and permitted a heretical work to be published. . . . We advise you to weigh your accusations *against us* with extreme caution . . . as our Bet Din found nothing so improper in the book as to warrant the extreme sanctions you threaten. . . . Consider with greatest prudence the harm that can result to the *Kehillot* of Israel if you proceed." This friction carried over into the Hayon controversy.[71]

Lay communal leadership could not easily dislodge the claims of the rabbinate to superiority in the Jewish community. The spheres of spiritual versus worldly matters in Jewish communal affairs had never been clearly delineated. The gray area between the clearly ritual and the overtly political was the object of a constant struggle for control between lay leaders and rabbinate. In this conflict the itinerant rabbi played a crucial role. Any lay council could effectively neutralize rabbinic interference by claiming that it would submit all its affairs to its own local rabbi. Compliance with lay wishes was virtually assured because the local rabbi depended on the goodwill of the lay leaders who had appointed him to his position. Hagiz complained that "those who occupy rabbinic positions responsible for the public welfare, have joined the iniquity first." The itinerant rabbi was the discordant note that jarred this comfortable arrangement. Residing in the city, but holding no official position in it, he often asserted that his authority was superior by virtue of greater piety, scholarship, or provenance from Erez Israel. This placed him at odds, not only with the lay leadership whose ends he was not bound to serve, but also with the local rabbi as well, who claimed that the usurper had no right to infringe upon his sphere of jurisdiction.

Hagiz understood this relationship perfectly. He often expressed his position that rabbinic authority was vested in personal piety and scholarship, that it knew no geographic bounds, and that its power derived from rabbinic consensus—not lay appointment. This context formed the background of tension between the Amsterdam parnassim and the itinerant Hagiz, as well as Solomon Ayllon, chief rabbi of the Sephardic Kehillah in Amsterdam, and the ad hoc Bet Din in the Hayon controversy. The Bet Din, appointed by the ma'amad to be its juridical arm specifically for the case of Hayon was in a position analogous to that of the local rabbi. The ma'amad repeatedly emphasized that it would not reconsider the verdict regardless of the merits of the appeal because "it is imperative to uphold the honor of our Bet Din." In cities where the lay leadership opposed Hayon, the relationship between rabbi and lay leaders was the obverse of Amsterdam. In Florence, the rabbi J. Ghiron, was shut out of the deliberations and his opinion of Hayon was not solicited because he was known to be a Sabbatian sympathizer. He was threatened with loss of his position and his status if he did not comply with the wishes of the lay leaders that he add his name to the ban against Hayon. Ghiron capitulated. His herem was signed on July 14, 1714.[72]

It is no mere happenstance that a similar constellation of conflict between lay leadership and rabbinate also shaped the career of Hakham Zebi Ashkenazi, Hagiz' first partner in the Hayon controversy. Born in Moravia in 1660 to a renowned Ashkenazic rabbinical family, his father sent him to Salonika in 1676 to study in the Sephardic yeshiva of Elijah Covo. During his years there and in Belgrade, he adopted Sephardic customs as well as the Sephardic rabbinic title "Hakham." In Sarajevo, he was appointed Hakham of the Sephardic community. While gaining renown as a brilliant halakhist, Hakham Zebi proved extremely unyielding and intractable in his interpersonal relations, especially with prominent lay members of the community.

One clash during his tenure at Sarajevo was to assume greater significance many years later. Hakham Zebi became involved in a dispute with a pair of affluent businessmen, Samuel Almoli and Hiya Hayon, known as Hiya ha-Arokh. Almoli and Hayon interceded with the government and succeeded in having Zebi exiled from Sarajevo. The rabbis of the community retaliated by putting Almoli under a ban, from which he was later released from by R. Aron Ha-Kohen Perahya. Years later, when Zebi heard that a certain Nehemiah Hiya Hayon of Sarajevo had arrived in Amsterdam, he assumed that the newcomer was his old adversary, and quickly joined the campaign against him. Shortly thereafter, the two antagonists faced each other. The only account of this meeting comes from the pen of Solomon Ayllon. "After three days, Hayon met and spoke with Hakham Zebi, and after the meeting, Hakham Zebi retracted, saying that this was not his old adversary. Scarcely three hours later, he reversed himself again, upon the urging of Hakham Hagiz who claimed that he had just seen Hayon's book and it was filled with heresy."

Ayllon's account of this meeting and the swift reversal have been accepted at face value. But there are a number of reasons to call it into question. Ayllon was a partisan of Hayon in the controversy, and his motive was to show Hakham Zebi in the worst possible light. He attributed Zebi's second change of heart to the undue influence of Hagiz, but this is doubtful. Zebi was not easily swayed by anyone's advice. Hagiz himself responded incredulously to the charge of the lay leaders that he had exerted undue influence on Zebi and dragged him into the controversy. "Is it not known to the entire Diaspora that Zebi is intransigent, and nothing can dissuade him from the truth?" Ayllon's credibility is further eroded when we note that in the same letter to his anonymous correspondent he deftly concealed the truth about another, unrelated, matter. The burden of evidence seems to vindicate Zebi's original—and final—identification of Hayon. In Hayon's *Moda'ah Rabah*, we learn that he married the daughter of Samuel Almoli in Sarajevo. This is sufficient evidence to state that at the very least, Nehemiah Hiya Hayon was closely related to one of Zebi's former adversaries. The facts that the name Nehemiah was added to Hiya Hayon only after an illness, and that more than a quarter of a century had elapsed since the incident occurred in 1688, indicate that Nehemiah Hiya Hayon was most likely Zebi's old adversary.

Zebi left Sarajevo, and eventually became rabbi of Altona, where he served for many years. He was forced to resign in 1709 in the course of a celebrated halakhic dispute, and he was invited to serve as rabbi of the Ashkenazic community of Amsterdam in 1710. His tenure there was fraught with conflict from the start. One of the most important bones of contention were the terms of Zebi's contract. The parnassim appealed to the burgomasters of Amsterdam to intervene. They ruled in Zebi's favor, and Zebi remained on, in an atmosphere charged with resentment. When the Hayon controversy developed, the Ashkenazic adversaries of Zebi lost no time in joining Zebi's detractors from the Sephardic community, and they revived the issue of Zebi's contract, submitting it to several celebrated Christian Hebraists for analysis. Zebi's earlier struggles converged with the issues in the Hayon campaign. Solomon Ayllon derided Zebi's authority: "He [Zebi] ordered them [his Ashkenazic Kehilla] to declare a ban in their synagogue, but they paid him no heed . . . If he cannot prevail over his own congregants, who is he to speak to outsiders [the Sephardim]?"[73]

When Hayon arrived in Amsterdam, he submitted the books which
he had published in Berlin to the ma'amad to receive permission to distribute them. The ma'amad remanded the books to their Hakham, Salomon Ayllon, for approval. Ayllon, unwilling to bear sole responsibility,
convened an ad hoc committee of six knowledgeable laymen to ascertain
the nature of the books. Before the committee was ready to release its
opinion, Hagiz and Zebi published a ban against the books, and sent
letters asking many of their rabbinic colleagues to join them. The lay
leaders regarded this action as a usurpation of power by Hagiz and Zebi,
and was one of the reasons why the lay leaders aligned themselves with
Hayon. The leaders acted not so much out of sympathy for Hayon as
out of determination to utterly subjugate the unruly Hagiz and Zebi.

The first proclamation of the ma'amad rendered no judgment on the
books of Hayon, but ordered the premature proclamations of Hagiz and
Zebi to be banned and confiscated because they were issued before the
Bet Din had concluded its deliberations. In the winter of 1713, the ma'amad
wrote to Judah Briel who had polemicized against Hayon's books solely
on the basis of Zebi's description. The ma'amad vehemently opposed this
rabbinic intrusion into its affairs: "Your Honor is surely aware that in
this city there is a Portuguese Kehilla, more noble and venerable than
that of the Ashkenazim [of which Zebi was the rabbi]. *It is not subject to
anyone, nor is it obligated in its conduct of daily affairs to follow the opinions
offered by anyone* other than its own Bet Din, in accordance with God's
law" [my emph]. The ma'amad invited Zebi numerous times to join them
to deliberate on the matter, but he consistently refused their overtures.
The ma'amad complained, "He only sows discord in this city, and
throughout the world. [His refusal to meet with us] proves clearly that
his intentions are not . . . pious and motivated by zealousness for
God. . . . We hereby declare to you that *their honor* [Ayllon and the Bet
Din] *is our honor.*"[74]

Hagiz suggested that the ma'amad convene a panel, including rabbis
Judah Briel, Naphtali Kohen, and Gabriel Eskeles, to mediate between
Zebi and the ma'amad. The parnassim refused to consider a convocation
from outside their own city, and rightly objected that the latter two were
related to Zebi. When Briel did not retract his support for Zebi, the
Ma'amad grew more abusive and impatient.

> Although he [Zebi] is renowned and fancies himself an expert, he
> is, after all, merely human and he can err, as he has proven in this
> case. You [Briel] are in no position to judge impartially. . . .
> Moreover, we are amazed that you rely on scandalous judgments

which constitute *an extreme affront to our Hakham and his Bet Din, whose honor*, as we had earlier informed you, *is inseparable from the honor of the community*. . . . Although you are undeserving of a reply because you slighted our Hakham, we will include one regardless. Please do not pester us further with your letters because you have not fulfilled the divine command to judge impartially. You will never convince us to abandon the precept of God to follow our own Bet Din in case of doubt. . . . We hereby warn you: just as we feel we do not have the right to interfere with the sovereignty of other *Kehillot*, so we will not tolerate anyone who dares to impinge upon ours.[75]

On November 6, 1713 the Ma'amad sent its notary to Hakham Zebi with an official warning. It underscored the fact that their quarrel with Hakham Zebi was over breach of jurisdiction rather than interpretation of Hayon's books.

While our Bet Din was in the midst of its deliberations, you took liberties and impudently expressed your opinion prematurely, in Hebrew and in Spanish . . . you libeled and cursed the book and pronounced the author under ban *although he is not of your nation or jurisdiction* [Zebi was rabbi of the Ashkenazic Kehillah] . . . Even after our decision was rendered in favor of the book, you continued to promote your opinion, not only locally, but to rabbis in other lands.

The Ma'amad ordered Zebi:

To lift the ban, which you have unjustly imposed on Hayon, within three days, in the same fashion as you denounced him in print. At the least, you must recant in public, in your synagogue, so that your remorse will be apparent to all. Moreover, you must provide us with open letters to all the scholars who received your libelous account of Hayon, in which you will state that you had erred in banning Hayon, that you are retracting your ban, and they should follow suit.[76]

The Ma'amad threatened to use its ultimate weapon, herem, the ban of excommunication against Zebi if he did not recant.

Zebi issued a notarized response (in Dutch) three days later. It was a formal protest directed at "Solomon Ayllon, representative of the plaintiff's of the Bet Din of the Portuguese Jewish Community." Zebi responded that he had never desired to interfere in this matter and that his opinion, like that of Hagiz, had been solicited, as on many prior occasions, by the treasurer of the Sephardic Kehillah, Abraham Franco Mendes. Zebi testified that he was loathe to become involved but Franco Mendes pressed him to issue a written opinion. He was abetted by Dr. Solomon de Mesa who likewise pressed Zebi for an opinion in writing. Although Zebi had argued that he did not wish to issue any opinions before they had consulted their own rabbi, de Mesa prevailed by arguing that he spoke in the name of the entire lay council. De Mesa translated Zebi's verdict into Spanish, and Zebi testified that he was astonished to hear that the Ma'amad had then ordered that his opinion be suppressed. Zebi concluded that he would have been willing to refer the matter to impartial arbitration—but not under threat of herem. He protested the treachery to which he had been subjected.

On the same day, three of his supporters in the Ashkenazic community registered their protest at the shabby and degrading treatment Zebi had been accorded by the Sephardim. Hagiz, who had agreed to hold his peace until the Bet Din had concluded its deliberations, now contended that the matter was in the public domain and he could say anything he wished to anyone he pleased. The parnassim disagreed. *"Because it is imperative to prevent the aforementioned from interposing themselves in the affairs of our community,"* the Ma'amad and the Bet Din on that same day, Nov. 9, 1713, issued the ban:

> It will henceforth be forbidden for any member of our 'nation' to assist, or take counsel with Hakham Zebi, nor may anyone obtain or give any favor to him, directly or indirectly . . . The members of the Ma'amad are also enjoined from speaking with him, or with Moses Hagiz, as they have been disobedient to the Bet Din.

On December 6, 1713, the Ma'amad issued a second, harsher ban, in reaction to the apparent violations of the first one.

> We must preserve our unity and maintain our independence. No man dare interfere with our sovereignty . . . so we must act with the authority vested in us by the community *and the municipal* authorities . . . We reiterate and reaffirm our previous herem, that no member of our community may have any association with Zebi or Hagiz, nor may they remand their sons to their tutelage.

Transgression of the ban carried the penalty of excommunication. On February 12, 1714, Abraham b. Mordecai Senior was excommunicated for two weeks for violating the ban. When Abraham Yizhaki protested the treatment accorded to his proteges, the ma'amad provided its (by then formulaic) response: "We acted impartially and we have no regrets over our actions. *We are bound to follow our Hakham, and his Bet Din* and none other, as the Lord has commanded us."[77]

The arrogance of the ma'amad infuriated Hagiz. Who were they to claim, "that their community is supreme and sovereign unto itself; that no outsider can come and rule over them? Is the community of Amsterdam and its parnassim superior to the ancient kings of Judea and the inhabitants of Jerusalem who accepted reproof from the prophets who did not defer to them?" In his search for rabbinic allies in this controversy, Hagiz felt most assured of the cooperation of rabbis who did not depend on their salaries for their daily bread. "Hakham R. Joseph Ergas . . . who is *wealthy and independent* and R. Eliezer HaKohen who is *rich and powerful* . . . will certainly do their share." However, some rabbis were relieved that the parnassim wished to stifle the controversy. Benjamin Finzi complained that the acrimonious debate gave the rabbinate a contentious public image, while it achieved nothing.[78]

An anonymous source close to the controversy recalled how Ayllon had pressured the ad hoc Bet Din to approve Hayon's work as a legitimate Kabbalistic work: "Our Hakham [Ayllon] was greatly attracted to this lore [Sabbatian Kabbalah] and esteemed it highly; he tried to obtain a unanimous consent. . . . After he obtained the signatures, he added a preface of his own words, which was highly improper. But the *Parnassim* did not object. Never has any community been served by such an inadequate scholar as he [Ayllon]. It was his good fortune that he was brought into this position by the influence of others, rather than on the basis of his own merit." The same source later attributed the unauthorized preface to one of the *Parnassim* directly, as though the rabbi and the *Parnassim* belonged to one cabal, and it mattered little who actually wrote it. He tried to persuade the lay Bet Din to reverse its verdict in light of Hayon's blatant heresies, "but six of them were laymen, and the other a pseudo-scholar, and they will not reconsider, except to respond, 'We must guard the honor of our Bet Din.'"

A supporter of the lay leaders reflected: "What shall we say? That our Bet Din of seven wise and pious men is too dull to comprehend? Or are we to believe that they are wicked men? That they deliberately supported an evil doctrine? Upon whom shall we confer binding authority if we remove it from those whom the public has empowered? Who shall be considered wise if our best men are not trustworthy? They have decided that Hayon's inquiries were in accordance with tradition, without heresies . . . so anyone who wishes to oppose him had better be prepared to contend with a mighty force."[79]

Every one of the *Parnassim* was extremely wealthy. Collectively, they played an important role in the commercial life of the city. Some served as local consuls for other countries, such as Portugal and Sweden. The Ma'amad represented the Jews to the civil government, and it guarded its image with great care. Any upheaval within the Jewish community that could reverberate outside of its confines and jeopardize their valuable position was harshly suppressed. Because their sense of fairness demanded it, the lay leaders accorded Hayon full public restoration of his honor: an afternoon sermon and an aliyah to the Torah with unusual honorifics. But there is no greater proof of their lack of inherent interest in the substance of his case than their great anxiety to be rid of him as soon as possible. Less than two months after the departures of Zebi and Hagiz from Amsterdam, on March 14, 1714, they induced Hayon to depart for the Holy Land by offering him an annual stipend. Later, during a revival of the controversy over his works in 1725–26, Hayon was offered a large lump sum (400 florins) and an increased stipend if he promised never to return to Amsterdam. When Hayon held out for an even greater sum (600 florins), it too was granted, on the condition that he support his promise by an oath of herem. Hayon agreed. Two years later, in 1728, when Hayon violated all these promises and returned to Amsterdam, even Ayllon did not greet him. Throughout the controversy, the lay leadership appears to have been acted to protect its own interests within the larger society, by maintaining tight control over all sources of conflict within the Jewish community.[80]

Another undercurrent which surfaced during the Hayon controversy was the tension between the Sephardic (Portuguese) and Ashkenazic communities of Amsterdam. Ashkenazim had come to Amsterdam in small numbers after 1620 and their population was greatly increased by Polish Jews fleeing the Chmielnicki pogroms and the Swedish invasions of the mid-seventeenth century. By 1660, they had formed their own kehillah, with completely separate communal apparatus. By the eighteenth century, Ashkenazic Jews far outstripped the Sephardim in numbers, but not in wealth and influence. The Sephardim were concerned that their conspicuous and poverty stricken Ashkenazic brethren would arouse the contempt of the Dutch and jeopardize their highly prized success. That is why Hakham Zebi's scathing rejection of the Sephardic rabbi and his court rankled so. In their proclamation, *Kosh't Imrei Emet*, they referred to Zebi, who had served as rabbi of the Ashkenazic community since 1710, as the *rabbi* of the Ashkenazim, never by the Sephardic title Hakham which he had adopted. They remonstrated to Judah Briel that he must support their position, for their Kehillah is more ancient and venerable *than that of the Ashkenazim*. According to the account of Zebi's son, Jacob Emden, Solomon Ayllon was driven by jealousy over Hakham Zebi's greater esteem even in the Sephardic community, and it was he who persuaded the ma'amad to repudiate Zebi as a matter of Sephardic pride. "Ayllon importuned the Parnassim not to increase the measure [of esteem] of the rabbi of the Ashkenazim over the Hakham of the Sephardim . . . to protect their honor and that of their Kehillah, not to accept the decree of the Ashkenazi rabbi." It was to be Hakham Zebi's misfortune that his own Ashkenazic communal leaders were mortified that he had antagonized the powerful Sephardim upon whom they depended in many ways, and they repudiated him too.[81]

The *herem* (ban of excommunication) was an important symbol in the conflict between Hagiz and the communal lay leaders. Hagiz believed that particularly in cases of ideological deviation such as that of Hayon, the power to pronounce a ban belonged exclusively to the rabbinate. He and Hakham Zebi were the first to issue a herem in the controversy. They were soon made aware that their solitary ban had very little effect, while the counter-ban issued against them by the ma'amad was so powerful that its influence extended beyond the Jewish community. "Solomon Ayllon together with the parnas Aaron de Pinto and his comrades, have interceded with the princes of the land to have Zebi and Hagiz evicted from this land." Hagiz complained that "Ayllon tried to coerce us to capitulate to his words, by threat of the Gentile courts, by declaring that no one may speak with us, and after we left, that no one may correspond with us." To counteract this power, Hagiz denied the validity of the ban of the Bet Din and called for massive rabbinical support for *his* ban: "Whoever disregards [the ban of the Parnassim], and honors Zebi and Hagiz, has fulfilled several Biblical precepts. . . . Because we are aware that their herem is very potent . . . we are acting cautiously, and requesting discreetly that all Sages, in every city and every province, come forward and dispatch their pronouncement on this matter . . . and the truth will out." The final phases of the controversy were punctuated by a confusing staccato of ban and counter-ban. Samson Morpurgo reflected on the futility of pronouncing additional bans in the welter of confusion: "What impact can I have on the citizens of Amsterdam, if they have not heeded the barrage of bans, excommunications, and violent maledictions which plastered the streets?"

Hagiz did succeed in amassing many rabbinic bans of Hayon, but he could not wrest the real power of this weapon of social control from the lay councils. In the Ashkenazic Kehillah of Amsterdam the Hayon controversy produced a ban, recorded in Yiddish in the register of the Ashkenazic community, dated August 19, 1715. It was the first ban to be pronounced by this Kehillah in which the lay leaders did not seek to affix the signature of even one rabbi. The signatures of the seven lay leaders of the council stand boldly, defiantly, alone. It is a ban against Moses Hagiz and his polemical writings.[82]

RABBI SOLOMON AYLLON

As the rabbi of the Portuguese Kehillah of Amsterdam throughout the years of the Hayon controversy, R. Solomon Ayllon (b. Salonika, c. 1655), was caught at the center of the maelstrom. Ayllon, a Sabbatian since his youth, had enjoyed personal ties to Nathan of Gaza, Sabbatai's prophet. In 1680, he settled in Safed; he later traveled to Europe as an emissary of that community. He established close ties to the Sabbatians of Livorno when he traveled there in 1688, although he took care to keep his Sabbatian ties out of the public eye. Ayllon was appointed rabbi of London when he arrived there in 1689, a controversial appointment. In 1700, he was selected to be chief rabbi in Amsterdam. Except for the banning of Hagiz' *Sefat Emet* in 1708, an incident in which Ayllon played no important role, there was no sign of overt conflict between Hagiz and Ayllon. In fact, there were cooperative efforts, such as "Hilkhot Missim."[83] Yet, the malevolent feelings which surfaced almost immediately at the outset of the controversy belie the amicable facade. Less than six weeks after Hayon's arrival in Amsterdam, Ayllon complained to a friend of the tumult caused by Hagiz and Zebi, "who have always sown divisiveness and ill will . . . and are arrogant without giving a thought to profanation of the Name." Ayllon admonished Judah Briel for supporting Hagiz and Zebi. "I stand inside [at the center of the controversy] and I know how great is the power of these quarrel mongers to alter the facts. . . . Everyone knows that they are motivated by malice and by love of controversy."

Hagiz, likewise, claimed to have known of dark stains on Ayllon's past. He put Ayllon's associations with the Sabbatians of Salonika to very effective polemical use.

> Ayllon . . . was one of those smitten by the unclean plague of Querido, Filosof, and Florentin . . . He held fast to the abomination [his wife] after she had already sinned with another man from their abominable sect who took her from her husband on the

pretext that she was not his true mate. . . . After their apostasy, it is said that they divorced and married without the mediation of the rabbinate.

He publicly declared in his sermons that he has the soul of King David . . . that her first husband had been the primeval serpent, while the second was Uriah, and those who understand, will not object. . . . If I had not heard it with my own ears, I would not have believed it. I also heard from his mouth how an aged "sage" had envisioned thirteen long rays emanating from Ayllon's beard . . . I will not reveal their meaning in order not to violate the paper on which I write . . .

When he [Ayllon] took an oath on a sacred object, he later claimed that he had replaced the sacred phylacteries with two onions.[84]

Hagiz' charges that Ayllon was an apostate and member of the antinomian Donmeh sect have not been substantiated. Hagiz does not discuss the Sabbatian ideology in Ayllon's writing, and he was apparently unaware that it existed. Judah Briel likewise appears to have been unaware of Ayllon's Sabbatianism when he vainly implored Ayllon to condemn Hayon as a Sabbatian.[85]

Hagiz attributed the most extreme characteristics of some Sabbatian groups to Ayllon. But it was not Sabbatian foibles, nor Ayllon's doctrines which earned him the distinction of being numbered in the calamitous trio which formed the main target of Hagiz' polemical opus, *Sheber Posh'im*. Ayllon merited a place in Hagiz' pantheon of ignominy because Hagiz perceived him as a rabbinical lackey of the lay leadership in Amsterdam, whose interests directly opposed those of Hagiz. Hagiz did not condemn Ayllon for his heretical ideas, but for using his rabbinic position to promote the heretical ideas of others. "The third rebel is Ayllon who upheld their [Cardoso and Hayon's] work." Hagiz accused Ayllon of tampering with the established rotation of parnassim to secure a Bet Din that would support Hayon. Hagiz argued that when Ayllon had approved the works of Cardoso for publication a short while earlier, he had nearly exposed himself. When the Parnassim overruled him, he should have stood forewarned "not to camouflage the subversive intent of the works of Cardoso and Hayon." "I swear that I [Hagiz] never had the slightest doubt that he [Ayllon] would condemn Hayon's book, despite the fact that he had approved the works of Cardoso. I thought to myself, as one of the apostates of Salonika surely he would withdraw himself from the case. Who would have imagined that he would have the temerity to mislead the Parnassim!"

The conflict between Hagiz and Ayllon reached a dramatic public denouement. In Ayllon's sermon one Sabbath, Hagiz detected criticism leveled at himself for slander. Ayllon had made thinly veiled comparisons of himself to King David, of the parnassim to King Saul, and of Hagiz to Do'eg the Edomite who was barred by the Talmudic Sages from a share in the world to come because he had peddled gossip. That same day, in the course of the afternoon services, Hagiz retaliated. In his sermon he delivered a scathing attack on Ayllon. He compared him to Jeroboam whose arrogant comparison of himself to King David led him to introduce idol worship. This sermon provoked the anger of the audience, who felt that the honor of their rabbi had been publicly violated. Hagiz realized only later that this confrontation had cost him dearly in terms of public support.[86]

In his written polemics, Hagiz emphasized those aspects of Ayllon's conduct which rendered him unfit for the rabbinate. He listed numerous occasions on which Ayllon had made a mockery of his own oaths. In the perverse Sabbatian world where sin was holy, oaths taken to be violated, and dissembling replaced honesty, how could Ayllon dispense justice to the constituents who came before him to settle disputes? "Hayon and his cohort Ayllon postulated that the study of Talmud and Codes is worthless. . . . He who can betray his faith can easily betray his own words." By showing that Ayllon's appointment to the rabbinate was a travesty, Hagiz was able to score other polemical points. The appointment of such a seriously flawed figure to the position of chief rabbi demonstrated the fallibility of the lay communal leadership. It seemed to prove Hagiz' point that rabbinic authority should derive from a higher source than lay appointment.

Ayllon was able to parry some of the accusations against him by outright denial: "You have written that Hayon's work reeks of Sabbatianism. What idiocy! Who would wish to support those sinners? I inquired into the allegation until I found a sermon in *Diberei Nehemiah* which condemns that generation [the apostates]." He did not respond to the accusations of his own past affiliation with Sabbatianism. According to Hagiz, he pleaded with the Parnas Aron Pinto to defend his honor, "for that is the honor of the Portuguese community." The relationship between lay leaders and communal rabbi was Ayllon's ultimate defense.[87]

THE MIGHT OF THE PEN: THE BATTLE TO CONTROL THE PRESSES

As accusations, bans, and testimonies proliferated, the effort to muster influential support often depended on the speed with which material could be printed and circulated. Both sides had easy access to the presses, which undoubtedly contributed to the magnitude of the controversy. Polemical literature often appeared first in ephemeral form—broadsheets, placards, pamphlets and correspondence—to facilitate immediate response as well as to promote wide, inexpensive circulation. Many important documents were later reprinted in more permanent form. Hagiz' long association with the presses in Amsterdam was invaluable, although the publishing house of Foa closed its doors to him because Netanel Foa was a son-in-law of Solomon Ayllon. Printing and distribution of materials was a great expense. The Kehillah, a wealthy institution, could easily afford it, but as Hagiz found to his chagrin, it was a tremendous financial strain for an individual. The parnassim were able to use superior distribution channels to those of Hagiz, perhaps those developed for commercial purposes. The strategy of the ma'amad was to distribute its material abroad first, and release it locally only later. By the time Hagiz could react to damaging material circulated in Amsterdam, it had already preceded him abroad, sometimes by several weeks. The parnassim were able to effectively suppress the writings of the opposition; the rabbinate was unable to retaliate in kind. Judah Briel lamented: "I pity the parnassim who declare that their only wish is to unearth the truth, while they close all the windows through which it can penetrate. How can one arrive at a balanced view of the opposing sides, when for political reasons, they have suppressed the writings of the opposition?" When the parnassim accused the rabbis of condemning Hayon's book without having seen it, Hagiz retorted that, to the contrary, he and Zebi had sent copies of the work to every rabbi whose opinion was solicited, although they were individuals with limited resources, whereas the parnassim, who had access to unlimited public funds, conspired to conceal it.[88]

Another aspect of the contest to control the printed material was Hagiz' campaign for the exclusive right to grant approbations. Hayon had printed several rabbinic letters of approbation (*haskamot*) at the beginning of his works. In the first stage of the campaign Hagiz and Zebi contacted the writers of the approbations and persuaded them to retract the haskamah or deny that they had issued it. Their responses provided Hagiz and Zebi with their first substantive polemical weapons, evidence of Hayon's lack of credibility. This shrewd appeal calculated that most rabbis would feel obligated to respond immediately, lest they be held guilty by association with Hayon. It was an opening wedge to procure the active participation of individuals who might have preferred to observe the controversy from the sidelines.[89]

Beyond its utility for the campaign against Hayon, the call for repeal of the haskamot also served a more profound objective for Hagiz. He believed that rabbinic scholars had relinquished an important prerogative when they relaxed their pre-publication censorship. His petition to repeal the haskamot was an attempt to recover this power for the rabbinate. Hagiz and Zebi urged a renewed emphasis on the aspect of consent and approval in haskamot. It is appropriate that Hayon, who was protected by the lay leadership, urged them to counteract this bid by extending *their* powers of censorship into the prepublication period. As the perfect example he chose the *Sefat Emet* of Hagiz which was first published, and *then* banned in Amsterdam: "It is puzzling that in a place of justice and righteousness [Amsterdam] works are published indiscriminately. . . . You cannot be blamed, for the reason is obvious. [Moses Hagiz] showed you an unblemished version when he obtained permission to publish, and then he printed whatever he pleased."[90] Hayon argued that the lay leadership should initiate a rigorous prepublication censorship, as his opponents sought to recover this power for the rabbinate.

The appeal to retract the approbations that had been issued for Hayon's book elicited a swift and encouraging response. Zebi's first pronouncement against Hayon, *le-Einei Kol Yisrael*, was issued in mid-July, 1713, during the deliberations of the ad hoc Sephardic Bet Din. Zebi outlined Hayon's heresies, especially those in the introduction to *Oz le-Elohim*, and accused him of being a Sabbatian. He appealed to "Every man who is free of this pernicious faith and not joined to these heretics, to make a conflagration and burn them." On July 27, 1713, the Bet Din issued its verdict exonerating Hayon, followed immediately by another (undated) proclamation of Zebi against Hayon. This pamphlet contained many explicit quotations from *Oz le-Elohim*. In addition to enjoining the public to burn Hayon's book, it also contained an appeal "To the great sages and eminent rabbis everywhere: It is your responsibility, in view of the serious nature of the subject, to enlighten and warn all Israel who rely upon you . . . to alert all the farthest reaches of the Diaspora, as I have done in my earlier proclamation."

The personal letters that accompanied Zebi's printed proclamations have not survived. It appears that some of these were signed by Zebi only, and others by Hagiz as well. The first letter of support, from Judah

Briel of Mantua, was addressed to Hakham Zebi and to Hagiz. Briel's letter was not a retraction of an approbation but an enthusiastic response to the call of Hagiz and Zebi to join their campaign. Briel wrote that he had been confined to a sickbed, "but when I was called upon to participate in this great *mizvah*, to denounce and pursue these evil heretics, my strength returned. . . . I hereby curse, excommunicate, and consign to eternal oblivion the author of the book, and his supporters. . . . The book should be burned, and the people should be expelled from the Jewish community."

The first retraction came from Venice. An approbation by the rabbinate, (Solomon Nizza, David Altaras, and Raphael da Silva) had appeared in Hayon's first printed work, *Raza de-Yihuda*, (Venice, 1711), as well as in the *Oz le-Elohim*. Hagiz and Zebi turned to the sons of Samuel Aboab, an early opponent of Sabbatianism, to pressure their Venetian rabbinic colleagues to withdraw the support of Hayon implied in their haskamah. Jacob Aboab, in the name of his brothers, replied on August 14, 1714: "When Hayon had appeared in our city last year for a brief visit, we learned of his clandestine abominations and alien doctrines, so we distanced ourselves from him and did not speak with him. After he left, we heard of a small book he had printed, *Raza de-Yihuda*. . . . When we received your letter, stating your objections, we immediately turned to the sages of our yeshiva to investigate how this occurred, what they had known of Hayon, and how they had consented to the publication of his work. When confronted, they were astounded . . . then they replied, all three as one, that *they had never seen the book* [*Oz le-Elohim*], *and did not sign this haskamah*, even the small book (*Raza*) they had barely glimpsed. The haskamah was surely forged: no good Jew could suspect that these sages had seen these books and then approved them . . . Hayon wished to honor himself by embarrassing the sages." Hayon later claimed in his defense, that the rabbis had been intimidated by Hagiz and Zebi into prevaricating, and that the signatures of the communal scribe of Venice on these documents were authentic. Given the known Sabbatian sympathies of two of the three rabbis, Hayon's defense cannot be discounted, although it came too late to salvage his reputation. Two days later, on August 16, a response was issued by R. Gabriel Eskeles of Nicholsburg whose haskamah appeared both in *Diberei Nehemiah* and *Oz le-Elohim*. The letter was addressed to Zebi alone and referred to Zebi's letter of August 4. Eskeles wrote that he was horrified to hear about the publication of Hayon's book. "I have never issued a *haskamah* for this book, nor any that resembled it, for I am extremely cautious about approving new books *and my signature is undoubtedly a forgery, for I have never signed this appro-*

bation. Today I will write to Berlin to forbid the continued publication of this book. . . . My scribes affirm that I have never issued an approbation to the book, but I did write a personal letter of recommendation for him because of his persistent entreaties."[91]

R. Naphtali Kohen, eminent halakhist and renowned kabbalist of Frankfurt, replied on that day (August 16) as well. The Hayon controversy came at a period of grave personal difficulty and upheaval in Kohen's life. In 1711, at the height of his successful rabbinic career, while serving as rabbi of Frankfurt, a fire destroyed his house and his possessions. His enemies maliciously slandered him, saying he had done nothing to prevent the spread of the fire so that he could first test the effectiveness of his amulets, as he was deemed a great expert in practical kabbalah. Kohen was jailed on these charges. In 1711–13 he sojourned in Prague, where he first met Hayon. If the lines of his apologetic and somewhat disorganized letters in the Hayon controversy seem confused, we must attribute it, at least partially, to his recent losses of wife and property. His letter is permeated by a sense of guilt and shame for having permitted his imprimatur to support a Sabbatian work.

> Although I am unworthy . . . I will speak, because they are propping up their putrescent views with a debased person such as myself. I am responsible for this obstacle, for I did give him a haskamah on his heretical book. I sinned out of ignorance . . . [There follows a description of the deceptive appearance of Hayon while in Prague, and the widespread adulation he received.] I tried to retrieve my haskamah . . . but I was living modestly in Prague and my associates were not with me as in the past. If the *Ab Bet Din* [David Oppenheim] had been at home at the time surely he would have given zealous pursuit, but he was away, and his sons were beguiled by Hayon's smooth tongue . . . Later, in Berlin, I met Hayon . . . and I intended to retrieve my haskamah by crafty means . . . but he was very popular, while I was an alien, and I was afraid. . . . The treatise called *Mehemnuta de-Kola* I have never seen, nor his two commentaries which frame it . . . I only saw a few innocuous pages . . . and now, upon reading the excerpts from that work [*Oz le-Elohim*] in the copy you sent me, . . . I can wrench the hair out of my head over my blunder in this matter.

In his *Moda'ah Rabah*, Hayon vehemently denied all of Kohen's defensive statements, and claimed that Kohen had willingly and knowingly given his approbation. Hayon claimed that Kohen had ample opportunity to ask for the return of his haskamah, but he never showed the slightest inclination to do so.[92]

By mid-September of 1713, Zebi and Hagiz had assembled enough retractions or repudiations to print a small pamphlet, which included the letters of rabbis Naphtali Kohen, Judah Briel, Gabriel Eskeles, Jacob Aboab, and part of a letter of David Oppenheim. The Amsterdam ma'amad, which had already declared Hayon innocent of all charges, issued a rebuttal "Kosh't Imrei Emet," [in Portuguese, "Manifesto"] of this attack on Hayon's integrity. Hagiz soon responded with a "Risposta dell Manifesto."[93]

The publication of the first letters engendered more support for the cause of Hagiz and Zebi. Hagiz was not content to let the matter rest at that. He intended to overwhelm the opposition with a massive and unprecedented display of rabbinic unity. The letters of support he continued to solicit would be the bricks to create a solid wall of protest against Hayon; they would be garnered from every corner of the Jewish world. While it was impossible for Hagiz himself to contact and pressure every potential supporter, he concentrated on winning over key rabbinic figures who could act as his deputies on the local level where their influence was greatest. In his allies Hakham Zebi and Judah Briel, Hagiz was fortunate to have figures of towering stature among Ashkenazic and Italian Jewry, respectively. Their association with him from the embryonic stages of the controversy gave his campaign impact and scope that he could scarcely have attained singlehandedly.

CHAPTER 5

Expansion of the Hayon Controversy

 TO REGAIN ground that had been lost to rabbinic divisiveness and passivity Hagiz believed that the rabbinate must cement the breaches within its ranks and become an aggressive force. Then it could begin to assume its rightful position, in Hagiz' idealized view, at the helm of Jewish communities. The contents of the polemic, rejection of lay claims and Sabbatian interpretations were ancillary to Hagiz' main goal: to revitalize the rabbinate and resurrect its authority. In order to do this, he needed to enlist the support of many influential rabbinic figures.

FORGING ALLIANCES

Scorned by some of his own fractious congregants, Hakham Zebi's word nevertheless commanded respect in many reaches of the rabbinic world. Zebi was instrumental in attracting the support of major rabbinic figures, especially in Central Europe, to the campaign against Hayon. Many contacts were facilitated by Zebi's ramified family ties to other rabbinic figures. Kinship bound Zebi to Naphtali Kohen. Zebi solicited and received a strong denunciation of Hayon from another relative, R. Jacob Kohen Popers of Koblenz. Popers issued his first proclamation of the ban against Hayon at the end of October 1713. Although we do not have Zebi's reply, its contents can be inferred from Popers' subsequent communi-

cation. Once assured of Popers' personal commitment, Zebi proceeded
to build on this success. He asked Popers to intercede with the rabbinate
of Frankfurt, whose approbation had appeared in Hayon's book. Popers'
reply of December 21, 1713, informed Zebi that his efforts in Frankfurt
had not yet met with success, but he would continue to pursue the matter. In the absence of the complete correspondence, we must again rely
on deduction to learn that Hagiz then urged Popers to exert himself further to press for a ban and retraction from the rabbinate of Frankfurt.
On March 8, 1714, Popers wrote to Hagiz that he had finally obtained
a copy of *Oz le-Elohim*, and had submitted a detailed refutation to the
rabbinate of Frankfurt, which he enclosed in his reply to Hagiz. When
the rabbinate of Frankfurt issued its condemnation (but not ban) of Hayon,
and a denial that they had ever approved his book, Popers' name was
mentioned as an important influence.[1]

R. Gabriel Eskeles was chief rabbi of Moravia and head of the yeshiva
of Nicholsburg [an office he shared with David Oppenheim]. Like Popers, Eskeles was also related to Zebi by marriage. His letter to Zebi of
August 27, 1713, denying that he had issued the approbation that appeared in Hayon's book was one of the earliest responses to Zebi's campaign. On September 3, 1713, the Bet Din of Nicholsburg, headed by
Eskeles, issued a ban and anathema against Hayon and his books. Zebi
asked Eskeles to persuade the chief rabbi of Berlin, Aaron Wolff, to issue
a ban and a repudiation of his haskamah to Hayon's book. Eskeles reported to Zebi that he had not only contacted Wolff but also tried to
elicit support for their cause from Samson Wertheim, the renowned court
Jew and financier, whose daughter was married to the son of Eskeles. It
is not known whether either overture met with a positive response.

The most conspicuous omission from Zebi's roster of supporters in
Central Europe is R. David Oppenheim. Scholar, bibliophile, and chief
rabbi of Moravia and Prague. Oppenheim had provided Hayon with a
haskamah for *Diberei Nehemia* (which Hayon printed in *Oz le-Elohim*) although he stipulated that he had not examined its contents. Oppenheim's
son, Joseph, had provided hospitable lodging for Hayon during his stay
in Prague, and he had conveyed to his father his impression of Hayon's
saintly character. Both parties to the controversy, Hayon and Zebi, implored Oppenheim for his valuable support. Their exploitation of his name
left Oppenheim with unsavory feelings toward both. In a private letter
to his relative Leib Hamburger, on October 25, 1713, Oppenheim explained that he had been apalled to see both sides take liberties with his
name. Hayon had brazenly admitted to transferring the approbation given
to *Diberei Nehemiah* to his other work which he had never shown Op-

penheim. Zebi had published excerpts from an earlier letter of Oppenheim's, and disguised the true intent of Oppenheim's entire letter, which was not supportive of Zebi. Thus, unlike his contemporaries who decried the strife but did not decline to contribute to it, Oppenheim did not support either party. Although he did not defend Hayon, Oppenheim argued that he deserved a fair and impartial hearing. As for the rabbinic bans and accusations that proliferated with ever greater momentum, Oppenheim remained in vehement opposition to that conduct. "I am astounded that great scholars such as they have committed their complaints to publication . . . accessible to all, even school children. . . . What will the future generations think? . . . How will the masses malign the sages! . . . They will call us petty and contentious." Oppenheim chided the rabbis for rushing to join the combat without first considering more peaceful alternatives. Instead of signing mutual defamations, partisans of both sides should have insisted that the matter be tried by a scrupulously impartial rabbinic court, which would render a verdict "between the rabbi of the Sephardim and the rabbi of the Ashkenazim." Oppenheim's sane suggestion was drowned out by the clamor of the controversy. Zebi never forgave Oppenheim for his refusal. Years later, when they met in Poland, Jacob Emden recalled that his father, Hakham Zebi "reproved him [Oppenheim] to his face in the presence of all the nobles standing there, for having secretly abetted and supported Hayon."

Zebi proved to be a tireless partner in the effort to enlist rabbinic support in Italy. Jacob Aboab of Venice, in the name of all his brothers, responded immediately to Zebi's call on August 25, 1713. Gabriel Pontrimoli of Torino wrote that his ban of Hayon was being issued at the request of Zebi. His painstaking diligence and tireless zeal left no potential supporter untapped. With a prestigious rabbinic position at stake, and a very large family to provide for, the disfavor of the Sephardic lay leaders entailed greater personal sacrifice on the part of the Zebi than of most other participants. That he persisted nonetheless demonstrates Zebi's unbending posture in the face of great pressure.[2]

THE ITALIAN RABBINATE: RABBI JUDAH BRIEL

I am certain that when they [the Italian rabbinate] will form a solid phalanx by affixing their signatures boldly . . . then surely this recalcitrant kehillah [the Portuguese of Amsterdam] will pay attention. . . . This will happen due to the prestige of the Italian rabbinate, which will have brought them to this admission against their will."[3]

A most important strategic and psychological goal of Hagiz' campaign was to enlist the entire Italian rabbinate on his side. The enthusiastic collaboration of R. Judah Briel, elder sage of Mantua, was vital to the success of this endeavor, as his opinion carried great weight throughout Italy. Why did Hagiz elevate the Italian rabbinate above all the others? In Amsterdam, every official segment of the Portuguese kehillah, lay and rabbinic, had joined in the rejection of Hagiz' claims. No individual, regardless of his personal eminence or influence, could breach the inviolable sovereignty of the Kehillah. Briel's individual entreaties resulted in an impatient, insolent brushoff. Hagiz believed that only the opprobrium of another venerable Jewry could effectively pressure the Amsterdam community. The variegated collective of Italian kehillot was the only body in Europe that could lay claim to such obeisance. Italy was the home of the most ancient and venerable Jewish communities in the West. Hagiz had opened his *Milhamah la-Shem*, a grand collection of proclamations of the Italian rabbinate, with that of the Roman rabbinate. The Amsterdam kehillah had always looked to Venice as a model, and even when Amsterdam outstripped Venice in wealth and influence, they still maintained close ties.

Many Italian rabbis were disinclined to embark on a raucous, aggressive campaign of this nature for a variety of reasons. Foremost among these was the fact that Italy was a major center of Sabbatian activism, and many rabbis were sympathizers or outright adherents. R. Jonathan Ghiron of Florence wrote of the advice he received from R. Benjamin Kohen of Reggio: "He advised me to sit and do nothing [refrain from joining Hagiz' campaign]. One of his reasons he gave was that Hakham Ayllon is known to him as a great kabbalist of the true esoteric lore, unlike his adversaries."

R. Benjamin Kohen of Reggio, a sympathizer of Sabbatian kabbalah, expressed his surprise and displeasure that he was not directly consulted for an opinion on Hayon. He stated that he did not believe Hayon's works to be false or heretical, nor did they deserve to be consigned to the flames. But he agreed that Hayon's statements could be misleading to the public, and he agreed to join the local herem against the books and their author *at the request of Briel*. He provided a withering letter, denigrating Hayon for his "queer ideas," and his little treatise printed in Venice (*Raza de-Yihuda*) which was short in "quantity and quality." R. Elijah Mujajon was a native of Salonika who transplanted his Sabbatianism onto Italian soil. He became a member of the rabbinical court in Ancona. There he served together with Joseph Fiametta, another expert in Sabbatian kabbalah who was torn between the two sides of the Hayon controversy. Both Hayon and Ayllon corresponded with him in the hope of securing his support, but the presence of Briel eventually won his grudging support for Hagiz' campaign.[4]

R. Samuel de Pas, a Sabbatian rabbi in Livorno who was a correspondent of Abraham Cardoso's on the subject of the "Mystery of the Godhead" ["sod ha-Elohut"] represented many of his Livornese brethren in their Sabbatian activism. Supporters of Hayon in Amsterdam kept up a steady barrage of pro-Sabbatian propaganda literature, which circulated in the Italian cities in Italian. A sample of this literature is ample evidence of its compelling style:

> From which school did Abraham our Patriarch emerge with knowledge of the one God, if not that of his father and teacher, the idolater? Did not the receiver of the Torah [Moses] drink the pure milk of his visions in the academies of Memphis and Egypt? The taste of a rose is bitter, but the active bee can transform it into the sweetest honey; from the most poisonous venom one can extract the most powerful antidote. Knowledge of evil is the surest medium to recognition of the good. Righteous men learn from contemplating the failures of the wicked.
>
> The subject of the [Hayon's] book is kaballah, and those who have investigated it have declared that its deliberations remain in accordance with the true principles of tradition. They have not found the heresies which were unjustly attributed to him; they concluded that his words had been distorted.[5]

Another source of resistance to Hagiz' campaign was the tradition of anti-kabbalism which had deep roots in some segments of Italian Jewry. From Elijah Delmedigo (*Behinat ha-Dat*) in the fifteenth century, to Leone Modena (*Ari Nohem*) in the sixteenth and the Frances brothers in the seventeenth, a strong current within the Italian rabbinate disapproved of the study of kabbalah altogether, particularly for the masses. Many of these rabbis felt that the Hayon controversy was a debate over the legitimacy of various schools of kabbalistic thought, and they had no desire to vindicate either side, when in fact, they rejected both. In addition, many Italian rabbis were concerned lest the material publicized in the polemic become grist for the mill of the Christian polemicists. They had no desire to revive the unsavory memory of the Sabbatian movement, for which Jews had paid a high price in the polemical debate with Christians.[6]

Despite these obstacles to success, Hagiz gathered statements of support for himself and repudiation of Hayon from every major Italian Jewish kehillah; almost all his potential opponents had capitulated and provided the necessary statements. Hagiz published these documents as a pamphlet, *Milhamah la-Shem*, in mid-1714. Hagiz titled its final, triumphant portion of it "A Gathering of Elders of Israel, the Illustrious Rabbis of Italy, may the Lord keep them." It contained the proclamations of Isaac Cantarini, Isaac Lampronte, (a reference to the statement of) Samuel de Pas, Samson Morpurgo, and Joseph Fiametta, among others, all rabbis who had resisted joining Hagiz' campaign at first. There were some individuals, such as R. Meir Baki, who never did participate in Hagiz' campaign. Their refusal was greatly publicized; some later felt constrained to offer apologetic explanations. The handful of exceptions does not detract from Hagiz' success in gathering Italian support.[7]

Hagiz achieved his goals in Italy through his skill as a persuasive polemicist, and his astute deployment of loyal associates. The most crucial figure in his Italian campaign, a most valuable and active ally, was Judah Briel, rabbi of Mantua. Briel, a septuagenarian when the controversy broke out, was renowned as a halakhist and anti-Christian polemicist. When Hagiz and Zebi turned to him at the outset of the controversy, Briel's reply was immediately forthcoming:

> I have been called upon to partake of this great duty, to publicize the wicked and their evil deeds, and to pursue them until they are destroyed . . . I arose and girded myself with strength. . . . I hereby curse and vilify the author of this book [Hayon] with all the maledictions of the Torah, and his supporters will bring the ban of excommunication on themselves. . . . The Lord will surely call into account the teachers of the Torah who have closed their eyes to the harm of teaching kabbalah to the ignorant, or have forgotten the fundamentals of our faith. . . . I order every rabbi and director of a community to proclaim this. I know that I have overstepped my boundaries. . . . The zeal of the Lord, to destroy the heretics, has effected this.

When Zebi published Briel's letter in his pamphlet which formally initiated the controversy, "le-Einei Kol Yisrael," the wrath of the Amsterdam ma'amad descended upon Briel. In mid-September of 1713, Briel reaffirmed to them that his original letter published by Zebi was a true reflection of his convictions, not given in a haphazard or flustered state of mind: "I hereby affirm and substantiate the epistle "le-Einei Kol Israel" . . . which . . . Zebi . . . and Hagiz have published. When I saw that the Sephardic community, with their king, R. Solomon Ayllon, at their head, came to defend Hayon and his book, despite detailed refutation by Zebi, I felt obliged to declare: I have always loved Solomon Ayllon, and the entire Sephardic community . . . and I will forever bind their love as a garland to my crown. But the truth is dearer to me. . . . The words of Hayon are absolute heresies, and Zebi has written the truth." In early October 1713, Briel wrote a private letter to Ayllon in which he defended his position and entreated Ayllon to retract. He was apparently unaware of Ayllon's Sabbatian sympathies, as his tone to Ayllon is one of great deference and respect. Briel repeated his declaration of friendship to Ayllon and argued, "Even if you say there is hidden merit in Hayon's work, the overt meaning is evil, a heretical remnant of Sabbatai Zebi, and should be silenced . . . You alone hold the power to destroy this evil, to preserve all Israel from calamity, by announcing that the ruling [of the *Bet Din*] was based on [Hayon's] deception. The testimony of R. Naphtali Kohen [who had retracted his first, favorable opinion of Hayon] is compelling. Admit your error and do not concern yourself with pride . . . Should anyone object that I am speaking out of place, I answer that in the case of profanation of God's name, when many souls are at stake, I could not hold my peace." On October 21, 1713, Ayllon responded, carefully and forcefully to Briel. It was not he who had been misled by Hayon, but Briel who had been misguided by Zebi and Hagiz, the inveterate troublemongers.[8]

Briel's reply of November 3, 1713, was terse and urgent. Hayon's books, "provided our enemies with material to dispute us on the fundamentals of our faith." As an anti-Christian polemicist, Briel was particularly sensitive to the uses which Hayon's trinitarian conception would be put by Christian polemicists. In a call for a truce, he begged Ayllon to join them in concealing the books from the public to extinguish the bitterness and contention that raged among the rabbis. In Briel's final message to Ayllon, on December 22, 1713, he seemed resigned to the irremediable state of the conflict. He admitted that although his initial proclamation had been issued on the basis of hearsay from Zebi, he had since examined the book and found it even worse than Zebi had described. He informed Ayllon that he had decided to gather a 'multitude of shepherds' [rabbis] against the book, to pursue and destroy it. "I never would have believed that in your venerable and renowned Kehillah, there could be found people who would defend bearers of heresy and distorted doctrines, unless they shared the convictions of the author." He closed with a blessing to Ayllon for restoration of peace among all participants after the conflict had taken its course.

On the same date as he wrote his penultimate plea to Ayllon (November 3, 1713), Briel also bravely directed a call for peace to the lay leadership: "Let it not appear strange that you receive this writ from an unknown person who is far from your community . . . for I have overcome all human considerations to beseech you to accept my words with grace." Briel apologized, and claimed that he had been unaware that the ma'amad's Bet Din had been in the process of deliberation over Hayon's work, when his first hostile evaluation of Hayon had appeared in Zebi's *le-Einei Kol Israel*. Briel underscored two objections to the conclusion of the Bet Din. First, regardless of Hayon's intentions, the work was misleading the ignorant Jewish masses. Second, Christian polemicists found material in Hayon's work to bolster their claim that Kabbalah had always affirmed elements of Christianity. Briel did not urge any sanctions against Hayon, but merely urged that the works be buried in the sealed communal archives to forestall their deleterious effect on the public welfare.

The response of the ma'amad as we have seen, was imperious and unyielding. The final, abusive rebuff of the ma'amad (late February/early March, 1714) quelled any hopes of Briel that his efforts to effect a truce would be fruitful. Briel's tense exchange with the ma'amad was very similar in essence to the ma'amad's hostile relationship with Hagiz and Zebi. As with Hagiz and Zebi, the high handed manner of the ma'amad fueled Briel's decision to fight back, and reclaim control over ideology and dogma—including the power over censorship and ban—for the idealized rabbinate.[9]

Hagiz orchestrated Briel's campaign to complement his own tireless effort to recruit allies among the eminent rabbis. Briel would contact, cajole, or pressure members of the Italian rabbinate who showed resistance to Hagiz' overtures. Although many of the records of these activities have not been preserved, the remainder provides some illuminating examples. On January 19, 1714, Hagiz wrote to R. Joel Pincherle in Alessandria to sustain his earlier efforts and to persuade him to accept a larger role. "I am certain that . . . you will galvanize all the rabbis and scholars in the surrounding communities to gather together, each one with his Bet Din, to curse, anathematize, and annihilate all the heretical books published by, or through the office of . . . Hayon and his cohorts . . . They should be condemned to the flames, and never again be numbered among the sacred Jewish books . . . as the rabbinates of Jerusalem, Smyrna, Syria, and Frankfurt have already declared. . . . It is especially incumbent upon Italy, so close to the center of activity. . . . I greatly question those rabbis whose quill-strokes have been tardy . . . Therefore I urge you to complete the task you have begun . . . and *you will take counsel and plan strategy with the great sage Judah Briel,* who was the first to draw his sword from its sheath, and who fears no man." When he sensed that R. Samson Morpurgo was wavering in his resolution to join the campaign, Hagiz asked Briel to exert extra pressure on Morpurgo, who chafed at this attempt to manipulate him. Many other Italian rabbis threw aside their reservations at the behest of Briel. Benjamin Kohen of Reggio wrote to Briel of his tentative support. Joel Pincherle issued his first ban and Netanel Halevi of Pesaro broke his long silence at the urgent request of Briel. The long awaited denunciation from Joseph Fiametta of Mantua explicitly mentioned the influence of Briel. While Fiametta did not mention Hayon by name, he agreed that sensitive kabbalistic works should not have been published, and he issued a denial that he had ever given an approbation to Hayon's work. To persuade Fiametta to retract, the efforts of Hagiz, Morpurgo, and Joseph Ergas were not as effective as the request of Briel. In a correspondence with Benjamin Finzi in Amsterdam in September 1713, Briel gave a succinct analysis of Hayon's theses, which he reduced to eight major heresies. This formulaic analysis formed the basis of Briel's effective polemical writing.

In the last week of November 1713, Briel issued an open call for a rabbinic ban of Hayon: "I hereby call in a great voice to all the sages and judges of the land, and the nobility of every locale, . . . to pursue Hayon and his books, and his supporters, in order to save many Jewish souls. Whoever supported Hayon in the past must do public penance in the presence of at least five rabbis." Briel's call stimulated a new round of bans among Italian rabbis. On January 16, 1714, Isaac Cantarini wrote a ban against Hayon *at the request of Briel.* On January 13, 1714, the rabbinate of Rome wrote in accordance with Briel's request. The rabbis of Ferrara had issued a statement against Hayon on December 3, 1713, signed only by a student, Jacob Daniel Olmo. After the circulation of Briel's appeal, they issued a ban of Hayon signed by the entire rabbinate, including the chief rabbi, Isaac Lampronte.[10]

While Judah Briel did not leave any full length polemical work against Hayon, Hagiz' *Milhamah la-Shem* remains a tribute to the dedication and effectiveness of Briel's efforts. Abraham Segre referred to a "convocation of elders whom Briel addressed with persuasive arguments." Apparently, Briel used the occasion of a live audience to collect more writs against Hayon, which Hagiz then added to his growing collection. Briel's eight-point analysis provided his audience with the most coherent attack on Hayon's work and the most succinct explanation of his heretical dogmas in the entire literature.[11]

One of the most active lieutenants to join Hagiz' Italian campaign was a young scholar, Abraham Segre. Born in Turin, Segre served as rabbi of Casale, Monferrato at the time of the Hayon controversy. He was genuinely moved by the combined call from Briel, Zebi, and Naphtali Kohen: "A crisis had befallen Israel, their shepherds have betrayed them; and the innocent flock, how have they sinned?" Once aroused, Segre enthusiastically joined the campaign. He wrote, "A weakling such as I, must gird his strength. I will arise and say to God, 'Behold, I am prepared to join the holy war, to undertake the tasks of Your Kingdom among the ranks of the mighty warriors.' " He was active in so many spheres of the campaign pressing other rabbis to lend their names, that Hagiz later wrote of the Italian effort: "The Italian rabbis did not fulfill their obligations, except for Abraham Segre of Casale who has written against Ayllon." One of Segre's strongest efforts was directed at R. Meir Baki. Baki had been contacted by Solomon Ayllon's nephew, the Amsterdam publisher Netanel Foa, who sent him a copy of the ma'amad's *Kosh't Imrei Emet*. Baki explained that he had already promised Foa that he would not intervene in the controversy, and he ultimately resisted joining the campaign, yet he felt constrained to tender an apology to Segre.

Baki's refusal triggered other setbacks. Isaac b. Solomon Nizza of Florence excused himself to Segre on the grounds that Meir Baki and Benjamin Kohen had not yet joined. He also argued that the ban which had been pronounced in Livorno forbade the reading of Hayon's book, but did not excommunicate Hayon. He concluded with another excuse: a communal ordinance in his city stipulated that no individual, rabbinic or lay, could ban any other individual.

Segre shared many of Hagiz' views with respect to Hayon. Unlike many other Italian rabbis, he believed that the content of Hayon's doctrines should be publicized so that his heresies would be manifest to all. He reserved great contempt for the lay leadership in Amsterdam: "If we must accord honor to the lay appointed court, how much more so to the heavenly court. They issue long screeds proclaiming their inviolability. How they have erred! For in matters of pertaining to Jewish law we [the rabbinate] are all members of one city." Because he believed that the appropriation of classical kabbalah camouflaged the Sabbatian intent of Hayon's work, Segre made a point of the Sabbatian origins of the *Mehemnuta* in every manifesto he wrote. Segre planned to write a full length polemic against Hayon's *ha-Zad Zebi*. This work was never completed, perhaps due to the influence of other Italian rabbis. Samson Morpurgo, for example declared his intention of deterring Segre from writing a polemical work in the interests of quieting the controversy.

Segre shared his concern over the integrity of the kabbalah with Joseph Ergas. Though Ergas was his senior, Ergas asked Segre to provide him with kabbalistic sources to confute Hayon's claims, especially in the work written against him.[12]

At age twenty-five, Segre moved to Safed. On a mission to collect funds for Safed in North Africa, Segre provoked a great outcry when he insisted that these funds not be channeled through Livorno. Perhaps he had deduced from the problems with the bequest to Hagiz that influential figures there would divert funds earmarked for anti-Sabbatians in Erez Israel.

R. SAMSON MORPURGO, VOICE OF MODERATION

The texture of Hagiz' communications to individuals is difficult to reconstruct from the snatches of sources that remain. One fortunate exception is his extensive exchange with R. Samson Morpurgo. It provides a rich study in contrasts as the zealous Hagiz attempted to draw the cautious and temperate Morpurgo farther and farther into the maelstrom of controversy.

Although a decade-long friendship had flourished between them, Samson Morpurgo, eminent physician and rabbi of Ancona, had first resisted Hagiz' overtures, for reasons of both temperament and ideology. Judah Briel opened the aperture through which Hagiz could exercise his own powers of persuasion. Hagiz' tone alternated between cajoling and demanding that Morpurgo crusade with greater vigor; Morpurgo responded with sober, deliberate justifications for restraint. To Hagiz' stern opening threat that "the waters of contention can destroy bonds of brotherly love," which hinted that their continued friendship depended on Morpurgo's willingness to participate, Morpurgo gently chided in return; "Moses, zealot son of a zealot, great affection and special friendship I feel towards you." Hagiz tried to convey to Morpurgo the intensity and scope of his projected campaign, "*All* the rabbis of Italy must band together, so their numbers will have greater impact . . . to jolt the minds of those who are not impressed by greatness, but by quantity." He tried to overwhelm Morpurgo's hesitancy with the strength of precedents and the comfort of numbers. Morpurgo replied with an eloquent plea for moderation: "It is not our approach to come with shouting hordes. Our wish and our intent is to heal and not to harm, to embrace rather than to reject. Perhaps those who strayed will repent and mend their erroneous ways."

The members of Morpurgo's yeshiva agreed with him: "Many of us *Haberim Makshibim*, engaged in the dialectic of Torah, have deemed it best not to fight with loud saber-rattling and force of numbers. . . . The quality of our argument rather than the quantity of our signatures should be decisive." Morpurgo disagreed with Hagiz' assessment of Hayon, as well as the timing of the campaign. While he conceded the obligation of rabbis to segregate the "idolaters . . . who strayed after the notorious false messiah," he believed that Hayon still remained within the fold. "We have met Hayon, and we loathe his pretensions and illusions. Nevertheless, we ask those who prepare for war, to speak in peace. Perhaps he [Hayon] will conceal the book and admit that he had never intended to sunder his ties with the House of Israel or undermine the foundations of our Divine faith, for we share with him a belief in the unity of God and His Providence . . . especially at this time when the hand of the state is heavy upon us."

Shortly after Morpurgo wrote his first letter to Hagiz, he received a copy of *Kosh't Imrei Emet*, the account by the lay leadership of Amsterdam of the genesis of the rupture over Hayon. The account accused Zebi and Hagiz of pursuing Hayon for personal rather than ideological reasons and Morpurgo was appalled to learn from this document that the controversy had been brought to the attention of the government. He bitterly remonstrated that a controversy which spawned such literature defeated the central purpose of Hagiz' campaign: "This document distressed me greatly. After it had been distributed, and its contents became known to the public, they said, 'Behold these rabbis—it is not the fire of Torah which rages within them, but their own petty jealousies. Some say that Hayon has been falsely libeled, the others maintain the contrary. Both sides agree that the rabbinate is fit only for ridicule. . . . If the Sephardic Bet Din is willing to pursue harmony and truth, we should seek it as well, for we are all comrades to restore the glory of the Torah to its former luster. I will stand my ground, to pursue peace, to calm the confusion, and to still the complaints lodged by Jews against their rabbinate which has lowered its own esteem."

Hagiz defended each of his positions to Morpurgo, even parrying Morpurgo's salutation. "Fortunate is the generation that can count 'zealots, sons of zealots' among their numbers, for they are incorruptible." On the choice of Hayon as subject of his campaign, Hagiz argued that

Hayon's opinion of the Ein Sof as an amorphous Deity devoid of knowledge, will, and desire, was more heretical than that of the Deists. The lay leaders were seekers neither of truth nor peace. "They did not consult us before rendering their decision. Moreover, in the scurrilous pamphlet which they published, they omitted this: That I myself came down to their chambers time and again and begged them to let us examine Hayon's book . . . and we would have been ready to admit the truth had we been wrong, for it was our sole objective. At that time, I fell on my knees in submission to them, all in order to quell the controversy. But they refused." Hagiz warned Morpurgo not to shirk this historic duty, which he must discharge out of love for Israel.

Hagiz proceeded to outline the steps Morpurgo should take: First, it was incumbent upon Morpurgo to obtain a condemnation of Hayon from his father-in-law, Joseph Fiametta. Fiametta was the only rabbi who had yet to repent of his approbation to Hayon's book, and Hagiz threatened that unless he would do so forthwith, his name would be linked to the reprehensible book. Hagiz wrote that he knew Fiametta to be "an expert in some aspects of their corrupt faith [Sabbatianism], but not in all, for he was not in the locale of the apostasy." This may be a tacit acknowledgment by Hagiz of Fiametta's 'moderate' Sabbatianism, perhaps in contrast to those, like Ayllon, whom Hagiz accused of apostasy. Hagiz instructed that Fiametta's repudiation be issued in concert with those of Briel and Segre, so that together they would constitute the nucleus of this campaign. "Our entire success depends upon accumulating these signatures. For our words are not directed to wise men, but to an audience which speaks a foreign tongue . . . and counts signatures." Tepid pronouncements would not suffice. "I urge you, let your words be written in a clear and succinct style. Elegant literary allusions are riddles, except to the most erudite experts, and they are most confusing in translation."[13]

In the interim, Morpurgo compared Hagiz' account of the first steps in the controversy with the account of the Amsterdam Bet Din. He found the version of the Bet Din lacking, which greatly perturbed him. This created a more fertile climate for Hagiz' exhortations, and in the subsequent reply of Morpurgo (of February 18, 1714), a change of tone can be detected. Morpurgo appeared more compliant to Hagiz' demands, and his own attitude toward Hayon betrayed a newly conceived hostility. Morpurgo felt constrained to excuse his earlier lack of participation in the campaign. He claimed that he had tried to unite the sages of Italy with all his might, "but most of them are bound by inertia. Perhaps after the rabbis of the East and Poland join the campaign, they will have no more subterfuge."

He observed that Hagiz was unaware of the strong influence Sabbatianism still exerted among Italian Jewry and its rabbis. Given this circumstance, Morpurgo argued, efforts to combat Sabbatianism must be measured by a different yardstick: "I have disputed many fools who still guarded Nathan's [of Gaza] writings in safeboxes as though they were sacred prophetic writings. . . . I prevailed upon them to remove them." With regard to the participation of Fiametta, Morpurgo's apologetic tone intensified. Fiametta had relied on David Oppenheim, who had expressed disapproval of Zebi's intransigence in the Hayon affair. Fiametta was still awaiting a reply to Hagiz' accusations from Solomon Ayllon. Moreover, both he and Fiametta had been engaged in caring for a relative who had fallen ill. Morpurgo feigned umbrage that Hagiz had asked Briel to keep special watch over him as though he were a man of irresolute faith. Morpurgo's change of heart prompted him to take the action that Hagiz had urged. A few weeks later, the Bet Din of Ancona, headed by Morpurgo and Fiametta, issued a ban of excommunication against Hayon.

Nevertheless, Morpurgo's concession to Hagiz remained a grudging one. He never abandoned his reluctance to engage in shrill polemical warfare, always preferring a more dignified and subtle approach. Even after Hagiz had fled to London, Morpurgo wrote, on July 10, 1714: "I am greatly distressed over those who turned this shameful affair into a disputation and dialogue . . . responding to every jot and tittle with masses of confutations and retorts. Let it be known to you, that when it reached my ears that Abraham Segre was preparing a major refutation of Hayon, I begged him to cease his labor . . . for those detailed polemics help spread the ideas of our opponents." Morpurgo felt that the methods used in Venice and Livorno, where the bans from Constantinople were read in their synagogues, were sufficient for the rest of the communities. Even as Hagiz prepared to release a new avalanche of polemical works from London, Morpurgo advised, "Gather them all in one volume, to be preserved as a warning for future generations."[14]

Morpurgo's reluctance to enter the controversy with full force was nourished by sources beyond personality and awareness of the Sabbatian dilemma of the Italian rabbinate. A decade earlier Morpurgo had published a text by Yedaiah ha-Penini, *Behinat Olam*, with his own commentary, *Ez ha-Da'at* [*Tree of Knowledge*], (Venice, 1704). It is a paean to the sober, yet exhilarating life of the mind, taking philosophy as its guide to the truth, and Maimonides as its model. In his introduction, Morpurgo praised philosophy as an antidote to the spiritual malaise of his time. He praised ibn Ezra's philosophical polemics against the Karaites, "who swear falsely, and have violated the covenant seared into their flesh, who have slept with strange women and hugged abominations close to their bosoms." The term Karaites in this citation seems to be a generic one for heretics. Morpurgo reprinted the caustic, satirical poem of Jacob Frances, "*Ashrei ha-Goy*" ["Fortunate is the Nation"], against the vulgarization of the kabbalah, as an epilogue to his *Ez ha-Da'at*. Although Frances did not openly deny the validity of kabbalah, he stated it had been diluted and distorted when it became accessible to the untutored masses. Frances' poem had been banned and burned in Mantua when it was first published; its reprinting by Morpurgo leaves no doubts as to Morpurgo's own desire to limit the spread and influence of kabbalah. Morpurgo himself has suggested the parallel between his anti-Sabbatianism and that of Frances, which was sustained by a rejection of kabbalah in its popular manifestation.[15]

JOSEPH ERGAS AND THE DEBATE OVER THE ROLE OF KABBALAH

R. Joseph Ergas of Livorno had, like Samson Morpurgo, expressed initial reluctance to enter the Hayon controversy. The motive behind his eventual participation stands in sharp contrast to that of Morpurgo. Although rich epistolary material like that in the correspondence between Morpurgo and Hagiz is lacking, there is sufficient evidence in Ergas' two full-length polemical works to demonstrate that Hagiz' heavy hand was persuasive. Ergas inserted a revealing disclaimer in his first polemical work, *Tokhahat Megullah* [*Public Admonition*]: "Even the little which I have written, I penned at the request of my dear friend [Hagiz]." Ergas' second full-length polemic, *ha-Zad NaHa"SH* was written as a response to Hayon's vicious attack in *Shalhebet Yah*. By the time it was written, Ergas had been drawn into the full heat of the controversy. A report circulated in Livorno that upon receiving a copy of Ergas' *Tokhahat*, Hayon wrote to an associate in Livorno that he would force Ergas to recant or he would publicly revile him. This bold insult to Ergas moved the Parnassim of Livorno to denounce Hayon. Hayon, undeterred, published his vituperative polemic against Ergas (*Shalhebet Yah*).

It comes as no surprise that Ergas' retort to Hayon, *ha-Zad NahaSh*, considerably exceeded his first work in the fury and asperity of its tone. As Ergas' own outrage mounted, the role of Hagiz receded. "Because they have assembleda conglomeration of falsehoods, let them be barred from the congregations of Israel. . . . My arm will remain outstretched until his [Hayon's] memory will be effaced from the earth." Ergas' first polemic dealt almost exclusively with the substance of Hayon's argument, the second contains much more of the ad hominem invective which characterized the polemics of Hagiz. Ergas' title, *ha-Zad NaHaSH*, [To Ensnare a Serpent] was a retaliation for Hayon's defamation of Hakham Zebi in *ha-Zad Zebi* [To Ensnare Zebi = a Hart]. Ergas' two works were printed in one volume in 1715 by Hagiz in London, and he served as their publisher, editor, and proofreader. In the foreword he added, Hagiz could not conceal his pride at having secured the support of Ergas for his campaign.

Ergas was an active voice in the debate between the advocates of esotericization and those who endorsed the popular dissemination of Lurianic kabbalah. This dilemma was raised anew in 1713, and was nowhere articulated more clearly, and with greater anguish, than in the works of Joseph Ergas.[16]

Ergas must have arrived at his anti-Sabbatian position after much soul searching for, like others in his generation, his biography would indicate a predisposition toward Sabbatianism. His maternal grandfather, Moses Pinheiro, was one of the earliest adherents of Sabbatai Zebi, one who had remained an ardent follower all his life. As a youth, his father, Emanuel, remanded him to the tutelage of Samuel de Pas, a Sabbatian rabbi in Livorno. After his marriage, he traveled to Reggio, where he studied under the Sabbatian sympathizer Benjamin Kohen, and he immersed himself in the study of Lurianic kabbalah. Upon leaving Reggio, he journeyed through cities and towns, "preaching and enacting customs and ordinances." He settled in Pisa where he established a yeshiva, *Neveh Shalom*, which he financed from his own personal resources. Its fellows were "attentive comrades, all holy, all beloved," who gathered at the yeshiva to "foster harmony between themselves and their Heavenly Father." Presumably, the yeshiva was a conventicle for mystics, and kabbalah was their primary occupation. Ergas also founded and underwrote two charitable societies in Pisa, *Malbish 'Arumim* (Clothing the Naked) and *Mohar Betulot* (Dowering the Maidens). He was subsequently appointed to a rabbinical chair in Livorno, where he was to remain for the rest of his life. His favorite disciple was Malakhi HaKohen, who rose to prominence in the rabbinate of the next generation.[17]

Ergas' anti-Sabbatianism seems somewhat anomalous considering that his forebears, his earliest teachers, as well as his most prominent disciple, seem to have favored Sabbatian positions. In fact, when Hayon visited Livorno in 1710, he erroneously assumed that Ergas belonged to an Italian school of Sabbatian kabbalists. Hayon was greatly surprised when he became aware of his error in the course of their debate: "I realize from reading between the lines of your questions that you are not a believer in Sabbatai Zebi; for if you had been one of the faithful, you would never have countered my words with quotations from Luria, as Sabbatai has the authority and the merit to oppose Luria." Ergas believed that Hayon's *Mehemnuta de-Kola* was identical to the manuscript circulating in the name of Sabbatai, *Raza de-Mehemnuta*, and Hayon did not deny this. This account of a meeting with Hayon in 1710 establishes that his opposition to Sabbatianism on ideological grounds predated the controversy of 1713, but only the prodding of Hagiz converted Ergas into an active polemicist.[18]

Hayon had introduced his *Oz l'Elohim* with an appeal for the further popularization of kabbalah, and an argument that would legitimate all sources of kabbalistic doctrine. Crypto-Sabbatianism could not be sustained without the maintenance of kabbalah within the public discourse. If Kabbalah were to become highly esotericized again, Sabbatianism would eventually fade along with it. Hayon's virulent attacks on "philosophy" may have stemmed from a traditional perception of kabbalah and philosophy as antithetical orientations. Contemporary expressions of the irreconcilable nature of these two disciplines abounded, from Aviad Basilea's *Emunat Hakhamim*, which defended kabbalah and attacked philosophy, to Morpurgo's introduction and epilogue to *Ez ha-Da'at*, in which these positions were reversed. Rabbi J. Ghiron relied on this dichotomy as an excuse for refusing to ban Hayon: "It would be a wasted effort for this community [Florence] to take any further steps [against Hayon] . . . These books have not appeared here . . . and it is unlikely that they will because it is in the nature of our scholars to desire and embrace philosophical works, while doubling their distance from kabbalistic works."

In both Ergas' polemical works, he argued that Sabbatian kabbalah was an illegitimate offspring and distorted interpretation of Lurianic kabbalah. According to Ergas, Luria had intended his descriptions of Divine attributes and activities to serve as metaphors, to explain how limited, corporeal beings issued from the infinite *Ein Sof*. Ergas objected to Hayon's literal, anthropomorphic interpretation of Divine attributes, and particularly the Lurianic notion of *zimzum* (withdrawal). Although he is not the first to oppose a literal reading of Lurianic kabbalah, Ergas is the first to do so as a means of negating the entire foundation of Sabbatian kabbalah: "How sweet is this mystery to those who are submerged in the lore of Luria, in his homily on emanations, where he expounded on the spiritual matter (hyle) which mediated between the *Ein Sof* and the emanations. . . . The sinners who followed Sabbatai have completely destroyed its meaning, as is evident from their works."

Hayon countered Ergas' interpretation by arguing that even Luria's closest disciples did not adopt it: "You claim to understand the words and doctrines of Luria. You betray yourself when you admit that even his students did not understand the material in the manner you propose. You are forced to admit that the words of Luria are meant to be understood literally, and not simply as a metaphor." Ergas replied that Luria had spoken of individual attributes, the emanations, with many cautionary admonitions, "But you have dared to violate their primeval source . . . and have attributed to Him three different natures. . . . This is outright heresy, for He is simple and indivisible."

In both his works, Ergas refuted the legitimacy of Sabbatian kabbalah. He accused Hayon of falsely attributing his heretical views to the *Zohar* and the [Lurianic] kabbalists, with utter disregard for the tradition. To counter the contention that kabbalah had successfully sustained novel interpretations in the past, and eventually integrated them, Ergas was forced to resort to a juxtaposition to halakha. He quoted from the responsa of Levi ibn Habib, "It is not our way to invent interpretations of the Law which have not been cited by our predecessors. If we should happen upon some novel interpretation, even if it seems correct, we try to challenge it from every angle, for if our predecessors did not see fit to bring it, surely it is incorrect."[19]

To support his nonliteral reading of Luria's doctrines, Ergas turned to the treatise *Sha'ar ha-Shama'im* [Portal of Heaven] of Abraham Herrera, in which Luria's doctrines were correlated to Platonic emanations. Hayon sharply attacked Ergas for resorting to a work heavily influenced by Platonic philosophy to bolster his argument. On the title page of *Shalhebet Yah*, his polemic against Ergas, he added that he had come to "prevent others from stumbling over the faith of Plato and his ilk, an alien faith."

Hayon argued that the greatest of Gentile philosophers had never attained true knowledge of God, so it was a travesty to cite their works as valid sources for interpretation of Luria. Ergas disagreed:

> Hayon has attacked me for citing the *Sha'ar ha-Shama'im* which maintains that the mystery of *zimzum* [Divine Withdrawal] is not literal. He is unaware that a great figure has supported *Sha'ar ha-Shama'im*—none other than R. Jacob Zemah. He [Zemah] has annotated the Spanish original of Herrera's work, and in an epilogue, he wrote, "There are a number of philosophical works which do

not oppose the doctrines of Luria; to the contrary, they facilitate our understanding of various matters in the Zohar and other rabbinic writings." Zemah's great stature [as a kabbalist] has been long established from his glosses on Luria's writing, which have become universally accepted. Zemah has himself written that the "withdrawal" is not to be understood literally, heaven forbid. And note too, that R. Isaac Aboab of Amsterdam devoted himself to translation and publication of Herrera's work because of its great value.

Nevertheless, Ergas had to admit that despite the occasional accord between philosophers and kabbalists, they were strange bedfellows. Ergas even turned the tables and accused Hayon himself of appropriating, and disguising, philosophical notions: "It is apparent that his [Hayon's] disease has been caused by the poison of Greek philosophy, and he has written that the sustenance of the soul and its eternality derive from wisdom." Samson Morpurgo also traced this element of Hayon's Introduction to pagan philosophy. "They both claimed that the contemplative life, regardless of the outcome of the contemplation, was sufficient to guarantee immortality of the soul." Joel Pincherle echoed the charge against Hayon in a less specific way: "Why do we go to seek faults with pagan philosophers if we have blasphemers within our own camp?"[20]

Ergas' most profound concern was that Sabbatian Lurianism would cause an undifferentiated repudiation of all kabbalah, especially by the masses who were confused by intricacies and could not distinguish between legitimate and heretical developments. His brief account of the rapid spread and popularization of Lurianic kabbalah, constituted a plea and a lament for an "orphaned generation" to recognize the difference between other legitimate schools and the Sabbatian kabbalistic system. His second polemic opened with a mournful dirge on the reputation of the kabbalah:

> O, what anguish, sweet beloved, charming bride, precious hidden treasure! The deceits of that serpent [Hayon] have caused you to sink to the lowest rank, scorned by the multitudes as strange fruit. Torah! Torah! illumination of all the worlds. How have your lights dimmed as in a tenebrous land.[21]

The original verdict of the lay Bet Din in Amsterdam on Hayon's *Oz le-Elohim* attempted to blur any distinctions between Sabbatian and other schools of kabbalah: "They concluded that the book was based on the Zohar and other rabbinic dicta, and while it would have been proper to refrain from publishing esoteric material . . . nevertheless, *let it be numbered among the works of kabbalah.*" This verdict strengthened the cynicism of those who were already disinclined to kabbalah.

> I read the work [*Oz l'Elohim*] and truly, I found it to be riddled with heresies and doctrines that had been prevalent in the time of Sabbatai Zebi . . . written by a heretic named Abraham Cardoso, an adherent of Sabbatai then in Smyrna. When the Bet Din convened, they decided to categorize the book as a "work of kabbalah" since important persons had approved it . . . I have never truly inclined toward kabbalah, for my foremost teacher in Venice, R. [Simhah] Luzzatto, an eminent man, told me that in our days, KABBALAH should be renamed CABOLA [cabbola, in Italian, a game of chance], for with the absence of Divine inspiration, who can lay claim to knowledge of Divine matters? He mocked those who considered themselves kabbalists. I know several people who dabbled in that lore, and they were all men of inferior character."

At the outset of the Hayon controversy, Ergas expressed his profound reservations on the desirability of engaging in open polemical warfare, which would further erode the public image of kabbalah. His formulation of this dilemma was representative of many others—Sabbatian and anti-Sabbatian alike. Judah Briel wrote to Ayllon, "Even if we were to agree that Hayon's statements are all grounded in valid sources, elaborate commentary on these matters is still very detrimental. If even one Jew has been led astray by his hallucinations—to us that is a whole world." Briel voiced a similar objection to the ma'amad in Amsterdam. "It is possible that these kabbalistic opinions *are* subject to different interpretation—very few truly understand them. But in the face of imminent danger, prudence and Divine law require the erection of fences. It is forbidden to take lightly the ways of the esoteric Torah. . . . Let us remove the obstacles by remanding the book to the secret archive of the kehillah." Fiametta objected that even if Hayon's works were to be given the benefit of doubt by interpretation in the least radical mode, Hayon was still guilty "of having opened a Pandora's box among his people."

Ergas had been an enthusiastic advocate of popular dissemination of kabbalah prior to the controversy. The publication of Hayon's work and the public debate that followed forced him to reevaluate his position. In this predicament, Ergas found a partner in Hagiz, who had also actively encouraged the popularization of kabbalah throughout his early career. Hagiz' concern "lest the kabbalah be employed as a camouflage for the ideas of hypocritical fools and ignoramuses," suddenly loomed large with the publication of Hayon's *Oz l'Elohim*. Their shared concern for the fate of kabbalah notwithstanding, Hagiz and Ergas diverged in their final verdict. As a result of the controversy, Hagiz reversed his opinion. Although he never retreated from the position that kabbalah was a fundamental core of Judaism—"Take heed lest you doubt true kabbalists and never contradict them, for this lore is our faith"—he altered his stance with regard to the accessibility of kabbalah. He now advocated restricting it to the scholarly elite: "Kabbalah was not given to simpletons or the fickle minded. Do not trust everyone who declares 'I am a kabbalist, come let me reveal the mysteries of the Torah.' Transmission of this *esoteric* lore can be made only by a prudent and respected sage who has already digested the meat and wine of Torah, its laws and customs." All the major polemicists (Zebi, Briel and Hagiz) attacked Hayon for stating in his introduction that man is obligated to subject the most profound mysteries to rational investigation, regardless of the conclusion. Ergas maintained that those who had acquired solid foundations in the study of kabbalah were permitted to contemplate the mysterious, *"even if they should err."*

While Hagiz ceased to publish kabbalistic works after the controversy, Ergas devoted the remainder of his literary productivity to strengthening the foundations of the kabbalah. His *Shomer Emunim (Guardian of Faith)* took the form of a dialogue between a talmudist who championed mastery of the Law as the ultimate attainment, and a kabbalist who argued that only through study of the esoteric lore could one attain religious perfection. *Mabo Petahim* was an alphabetical index to key terms in Lurianic kabbalah which Ergas wrote to facilitate its dissemination.[22]

Ergas' misgivings concerning the damaging effect of Sabbatianism on kabbalah grew after the Hayon controversy. When Hagiz later presented him with the obligation of another heresy hunt, against Moses Hayim Luzzatto, Ergas' response was similar. He refuted Luzzatto's claims to mastery of kabbalah.

IN LONDON: R. DAVID NIETO

The second herem of the Amsterdam Bet Din made it very difficult for Zebi and Hagiz to function effectively, as they were cut off from all sources of income and channels of communication. By February 1714, less than a year after the eruption of the controversy, Hagiz and Zebi felt that they had no recourse but to leave Amsterdam and continue their crusade in a less hostile atmosphere. Hagiz later turned this flight to polemical advantage, claiming that while he and Zebi would surely have emerged victorious if their case had been tried by the magistracy, they preferred to leave rather than argue their case before the Gentile court.

We knew that our cause would be found just in court, because it would have become apparent in the process of argument that the faith of Cardoso, Ayllon, and Hayon [Sabbatianism] undermines not only our faith, but confutes the Christian and Muslim religions as well. Surely, they would have consigned the book [Hayon's *Oz l'Elohim*], its author, and Ayllon . . . to the flames. Nevertheless, we have resolved to bring our case only before the Sages of our Nation . . . and not to Gentile courts. . . . We will pay no heed to their persecutions and blasphemies.

Although Hagiz appeared the least concerned of all his contemporaries with the effect of the controversy on Jewish-Christian polemic, he nevertheless tried to evoke the medieval Jewish opprobrium toward acts of 'informing' and 'betrayal' against a fellow Jew. He insinuated that the lay leaders of Amsterdam had violated an ancient code of honor by referring the case to the Gentile authorities. "We were forced to choose the lesser of two evils [and flee] rather than submit such a weighty matter to their [Gentile] consideration." Hagiz melodramatically compared this 'betrayal' of himself and Zebi by the Parnassim, to the Christian intervention during the Maimonidean conflict, which had resulted in dire consequence for both sides. In fact, his indignant accusations must be regarded as greatly overstated. While informing had been a cardinal sin within medieval Jewish communities because the slightest pretext often served as an excuse for hostile powers to inflict grievous reprisals, this was hardly the case in Amsterdam, where even the pettiest of internal disputes was routinely brought before the magistrate.[23]

Zebi sent his family to Emden, while he and Hagiz left for London, to which they had been invited by the rabbi, David Nieto. Nieto was born to a Sephardic rabbinic family in Venice. After receiving his medical degree from the University of Padua, he became physician and head of the *Reshit Hokhma* academy in Livorno. When Solomon Ayllon moved to Amsterdam, Nieto was appointed in 1701 to fill his chair as chief rabbi of London's Sephardic community. In London, Nieto established charitable societies, published material to aid in the integration of Marranos into his community, and corresponded with many of the leading Christian Hebraist scholars of his day. When Nieto preached a sermon in 1703, some of his leading congregants claimed that it contained pantheistic elements. The controversy over Nieto's doctrines raged close to two years and split the young London community into two factions. There is some support for the conjecture that the faction opposed to Nieto, former supporters of Solomon Ayllon, included many crypto-Sabbatians who were chagrined that Nieto did not share their sympathies. The key to restoration of peace to the divided community was provided by Hakham Zebi, when both parties turned to him for arbitration in 1705. Zebi's response completely exonerated Nieto, and Nieto did not forget this kindness.[24]

In London, Hagiz continued the battle against Hayon without skipping a beat. He published Joseph Ergas' first polemical work, *Tokhahat Megullah*, together with Ergas' second work against Hayon, *ha-Zad NaHa"Sh*. Shortly after his arrival, he published his polemical magnum opus against the triple calamity, "Hayon, Ayllon, and Cardoso," *Sheber Posh'im*. The printing was apparently started in Amsterdam, and completed in London. Hagiz' speedy entry into the polemical fray immediately upon his arrival in London was due to a sympathetic lay leadership as well as to Nieto's close ties to the Hebrew printing presses in London.

The induction of R. David Nieto into the controversy was the most important result of Hagiz' move to London. Within months after the arrival of Hagiz and Zebi in London, Nieto published a full-length work which equaled any of the major polemics of the Hayon controversy in the zeal and thoroughness of its attack. Nieto's *Esh Dat* [*Fire of the Faith*] appeared with a simultaneous Spanish translation [*Fuego Legal*] "at the behest of the London Ma'amad." Nieto wrote it as a dialogue, one of his favorite literary forms, "in imitation of our sacred Bible . . . Canticles, and Job . . . as required by the profundity of the material. . . . I have used the same form in my *Pascalogia* in the Italian language, in my *Divine Providence*, and *Mateh Dan*." In the latter book, the figure of DaN [acronym for *David Nieto*] is the voice of Nieto, responding to the provocative questions of the interlocutor, Naphtali. In a preface to the Spanish edition (not present in the Hebrew version), Nieto outlined the scope and contents of his work:

It consists of two Dialogues: the first confutes; the second instructs. That which confutes, demonstrates with incontestable authority that the dogmas which Hayon presented as legal, legitimate, and revealed are, to the contrary, newly invented, spurious and false. Consequently, they contradict our Holy Law, and the true doctrines of our Sages, Talmudists, and Kabbalists, as well as our in-

fallible Tradition, preserved unaltered and intact for over thirty centuries amidst many persecutions and calamities . . .
The section which instructs confirms that which we all believe; that our mystical theology, which we call kabbalah, is so enveloped by abstruse anthropomorphisms and metaphysical terms that it is impossible to fathom its true meaning without Divine inspiration, angelic revelation, or accredited Tradition.

In order to analyze Hayon's heresies, Nieto provided an encapsulated history of the kabbalah. Nieto's polemical taxonomy of kabbalah consisted of two major categories—the "ancient" traditional esoteric lore from pre-Talmudic times through Luria and his disciples; and the "novel," which consisted of Sabbatian kabbalah. He made an impassioned plea for the extirpation of Hayon's heresies as a means of preserving a unified Jewish doctrine.

Nieto's refutation of Hayon generally reiterated doctrinal points that had already been expressed by other polemicists, especially Zebi and Hagiz. Nieto diverges from them in his emphasis on the potential for the controversy, and Hayon's views in particular, to inflict grave harm on Jewish-Christian relations. Nieto was not the only polemicist to look beyond his Jewish audience. Many rabbis who had previously engaged in theological debate with Christians, especially in Italy, feared that material which would be brought to public scrutiny in the course of the controversy would be used against them. Judah Briel had written, "In our time, and *particularly in this land*, scholarship is flourishing and many Gentile scholars from foreign lands study our Holy Tongue and translate the works of our authors. Whenever possible, they trumpet forth triumphantly over statements that had been written or printed in haste, and they desecrate the Name of our Lord. . . . The fear of this grave danger aroused me to take up my quill." Joseph Fiametta of Ancona had protested to Solomon Ayllon, "If, heaven forfend, his [Hayon's] work should become known among the nations, woe! They will sally forth, from their castles and courtyards and proclaim, "The Lord has forced [the Jews] to admit the truth of our faith!" And how many [Jewish] fools will apostatize." Rabbi J. Ghiron in Florence, essentially sympathetic to Hayon, nevertheless concurred that publicity should be avoided at all costs. "Ridicule will follow upon the heels of this controversy, the Sages of Israel will be maligned as confused and divided over the principles of their faith, especially by the Gentiles of Italy." The rabbinate of Rome justified its ban of Hayon saying: "Let not the Gentiles say, 'so this is the nation of God! They are exactly the same as we are.' " Hagiz later offered a similar argument—the Jewish faith would seem bizarre if Sabbatian doctrines were permitted to represent it: "The manuscript which begins, 'And I come today to the spring (*Ve-Abo ha-Yom el ha-'Ayin*),' is filled with lewdness and superstitions the likes of which have never crossed the mind of any sage or philosopher, even among the Gentiles and the ancient pagans." While it is clear that Nieto was not alone in his concern, the issue of Jewish-Christian relations is raised to a preeminent position in his polemics.

In *Esh Dat* Nieto emphasized the most extreme doctrines of Hayon and declared that they were contrary even to natural religion. "I have investigated all the religions and customs of the world, and I have discovered that not only Christians and Turks hold the same three principles in common with our faith, (the existence of God, revealed legislation, and reward and punishment) but also most of the peoples of the East and West Indies, and the black and Berber natives of Africa." Hayon's doctrines were a perversion of all religions, and Nieto urged all Jews to unite in their denunciation of Hayon. "Hayon boasted among the Christians that he is proclaiming the Trinity among the Jews. . . . In fact, Christian doctrines are closer to Jewish ones than Hayon's are." Nieto, an apostle of rabbinic Judaism to former Marranos, made a special appeal to their emotions in his polemic against Hayon. "By denying the unity [of God], Hayon has robbed all Jewish martyrdom in Spain and Portugal of any meaning."[25]

Although Nieto deliberately muted his political arguments in *Esh Dat*, at the very end of his Spanish introduction he hinted that he had written more polemical material of such a sensitive nature that he would not print it, but he would reserve it for limited, judicious circulation in manuscript. "I could say much more of the pernicious consequences of this schism, but I have omitted it for very potent reasons. However, in order not to deprive *my nation* of that which is so vital to it, I will reserve it in manuscript, in my possession. I offer it with deep affection to anyone who desires to read or translate it." The Spanish manuscript was bound into some copies of the *Esh Dat*. Titled "Theological, Political, and Moral Reflections on the Execrable system of Nehemiah Hiya Hayon," it dealt almost exclusively with the political harm to Jewish interests that could result from Hayon's theology. These "*Reflexiones*," which Nieto did not translate into Hebrew, were directed to the former Marranos of his community. "Ah, brothers and gentlemen, I beseech you and beg you by the bond of blood which unites us, by the common interest . . . which obliges us . . . to examine these *Reflections* . . . with the attention and care that the importance of the subject requires, that you consider that they issue from an author who is your brother by blood and by religion, who loves and esteems you as brothers."

Nieto argued that Hayon's doctrines, leading to abrogation of Jewish law and tradition, could appear to be a breach in the social contract between the Jewish community and the Gentile nations among whom they dwelled. In Catholic countries, where freedom of conscience was not granted to all citizens, the Inquisition would persecute all those Jews who deviated from articles of faith common to both religions. Hayon's works would make the Jews susceptible because he separated the Creator from the First Cause, and because he taught that the ceremonial, judicial, and moral laws of the Torah may be suspended except for idolatry; whereas Christianity suspended only the ritual, leaving the judicial and moral law in force. Nieto argued *ad absurdum* to illustrate the far reaching consequences of Hayon's teachings. If all the laws of God could be betrayed, the prohibition against false oaths would also be violated. Once Hayon's diabolical dispensation to commit perjury would become known among the Gentiles and their princes, their tentative hospitality to Jews would be turned into fury.

What will happen to us? What will they do to us? What concept will they form of our behavior, of our promises, of our consciences? What scandal will be caused, what profanation of God's Name? What faith, what peace, what love, what unity will they have with the nation in general. . . . After having been teachers of the Christians and Mohamedans, after having removed them from the darkness of paganism . . . , are we to degenerate by making ourselves instructors of heresy, teachers of libertinism, and professors of atheism?

What won't they say, and what won't they write against our poor downtrodden nation? What prince would allow us in his lands, what state would admit us? Won't the Jewish name be left more hateful and more opprobrious than ever?

Nieto recalled instances of the fickleness of Gentile hospitality to Jews, and he implied that the foothold of Jews on English soil was still exceedingly tenuous. Of all the polemicists to extrapolate political consequences from the Hayon controversy, Nieto took the argument to the furthest extreme.[26]

POLEMICAL PRECEDENTS

Hagiz' sharp break with earlier rabbinic policy toward Sabbatianism necessitated radical formulations. His goal was to force Sabbatianism into the same byways of Jewish history as other ancient sects: "The Samaritans, the Sadducees, and the Boethusians (from whom the Karaites emerged) passed through Israel . . . and in 1666, the plague began anew." Hagiz dwelled on a tendentious analogy between Sabbatians and Karaites: "Hayon and Ayllon have broken from the mainstream and eschewed the fundamentals of Judaism, modeling their opinions on those of the Karaite sect." The identification of Sabbatianism with Karaism was not merely a means of affixing old labels on new wine. While there was precious little resemblance between the sects, the comparison allowed Hagiz to identify his campaign with that of the rabbinate during an era of its greatest hegemony—the Geonic period.

This choice reveals Hagiz' perceptions of his role, and his chimerical aspirations for the rabbinate of his own time. Magnified by historical perspective, Hagiz' own role in the campaign "would be inscribed in an enduring record for all eternity." In Hagiz' polemic, the Sabbatians differed from the Karaites in but one respect: "They are more audacious than the Karaites, for the Karaites had spoken respectfully of the Sages even while disagreeing with them, unlike these wicked heretics." Because they did not fear to tread on the sacred honor of the rabbinate, "they must be utterly expunged from the Book of Israel. . . . For in the measure that they have dealt, so must they be measured, expelled from the House of Israel, beyond the communities of the Dispersion, for they have accused the Sages of Israel of misconstruing knowledge of the true God."

The Donmeh, the radical Sabbatian branch whose members converted to Islam, provided Hagiz with a most useful polemical tool against Sabbatians of every hue. Joseph Ergas echoed Hagiz' prescription for extreme ostracism: "Henceforth, let them become separated from all Israel. They may not be counted in the quorum for sacred purposes; their daughters will be considered as heathen women; likewise, their bread, their wine and the meat they slaughter will be unfit. They will be cut off from the House of Israel as were Zadok and Boethus."

Hagiz' emphasis on the novelty and historic importance of his campaign is the cause of a curious aspect of his polemics—his choice of material for the "usable dissenting past." While Hagiz eagerly sought parallels in the exclusion of schismatics in earlier centuries, more recent predecessors in the polemic against Sabbatianism remain conspicuously absent from his work. A striking example is the lack of any reference to the work of Jacob Sasportas, who in the late seventeenth century had conducted a campaign against Sabbatai Zebi and his adherents very similar to that of Hagiz. In both campaigns, endless rabbinic denunciations were accumulated, and both were interested in preserving records of their polemical activity "to serve as a warning for posterity." Jacob Hagiz had been a crucial ally of Sasportas, and their correspondence regarding Sabbatianism was carefully preserved by Sasportas. Although Sasportas had died before Hagiz reached Amsterdam, his son Moses Sasportas may have been known to Hagiz as he was an emissary of Erez Israel. Another son, Isaac Sasportas, corresponded with Hakham Zebi. Sasportas' painstakingly preserved archive lay in the hands of another son, Abraham. The material had been prepared for publication by Jacob Sasportas, but it was suppressed by the lay leadership of Amsterdam because it implicated many prominent pillars of the community as believers in Sabbatai. In 1737, when Abraham Sasportas printed his father's responsa, *Ohel Jacob*, he appended an abridged version of Sasportas' polemical work. This *Kizur Zizat Nobel Zebi* was confiscated by the ma'amad, which ordered the offending section torn out of every copy.

Hagiz was surely aware of the existence of Sasportas' material, and perhaps even had access to it. But the only reference to Sasportas in his entire polemical oeuvre is to a work by another author (R. Moses Albaz, *Sefer Hekhal ha-Kodesh*) which Sasportas had brought to press. Perhaps Hagiz wished to stress the gulf between the active, openly messianic phase of Sabbatianism which Sasportas had combatted, and the heretical crypto-Sabbatianism which confronted him in the eighteenth century. This would explain why he referred to crypto-Sabbatianism as a "deviation which has newly arisen, its *first generation* became manifest *in our days*," and why the only recent polemicist whose work he acknowledged was Yizhaki, who campaigned against the heretical writings of Cardoso.

Hagiz' failure to appeal to the polemical precedent of R. Samuel Aboab is another notable omission. The image of Aboab would have been especially valuable to Hagiz' effort to draft the Italian rabbinate to his cause. Hagiz was in close contact with Aboab's sons, who had given him access to their father's library. He referred often to Aboab's responsa in his halakhic works. Yet in his entire polemical corpus, there is only one desultory reference to Aboab's anti-Sabbatian activity: "A reminder of this evil affair can be found in *Sefer Debar Shemuel*."[27]

The only material to have originated with another polemicist which Hagiz incorporated into his polemical writing was a citation from Nahmanides' letter to the rabbis of France written during the Maimonidean controversy many centuries earlier. Samson Morpurgo referred in his polemics to the Maimonidean controversy, as well as to a more contemporary issue, the Italian controversy over Gentile wine. "If the great and compassionate R. Abtalion of Consilei had been attacked for innocently defending the Jews who engaged in this practice . . . surely Hayon should forfeit his life for exposing these matters to the public eye."[28]

The Hayon controversy left in its wake a relatively large number of printed, bound, full-length works. This was due largely to Hagiz' sense of the historic value of this confrontation, as well as his strong bonds to the Hebrew publishing world. The extension of Hebrew bibliophilia to printed matter prompted collectors to preserve much material that might have eventually been lost after the controversy was stilled. Samson Morpurgo requested of his correspondents, "Send me all the books that have been published hitherto, and those that will be published in the future pertaining to this controversy . . . the full and complete editions. I will store them in my library as a keepsake for generations." Morpurgo had a copyist preserve unpublished materials. Judah Briel too, collected all the available material and forwarded copies to Morpurgo, in addition to the material sent by Hagiz. David Oppenheim gathered all the material for his renowned private library; some items survived uniquely in his collection. David Nunez Torres, bookseller of The Hague, included many works of the Hayon controversy in his catalogue of Hebrew books.

Polemical writing appeared in a variety of genres—narrative, epistolary, poetic, records of debates. Its tones ranged from the politely factual to apologetic, quarrelsome, vituperative, and sarcastic. The polemics against Sabbatianism ran the entire gamut of literary genres. The poetry of the Frances brothers, and the wicked anti-Sabbatian parody, *Haggadah le-Tish'a be-Ab*, are examples of the most creative anti-Sabbatian writing. The most popular vehicle for anti-Sabbatian polemic was a combination of chronicle and documentary history whose objective was to show how much Sabbatianism deviated from normative Jewish doctrine. In Elijah Kohen's distorted chronicle, *Sefer Meribat Kadesh*, accuracy and detail were sacrificed to stylistic considerations such as rhyme, alliteration, and biblical or talmudic *meliza*. It was a violently bilious attack on Cardoso's messianic pretensions, written in the year after his death. Immanuel Frances' "A Brief Chronicle of the Activities of Sabbatai Zebi and Nathan of Gaza," follows the tradition of a cynic's account of a failed messianic movement.

Jacob Sasportas' *Zizat Nobel Zebi* is the prototype of all serious polemical works against the Sabbatian messianic movement, a massive collection of important sources. The polemical works of Jacob Emden, especially *Torat ha-Kena'ot*, are likewise remarkable for the painstaking accumulation of documentary evidence to support their argument. The Hayon controversy produced no single work of similar dimensions. Hagiz' *Sheber Posh'im* together with *Milhamah* and the later *Lehishat Saraf* are contributions to the source collections, but do not take the entire Sabbatian movement as their scope.[29]

Whether it attempted to be scholarly and sober, or shrill and inflammatory, polemical literature was governed by a different set of rules than other literature. It was certainly very different in tenor from other rabbinic writing. Whereas Moses Hagiz the halakhist had to be juridical and precise, measure hairline distinctions, and interpret the words of earlier authorities to yield their most subtle nuances, Hagiz the polemicist could use bombastic rhetoric, circular reasoning, and hurl hideous allegations with insufficient evidence to support them. An example of circular reasoning is Hagiz' statement that "Hayon's guilt is proven by the fact that he was pursued by rabbinic leaders—surely they would not have pursued him without sufficient reason." Hagiz cited fragments out of context from Hayon's work, or neglected to say that a passage he correctly attributed to Hayon had originally appeared in the Zohar. Both Hagiz' audience and his target understood that the polemical works must be decoded and could not always be taken literally. "All my words are written in a flighty and cursory manner. I cannot deliberate at length to clarify all the intricacies and profundities with strong and sufficient proofs, for time is of the essence. It is preferable for our cause, and for the glory of God, to gloss over the fine points and be brief."

Although Hagiz was thoroughly acquainted with the entire spectrum of eighteenth-century Sabbatian ideologies, complex distinctions were largely obscured in the course of the polemic. It was easier and more dramatic to simplify the welter of different voices into one starkly drawn adversary. "The villains are *all those*, from the upheaval of Sabbatai Zebi until today . . . and anyone following any of their wickedness, or nuance thereof." This was Hagiz' definition of the sect to be ostracized. By generalizing the polemicist could project the most aberrant characteristics of some individuals in the group onto the entire group. Antinomianism, especially in the area of sexual license and apostasy, is the most conspicuous case of extreme behavior practiced by some Sabbatians, and attributed to all of them. "Anyone knowledgeable [of Sabbatianism] in all its permutations knows their sinful intent, to permit the forbidden, idolatry and promiscuity. . . . Ever since the mass apostasy in Salonika, the fate of this entire licentious sect has been sealed. . . . They have turned the prohibition against illicit fornication into a positive precept, and they punish those who do not violate the Torah."

Nowhere in his works did Hagiz admit to the existence of Sabbatian believers who were devout and scrupulously observant Jews. The entire rabbinic polemical discourse could not comprehend, or would not admit to, a Sabbatianism which did not possess all the extreme tenets of the more radical segments. Joseph Ergas, who was well acquainted with many Italian rabbis who were Sabbatians, nevertheless underscored that the teachings of all Sabbatians, even the most moderate, were conducive to antinomianism. "This has caused the loss of many Jewish souls, from the time of Sabbatai Zebi when they falsified doctrines to bolster their corrupt faith, to abandon their religion, to exchange their wives, and to commit the most abhorrent transgressions."

There was a limit to the extent that the antagonists could take liberties with the documentary evidence. Their claims needed some foundation in truth to maintain credibility in literature intended for a large audience. This led to the phenomenon of "creating documentary evidence" when none existed that was suitable for the polemicist's purpose. Both sides of the controversy engaged in this practice, known as *Gebiyat Edut* [Gathering Testimony]. Persons of stature in the community were called before a rabbinic council, and testified under oath to queries presented by the council. This testimony was scrupulously recorded, and cited as evidence in the polemical writings.

To convey the impression that they presented information with scrupulous accuracy, both sides assiduously cited chapter and verse for every quotation in their principal works. Hagiz' *Sheber* contains copious accurate quotation from Hayon's book, perhaps to confute the allegation made early in the controversy that he had condemned Hayon's book without access to the text. Despite this, each side accused the other of forgery or misrepresentation. Hagiz charged:

> Hayon and Ayllon fabricated material when they presented the words of *Magen David* (Ibn Zimra) . . . In *ha-Zad Zebi*, they omitted the crucial line, #36 . . . "This is the method of the serpent [Hayon] in his proofs: He cites fragments that support him, and deletes the most important passages. Just as belief in the trinity is dear to him, so too the polemical methodology of the Christians: omitting texts and inventing libels.

In his *Moda'ah*, Hayon reproduced in abridged form the letter of denunciation written against him by the rabbinate of Smyrna which had been printed by Zebi. Hayon then accused Hagiz and Zebi of forging the letter—"This writ which they claimed had arrived from Smyrna, is completely fabricated, it never really existed." Hayon's proof is another letter from Smyrna attesting to his honorable departure from the city, a direct confutation of the letter printed by Hagiz and Zebi. In fact, elsewhere in the same work Hayon admitted to the existence of the first letter and blamed its jaundiced opinion of him on the malice of his enemies. "If the Smyrna letter exists, it can only be due to the vicious slander of R. Yizhaki of Jerusalem, who influenced them against me, as was his wont all the years, as he has even vilified me in Amsterdam." It is very likely that both letters were authentic, as the letter in Hayon's praise was provided by his lay supporters in Smyrna, e.g., the Arditi brothers, whereas the letter printed by Zebi was from the rabbinate of Smyrna. It is perfectly possible that Hayon's lay supporters bade him an elaborate farewell, even while his rabbinic detractors banned him. Hayon used the apparent contradiction to cast doubt over the integrity of Hagiz and Zebi's documentary evidence. Although Hayon's *Moda'ah* was avowedly autobiographical, he often wrote in the third person to enhance the impression of dispassionate objectivity.[30]

Some polemical works singled out particular groups of Sabbatians for special obloquy. Hagiz wrote *Sheber Posh'im* against "the triple calamity, Hayon, Cardoso and Ayllon," and the author of *Meribat Kadesh* referred to "an evil triumvirate of Sabbatai Zebi, Nathan of Gaza, and Abraham Cardoso." Benjamin Halevi, an inveterate foe of Sabbatianism in Smyrna, wrote against Daniel Bonafoux, Jacob [Elijah] Tarragon, and Cardoso. The polemicists' tripling of villains was a cynical allusion to the "three bonds of faith" which figured prominently in Sabbatian thought.[31]

The use of dysphemism, particularly by inverting or rearranging the opponent's name, was a favored means of expressing utter disdain for the enemy. This ubiquitous technique added to the shrill tenor of the controversy, and turned the most serious argument into petty ad hominem diatribe. Thus, Cardoso was referred to alternately as *Hokh*, *Kimosh*, and *Atad* [brambles], a play on the meaning of 'Cardo,' in Italian. Hayon was referred to as *NaHa"Sh* [serpent], also an acronym for Nehemiah Hayon Satan, or "Nehemiah Hayon *Shemo* [is his name], for the sorcerers precede their name." In his appendix to *Sheber Posh'im*, Hagiz rearranged the letters in Solomon Ayllon's name to form many rude combinations, e.g., Solomon became "*zalma*" [an idol], Ayllon became "*Ayil Yavan*" [the Greek ram]. When not using their names, Hagiz referred to Hayon as "that abomination," and to Ayllon as "the adulterous apostate." *Hayim Mevorakh* [lit. blessed life] became "*Mavet Mekolal*" [accursed death]; the surname Senior was parodied to *"Lo Ra'a Or"* [Has never seen light]. Their disciples (*talmidim*) were transformed into "destroyers" (*tashmidim*); their books (*sefarim*) into eulogies (*sefadim*). The rabbi of the Sephardim [Hakham ha-Sepharadim] became sage of the toads [Hakham ha-Zefard'im], and Naphtali Bacharach's work *Vale of the King*, was referred to as *Vale of Tears*. The rabbinate of Rome referred to Hayon's work *Mehemnuta de-Kola* as *Minuta de-Kola* [total heresy], and the rabbinate of Ferrara as *Mehemnuta de-Kula Ra'ah* [completely evil faith].

Hayon proved to be an equally adept desecrator of names. Ergas became *"I-Rogez"* [Isle of Rage] or *"Ayar Gas"* [a corpulent ass]. His exegesis on the name *Joseph* (Ergas), included gems such as: "Joseph, from the [Hebrew] root 'to gather'—like a school of fish. Thus, one may spear him like a fish." Hayon took special delight in perversely applying all the derogatory appellations that had been used to refer to Sabbatai Zebi, against Hakham Zebi, i.e., *Zebi Mudah* [the Rejected *Zebi* (Hart)] in his work *ha-Zad Zebi*.[32]

THE AUDIENCE

For whom was the vast outpouring of polemics written? Many of the polemical tracts were directed at more than one audience, not necessarily the target they had specifically designated. The virulent screeds that were published were not intended to convert the opponent, as was the case sometimes with Christian anti-Jewish polemic. Hagiz specified that he had no desire to engage his opponents in actual dialogue: "My words are not directed at the serpent and the ass [Hayon and Ayllon], the rebellious heretics, and those who follow them. . . . When I addressed the sons of Israel with restraint, I simply took the opportunity to smash the skulls of the wicked."

Much of the polemical writing of both Hagiz and his circle, as well as Hayon, was in Hebrew. This closed their works to most Gentiles who were not Hebraists, as well as to many Jews. The only audience that was erudite enough to follow their complex exchanges in rabbinic Hebrew were their rabbinic colleagues. Some rabbis felt that works written in the vernacular were intended for the masses, and regarded them with disdain. R. Judah of Mainz referred condescendingly to "an abridged Judeo-German translation, not appropriate literature for a scholar." Thus, other rabbis constituted the upper tier of the audience to which the polemics were directed. But there was another audience, for whom polemics were written in Spanish, Portuguese, Italian, and Yiddish. The lay readership, who could not follow the Hebrew text with facility, was a more amorphous body, whose opinion was crucial in determining the outcome of the controversy.

Even Hagiz reluctantly acknowledged that public opinion carried more weight than victories in arcane scholarly circles. He wrote that the Ashkenazic lay leaders did not agree with Zebi to ban Hayon "because they knew that this was not the opinion of the public." Some observers attributed the stance of the Sephardic *ma'amad* to the weight of public opinion. Hagiz stated that the most important goal "was to vindicate my position to the members of the community." A victory in the arena of public opinion would be a slap in the face to the arrogant lay leadership, one which Hagiz felt was richly deserved. He appealed directly to the public in his *Sheber Posh'im:* "Don't allow the unity of your community disintegrate over this issue. Even if you justify your actions by saying that they were politically desirable . . . don't let yourselves be swayed or your spirits cowed and broken by the herem which your *laymen* have decreed in the name of a Bet Din . . . for in this matter, even if one as insignificant as I were to ban them, the *nasi* and all Israel would be obliged to respect my ban. . . . Do not rely on the pronouncement of your Kehillah that she is sovereign . . . for in this matter, they are like any individual."

If Hagiz could secure public favor by appealing to the masses over the heads of their lay leaders, this would demonstrate that the rabbinate held greater sway over the opinions of the flock than their lay leaders did. Hagiz charged that the lay leaders forbade him to circulate his polemics in order to suppress the truth from the public. "Only to blind the innocent public, lest they become enlightened . . . for the masses, burgher and noblemen alike, are after all, Jews. . . . If they only knew the truth, they would surely uphold it. But in order to perpetuate their power, the lay leaders have imitated the tactics of the Gentiles. They have refrained from teaching Hebrew to their children and grandchildren in order to maintain their falsehoods among the masses."

Although Hagiz desperately needed the support of the public in order to prevail, he could scarcely conceal his patronizing attitude toward "the masses," as he unflatteringly referred to them. In this regard, his rabbinic elitism intruded on his polemical acumen. "And if the spirit of the Lord has set me down in the valley, among the ignoramuses, it is not to my detriment, but to their benefit." From the depths of Hagiz' polemics there emerges a vision of "the masses," a malleable, credulous, and amorphous body, a myth created by wishful thinking, and directly related to his ideal paradigm of the rabbinate. The function of the rabbinate was to inform and shape the opinions of this "flock." In Hagiz' opinion, much of the malaise affecting his generation was due to the usurpation of this rabbinic role by the powerful lay leaders. "Regrettably, the words of our Sages fall on deaf ears because the tyrants have lent support to the heretics."

Another layer of Hagiz' polemics was addressed directly to rabbis. An articulate and knowledgeable rabbinate would then be prepared to stir the masses to a "grassroots" movement against Sabbatianism, much like local parish priests were directed from above to engender enthusiasm for a crusade. "I said to myself, 'The time has come to fight the battles of the Lord.' It is better that it [the campaign plan] be concealed from the masses, and revealed only to the remnant called by God [the rabbis] in order that every scholar in his city will do his share to persecute the abominable one . . . all in secrecy, away from the eyes of the Gentiles and the masses." Hagiz' original plan called for great discretion in the campaign against Hayon, so that the masses would never suspect that they were being manipulated. Hakham Zebi shared Hagiz' attitude toward the public. As an argument to prove his original reluctance to enter the controversy, Zebi recalled that when the Portuguese Bet Din had beseeched him to identify the heresies in Hayon's book, he had replied, "It is not befitting my Torah-scholarly demeanor. I am a rabbi and a legislator, *but not a scribbler of opinions for lay audiences*, who tend to distort the truth."

As the support of the rabbinic elite was crucial to the outcome of the controversy, Hayon was forced to compete with Hagiz for the support of this group. Hayon's *Moda'ah* is addressed by the author to *all the rabbis* who did not accord him fair treatment. "Pay heed, *rabbis*, to the proofs I have adduced that he [Hagiz] is motivated solely by jealousy and hatred." Only the polemics of Briel and Nieto emphasized that their direct concern was to save souls from the consequences of wickedness or ignorance.[33]

Why did Hagiz choose to channel his greatest polemical energies against Sabbatianism rather than the prevalent open skepticism toward religion and the rabbinate? We have already seen that Hagiz did not react as much to Hayon's reinterpretations of classical kabbalah, as to the thinly veiled challenge to the entire notion of a sole rabbinic truth, authority, and hierarchy. Sabbatianism, possessing its own inner hierarchy of rabbis and kabbalists seemed to Hagiz to pose the greater threat because it appeared under a legitimate guise. Perhaps it seemed simpler to isolate Sabbatians and Sabbatianism than to fight against a general apathetic attitude.

Did Hagiz' campaign achieve its goals? The Hayon controversy did succeed, if for a brief interlude, in bringing together a large number of rabbinic leaders to act in unison. It signified a decisive change in policy of the rabbinate vis-à-vis crypto-Sabbatians. Hagiz did not regard it as an isolated episode, but as the starting point in a long continuum of anti-Sabbatian activity. He used the experience gained in the Hayon contro-versy to refine his technique in the future, discarding methods which proved unsuccessful, amplifying those that worked, and establishing net-works of allies, channels of communication, and modes of action. In 1725, during the first rabbinic pursuit of R. Jonathan Eybeschutz, Hagiz de-clared, "What we have not accomplished then [in the course of the Hayon controversy], we must complete now." The controversy left its imprint in the many works reflecting on the nature of Sabbatianism, kabbalah, and Jewish dogma.

Although crypto-Sabbatianism persisted, and remained vital well through the eighteenth century, it could never again make open appeals for public acceptance like those of Hayon. In *Meziz u-Meliz*, a small po-lemical tract printed in 1715 concerning a dispute over the correct can-tillation of the priestly blessing, and a monument to rabbinic conten-tiousness in the eighteenth century, R. Nehemiah Kohen of Ferrara accused R. Isaac Lampronte of suspicious irregularities because his denunciation of Hayon was late in coming. Already in this brief interval, position in the Hayon controversy had entered the polemical vocabulary as a test of orthodoxy. In his self-appointed task of separating all Sabbatians as dan-gerous sectarians, Hagiz succeeded admirably. In all future controver-sies, those suspected of Sabbatianism could not defend their views as Hayon did; they had to deny categorically that they held such views.

Yet these can be termed successes only in a limited sense. The con-troversy ultimately failed to become the springboard which would have propelled the rabbinate into a position of cohesive leadership of the Jew-ish community. In the long view, it further eroded the image of the rab-binate to a public who regarded it as another manifestation of rabbinic contentiousness. And the question remains whether crypto-Sabbatianism might have faded earlier if not for the stimulus of rabbinic persecution.

After reviewing the material concerning Hagiz' pursuit of Hayon, we are better equipped to address the question of his primary motivation. Although elements of personal animus can be traced in his choice of tar-gets in this greatest controversy of his career, in the final analysis, Hagiz' idealized typology for the structure of the Jewish community must take precedence. Jacob Emden, writing at a time when he had little affection to spare for Hagiz, nevertheless granted that Hagiz deserved to be numbered among the uncompromised zealots "who overrode concern for their honor and their livelihood, . . . in order to foster the realization of their ideals."[34] It is in the essence of zealotry to make no accommodation to reality, but to pursue a vision and try to change the world.

CHAPTER 6

The Campaign Against Sabbatian Emissaries: Central Europe, 1725–1726

WITH HAGIZ'S flight to London, the "exile born in Jerusalem" was banished even from his adopted city, Amsterdam. He responded characteristically to this doubly profound exile. Barred from the capital of the Sephardic Diaspora in the West, he gravitated toward new audiences in Central and Eastern Europe. In the next decade he would struggle to enlist the once mighty rabbinic synods of Eastern Europe to expand his claim of rabbinic unanimity in the struggle against sectarianism.

LONDON AND EMDEN: A DOUBLE EXILE

Hagiz hoped that London would serve as a temporary haven until the emotions aroused by the Hayon controversy subsided and he could return to Amsterdam. In a letter to R. Eliezer HaKohen of Livorno dated May 21, 1715, Hagiz wrote, "My desire, as always is to return to the Kingdom of Holland. There I would continue to monitor the community closely and teach the public to distinguish between the tainted and the pure."[1] He suspected that Solomon Ayllon, the Sephardic rabbi of Amsterdam who had been his adversary in the Hayon controversy, was behind the effort to prevent his return to Amsterdam. While it is true that Ayllon had retained his coveted position as chief rabbi, and had even established a hesger in Amsterdam, it was the lay leadership which refused to permit Hagiz' repatriation.[2]

In addition to the polemical tracts which he published in London, Hagiz issued another work, a second edition of his father's *Petil Tekhelet*. In his introduction, Hagiz acknowledged his gratitude to David Nieto:

> My dear friend and great sage . . . rabbi of this city and author of the renowned *Kuzari ha-Sheni* understood my intention to restore the crown to its former glory. . . . The book had become unavailable . . . "And David acted with justice and charity" and permitted me to publish it within his domain.

Hagiz' edition contains several anomalies. He did not add his own notes, as was his custom when reissuing his father's books, perhaps because in August of 1714 he had been devoting all his energies to the Hayon controversy. Even more curiously, Hagiz' edition bears no haskamot, neither that of Nieto nor of the Bet Din of London customary *reshut* (permission) of the ma'amad. It does not even mention the name of the printer. After offering refuge to Hagiz and Zebi, the communal leaders of London did not wish to antagonize the Amsterdam ma'amad by openly supporting Hagiz. Nieto never mentioned Hagiz in his anti-Sabbatian polemic, *Esh Dat*, for the same reason.[3]

By the summer of 1716, Hagiz realized that he could not return to Amsterdam as soon as he had hoped, and that he could accomplish nothing further by remaining in London. In the fall of 1716, he moved to the city of Emden, then under Danish hegemony, along with the members of his household and some adherents.[4] Emden was close to Hamburg, which contained a large Portuguese Jewish community, whose communal leaders were very hospitable to Hagiz. Hagiz' most pressing problem in Emden was financial. He had borrowed heavily to finance the Hayon campaign and he had no income to provide for his living expenses, let alone to offset the debts. His former occupations seemed closed to him. The Jewish community of Emden was too small to support him as a tutor, and the volumes of his own work *Leket HaKeMa"H* which he had prepared for publication languished for lack of funds. Out of desperation, Hagiz drew plans for an ambitious project designed to generate an income.

THE MISHNAH PROJECT

Hagiz' plan was to reprint a classical mainstay of any Judaica library—the Mishnah. While the Mishnah had already been published nine times, most recently in Wilemsdorf, 1715, Hagiz planned to include Jacob Hagiz' *Ez Hayim* in addition to the classical Mishnah commentaries. He hoped to enlist a large number of subscribers whose prepayment would guarantee all his costs before going to print. Additional volumes sold after printing would earn a clean profit for him. This potential solution to Hagiz' problems was not unprecedented. Following his campaign against the Sabbatian messianic movement in the 1670s, Jacob Sasportas had embarked on a similar project in which he reprinted the Pentateuch with classical commentaries.[5]

Hagiz would need many hundreds of subscribers to make the effort worth his while. He promised to publish the name of any individual who could secure at least five hundred subscriptions. As he could never achieve this goal single-handedly, Hagiz called upon the network of allies that he had forged during the Hayon controversy. He emphasized to Judah Briel that the purpose of the project was "to alleviate the burden of debt that I have incurred *as a result of the tumult.*" He implied that the debt should not be regarded as a personal one but as the collective responsibility of all those who had participated in the campaign. He thanked those who would support him "and complete this *mizva,*" a reference to the Hayon campaign. Hagiz asked Samson Morpurgo and Judah Briel not only to enlist subscribers but also "to write to other noble individuals who hearken to their words," to do the same. Hagiz hoped that his sympathizers, particularly those in Amsterdam, would rejoice at this opportunity to demonstrate their support in a neutral way, since they were unable to support him directly without invoking the ban of the ma'amad.

The community of Emden was especially gracious in its efforts on his behalf. The communal leaders and head of the yeshiva provided warm letters of support for Hagiz' undertaking. Two wealthy merchants, Leib Emden and Jonathan Levi, offered their offices in Amsterdam and Hamburg to issue receipts to subscribers in which they would personally guarantee all prepayments made to Hagiz. Hagiz felt that this would provide an antidote to the cynicism of householders who would be wary of paying in advance, complaining, "Who would want to be part of a scheme with pedants and scholars who are all thieves?"[6]

The first auguries were encouraging. Hagiz received initial support and approbations from his friends. Samson Morpurgo suggested that Hagiz

should omit the commentary of Rashi, which was reiterated by Berti-
noro's, and replace it with Maimonides' to provide a more complete selection.[7] Hagiz prepared a sample folio of his future edition to assure
potential subscribers of the quality they would receive. At this point,
Hagiz permitted himself to dream that soon, with his debts settled and
his *Leket* printed, he could return to Erez Israel.

The pleasant visions of success did not materialize. Morpurgo had
managed to obtain only fifty subscriptions for sets of Mishnah "bound
in leather with covers of wood."

> But as to the thought of selling them by the hundred or half-thou-
> sand, what can I say? In our time when the entire world is wal-
> lowing in misery and poverty is rampant . . . particularly in these
> war-ravaged parts where the roads are fraught with danger and famine
> lurks everywhere, people cannot be expected to pursue the ac-
> coutrements of leisure and repose.

The few subscribers he had enlisted came by dint of great effort. Morpurgo enclosed his approbation as well as that of his father-in-law, Joseph
Fiametta, as a consolation. Hagiz received similar replies from others to
whom he had appealed—the time was not propitious. Briel wrote that
prospects for finding subscribers were so dismal, "I was reduced to
searching in the marketplaces and roads of Italian cities for customers. I
found but one solitary buyer."[8]

People of means were continually besieged by requests to buy books
they did not really need. So great was the number of individuals ped-
dling books in some towns that ordinances were passed to prohibit door
to door canvassing for prospective customers.[9] Editions of the Mishnah
already abounded, and in difficult times people were unlikely to buy a
new edition that included the contents of several volumes they already
owned. Hagiz' proposal was not unique enough to attract jaded contributors. By early July of 1716, he sadly abandoned his plans to publish
the Mishnah, and he notified the lay leaders of Emden of this decision.
The printer, Zev-Wolfe Mireles (a brother-in-law of Hakham Zevi) who
had moved to Emden especially to work on this project, returned to his
hometown. To compensate him for his efforts, Hagiz apparently ceded
to him the publication rights to Jacob Hagiz' *Ez Hayim*. Mireles published the Mishnah with *Ez Hayim* later that year in Berlin.[10]

Hagiz was bitterly disappointed by the failure of the Mishnah project.
He did not wish to be a continuing burden to the small but hospitable
Jewish community of Emden. He wrote dispiritedly to his colleagues
that his health had begun to fail him and the new climate disagreed with

him. In a letter to his Christian correspondent, Christof Teofilo Unger, David Nieto wrote, "I have dispatched your letter to H. R. Moses Hagiz to Emden, where he has been living during the past year. I have not yet received his reply, as he is ill due to the climate which does not agree with him. When it arrives, I shall forward it immediately." Hagiz published only one responsa in 1716, to Isaac B. Gershon Khalfon. In it he wrote, "I am under great pressure at this time, and my mind is not clear enough to reply."[11]

Desperate and dejected, Hagiz turned to the ma'amad of Amsterdam. Laying aside his dignity, he beseeched the lay leaders to forgive past differences and revoke the ban they had issued against him. His missive of December 15, 1716, addressed to the Srs. Souzas, is uncharacteristic of Hagiz in its imploring, obsequious tone:

> As an honorable man, as a Jew, and as a Hakham, I was obliged to behave as I did, as God is my witness . . . Your Honor knows well how I have suffered from the controversy. . . . I had sought peace with all true humility and for no ulterior motive . . . but it was rejected because of the fury of the Parnassim, particularly Aaron de Pinto and Joseph Pardo. I can prove that he [de Pinto] has unjustly pursued me since the day I entered Amsterdam . . . But I will set aside this injustice now for the sake of securing communal harmony. . . .
>
> If the leaders of the community would consent to relegate the past to its rightful place, to be clement and forgiving, to lift all the bans that have been promulgated during this upheaval, to remove all strictures that have been issued against me, to forbid a regrouping of either side of the controversy, and to establish laws against any who threaten to divide the Kehillah with the same penalties that are customary among the magistrates, then I will be prepared to do anything necessary for the honor of the Srs. of the Kahal, whom I have always respected, to show that I have never transgressed beyond what Jewish law prescribed. I will beg their forgiveness as they require. . . . Please relay my message to them so that I could begin the process. . . .
>
> I beseech you to convey to the ma'amad in my name that I implore, supplicate and beg them to accept and embrace my submission at once, as it is dedicated to God and tranquility of the Kehillah. If they deem otherwise, they will be in the wrong and I will be forced to seek and to preserve my life and my honor.[12]

Hagiz' humble capitulation was forcefully rejected. He remained in

Emden several more months, until he found an alternative destination and completed his preparations for departure. From Emden, Hagiz traveled to Hamburg, where he arrived by November 15, 1718. At the time of his arrival, the Sephardic community was depleted, but it was still larger than that of Emden. Hamburg also contained a sizable Ashkenazic Jewish community, although its rabbinic seat was in nearby Altona. Wealthy Jews of Hamburg had been fleeing a precipitous rise in the annual tax levied against the Jewish community for two decades before Hagiz' arrival.

Hamburg had been home to a Hebrew printing press since 1586, and Hagiz took an active interest in the books published there. According to one source, all books printed in Hamburg at this time were subject to Hagiz' approval, although he wrote only one haskamah in Hamburg, to Solomon Zalman Katz' *Sha'arei Torah* (*Gates of Torah*) on November 4, 1717. In Hamburg, Hagiz published another volume of *Leket HaKeMa"H*, his halakhic digest, on *Eben ha-Ezer*, the third segment of the Shulkhan Arukh. It was to be the last volume in this series which Hagiz succeeded in publishing. Because of its tepid reception and slow sales, the fourth and final volume, on *Hoshen Mishpat*, was never published. To Hagiz' chagrin, the Hebrew press at Hamburg was forced to close in 1722, during the time that he resided there.

Hagiz' six years in Hamburg passed quietly; relatively little information about his activities has reached us. On May 2, 1718, his friend and ally, Hakham Zebi, passed away. In the following year, he wrote a responsum to Samson Morpurgo (July 1719) which revealed that he remained depressed: "It was not in my heart to take up the quill and write halakhic opinions nor to render judgments, for reasons known to me alone. My mind has become confused because of recent events, troubles, fatigue, and aching limbs . . . Each day exacts its toll."[13]

In 1725 Hagiz moved from Hamburg to the neighboring German city of Altona. Upon his arrival, Hagiz was granted permission to convene prayer sessions in his own home. Many communal leaders had protested the practice of conducting prayer services on private premises, and wished to coerce all individuals to pray at the main synagogue. When Jacob Emden arrived in Altona, he too was granted permission to pray with a private quorum.[14]

THE ROLE OF NEHEMIAH HAYON IN THE
ANTI-SABBATIAN CAMPAIGN OF 1725–26

Shortly after his arrival in Altona, Hagiz found himself at the vortex of another campaign against crypto-Sabbatians. The direct cause of his renewed interest was the reappearance of Nehemiah Hayon in Europe. Some of Hayon's opponents had continued to monitor his movements after the controversy of 1714, and they kept Hagiz well informed. Hayon had left Amsterdam in 1715, taking with him letters of support from his protectors. He planned to take the letters to Constantinople where the first bans had been promulgated against him. Joseph Ergas reported, "I have heard that the serpent [Hayon] embarked on a ship sailing for Constantinople to challenge the rabbinical court that had issued [bans] against him. . . . He carried affidavits with him, addressed to Jewish and Gentile contacts with the request that they use their powers to help him." Ergas immediately notified R. Benjamin Halevi, their anti-Sabbatian ally in Constantinople, of Hayon's intentions, and instructed him to alert the rabbis of his city against Hayon. According to another account, Hayon left Amsterdam on July 25, 1714, for Livorno, where the Jewish lay leaders prevailed upon the Duke to bar his entry because it would foment unrest among the inhabitants of the city. "They condemned his books to the pyre and produced a declaration from the lords of the land that Hayon was not to be granted entry to any portion of the Duchy."[15]

On September 25, 1716, Judah Briel communicated to Hagiz that he too had been following Hayon's activities. He had received word that Hayon reached Safed together with a group of adherents. There he had succeeded in establishing an institution which Briel described only as "a monstrous bastion of idolatry," perhaps the yeshiva devoted to Sabbatian-kabbalistic studies of which he had long dreamed. Briel informed Abraham Yizhaki, the veteran anti-Sabbatian in Erez Israel, and begged him to uproot this idolatrous growth from the soil of Israel with all his strength.[16] The letter was sent through Sr. Suleima of Livorno. During this period in Erez Israel, Hayon secured a letter of approbation from Abraham Ze'ebi, rabbi in Hebron, for his books *Oz le-Elohim* and *ha-Zad Zebi.*[17]

If Hayon's yeshiva did exist, it was short lived. According to his own account, he proceeded with Ze'ebi's letter to R. Hayim Kimhi in Constantinople. The letter exonerated Hayon from all charges of heresy and urged Kimhi to intercede with the rabbinical court of Constantinople on his behalf. R. Hayim Alfandari (whom Hagiz accused of being a supporter of Hayon) conveyed the letter. After tireless effort, Hayon eventually effected the recision of the Constantinople bans.[18]

The circumstances under which Hayon was able to have the bans revoked are obscured by conflicting accounts. Hayon claimed that the scholar R. Judah Rosanes declared his work untainted by heresy, and this paved the way for a hearing at the rabbinical court in Constantinople. Hayon published his account of this dramatic confrontation:

> The rabbis of Constantinople summoned me and asked, "Why do you demand a judgment?" I replied, "I want a hearing so that you can permit that which you have declared forbidden." They said, "How can we, the tender flock, permit your work when the great shepherds, R. Zebi [Ashkenazi] and R. Naphtali [Kohen], have 'misconstrued' your intentions? However, if you repent, and swear never to teach the esoteric lore to any person, then we will lift the bans." I told them that I would take an oath even to refrain from studying the esoteric lore myself. They replied, "Heaven forbid— it is proper and fitting that you study the lore, but you must not uncover the mystery for others." I retorted: "Then you will have permitted me to become steeped in heresy and blasphemy, for that was your opinion of my work which you published in your bans."

Hayon reported that the bans were lifted directly after this exchange, on July 18, 1724, with the aforementioned strictures.[19] Hayon also wrote that during his stay in Constantinople, he confronted R. Naphtali Kohen, his erstwhile enemy, who conceded to him and became reconciled with him.

From Constantinople, Hayon hastened to Amsterdam where on January 5, 1726, he published the supportive letters from Hebron, Salonica, and Constantinople, in a self-vindicating tract entitled _ha-Kolot Yehdalun_ [_The Voices Shall be Silenced_]. Hayon hoped that this evidence would suffice to nullify the bans which had been pronounced against him a decade earlier in every major Jewish community, and lead to reconciliation. Sadly for Hayon, his actions produced the reverse effect. He was not permitted to remain in Amsterdam. Even Solomon Ayllon refused to greet him, as he had broken his promise never to return to that city. According to Hagiz, Hayon led a hunted and desperate existence:

> He began to wander, spurned and rejected, from city to city, from state to state. He arrived at the capital city, Vienna, but the communal elders refused to admit him. He sat in the courtyard reserved for the Ottomans, claiming to be a Turk. The Sages tried to per-

suade his adherents to abandon him. From there he went to Glogau, where he was recognized. They searched for his writings, but
he had craftily concealed them in the mailhouse. They expelled
him. On that day, he arrived in Berlin where he wrote to a former
adherent that if further antagonized "the waters would engulf him"
[he would be baptized]. Because of this, they gave him two Mark
and dispatched him from there, and he remained within the Jewish
fold. He arrived in Hanover where he disguised himself . . . but
he was recognized, and he admitted that he was . . . Nehemiah
Hayon . . . whereupon they immediately decreed against him in
the synagogue. On Saturday night, the sextons entered his room
to search his satchels. Most of his writings had been hidden, but
they found several documents . . . Sabbatian in nature, including
a correspondence with Jonathan Eybeschutz.

When Hayon arrived in Prague, he was barred from the city, and he
survived on its outskirts because the wife and daughter-in-law of R. Jonathan Eybeschutz felt compassion toward him and supplied him with
food. Hayon died several years later. According to Hagiz, there was an
even crueler coda to the story of Hayon's demise:

> We anticipated that with the death of NaHa"Sh [Hayon], the earth
> would be peaceful and they [the Sabbatians] would sink into obliv-
> ion. . . . But today, December 3, 1732, I received a letter inform-
> ing me of the travails of one of our brethren in the Diaspora, . . .
> For Hayon has an offspring who has left the fold [sheyaza la-huz]
> to take revenge and to persecute those who had persecuted his fa-
> ther . . . and he besmirched not only the name of all the *aggadot*
> and *midrashim* of the Sages, teachers of the twenty-four [books of
> the Hebrew Bible] but of the codifiers and ethicists, new and an-
> cient, until our odor became foul in the eyes of the Gentiles and
> he aroused an implacable fury.[20]

Hagiz' alarm at the spectre of Hayon's reappearance is understandable.
His careful account of Hayon's subsequent misfortunes, the wandering
and repeated rebuffs suffered at the hands of various Jewish communities, served to demonstrate the efficacy of the rabbinic effort of 1714.

When Hagiz received a copy of Hayon's self-vindicating pamphlet his
lassitude vanished and a decade of silence ended. He perceived the tract
as a direct challenge. If the public were to accept Hayon's claim that the
bans against him had been rescinded, all Hagiz' effort to gather them
would have been in vain. To counter Hayon's account, he would have

to destroy every vestige of its credibility. This he set out to do with a scathing rebuttal, entitled *Lehishat Saraf* [*Whisper of a Seraph*].

Hagiz' rebuttal presented a completely different account of Hayon's activities. Hagiz based his version on the testimony of a witness, Zerah B. Mordecai, who testified against Hayon on January 19, 1726, before the rabbinical court of R. Ezekiel Katzenellenbogen, chief rabbi in Altona. The witness reported that in Constantinople, Hayon had resided at the home of Abraham Samenon, a member of the circle of Court Jew Raphael Majolo, who served at the court of the Vizier. Hayon was able to reach the Vizir through these channels, and the Vizir agreed to intervene with the Jewish community on his behalf. He ordered the community to grant a stipend to Hayon out of the communal treasury, and to lift the bans they had pronounced against him. Thus, the bans of Constantinople were retracted by the rabbinate only *under duress*, and their original intent remained in full force.

Hagiz pointed out that the witness' story was corroborated by internal evidence in the document. In addition to the restrained tone of the proclamation, it had been signed by only three rabbis, the minimum quorum for a rabbinical court. The original bans had been signed by ten rabbis, and the procedure for revocation should have required at least an equal number. The absence of a plenum indicated that the document had been a product of external coercion, and was therefore invalid. Hagiz argued that even if the document had been voluntary and authentic, it would nevertheless have become null and void because Hayon had failed to heed any of the conditions specified in it. He cast doubt over Hayon's portrayal of R. Judah Rosanes. Rosanes had never professed to be versed in kabbalistic lore, and it would have been highly unlikely for him to have interested himself in Hayon's writings. The witness had also testified that R. Naphtali Kohen had resided at home during the entire incident, and contrary to Hayon's claim, Kohen had never even granted Hayon an audience.[21]

Although the only substantial polemical works to be published at this time were those involving Hayon, he occupied a minor role alongside the central characters and themes of the polemical war of 1725–26. We are fortunate to have other sources for this polemic, notably Joseph Prager's *Gahalei Esh* [*Fiery Coals*], still in manuscript. In the context of a more complete account of the 1725–26 controversy, the image of Hayon recedes to serve merely as a connecting filament between the two anti-Sabbatian campaigns. Before we outline the particular characteristics of the anti-Sabbatian pursuit of 1725, we must underscore the fact that it was a sequel to the first controversy, and contained many common elements. The campaigns must be evaluated as segments of a continuum rather than as isolated reactions to specific personalities and events. We begin to perceive elements which transcend the particulars of each campaign; some will become fixed features of subsequent rabbinic battles against Jewish sectarianism.

Hagiz' introduction to *Lehishat Saraf* was a brief updated history of the Sabbatian messianic movement and its sectarian offshoots. It is noteworthy that in this encapsulated account, in which Hagiz admitted to broader comprehension of Sabbatian sectarianism, the role of Hayon is diminished:

> In 1666 they [the Jews] were stricken with blindness . . . saying "This one [Sabbatai] shall redeem us" . . . but he became a rotting corpse, among the Ishmaelites. . . . He has claimed more victims in death than in life . . . for his influence continued long after his death. . . . After him, many sects appeared. . . . Each begins as though holy and pure, but their end is debasement, . . . with abominable words: "The desecration of the Torah is its fulfillment, like the seed which must first rot in the ground."
>
> The fate of hundreds of souls who adhered to him [Sabbatai] in Salonika and Adrianople is already well known. If only they had sunk along with him! For all those who have ostensibly returned to the fold served Israel only as obstacles. . . . They pose as pietists but their heart is not with God. . . . Take the case of Abraham Michael Cardoso, who described himself and signed his name Messiah ben Joseph, in addition to writing several heretical works. He inscribed his homilies *"Derush Megalleh 'Amuqot Minni Hoshekh,"* (Homily of Revelation of Profundities from the Darkness) . . . He mocks the Sages often, and describes several faiths that were born in 1666. He writes that they are at variance with those who claim to have received the tradition directly from Sabbatai Zebi, for they are excluded from the "mystery of the faithful," that is embodied in the work of his disciple, the serpent Hayon.
>
> As we have already elaborated in the epistles and books of 1713–1715, . . . when most of the Sages in the realms of the Diaspora, unanimously excommunicated and publicized the case of Michael Cardoso, and also agreed that the works of Hayon were works of sorcery . . . we will not elaborate here. Everything that has been written in the past still retains its validity, and this chronicle is being written only to report that which is novel.[22]

In this sketch, Hagiz has provided the link between the Hayon campaign of 1715 and those that followed it. In both Hagiz' *Lehishat Saraf* and Prager's *Gahalei Esh*, documents from the campaigns of 1715 and 1725 are intermingled with no distinctions, as though both campaigns were part of one unit. Yet while the rabbinic polemics of the Hayon campaign portrayed Sabbatianism as a one-dimensional heresy, the polemics of 1725–26 were fully aware of the multiple forms in which Sabbatianism appeared. In the course of the Hayon campaign, Hagiz had insinuated that crypto-Sabbatianism, and his campaign against it, were novelties. In the campaign of 1725–26, Hagiz characterized crypto-Sabbatianism as a recurring leprosy, and he did not disregard the role of the anti-Sabbatian zealots who had preceded him.[23]

SABBATIANISM IN EASTERN EUROPE

The setting and background of the second anti-Sabbatian campaign in which Hagiz participated, Eastern and Central Europe, differed greatly from its predecessor. After the apostasy of Sabbatai, Eastern European crypto-Sabbatianism remained pietist in nature like its Italian counterpart. Only after thirty years, in the last decade of the seventeenth century, did a more radical and antinomian strain of Sabbatianism percolate into Eastern and Central Europe. The transplanted lore from Turkey and Salonika took hold especially in Poland and the Ukraine. Itinerant Sabbatian missionaries, preachers, or even peddlers, were responsible for the dissemination of the radical doctrines. They became especially popular in Podolia, where communal leadership was weak and the reception for roving demi-messiahs and spirituals was warm. Salonika's radical Sabbatians established direct ties with Podolian Sabbatians. From Podolia, they sent emissaries to Prague, Fuerth, Berlin and Mannheim, where they transmitted their radical doctrines to the pietistic crypto-Sabbatian enclaves already existing in Central Europe.

The anti-Sabbatian rabbis in these communities had organized themselves to fight Sabbatianism, independent of Hagiz' efforts in the West. Their effort concentrated on exposing and denouncing the Sabbatian missionaries who posed as peripatetic illuminati. A herem in Lvov (Lemberg) in 1722 marked the start of a new era of vigorous pursuit of Sabbatians in Eastern and Central Europe. The first evidence of Hagiz' participation appears in the summer of 1725, by which time the indigenous campaign was well under way. Hagiz ignored this history of local anti-

Sabbatian activity, and attributed the renewed anti-Sabbatian efforts to the arrival of Hayon. Of one recidivist Sabbatian, Hagiz commented, "Now that the serpent [Hayon] has crossed his path, he had lapsed into his former wicked ways." To the Council of Four Lands, Hagiz characterized Hayon as "the root of all poisonous hypocrites, who has returned here."

Hagiz' account places much greater emphasis on the role of Hayon than warranted. The Sabbatian centers in Eastern and Central Europe from which the itinerant missionaries radiated had been active long before Hayon appeared there. In 1715, Barukhya Russo, head of the Sabbatians in Salonika, was declared 'santo Señor'—an incarnation of the God of Israel. In the wake of this new development, many emissaries were dispatched from Salonika to rekindle the faith. Hayon's arrival in Central Europe in 1724 coincided with the heightened activity of Barukhya's propagandists. Even after this became apparent to Hagiz, he insisted that Hayon remain a prominent and permanent target of anti-Sabbatian persecution. To one colleague he wrote on September 25, 1725, that when upholding the bans against other satans, Hayon and his cohorts should not escape.[24]

R. Jacob Emden offered a detailed account of how Sabbatianism spread among the scholars of Prague:

The house of study, the cloister that had been founded by the Sage R. Abraham Broda . . . went astray. This was established in 1724–26 by dependable witnesses who had originally been members of the [Sabbatian] circle. . . . They disclosed everything to R.D.O. [R. David Oppenheim], Chief of the rabbinical court of Prague. . . . He, in turn, notified the communal leaders of Central Europe and Poland. Some disciples of R.A.B. [R. Abraham Broda], with whom R.J. [R. Jonathan Eybeschutz] had studied for many years, acted similarly—they saw the evil and protested. . . . R. Benjamin, son of Michael Hasid of Berlin, who had sojourned in Prague and learned about the entire episode, sent his father a copy of the tainted work *ve-Abo ha-Yom* [attributed to Eybeschutz]. . . .

R. Jonathan wrote to Tosmaniz to summon the scholar . . . R. S. [Simon] Cracower. He implored and then bribed him to circulate the heretical writings in Podolia, and R. S. [Simon] was entrapped and agreed to the mission. When he arrived in Breslau, the matter was brought to the attention of R. Hayim Jonah . . . who had him [R. Simon] imprisoned, confiscated his heretical works, and revealed his shame to all. . . .

At the same time, the abominable ones [Sabbatians] . . . in
Zolkiew and Podolia, confidantes of . . . Eybeschutzer, sent a special emissary, Moses Meir, to entrap souls."[25]

Even if we discount Emden's emphasis on the role of Eybeschutz (whom
he saw as chief heresiarch of the crypto-Sabbatians), Emden's account is
still a valuable guide to the circles in which Sabbatian activists successfully proselytized.

THE EMISSARIES:

Leible of Prosnitz

The anti-Sabbatian campaign of 1725–26 was directed against several
conspicuous Sabbatian emissaries. Their names appeared in almost every
anti-Sabbatian ban, and they were listed by Hagiz in *Lehishat Saraf*. Leible [Judah Leib] of Prosnitz, (born c. 1670) was an uneducated peddler
until a spiritual awakening led him to study of the Mishnah, from which
he proceeded to Sabbatian Kabbalah. At first he led a quiet ascetic life,
but as he grew more confident of his powers, he began to preach his
Sabbatian faith publicly. He claimed to have been visited by souls of the
deceased, including those of Isaac Luria and Sabbatai Zebi.

R. Meir of Eisenstadt, a renowned scholar who became rabbi of Prosnitz in 1702, became a supporter of Leible. Jacob Emden claimed that
during this period Leible studied together with R. Jonathan Eybeschutz,
also a disciple of R. Meir. Other testimonies claimed that he later stayed
at Eybeschutz' home for a period of two weeks. Several pieces of his
correspondence with R. Jonathan circulated among Sabbatians, and they
revealed a sustained friendly contact.

Like other Sabbatians, Leible prophesied that Sabbatai Zebi would
return in 1706, and his agitation reached such a pitch that he was threatened with excommunication by the rabbis of Glogau and Breslau and R.
Meir of Eisenstadt withdrew his support. The renewed frenzy of Sabbatian activism in 1725 infused Leible's career with new spirit. Although
Hagiz attributed Leible's reawakening to Hayon, he had, more likely,
been in contact with Sabbatian emissaries from Salonika.

In 1725 a rabbinical court in Mannheim gathered testimony against
Leible. His son-in-law had sojourned in Mannheim at the home of Isaiah
Hasid, another Sabbatian activist. Hasid had revealed that Leible was
the Messiah son of Joseph and Jonathan Eybeschutz, the Messiah son of
David. Leible acknowledged his new messianic status by affixing his sig-

nature to documents as "Joseph ben Jacob." In Hagiz' account, "Leible Prosnitz . . . has prophesied to call himself Messiah son of Joseph. He has already been banned and excommunicated by the Bet Din of his city, with the concurrence of R. David Oppenheim. It is evident that Leible is a sorcerer and a black magician. When Hayon reappeared, he verified that Leible has been possessed by the unclean spirit." Hagiz cited examples of Leible's "lewd and heretical" thought. Regarding the rabbis who pursued him, Leible had decreed, "We must arouse all of Israel so that their hearts will be kindled against these evil classes." Hagiz considered Leible dangerous not only for his heretical preaching, but also because he used his network of Sabbatian contacts to push Sabbatians into positions of power within the community. In 1724 he had vigorously supported the candidacy of a fellow Sabbatian, R. Sender, for the rabbinate of Mannheim.[26]

Isaiah Hasid

A second Sabbatian emissary to play a role in the campaign was Isaiah Hasid, also known as Isaiah *Mokhiah* [the preacher], the son-in-law of R. Judah Hasid who had led a group of Sabbatian enthusiasts to the Holy Land in 1700. After the death of Judah Hasid, Isaiah assumed leadership of the remnants of the group. He played an important role in disseminating Sabbatianism within the Ashkenazic kehillah of Jerusalem. When Abraham Rovigo established his study group there in 1702, he chose its members on advice from Isaiah Hasid "and did nothing without consulting the opinion of the latter." He eventually returned with his adherents to the Diaspora, where in 1708 they established themselves in the study hall of Mannheim. This study hall became a center of Sabbatian activity in Eastern Europe. Jacob Emden published testimonies against Isaiah: "He swore to R. Abraham Broda that he would repent completely of the evil deeds he had committed in Jerusalem; but it became apparent afterward that he had continued to believe in Sabbatai Zebi." "When confronted with his abominations, he became an unwilling penitent . . . he flung himself on the synagogue in order to trample it." According to Hagiz' account, "He too was a pretender to the throne, calling himself Messiah son of Joseph."

Isaiah Hasid corresponded with Leible Prosnitz as well as with R. Jonathan Eybeschutz. According to one testimony, Leible urged him to support the candidacy of Eybeschutz for the rabbinate of Mannheim. Isaiah Hasid disseminated Sabbatian manuscripts with such great enthusiasm, that they often fell into the hands of their opponents. This carelessness was a source of tension between Isaiah and his fellow Sabbatians: "R. Isaiah gave a copy of all the Sabbatian writings of Jonathan of Prague and Leible Prosnitz to R. Joel Merish . . . A great outcry against R. Isaiah ensued. Why was he revealing the secrets of the sect to non-believers? R. Isaiah became enraged when it was learned that he had been the one to distribute the manuscripts."[27]

Moses Meir of Zolkiew

Moses Meir of Zolkiew, brother-in-law of Sabbatian emissary Feivel of Zlotchov, best exemplified the Sabbatian functionaries who were the focus of the 1725–26 campaign. He was not the author of any original works, nor did he develop new avenues of thought. The polemical literature characterized him as a distributor of Sabbatian writings, proselytizer and agent par excellence: "Moses Meir, messenger of sin, sent to lure the public with epistles from the evil sect." He was accused of trafficking with the Sabbatian manuscripts of R. Jonathan Eybeschutz to seduce scholars to join the sectarian faith. "In Prague, he stayed at the home of R. Jonathan who provided him with heretical manuscripts and letters of recommendation." The nature of Moses Meir's mission was discovered by rabbinic appointed poursuivants who searched the luggage of travelers sojourning at the inns.

Jacob Emden, sojourning in Pressburg in 1725, described the procedure: "The head of the *Bet Din* of Prague, in concert with the communal leaders and officials of Vienna, appointed guards to examine [the effects of] unworthy students who were returning from Prague with the novellae of their master. The same was done in Pressburg . . . The beadles of the community suddenly searched the room of the aforementioned guest, open his trunk and found the manuscript of the renowned seducer [Eybeschutz]. . . . *ve-'Abo ha-Yom*." They were especially thorough with the valises of those who were associated with the study hall of Prague. "When Moses Meir arrived in Frankfurt am Main, R. Jacob Katz of Prague investigated and searched, and he found the treacherous material in his possession. On June 14, 1725, he and all those who took his counsel, were excommunicated."[28]

R. JONATHAN EYBESCHUTZ

The most enigmatic and elusive figure in the campaign of 1725–26 was R. Jonathan Eybeschutz. His role in this campaign has been overshadowed by the controversy with Emden a quarter of a century later, but the conundrum of Eybeschutz cannot be approached without appreciating his role in this earlier campaign. A disciple of R. Meir Eisenstadt in Prosnitz, among others, Eybeschutz settled in Prague in 1715, where he was soon acclaimed as a brilliant Talmudist and skillful preacher. His exceptional abilities brought him prominence as head of the yeshiva of Prague, as well as the attention of Christian polemicists, particularly Cardinal Hasselbauer with whom he debated. Eybeschutz received permission to print the Talmud if he promised to omit all passages deemed contradictory to principles of Christianity. This provoked a public confrontation with R. David Oppenheim, then rabbi of Prague. Together with the rabbinate of Frankfurt, Oppenheim had the license revoked. Upon Oppenheim's death, Eybeschutz succeeded him as chief dayyan of Prague.

Eybeschutz avoided direct confrontation with the anti-Sabbatians in 1725, and even joined forces with them. Despite this, his role in the controversy was great. The most important new Sabbatian manuscript in circulation was attributed to him. R. Jacob Kohen Popers of Frankfurt wrote to his brother, Abraham Popers of Prague:

> The writings discovered in the satchel of Moses Meir were not signed by any author. But he swore upon pain of excommunication that one manuscript was the work of R. Jonathan of Prague. In this script, the name of Sabbatai Zebi is never once mentioned . . . It is Kabbalah which contains many astounding ideas, and which detracts from the notion of the unity of God. He divulges many omens and mysteries, and he writes them as though they had been revealed at Sinai. He does not say from whence they originated, it is as though the spirit of the Lord spoke through him . . . It appears from his own words . . . that he has a *maggid* which appears to him.

The Sabbatian treatise at the center of this discussion, *ve-Abo ha-Yom el ha-Ayin* [*And I Came This Day Upon the Fountain*], was an intellectual descendent of Hayon's *Oz le-Elohim*.

In the campaign of 1725, Eybeschutz was assumed by both Sabbatians and their opponents, to be the author of the manuscript. The editor of

Gahalei Esh described a demoralized Sabbatian sect which pinned its hopes on R. Jonathan and attributed greater powers to him. "R. Moses Leib Tributsch testified that R. Isaiah [Hasid] said of R. Jonathan, 'He is possessed of Divine inspiration and reveals more secrets of the Torah than Itzik Luria.' " Other Sabbatians saw in Eybeschutz a new incarnation of the Messiah. Hagiz sarcastically mocked the Sabbatians who regarded Eybeschutz as a new savior: "But perhaps he [Eybeschutz] is being truthful when he declares that he does not believe in Sabbatai Zebi . . . *because in his own mind he is Sabbatai Zebi* . . . I can testify to the fact that Eybeschutz has left the community of Israel, and has filled himself with the drivel of Leib Prosnitz." One of the letters attributed to R. Jonathan expressed a passionate and total desire for concealment of his role. The letter is addressed to Isaiah Hasid:

> I cannot elaborate, for "the desert is closing in on me" and my powers have not yet reached their plenum. . . . This letter does not come to innovate, but to inform—I have already told it all to Moses Meir and he will carry my complete reply. Please do not number yourself among the publicizers. Reveal only to the most discreet, and so instruct all your confidantes, because the barking of dogs and braying of asses is before me [the anti-Sabbatians]. Please be extremely modest and circumspect, like the verse [Isaiah 26:20] which instructs "enter your chambers and lock your doors" until there be no more evil in the world, and then you will be crowned with glory.[29]

Dissimulation of one's true faith was not unusual among Sabbatians. Many of Eybeschutz' predecessors and contemporaries, such as the highly regarded R. Heschel Zoref, specifically requested of their Sabbatian correspondents that their Sabbatian loyalty be concealed from the public.

Anti-Sabbatian rabbis were able to seize many pieces of private correspondence by intercepting the mail of suspected Sabbatian emissaries. These were assiduously copied and circulated, perhaps embellished upon. From this correspondence, they were able to reconstruct the network of contacts between Sabbatians and their influence upon one another. For example, "It is already widely known that R. Jonathan of Prague, who is presently head of the rabbinical court of AHW, spent many an evening in the home of R. Leible [Prosnitz]. Leible visited for over two weeks in the home of R. Jonathan and R. Jonathan and his sect supplied him with food and livelihood all his days."

When Nehemiah Hayon's identity was uncovered in Hanover, his presence was announced in the synagogue and the sextons searched his room that night. Among the documents found in his possession was a letter from R. Jonathan of Prague. It was a reply to Hayon's request that R. Jonathan publicly support the writ from Constantinople. Eybeschutz had responded that he would not become involved in Hayon's affairs. He asked Hayon why he continued to seek controversy that would compel him to become a perpetual vagrant.[30]

CONFRONTING A PARADOX: THE SABBATIAN TORAH-SCHOLAR

Although in 1725 Eybeschutz had not yet attained the renown that he enjoyed twenty-five years later at the time of the great controversy with R. Jacob Emden, he was already recognized as a brilliant young rabbinical scholar and an exceptional preacher. His presence in the controversy was highly significant both for Sabbatians and for their opponents alike. It necessitated a reformulation of basic assumptions of the entire anti-Sabbatian polemic. The towering presence of R. Jonathan in the Sabbatian camp would mean that the anti-Sabbatian polemicists could no longer portray Sabbatianism as the spiritual fare of the ignorant and unlettered. His presence would confer legitimacy to an ideology which they abhorred and persecuted in the name of the Torah. It would force them to confront the phenomenon of the Sabbatian cum Torah scholar, and in the case of Eybeschutz, preacher extraordinaire.[31]

Hagiz, confronted with the image of the Sabbatian as rabbi, found a precedent for this phenomenon in the earlier campaign: "R. Jonathan, head of the *Pe'or* [a Biblical idolatrous sect] is like Ayllon. Their words are the same, and it is as though they had taken counsel together against all the Sages of Israel. Indeed, they have [both] called the sages 'dogs and asses.' " Hagiz claimed that they had learned a valuable lesson from the example of Ayllon:

In the previous campaign against the serpent [Hayon], Ayllon was shown favoritism [because of his rabbinic status], and now they favor R. Jonathan of Prague. Since the earlier favoritism resulted in abomination, who can tell what horrors will emerge from this instance? What we have left undone in that campaign [of Hayon] must be completed during this controversy, and justice must be meted out *without regard to status.*

The analogy between Ayllon and Eybeschutz was imperfect. Eybeschutz rose to a pinnacle of esteem in Jewish scholarly circles that Ayllon would never begin to approximate. Nevertheless, the name of Ayllon was occasionally interjected into testimonies of the 1725 campaign, and his image remained influential even though he took no part in the campaign. One witness in 1725, Zalman Leipziger, testified that during his visit to the synagogue of Isaiah Hasid, Hasid would speak of Ayllon as a true Sabbatian.

Proselytization among young rabbinic scholars was one of the most important objectives of the Sabbatian emissaries in 1725. R. Jonathan's reputed presence in the Sabbatian camp was a trump card which the Sabbatians played to the fullest extent. An emissary who identified himself as a disciple of R. Jonathan found a receptive audience for his Sabbatian manuscripts among admirers of the great Talmudist. Many well-publicized conversions to Sabbatianism were attributed to the charismatic powers of Eybeschutz. In Poland, one witness testified:

> A great scholar, Solomon ben Samuel Cracower, a member of the anti-Sabbatian rabbinic party, lived in Buczacz. R. Jonathan wrote and asked him to come to Prague to fill his father's position upon his return from Prague. R. Solomon had changed from an enemy to an ally [of Sabbatians] and had befriended the wicked sect. R. Solomon also tried to bring R. Nathan [a confirmed antinomian Sabbatian] but he was prevented from doing so because of public opposition to the sect. In the course of their words, the public murmured that R. Jonathan, too, supported these wicked men until some leaders of the community asked to have R. Jonathan banned. I do not know why they did not do so. R. Jonathan also instructed R. Nathan to nurture his contacts with R. Solomon, "who was approaching holiness but was still in the hands of the head of the rabbinical court of Broda."

The witness added that he had seen Eybeschutz' letter with his own eyes and recognized it to be authentic. Some scholars were initiated into the lore of Sabbatianism only to be repelled by some aspect, and repent. The compelling figure of Eybeschutz remained to disturb their equilibrium:

> R. Feivel was a giant in both the exoteric and esoteric Torah. He testified to me that he had been seduced by Sabbatians in Zolkiew, but when he saw their corrupt ways, he repented. He went to R. Joshua, chief rabbi of Lemberg . . . and asked, "What am I to do, when I know with certainty that R. Jonathan of Prague is the head of all Sabbatians. It distresses me, for he is a Sage of Israel!"

Hagiz had urged his allies to wage total war against all Sabbatians without regard to their rabbinic status. Some rabbis could not bring themselves to comply. For example, on November 2, 1725, Hagiz wrote to R. Arye Leib, then in Rzeszow, "I have written to you once, twice and thrice, and I am puzzled that I have not yet received any reply." Many years later, in 1752, R. Aryeh Leib explained his reluctance to condemn Eybeschutz: "Although at that time [1725] R. Moses Hagiz and R. Jacob b. Benjamin [Reischer = Pol. Rzeszow], who was rabbi of Frankfurt, wrote to me in great excitement that I should pursue him [Eybeschutz] to the bitter end. . . . Nevertheless, I said to myself, he has erred and the light from within will make him repent." Behind the most vehement pursuit by those who agreed with Hagiz lay genuine distress and regret that targets of their venom included great rabbis and scholars. R. Ezekiel Katzenellenbogen, rabbi of Altona and a close ally of Hagiz, mourned over the attribution of a Sabbatian manuscript to Eybeschutz: "Alas, what can we do with regard to him [Eybeschutz]? For we have seen greater men than him ensnared by sin. Every word in the treatise . . . *ve-Abo ha-Yom el ha-Ayin* speaks profanity." Upon reading a kabbalistic work tinged with Sabbatian references, Hagiz reacted with dismay: "I was greatly distressed because I saw from the book that if the author had not been struck with this blindness [Sabbatianism] he would have been a truly great authority on the holy *Zohar* and the writings of AR"I."

Despite Hagiz' vow to persevere in the pursuit even of Torah scholar/Sabbatians, the phenomenon remained a profound incongruity to him. When a rabbi was identified as a Sabbatian sympathizer without concrete evidence, Hagiz would first try to dismiss the information, an anomalous exception to his policy. He did so *on the basis of the accused's rabbinic status.* When Hayon had claimed that R. Judah Rosanes supported his Sabbatian work *Oz l'Elohim*, Hagiz refused to accept this information. He wrote, "This is a notorious falsehood, for we know that . . . R. Rosanes has earned a reputation as a great Talmudic scholar. . . . Heaven forbid that we should believe that such a pious man uttered those words. . . . This hearsay is a fabrication and malicious distortion." The defenders of Eybeschutz were to advance similar arguments to vindicate him from charges of Sabbatianism, without success.

The position of Eybeschutz in the controversy of 1725 was further clouded by confusion because of the herem of Prague, issued against Sabbatians on September 16, 1725. R. Jonathan Eybeschutz was among those who signed the herem. To his ally, R. Michel Hasid of Berlin, Hagiz wrote: "The unpleasant news has reached me that the letter [the herem of Prague] has been published, replete with deceit and confusion. For this iniquity . . . which will blind the eyes of Israel and hide the truth . . . the heads of our generation will be held accountable. . . . I have seen the great damage that will ensue if the rabbis who have the power to reveal his shame do not do so immediately." Hagiz remarked that R. David Oppenheim, who had refused to join Eybeschutz in signing the ban, "had prophesied in his wisdom that this was just a trap to lure innocent souls." In fact, there were other, unrelated bones of contention between Oppenheim and Eybeschutz, such as the controversy over printing the Talmud.

Hagiz tried to combat Eybeschutz in the arena in which Eybeschutz had proven most effective—as a master who provided great inspiration to his disciples. In a letter to R. Arye Leib of September 26, 1725, Hagiz urged: "You should decree with the severest herem that no students from Poland should study with R. Jonathan."

The presence of rabbinic scholars within the ranks of the Sabbatians added a new dimension to the Sabbatian controversies which Hagiz did not have to confront earlier. Moreover, the campaign against Sabbatianism in East and Central Europe had always numbered prominent laymen, the Parnassim among the anti-Sabbatians. For that reason, too, this polemic could not be portrayed as a battle of rabbis versus ignorant laymen. In the entire *Pinkas* [Register of Communal Ordinances] of the Jewish communities of Altona-Hamburg-Wandsbeck, the only ordinances issued in the name of rabbis and laymen alike were those issued against Sabbatians during the campaign of 1725.[32]

GEBIAT EDUT: THE EVIDENCE OF HERESY

The fulcrum of the Hayon polemic had been the analysis of Hayon's Sabbatian text, *Oz l'Elohim.* In contrast, the anti-Sabbatian campaign of 1725 devoted very little attention to the most important Sabbatian text to emerge from it, *ve-Abo ha-Yom,* similar though it was in many ways to Hayon's work. Instead the primary source material was a colorful collection of anecdotes and attributions, part of a far reaching endeavor to gather testimony about the Sabbatians, the practice of *Gebiat Edut* [Gathering Testimony].

To what extent can these testimonies by their opponents be used to draw an accurate picture of the Sabbatians? As with any polemical hyperbole, allowances must be made for some degree of alteration and embellishment of the facts. But we cannot simply dismiss the entire corpus of testimonial literature as a complete fabrication by rabbinic opponents. The testimonies accurately convey the tone in which the campaign was conducted and when read with a cautious eye, they provide an unusual illumination of the inner world of the crypto-Sabbatians.

Some of these glimpses, which would never have surfaced in any other sources, are exceptional. A letter of Leible Prosnitz addressed to Eybeschutz was forwarded to Hagiz by Seligmann b. Baer. One passage contains an insight into the sectarian psychology of secret messianic expectation:

> On that night I beheld a vision, and lo, Our Master, the true Messiah [Sabbatai Zebi], stood beside me. The presence of the Lord hovered over him and told him that the time was ripe to redeem Israel. Thereupon he and Nathan his Prophet set forth to redeem Israel. Our Master exclaimed, "How can I go, if Israel hears of it they will surely kill me, for they do not have faith in me." The Lord responded, "In that case, redeem only those who have faith." Then our Master, Zebi, Crowning Glory of Israel, said, "If I must redeem only the believers I would rather turn back home, for surely that would be a mockery among the Gentiles. I will wait until they shall all repent and become believers in me."

A much later testimony, which emerged during the Emden-Eybeschutz controversy, took the development of the sectarian psyche under siege to its farthest reaches. R. Jonah Land-Sofer testified that a Sabbatian had told him, "Sabbatai Zebi declared: 'Since the God of Israel did not choose to fulfill my messianic destiny, I will punish Him by causing thousands to abandon his faith." The author of this excerpt seems to have abandoned hope of fulfillment of Sabbatai's messianic mission. This prompted Land-Sofer to remark that they had "overturned ideas which had emerged from the primordial crucible, as Jesus of Nazareth did." Hagiz reported to R. Aryeh Leib that "the hypocrite Aaron Antones, of the coterie of R. Netanel in Norden, came to the lay leaders of Amsterdam and their upstart Bet Din, and told them that Moses our Master had appeared to him and told him that the year of redemption by Sabbatai Zebi was at hand." A letter written by Isaiah Hasid to Leible Prosnitz during the campaign was described as a "letter of consolation" dated "in the messianic era."

In addition to the messianic hopes of the crypto-Sabbatians, the testimonies described their thoughts and practices at this stage of the development of the sect. Hagiz cited an example of Leible Prosnitz' "lascivious and heretical" ideas:

> In this coupling, the Lord will pay no heed to anything because His thoughts are occupied by the *Shekhinah* [the female element within the divine presence]. . . . Therefore he will have removed his Providence from the lower realms and will delegate responsibility for these worlds to the Righteous One. The Righteous One will only watch over those who adhere to him. The 'Righteous One' is their appellation for Sabbatai Zebi, to whom they direct their prayers. . . . Many members of the sects believe that the Torah has been abolished, and it will continue to remain devoid of *mizvot;* that its violation is its fulfillment.

In Mannheim, one witness testified that a crypto-Sabbatian, "showed me a calendar of their festivals of which there were one hundred and two, and their chief holiday is the ninth of Ab [the traditional day of mourning]."[33]

The depiction of Sabbatianism as a perverse ideology and its adherents as perverted individuals supported the contention of their opponents that they should be cut off from the Jewish community as dangerous sectarians. Hagiz had made this argument during the Hayon campaign, and he continued to advance it in 1725. For this reason, the testimonies that were gathered were replete with reports that Sabbatians had indulged in the most deviant and devious behavior. Hagiz reported to R. Arye Leib that when Hayon had sojourned in Vienna, he committed adultery with a married woman and had children from her.

"R. Wolf Lissa, a wicked man . . . wanted to copulate with a married woman while she was menstruant [thereby violating two Biblical prohibitions simultaneously] and the rabbi of Bumsali told him that this would be a great *Tikkun* [Restoration]." In Mannheim an opponent of Sabbatians "observed through a crack in the door that R. Hirsch Kohen [a Sabbatian] was masturbating [in the study hall] . . . In great consternation he went to R. Hayim Hildesheim to report that the guardians of the study hall are in fact its destroyers. . . . R. Hayim replied that he knew of many worse acts."

In Poland, one witness testified to a different sort of profanation of the sacred:

> R. Nathan, head of the study hall, had a Torah scroll from which the name of God was omitted. Instead, he inscribed the name of

Sabbatai Zebi. There were approximately fifty souls who knew of this, R. Hayim of Zolkiew among them, and they did the same with their phylacteries. When they investigated him, he tearfully confessed; when it was all found to be true, they burned the scroll and the phylacteries. The communal scribe had contaminated many people with these phylacteries, and the communal leaders exposed him and whipped him. . . .

Near this community, in a town called Nadborni, the entire community turned to heresy, adhering to Sabbatai Zebi. Two members of the sect from Buczacz went to Nadborni, where they swapped wives until the wickedness came to light. They [the opponents of Sabbatianism] tried to procure the support of the magistracy. The house of R. Nathan was burned, no remnant of his study hall was spared, and he fled.

The second ban issued in Altona-Hamburg-Wandsbeck against Sabbatians, of August 8, 1725, emphasized that all Sabbatians were still under the severest form of excommunication. One may not approach within their "four ells," they may not be counted for any sacred rites, their wine and bread was prohibited like Gentile wine and bread, one may not intermarry with them. Their sons are bastards, and regarding their daughters the scriptures say, "Cursed is he who copulates with animals." Their burial should be like that of an ass, their corpses flung over the fields. Even if they desire to repent, the path will be barred.

In a letter to R. Arye Leib, Hagiz echoed the condemnation of the AHW decrees, adding, "But whereas those decrees have left the gates of repentance open to them, I cannot approach them in a conciliatory manner. We must lock the door securely. If they return of their own accord, so be it—but at present we must quarantine them and all those associated with them. They are worse than the Karaites for they persecute Israel and prolong our Exile."

This harsh tone and extreme approach elicited calls for moderation and normal relations with Sabbatians. Hagiz forcefully rejected the arguments that persecution of the Sabbatians would aggravate divisiveness in the already splintered Jewish community. "These are not our brethren, this is not like a battle between Judah and Israel."[34]

BLUEPRINT FOR CONTROVERSY: TECHNIQUES OF THE POLEMIC OF 1725

The fact that it had become necessary to mount another massive anti-Sabbatian campaign only a decade after the Hayon controversy indicated to the adversaries of Sabbatianism that the measures they had taken had not been effective enough. The Hayon campaign had succeeded in suppressing crypto-Sabbatianism only to have it surface with greater vigor a short time later. The architects of the anti-Sabbatian campaign of 1725 expressed impatience with half measures and a desire to effect permanent results, "so that we will not have to repeat our efforts every two years." They hoped their actions would leave "a lasting imprint on future generations with ordinances and drawn swords, over the public as well as individuals." For example, when the community leaders of Frankfurt decided to remove from circulation all kabbalistic and ethical works that may have been tainted by Sabbatianism, they decided to employ a communal agent who would circulate among the unsuspecting public and ferret out copies of the books. The leaders of the anti-Sabbatian campaign rejected this method as haphazard and inefficient. They recommended stronger action which would be broad and permanent. They suggested that all communal leaders, once alerted to the existence of these works, should band together and reach an agreement whose power would bind the public and individuals under severest penalties. The agreement should be well publicized and perpetually binding.

As in the Hayon campaign, correspondence remained the most effective means of gaining and maintaining support and contacts, of exchanging information, evidence, and other material. Hagiz played a central role in the development of these channels. On September 26, 1725, he wrote to R. Arye Leib, "I will send you this work entitled *ve-Abo ha-Yom el ha-Ayin*. It is a work replete with such lewdness and blasphemy, its like has never occurred to any sage or philosopher, even among the Gentiles and early pagans. It was sent to me by the chief of the rabbinical court of Berlin, who sounded the alarm to his colleagues in Frankfurt to no avail. Until now, no action has been taken save for the letter which I sent you." Hagiz also included an emotional appeal to R. Arye Leib: "Pious man, embrace the ways of your holy forebears. . . . Try to persuade all the sages of Poland to join you and let them spread the message by posting it with special emissaries to Germany, Turkey, and the land of Israel."

In another letter of November 2, 1725, Hagiz admonished, "I have already notified you of all the news in Ashkenaz, of the return of the serpent Hayon, and one R. Jonathan Eybeschutz, and Isaiah, son-in-law of Judah Hasid in Mannheim, who have misled Israel with their sinful talk, as I have elaborated upon *thrice in previous letters*. I have received no reply from your honor, and I do not understand why. I am concerned about the great distances and postal expenses which I have already incurred. I have repeated my earlier missive, supported by various other writs which are enclosed. . . . When they reach you . . . be zealous for the Lord as befits Him. . . . If not now when? A wise man like yourself will know how to take action which will leave permanent effect."

R. Ezekiel Katzenellenbogen, one of the initiators of the campaign of 1725, in an early letter of September 10, 1725, argued that the process of gathering individual approvals for each anti-Sabbatian pronouncement was costing too much time and effort. Individual, local efforts were of little value in the face of the ubiquity of Sabbatianism. "What they [the rabbinate of Frankfurt] have accomplished is insufficient. They have not even sent us—nor any other community—copies of the evidence which they have compiled." Instead Katzenellenbogen urged that all rabbis make a prior agreement that after one or two authorities have pronounced a ban, the names of the others would automatically, immediately, and unanimously be appended. Such instantaneous and widespread action would be sufficiently effective to combat their foe, an echo of Hagiz' belief in the power of the rabbis to accomplish anything if they united. Katzenellenbogen's suggestion that individual rabbis dispense with their prerogative to judge each case on its own merit was not adopted. Instead, whenever decrees were promulgated against Sabbatians, they were quickly copied and circulated to other rabbinic figures in the hope that they would be inspired to emulate the action.[35]

Many of the techniques used to combat and defame Sabbatianism in the polemic of 1725 were the same as those employed in the Hayon controversy. The most conspicuous contrast to the Hayon campaign was the absence of published polemical literature. Much of the Hayon controversy was conducted in print and designed to reach the largest possible audience. The only published works to have reached us from the campaign of 1725 are Hayon's *ha-Kolot Yehdalun* and Hagiz' *Lehishat Saraf*. This exchange between Hayon and Hagiz was more of a final salvo in the Hayon controversy than the commencement of a new affair.

The retreat from the printed polemic did not signify that the foes of Sabbatianism had become less aggressive. To the contrary, the barrier of silence had already been breached, and in many ways the campaign leaders of 1725 sought opportunities and took initiatives to combat Sabbatians which their predecessors had avoided. Hagiz urged his allies, "The time has come to ferret out the leaven of Israel by the glow of candles in all the nooks and crevices, so that it should never more be seen or found. The time has come to destroy all those who have destroyed the faith of the patriarchs." Instead of concentrating on literary polemics aimed at undermining the intellectual foundations of Sabbatianism, the polemic of 1725 was concerned with the social excision of Sabbatians from the Jewish communities in which they thrived. Whereas Hayon's *Oz l'Elohim* had spawned perhaps a dozen literary refutations, *ve-Abo ha-Yom el ha-Ayin* was never accorded such treatment. Despite its affinity to Hayon's work, it was not subjected to critical analysis by anti-Sabbatians in 1725 because it was never published and because the author's name did not appear on the manuscript. Without books or authors to attack, the focus of the new campaign against Sabbatianism shifted away from the texts to the social manifestations of its sectarian teachings.[36]

The polemical vehicle which best exemplified the direction of the campaign of 1725 is that of *Gebiat Edut*, the gathering and transcription of oral testimony. Joseph Prager's manuscript *Gahalei Esh*, preserved long segments of page after page of testimonies. Each testimony usually contained an anecdote portraying a Sabbatian belief or practice, generally transcribed in overtly hostile or derogatory tones. A particularly salacious anecdote or blasphemous quote was as valued by the anti-Sabbatians as any authoritative ban. The testimonies were copied and transmitted with great solemnity. Each one established the chain of transmission of the evidence. An example of the pedigree of one such anecdote: "The two writs mentioned above, and the testimony cited above, were transmitted to me by R. Seligmann b. Baer Cohen of Hamburg. They were sent to him by the community of Vienna and I affix my signature in testimony thereof. Moses Hagiz, September 16, 1725, Altona."[37]

Prager also included correspondence and chronicles written by Sabbatians. He believed that their very preposterousness would transform them into polemics against their authors. Prager realized that his manuscript unintentionally preserved an excellent rendering of the inner world of crypto-Sabbatians. As an antidote, he appended an early anti-Sabbatian account from *Ma'aseh Tobiah*.

The campaign of 1725 was initiated as a reaction to the rise of Sabbatian emissary activity. Sabbatian missionaries were often equipped with letters of introduction which openly referred to their mission. These emissaries fell prey to the zealous anti-Sabbatian spies, who even conducted searches of personal luggage and confiscated incriminating documents.

The reason for installing search squads in the hostels frequented by traveling emissaries in cities such as Prague and Pressburg was not to prevent Sabbatian mail from reaching its destination, but rather to copy and circulate it, to expose the continued existence of crypto-Sabbatianism. In September 1725, R. Issachar Ber of Cracow, then rabbi of Nicholsburg, wrote to R. David Oppenheim, R. Abli of Kovely, and Madochai Kempne to investigate the origins of letters attributed to R. Jonathan Eybeschutz which had "fallen" into his hands. Seligmann b. Bear of Hamburg gave Hagiz a copy of a letter written by Leible Prosnitz to R. Jonathan. The copy was made by Isaiah Hasid.[38]

Both sides went to considerable trouble to establish reliable channels of communication, to prevent the interception of their correspondence. In a letter to R. Aryeh Leib of November 2, 1725, Hagiz wrote that he was pressed for time in writing the letter because the carrier, Simon b. Leib, was on his way to Jaroslav, and he had promised to safeguard the documents until they reached their destination. He also advised R. Leib of a safe channel by which to convey his reply. "If you are able, send it through Jaroslav to the notable Isaac Raskes of Lissa who will relay it to his father-in-law, Hayim Weider of Lissa who is a son of the rabbinical judge Jonah Segal who resides here. It will surely reach me in that way. If you know of an alternative safe route, please use it."

Securing a reliable courier ranked second in importance only to securing prestigious allies. "An earlier letter I sent you [Hagiz to R. Arye Leib] via Dr. Portes, a resident here, and I have also written to his brother, president of the council, and he has promised to publicize this affair as well as to serve as a courier for the documents." Confidantes on both sides resorted to cryptic codes to prevent their content from being read by hostile eyes. "I cannot decipher the last line; perhaps it is a secret among intimates, so that only certain individuals would be able to decipher the signs which they have transmitted to one another."

Even the timing of the controversies appears to be one of the components of a successful strategy. Both anti-Sabbatian campaigns led by Hagiz were initiated during the summer months. While this may be sheer coincidence, several documents of the 1725 campaign mention that special vigilance was always warranted within the Jewish communities in the season preceding the High Holy days. This seems to have been a factor in Hagiz' initial decision to join Katzenellenbogen in this campaign. "Although I had promised myself not to attend to this matter [persecution of Sabbatians] so as not to contaminate my soul during these special days, nevertheless the sage [Katzenellenbogen] has expounded in his sermon that this is an obligation, so I will devote myself to it exclusively." Summer was also the season of most frequent travel. Both the itinerant Hayon and the yeshiva students-turned Sabbatian emissaries were more mobile in the summer months.[39]

LEAD MIXED WITH GOLD: CENSORSHIP AND THE ANTI-SABBATIAN CAMPAIGN

Although no overtly Sabbatian kabbalistic works were published at the time of the campaign of 1725, there was a renewed interest in kabbalistic works written by Sabbatians. Many such works contained Sabbatian allusions which might not be recognized today, but which were known and eagerly sought by eighteenth century Sabbatian sympathizers. During the Hayon controversy, Hagiz had been the foremost advocate of rigorous prepublication censorship by the rabbinate. In 1725, together with R. Ezekiel Katzenellenbogen he revived censorship as a means of suppressing Sabbatianism. Katzenellenbogen, as chief rabbi in Altona, drew upon other precedents for anti-Sabbatian censorship within Eastern Europe. In 1681, R. Ber b. Elhanan, in an approbation to *Keneh Hokhmah*, a book of kabbalistic homilies by R. Judah Leib of Pinsk, asked that "no new works be published unless they are cleared with me first . . . in order to crush the jaws of the wicked. . . . They have published novel works which our ancestors had never foreseen."

The history of the ban against *Or Israel* [Light of Israel] is instructive. Published in 1702 by R. Israel b. Aaron Jaffe, the book was "a commentary on many dicta of the *Zohar* . . . , the mystery of the order of emanation and an explication of the sacred writings of the AR"I." It contained many prestigious approbations, among them that of R. Abraham Broda who wrote that although he usually refrained from approving new books, and works of kabbalah in particular, he decided to deviate from his usual practice because "many of the disciples of my yeshiva, people of profound understanding, have testified that the author is . . . pious beyond reproach." R. David Oppenheim also provided an approbation. He too declared that while he hadn't seen the work, he relied upon the testimony of others.

A while after the book had been published, Jaffe revealed himself as a spiritualist with messianic pretensions. He claimed to have had celestial visions and revelations by the Prophet Elijah. He felt that he had been called upon to work toward the final redemption, and he traveled widely, collecting adherents and exhorting his audience to repent. The author's eccentric activities sealed the fate of his book. Moses Hagiz scrutinized it closely. His verdict: "I have found this work, *Or Israel*, guilty. It is tainted by Sabbatianism, pervaded by confusion; it is lead mixed with gold." Lead is a reference to the numerous instances of crypto-Sabbatian allusions. It was the gold which caused Hagiz great distress. He lamented that if not for the tainted alloy, the author would have ranked as a great kabbalistic scholar.

In a letter to Hagiz on September 10, 1725, Katzenellenbogen reported that he had ordered that an announcement be made in the synagogue that he would confiscate all works rumored to have hints of Sabbatianism. Among the books which must be turned over to him were all prayerbooks with the commentary *Keter Joseph* [Crown of Joseph], the popular abridged edition of the *SheLa"H*, as well as *Or Israel* [Light of Israel]. He requested that Hagiz investigate *Or Israel*, "*as well as all kabbalistic works written and published after 1666*, bearing in mind the agreement by the rabbinates of Prague and Frankfurt to issue a total ban against the study of such works."

The attack against individual works had become the starting point for a campaign to ban all kabbalistic works published after 1666. On September 26, 1725, Hagiz wrote to R. Arye Leib, "Your decree, and that of the Sage of Berlin, against the prayerbooks of R. Joseph and *against all other kabbalistic works printed from 1666 until today*, has been very effective. May it be God's will to excommunicate all those who believe in Sabbatai Zebi." A year later, on April 16, 1726, Katzenellenbogen wrote to R. Judah of Furth that he should "instruct the aforementioned sages not to give approbations to any work until a thorough search has been made, after the printing has been completed, particularly for kabbalistic works."[40]

THE COUNCIL OF FOUR LANDS

Hagiz' most far-reaching effort to gain allies was his attempt to gain the support of the Council of Four Lands, the supreme rabbinic synod of Poland. Although its power had waned considerably over the past century, it remained the most prestigious rabbinic body. The Council had followed the development of crypto-Sabbatianism since its inception. In 1670, shortly after the Sabbatian movement had gone underground, the Council issued a decree in Gromniz against Sabbatians, accompanying the pronouncement with blowing of the *shofar* [ram's horn] and extinguishing the candles. The text of this ban has not survived, but it is mentioned in a second ban issued the following year, on September 7, 1671, by the Council at its annual meeting in Jaroslav. The text of this ban is remarkable for the very sharp tone it employed to ostracize members of the Sabbatian sect. It is the first document to use the term "sect" [kat] to refer to Sabbatians. It called the sect a danger to the welfare of Jews, and empowered local communal officials "to persecute those people, and punish them with abuse and monetary fines, with jail; and even to remand them to the justice of the Gentiles. These people should forever be separated from their communities. . . . If harm befalls them, they should not be rescued."

The effect of the bans on stemming the growth of crypto-Sabbatianism in Eastern Europe was negligible—even the scribe who penned them was a Sabbatian. In 1705, the Council issued another ban at the request of R. Pinhas Moses Harif of Lvov against Hayim Malakh, a Sabbatian emissary. During the Hayon campaign of 1714, Hagiz and Zebi had turned to the Council to issue a condemnation of Hayon's work, but no reply is to be found in their records.[41]

In 1725, when the geographical locus of the campaign shifted eastward, Hagiz was possessed by the need to obtain a condemnation of Sabbatians by the Council of Four Lands. In August 1725 Hagiz wrote to the Council and implored it to support the campaign. Fully half of Hagiz' letter to the Council (which covers four manuscript pages) is devoted to glowing honorifics. Even compared with standard rabbinic practice, this is a prodigious amount. Hagiz invested the Council's potential pronouncement with vast importance, far beyond its actual power within the community. For Hagiz, the Council was the contemporary institution that came closest to his ideal rabbinate. Hagiz pleaded with the Council: "All these people [Sabbatians] merit the death sentence at the hands of a rabbinical court. Alas, from the day we were exiled, we have lost our sovereignty and the four capital punishments were abolished. Nevertheless, the guilt of the people has not dissolved, and only you have the power to break their spell."

The physician Dr. Isaac Portes, a member of the Council, was predisposed to favor Hagiz' request, as his brother in Altona was a confidant of Hagiz. An anti-Sabbatian tradition recorded by Jacob Emden identifies Portes as a fellow anti-Sabbatian: When Dr. Portes discovered that one of his dying patients was a crypto-Sabbatian, he refused to minister to the patient any further.

Despite this influence within the Council, Hagiz' entreaty was in vain. The rabbi of Teplitz, a supporter of R. Jonathan Eybeschutz, wrote that the Council of Four Lands would have acceded to Hagiz' request, but for the already considerable influence of Eybeschutz during the 1725 campaign.

There was a great tumult in the [Council of] Four Lands of Poland, which sought to excommunicate him [R. Jonathan] and he defended himself mightily and saved himself. . . . There have always been sages in Poland who refused to render distorted judgments before they had heard both sides. Several sages of Poland corresponded with Eybeschutz, . . . and they surely clarified the matter and determined that he was innocent.

Regarding the letter of Moses Hagiz, may his memory be a blessing, we become weary with the thought of committing all our rebuttals to paper. And how much more so will the listener laugh upon hearing that R. Jacob [Reischer] had written to Poland.

Jacob Emden, who turned to the Council repeatedly during his campaign against R. Jonathan Eybeschutz recalled, "Hakham R. M. H. [Hagiz] also wielded his pen and wrote a mighty letter to arouse the Council of Four Lands, which we cannot cite here because of its length. It, too, was not effective because the sages permitted [the situation] to fester. . . . All was in vain."

Although the Council of Four Lands did not participate in the anti-Sabbatian campaign of 1725, its earlier bans against the sect were recalled. On July 18, 1725, the synagogues of Amsterdam issued a ban against Sabbatians which noted, "At that time, the . . . Council of the Four Lands of Poland avenged the honor of God and excommunicated the sect . . . and they did not rest until they had banished the evil sect from all of Poland."[42]

FOR THE SAKE OF HEAVEN: THE INDIVIDUAL ZEALOT IN THE CAMPAIGN OF 1725

The campaign against Sabbatianism in 1725 presents another opportunity to evaluate the role of the individual rabbi, working outside the official communal structure, in Jewish communal life. The historian Jacob Katz has commented that the role of Rabbis Jacob Sasportas, Moses Hagiz, Jacob Emden, and Elijah, Gaon of Vilna, was necessarily limited because they stood outside the communal organization and their authority was based on voluntary supracommunal recognition. From the case of Hagiz, we can argue that their power derived precisely from their freedom from communal constraints. Their function was to influence and activate those who held the reigns of power to use it in support of the causes they championed.

The first steps against Sabbatians in 1725 were taken by R. Ezekiel Katzenellenbogen, chief rabbi of Altona-Hamburg-Wandsbeck. Hagiz' first letter to him has not been preserved, but we can reconstruct the main points of its contents from Katzenellenbogen's reply. Hagiz had written to applaud Katzenellenbogen's efforts, and to suggest additional means to curb crypto-Sabbatianism, among them the rigorous censorship of Sabbatian books. In his reply of September 10, 1725, Katzenellenbogen placed the burden of the campaign squarely on Hagiz' shoulders. His reason:

> I am a very busy man, I have no leisure whatsoever, I am engaged in the study of the Torah and burdened by public affairs while your honor [Hagiz] is free from one of these obligations, for *you do not bear the burden of the public.* Therefore it is incumbent upon you to investigate thoroughly. . . . Use your leisure to inquire into all kabbalistic works written and published after 1666.

Katzenellenbogen argued that he was a professional rabbi, while Hagiz was the professional zealot who occupied a special role outside the parameters of the institutional rabbinate.

Hagiz had not been seeking to launch this anti-Sabbatian campaign at this juncture in his life. He had recently settled in Altona, and he desperately needed community support. Indeed, he later bemoaned the fact that this role in the campaign had cost him important good will:

> I have not undertaken this for my honor . . . I am a stranger in the land; I have not been appointed as an official, nor have I been granted citizenship. I have been repudiated in the eyes of the Sephardim. . . . I have suffered, yet I accepted it joyfully for the sake of Heaven.

Moreover, Hagiz often wrote during this period that his ailing health caused him to neglect important business. Nevertheless, once the battle had been joined, as in the case with the Hayon controversy, Hagiz could not restrain the inner imperative that pushed him to its forefront.[43]

CHAPTER 7

The Luzzatto Controversy

 THE CONTROVERSY over Moses Hayim Luzzatto was the last major campaign conducted by Hagiz. The affair began in late 1728, and was revived in 1735 after a hiatus of several years. It was during this time that Hagiz reached the apogee of his literary and polemical careers. The Luzzatto campaign was a fitting climax to the progression of polemical wars orchestrated by Hagiz. Luzzatto, the most complex target of all Hagiz' campaigns, was a creative genius, blessed with spiritual and literary gifts. He was posthumously hailed as the father of modern Hebrew literature, a precursor of Hasidism, an explicator of Lurianic kabbalah, and a pillar of the ethical *mussar* movement. Because his spirituality and its relationship to Sabbatianism was obscure to Hagiz and his rabbinic allies, it was necessary for them to redefine the objectives of their campaign against heresy. It would be impossible to deliberate the choices that confronted Hagiz in his campaign without portraying the object of his pursuit.

Moses Hayim Luzzatto was born in Padua, in 1707, to a prominent and affluent Italian Jewish family. No efforts were spared to give him the best education. Among his early teachers of classical Jewish subjects were rabbis Isaiah Bassan and Isaac Cantarini. He received instruction in contemporary Italian culture and classical languages and literatures. According to Bassan, he had started to study kabbalah intensively when he was fourteen. His first book, *Leshon Limudim*, a work on Hebrew rhetoric, was published when he was seventeen. In it, he wrote that every word in the Sacred Language (Hebrew) possessed a spiritual dimension in addition to its conventional meaning; the rich, imaginative inner spiritual world which he inhabited was evident in his earliest writing.[1]

THE MAGGID

Luzzatto believed that he was chosen for a special destiny, his mission nothing less than to facilitate the cosmic restoration. Such a destiny required divine affirmation; for Luzzatto in the form of visitations by a *maggid*, a divine apparition or angel appointed to respond to the questions of man. For years, Luzzatto prepared himself to receive these visitations by reciting *Yihudim*, formulae of unity.

Luzzatto recorded the circumstances of his first revelation in an intimate diary:

> It occurred on . . . [May 21, 1727] as I was immersed in one yihud. I fell into a slumber, and upon awaking I heard a voice saying "I am descending to reveal the hidden secrets of the Holy King." For a short while, I stood trembling, then I revived myself. The voice did not cease, but revealed a secret to me. The next day, at the same time, I tried to be alone in the room, and the voice returned with another secret, until it revealed to me that it was a maggid sent from Heaven. He taught me private yihudim upon which to meditate in order to procure his presence. I could not see him, only his voice spoke through my mouth, and later he gave me permission to ask things of him. After three months, he gave me private tikkunim [restorative prayers] to recite each day in order to merit the revelation of Elijah. Then Elijah appeared and announced . . . that [Metatron] the grand minister [of Heaven] would appear. . . . From that time, I recognized each one, although sometimes souls revealed themelves to me whose names I did not know.[2]

The name of the maggid was Shamuel "servant of the Lord and guardian of the portals of ultimate wisdom." According to one eyewitness account, Luzzatto "fell onto his face, resting it in his hands on the table approximately half an hour. Then he stood, quill in hand, writing rapidly in a very brief time . . . a folio . . . of the secrets of the Torah.[3] Luzzatto's soaring spirit did not stop at Elijah and Metatron, in themselves attainments of which his predecessors scarcely dared to dream. He reported the appearance of the souls of Abraham, Adam, the King Messiah, and Moses, the faithful shepherd. Contrary to claims made by his disciple, Luzzatto claimed that he had no control over, or foreknowledge of, which of these figures would appear to him.

In addition to a diary recording the appearances of the maggid, of which only fragments have survived, Luzzatto wrote other works at the behest of the maggid. According to his own testimony, three substantial works were already written before the first appearance of Elijah, in the first months of the maggid's association with him. Among the works written under maggidic influence Luzzatto listed a commentary to Ecclesiastes consisting of over one thousand closely written pages, a book of tikkunim over two hundred pages long, and many other treatises. All the works were written in the style and language of the *Zohar*.[4]

Shortly after receiving the maggidic confirmation of his unique mission, Luzzatto joined a secret circle, *Hebrah Mebakshei ha-Shem*, in whose confines he would conduct his intense spiritual life. The special vision which informed the structure and activities of the circle contains the key to integrating the various aspects of Luzzatto's legacy. Details of the secret proceedings and purpose of other closed circles within Italian Jewry are usually scarce; we are fortunate that the reverse is true of Luzzatto's confraternity. In addition to voluminous writings, many important features of the group have survived: the membership lists, the function and position of every member, their special seating configuration, their private annual calendar and daily schedules. From this material, we can learn much about the sources and precedents which influenced Luzzatto's vision.[5]

The association was formally bound by a "contract of unity" (*Shetar Hitkashrut*), which obligated the members to certain conditions and duties. The recension of this document, which has survived, was written in January of 1731 after the publicity and persecutions were well under way. There is an earlier record of the circles' membership: In a letter to his teacher, R. Isaiah Bassan, of January 15, 1730, Luzzatto listed the members of his inner circle. The signatures on the contract differ in sequence and substance from the earlier listing. There are references to a *Book of Covenant*, including details not found in this contract. Thus, it appears that an earlier contract, or several, preceded the contract of 1731.[6]

Although at first he had not revealed the secret of the maggidic visitations to any person, Luzzatto later began to initiate his contemporaries, with the approval of the maggid. The first two members of Luzzatto's circle "who were privy to every secret and could penetrate innermost" were Isaac Marini and Israel Hezekiah Treves. The father of Isaac Marini, Sabbatai Hayim Marini, had been Luzzatto's teacher. He was the chief rabbi of Padua, a disciple of Samson Morpurgo and Isaac Cantarini, as well as an eminent physician. Isaac's membership in Luzzatto's circle seems to have been the cause of tension between father and son at first, but Sabbatai later became a friend and staunch supporter of the group.[7]

Luzzatto's affection for Marini is evident in a long poem he composed in honor of Marini's wedding. Marini, in turn, showed great respect for Luzzatto, and became very protective of him. He defended Luzzatto's controversial writings, arguing: "Surely if we had come upon them without knowing who had written them we would have said, 'Only a holy man of God could have written these, for the truth is evident in them.' "[8] Marini interceded voluntarily to make peace between Luzzatto and Bassan when their relationship became strained. Marini's name does not appear in the same position in the "covenant of unity" because he was not in Padua at the time it was signed.[9]

The second initiate into Luzzatto's secret world was Israel Hezekiah b. Michael Treves, whom Luzzatto considered to be his closest confidant. In the contract of unity, Treves replaced Marini as the first in importance after Luzzatto. In the special seating configuration, Treves was seated first on Luzzatto's right side, to symbolize his first-rank status.

The third initiate into the circle, Moses David Valle, central figure of the *hebra* from which Luzzatto's circle evolved, occupied a position of particular eminence in the secret life of the group. Although he appeared third on Luzzatto's list of January 1730, his name was not included among those who signed the covenant one year later, nor was a seat assigned to him in the special configuration. Yet, it is clear that he still belonged to the group at that time—he was one of those appointed to monitor its daily sessions. Valle did not sign the contract because as a senior participant and the only member of the group to display true creativity in addition to Luzzatto, he was not placed in a peripheral position to Luzzatto.[10]

Other members of the inner circle include Jacob Forte [Hazak], whose special strength in the group was as "the scholar who could judge and was expert in the laws." Forte [Hazak] sat on the right side of Luzzatto in the special configuration. Another member, Isaiah Romanin, signed letters of praise as the scribe of the Yeshiva of Padua. Neither Romanin, nor the physician Mordechai Ferarese, the next initiate on Luzzatto's list, signed the covenant one year later. But the last two members listed, Yekutiel Gordon and Solomon Dina, both remained prominent within the group, especially Gordon.

REDEMPTION THROUGH THE EYES OF LUZZATTO

The maggidic revelations, and the carefully ordered bonds of his circle, were the vehicles for Luzzatto's spiritual mission. His sodality modeled itself after a hallowed paradigm in which a circle of illuminati gather around a central figure for the purpose of redeeming the world and restoring the primordial harmony. The original model for this mythical drama is the Biblical Moses and his transmission of the Law at the convocation at Sinai. Each successive attempt at redemption through dissemination of an illuminating lore was informed by this image of Moses.[11]

Two successive reenactments stand out in Luzzatto's writings: that of Bar Yohai in the Zohar, the canonical text of the kabbalah, and of Isaac Luria in the hagiographic account *Toledot AR"I*. The character of Bar Yohai is explicitly developed in the Zohar as a parallel to Moses, the Law giver, as in the following exerpts:

> R. Simon [bar Yohai] sat . . . and explicated the secret lore, his face illuminating as the sun, the words reaching the heavens . . . Thus they sat for two days, they neither ate nor drank. On this, R. Simon pronounced: "And he remained there with God forty nights, and forty days." If we were able to sustain ourselves for a short hour in this way, Moses . . . all the more so.[12]

> What is written about Moses? "And the entire nation would see a column of cloud standing at the entrance of the tent [signifying the presence of Moses] and the people rose and each bowed at the entrance to his tent." It is meet for Moses, faithful prophet, superior to all prophets in the world, and for that generation, who received the Torah on Sinai . . . But here, in this generation, it is due to the superior merit of R. Simon that miracles be revealed through him.[13]

In the Zohar Bar Yohai is referred to as "Holy Spark," meaning a spark of the soul of Moses. Both are givers of a Torah and both deliver their generation from darkness into light. According to the Zohar, the soul of Moses is reborn in each generation, and it will play a crucial role in the messianic era. Ultimately, Luzzatto would return to the compelling image of the original Moses as his primary identification:

> The innermost light was not brought forth until the advent of Rashb"i [Bar Yohai], . . . [because] he is a spark of Moses our teacher, may he rest in peace; but in truth Moses was the original and the more important. It is Rashb"i who was from his root.[14]

The Zohar contains several narrative segments in addition to its core of Kabbalistic lore. The most important for Luzzatto were the sections known as the *Idra Rabbah* [Great Assembly] and the *Idra Zuta* [Small Assembly]. The *Idrot* provide a reverently detailed description of a ceremonial assembly at which the participants were initiated into secrets pertaining to the final redemption. They were characterized by an elaborate oath of secrecy, an extremely selective choice of participants, and great hesitation before the secrets were revealed:

> These sacred teachings, which have not been revealed until now, I wish to reveal in the presence of the Shekhinah . . . Until now they were concealed within my heart so that I may enter with them into the World to Come. I will make the following arrangement among you: R. Aba will write, R. Eliezer, my son, will repeat, and the others will think it in their hearts.[15]

The generation of Bar Yohai, principal figure of the Zohar, was described as mired in darkness and devoid of knowledge of God. The secret lore which he disseminated became the turning point, at which the world began its ascent out of darkness and toward the ultimate illumination. The secret lore was not in itself the final redemption, but it served to sustain the world until that time.[16]

The Zohar proper concludes with the death of R. Simon bar Yohai. Two sequels, the *Tikkunei Zohar* and *Ra'aya Mehemna*, take place in the realm of souls. Any figures from the past can, and do, appear, especially Moses and Elijah. In these final segments, the theme of redemption linked to the spread of kabbalistic lore is fully developed. This illuminating wisdom is the vehicle for the cosmic restoration and permanent banishment of darkness, and its dissemination represents the triumph of the spiritual over the material world.[17] Luzzatto's identification with this paradigm is evident from the fact that he wrote a new Zohar, *Zohar Tinyana; Adir ba-Marom*, a commentary on the *Idra Rabbah*; and *Tikkunim Hadashim*, modeled after the *Tikkunei Zohar*.[18]

In his commentary to the *Idra*, Luzzatto emphasized the parallels between Moses and Bar Yohai, the redemptive function of Bar Yohai's written lore, the Zohar, and the important role played by Bar Yohai's circle.[19] Luzzatto regarded the circle of Isaac Luria [AR"I] in Safed as the closest attempt to bring the redeeming illumination after Bar Yohai's. Luzzatto's perception was not imposed on unyielding material—*Toledot AR"I*, the hagiography of Luria, which was widely circulated in eighteenth century Italy, linked Luria's role as disseminator of kabbalistic lore to his redemptive mission: "He will begin to redeem the souls of

Israel from the kelippot and the lore of the kabbalah will be revealed through him."[20]

Toledot AR"I asserted that there had been no worthy successors of Bar Yohai until Luria[21] and explicitly developed the parallels between Luria and Bar Yohai.[22] Luria's circle emulated the Zoharic circle of Bar Yohai. A gathering of Luria's disciples signed a covenant of unity and secrecy, promising not to reveal the secrets that had been unveiled to them, a faithful re-creation of the scene from the *Idra*.[23]

Luzzatto's work is replete with comparisons and parallels between Moses, Bar Yohai, Luria, and himself, or some of these to one another. Moses had a son, Eliezer, as did Bar Yohai. *Toledot AR"I* explicitly assigned the role of Eliezer to R. Hayim Vital, Luria's foremost disciple. The first two initiates into Luzzatto's circle, Isaac and Israel Hezekiah, bore the same names as members of Bar Yohai's circle.

Each potential redeemer believed that he would receive an illumination greater than that of his predecessor. Thus, according to *Toledot AR"I*, Luria was told that he would obtain a more profound understanding of Zoharic matters than Bar Yohai himself. When comparing himself to Luria, Luzzatto pointed out that his lore was superior to that of Luria in one crucial respect. Like those of Moses and Bar Yohai, his illuminating lore had been eternalized in a written canon, an achievement which Luria had never merited.[24]

The biographies of Moses, Bar Yohai, and Luria include periods of living without their mates so that they could consecrate their entire beings to the love and devotion of the *Shekhinah* [in kabbalah, Shekhinah is the feminine principle of the sefirot].[25] Luzzatto refused to take a wife long past the age deemed proper for him. In the Zohar, only Moses and Bar Yohai were privileged to consummate the union with the Shekhinah as a literal mythical act, not just in a symbolic manner. In his work *Tikkunim Hadashim*, written in 1729 while still a bachelor, Luzzato received a message from primordial Adam who had appeared to him. The message underscored the difference between Luzzatto's permanent mystical unity with the *Shekhinah*, and the more ephemeral unions attained by other mystics:

> The progenitor of all forefathers, primordial Adam, arose and said, "Fortunate art thou . . . for other human beings must sever themselves from that supernal place during their sojourn on earth, but although you have descended into the world, you do not separate yourself from the Shekhinah at all, just like Moses, Faithful Shepherd."[26]

Only after the *Shekhinah* had been partly restored did Luzzatto enact the consummation of his union with an earthly ceremony. When Moses Hayim Luzzatto married Zippora, daughter of R. David Finzi of Mantua, on August 29, 1731, the parallel to the Biblical union of Moses and his wife Zipporah was duly noted by participants in the wedding. More importantly, Luzzatto perceived his marriage on earth to be a reflection of the union between himself and a celestial bride, the *Shekhinah*.[27] It was no coincidence that Luzzatto's circle performed "a comedy of the war of Gog" [the apocalyptic battle] as the wedding entertainment.

Although many of Luzzatto's writings deal with the process of redemption and his own role in it, Luzzatto is understandably circumspect in this matter. In his other written works on the subject, especially *Ma'amar ha-Geulah*, "Treatise on Redemption" and *Adir ha-Marom*, Luzzatto invited his more perceptive readers to decipher his code. The works are replete with exhortations to read between the lines: "I will set forth the great mysteries of those times [redemptions] but because they are such great secrets I cannot be very explicit. I will say only the minimum . . . and you [the reader], comprehend very well."[28]

However, in several poems in *Tikkunim Hadashim* and in his treatise on his marriage contract, Luzzatto identified himself directly as the redeemer. In these works, Luzzatto progressed from believing himself to be an epigone of Moses to an actual transfiguration into Moses.[29]

Luzzatto's plan in "Treatise on Redemption" for the gradual unfolding of the redemption is of special interest. As with the previous redemptions of Moses and Bar Yohai, it would come at a time of "profound darkness for Israel, when they have no consolation for their anguish and distress." Elsewhere, Luzzatto had established that his own time was such a period of darkness.[30]

Israel's sins had caused a complete obstruction of the divine flow of illumination, manifested in the lower world as the exile of Israel. Luzzatto described the inner development of Jewish history as a struggle to restore the original flow:

> The channels of heavenly influence . . . were sealed at the time of its [the Temple's] destruction . . . How many 'restorations' were set for Israel during their exile. The restoration of the Mishnah . . . the Talmud . . . the Midrashim . . . all were necessary for their particular time . . . but the restoration of the *Zohar* stands out among the rest. The *Zohar* is the drop of seminal essence that flows from the yesod [one of the ten *sefirot*]. When sufficient merit

accumulates for the seminal drop to reach the lowest world, then the great Restoration will have been completed for all. Bar Yohai was worthy to be the vessel to continue this restoration, and so he composed the *Zohar;* but in truth only one fraction of illumination emerged from that level of restoration. It sustained Israel and the world during the period of exile. But the Ultimate Restoration should be a ceaseless flow . . . Yet after Bar Yohai the "other side" came and sealed it off. Thus, [the *Zohar*] was only a temporary restoration . . . Until AR"I, when there was an illumination similar to that of Bar Yohai . . . Now, in God's desire to bestow good upon his people, He wishes to release another restoration similar to the *Zohar*, a seminal illumination, *and in His kindness, He chose me.* [my emphasis][31]

LUZZATTO'S SELF-PERCEPTION as the conduit of divine illumination in his generation contained the seeds of conflict with members of the rabbinic and scholarly hierarchy. Shortly after he had established a regular routine with the maggid, Luzzatto had boasted: "I have been permitted to inquire and to know any matter pertaining to our Holy Torah, barring none."[32] Given such direct access to sacred knowledge, Luzzatto could circumvent the more conventional means of attaining it, leading to conflict with members of the rabbinic and scholarly establishment. Luzzatto's account of the sequence of illuminations implied that sacred knowledge before his time was essentially flawed. In his "Treatise on Redemption" he characterized the entire diaspora period as devoid of Torah: "The gravest damage wrought by the exile was the concealment of illumination; on account of this, the Torah was absent from Israel."[33] Further in the treatise, Luzzatto qualified this statement by allowing that several "tiny apertures" were left open through the mercy of the Shekhinah so that the world should not be engulfed in complete darkness. An imperfect lore emanated from these apertures throughout the exile. "The Shekhinah would materialize as the Sages of the generations, and in that form would shed light upon Israel."[34] At best, then, Luzzatto characterized the Torah scholars of the ages as purveyors of a flawed illumination. Those few among them who understood their role in the cosmic restoration could contribute to it if their study was devoted to that purpose: "The only effective engagement in Torah is that which is undertaken with the motive of restoring the Shekhinah."[35] Even other Kabbalists who did not attempt to restore the primordial illumination as Bar-Yohai did, were isolated and ineffective.[36]

IN THE PUBLIC EYE

As long as Luzzatto's views were confined to privately circulated writings, his opinions caused no disturbance. In the summer of 1729, the nature of Luzzatto's circle became public knowledge. The manner in which Luzzatto came to the attention of the rabbis and his subsequent interaction with the most prominent among them led to open conflict. In a step carefully orchestrated by Luzzatto himself, Yekutiel Gordon, "commander of the army" of the circle sent a letter describing Luzzatto's unique spiritual attainments to a Viennese rabbi.

The letter began as a reverent testimonial to Luzzatto, "A young man, twenty-three years of age, . . . my teacher and master, holy spark, man of God, R. Moses Hayim Luzzatto." It also contained specific information on Luzzatto's activities and goals:

> The angel revealed to him the secret of bringing the Academy on High down to him. It ordered him, with the approval of the Holy One, Blessed Be He, and the Shekhinah, to compose a book of splendor titled *Zohar Tinyana* [New Zohar] for the great restoration [Tikkun] which is known among us. . . . At his command, Elijah appears immediately and reveals his secrets, as well as Metatron, [Moses] the Faithful Shepherd, grandfather Abraham, Rabbi Hamnuna the Elder, and the known Elder, and often, the King Messiah and primordial Adam. He has already completed a work on Ecclesiastes, marvelous indeed, and now he is commanded to compose seventy *tikkunim* on the verse "and all the mighty arm," the last verse in the Torah . . . He has also composed three volumes on the Torah, all in the language of the Zohar. He knows the '*gilgulim*' [transmigrations] and *tikkunim* [restorations] of every soul . . . nothing is hidden from him . . . No one knows of this except our group. . . . *Moses and Metatron have shown that many verses that have been expounded to apply to R. Simon bar Yohai, author of the Zohar, can apply to him as well. They [Luzzatto and Bar Yohai] are comparable in every respect, as has become apparent to all, and no one has merited this distinction since the time of Bar Yohai.*[37] [my emphasis]

The reaction to the revelation of the secrets of Luzzatto's circle was divided. Rabbi Jaffe, the first recipient of Gordon's letter, reacted with alarm rather than delight. He sent a copy to R. Ezekiel Katzenellenbogen, chief Ashkenazic rabbi of Altona-Hamburg-Wandsbeck, with his own introductory letter that has not been preserved. Katzenellenbogen forwarded the letters, "To my friend, the illustrious R. Moses Hagiz, the acknowledged sage in zealotry for God."[38]

The information contained in Gordon's letter was the first introduction of Luzzatto and his circle to public, and rabbinic, awareness. Hagiz' knowledge of the existence of the circle and its activities was based solely on the information contained in Gordon's letter. Hagiz assumed that Luzzatto was a crypto-Sabbatian even though he had no evidence to that effect. The letter was addressed to R. Mordechai Margaliot-Jaffe, a scholar in Vienna. Hagiz charged that the letter had fallen into Jaffe's hands accidentally; that Gordon had intended the letter for a R. Mordechai Pizinek, "a wealthy man and a credulous fool," possibly Hagiz' euphemism for a Sabbatian. Although it might appear that a "wealthy fool" would make a more likely destination for a letter intended to garner support for the group, the text of the letter contradicts Hagiz' charge. It is addressed to R. Mordechai Jaffe, and even contains a play on his name. Moreover, a similar letter was sent to another rabbi.[39]

THE CONTROVERSY

On November 1, 1729, Hagiz sent a copy of Gordon's letter to the rabbinic leaders of several communities to which he had appended a postscript:

"It is incumbent upon you, bedrock of Israel, teachers and rabbis, sages and leaders of the Jewish communities in the Diaspora to rend [your garments, as a sign of mourning] *over this letter*, to inquire and investigate, and to uproot *this evil sect* before its harm spreads to the masses. Regard all the members of this evil sect as persecutors of Israel."[40] From Hagiz' note it is clear that he had no information regarding the Luzzatto circle other than that which appeared in Gordon's, and perhaps Jaffe's, letter.

Gordon's letter alluded to Sabbatianism by admonishing Jaffe in advance not to compare Luzzatto to other "false affairs." We cannot know whether Jaffe expanded upon this point. By referring the matter to Hagiz, an inveterate anti-Sabbatian, Katzenellenbogen implied that the activities of the group fell within Hagiz' purview.

Luzzatto wrote a letter of self defense to Katzenellenbogen. In it he enclosed a Kabbalistic treatise which he had written. Hagiz judged this document, "to contain blemish and doubt. . . . The essence of his words constitute an apology for the apostasy of Sabbatai Zebi, whom they called "our Lord."[41]

Hagiz employed the suspicion of Sabbatianism to recruit allies. To Morpurgo he wrote:

The upheaval began anew in Padua when one or two of the Polish men [Gordon] caused a commotion by writing deceitful letters to distant places. This is more harmful to the masses than all of the deceptions which have preceded. . . . I remember the valor . . . which you demonstrated in the holy war against the serpent [Hayon] . . . Whom shall we send . . . to examine the youth of Padua? Yourself . . . and R. Abraham Segre . . . and R. Joseph Ergas [all participants in the Hayon campaign] . . . We must lead the masses away from this false illusion, for we have no peace from them. When we ask them, "Why do we need this trouble, regardless of whether it is true or false?" They respond, "Because the essence of his words supports the faith of Sabbatai Zebi!"[42]

Once the battle was joined, Luzzatto's enemies found other blemishes in him. He had immersed himself in the study of philosophy and other profane sciences. Many detractors focused on lacunae in his personal piety. Joseph Ergas pronounced judgment on this basis:

I am told . . . that he is learned in exoteric and esoteric [lore] but the fragrance of piety has never wafted over him. I asked whether he was married, whether he performed the ritual ablutions of the Sabbath Eve, and whether he was careful never to trim his beard, even with scissors, and to all these questions the reply was negative. . . . Yet, these are the pillars of spiritual attainment. . . . Why hasn't his maggid chastised him about these? If he does not uphold these pieties, his maggid cannot be a holy one.[43]

Luzzatto did not defend himself against any of these individual charges. He focused instead on the larger question underlying them: What preparations were necessary in order to merit divine communication? His opponents presumed that a lifelong immersion in piety and asceticism were prerequisites to the attainment of divine illumination. Luzzatto responded that many great scholars, and famed pietists, Benjamin Kohen among them, had deliberately cultivated this type of visitation, yet failed to achieve it. Moreover, there was a vast difference in ascetic preparation among those who did receive illuminations, such as Bar Yohai and Luria. He maintained that there could be no fixed formula which could guarantee this spiritual attainment, for if there would be one, masses of others would have succeeded in attaining it. The arbitrary nature of these visitations was proof that the Lord chose whom He pleased and specific preparatory routines were irrelevant to the process.

Hagiz' letter to the rabbinate of Venice soon reached Padua. His tender age notwithstanding, Luzzatto was politic enough to understand that Hagiz' interference could mean serious trouble and adverse publicity for his group. Shortly after Hagiz' letter arrived, Luzzatto wrote directly to Hagiz (at the maggid's behest), imploring Hagiz to desist from marking him as the target of another hate-filled campaign.[44]

In his letter, Luzzatto swore in the name of the Lord of Hosts that he sympathized with the motivation behind Hagiz' action, suspicion of Sabbatianism. Luzzatto protested, "Surely Your Honor should know that that is not my approach to God. . . . I hereby give notice today that I do not associate with sinners, nor take council with the evildoers who inscribe on the horn of the hart [*Keren ha-Zebi*, a reference to Sabbatians], 'We have no portion with the God of Israel.' " Luzzatto denied that he had claimed to be a prophet: "I am neither a prophet, nor son of a prophet, nor do I perform miraculous signs."

But Luzzatto did not deny the divine illumination which had been bestowed upon him, and affirmed that the facts in Gordon's letter were true: "The God of Israel has blessed me, not in accordance with my merit, but with great mercy as R. Yekutiel [Gordon] had written *in truth* in his letter . . . The Lord did not turn away from Israel even during the time when His face is hidden." He asked Hagiz to consider this il-lumination like the one which had been given to Luria and other "pure of heart," which were never considered "abominations in the eyes of God." Luzzatto rebuked Hagiz for being swift to condemn without conducting an investigation. Hagiz had dubbed his circle "an evil group" without the slightest familiarity with the members or their deeds. He asked Hagiz to verify the facts with other Italian rabbis, particularly Bassan, "my teacher and master who raised me like a father."

This was the only direct exchange between the adversaries throughout the long years of their conflict. In his reply, Hagiz addressed Luzzatto as "my son," and signed himself, "Your friend, if you so desire." He introduced himself to Luzzatto as a guardian of the faith:

Particularly in our times, when we are in the Diaspora, scattered defenseless among the Gentiles, it is as though we are all members of one community, responsible to guard the word. . . . Those who know me, know that I do not succumb to flattery. . . . All my life, it has been my desire to foster peace between Israel and their

Heavenly Father. . . . The sinners who have strayed have met their punishment.

Hagiz wrote that he had conferred with others regarding the contents of Luzzatto's letter, particularly with R. Ezekiel Katzenellenbogen. All concurred that Luzzatto's letter was replete with internal contradictions and vanities, but they agreed to judge him leniently because of his youth. Hagiz counselled Luzzatto, "for your own benefit and that of your circle . . . take my advice and abandon this entire path . . . If you have been given wisdom, don't rush the hour, for the fruit of haste is regret."[45] Hagiz did not disregard Luzzatto's personal appeal, but his reply rejected Luzzatto's claims and pleas.

Luzzatto wrote similar letters of self defense to others of Hagiz' allies—the rabbinate of Venice, and Samson Morpurgo—with similar results. Each side was already too committed to its position to allow the tentative words of conciliation to take root. The only exception was R. Emanuel Calvo of Livorno who answered with a glowing affirmation of faith in Luzzatto's illumination. Apparently, Calvo and some associates in the Livorno rabbinate were already predisposed to accept news of a maggidic appearance, although Calvo cautioned Luzzatto on the need for discretion. The obsequious tone of Luzzatto's direct letter to Hagiz: "From the lowliest of people, callow and debased . . . ," contrasted sharply with his arrogant and disparaging attitude toward Hagiz in other correspondence to other rabbis, just as Hagiz' soft tone to Luzzatto is belied by letters he wrote to other rabbis, such as that to R. Jacob Kohen Popers of Frankfurt. Luzzatto dismissed Hagiz' response coldly: "Here is the letter which the Hagis [a disparaging form] sent to me; you can see immediately that it is devoid of sense." And in another letter: "This fool Hagiz publicized the matter in his anger, without knowledge or wisdom, because he is a person who seeks controversy. I hope I will have muzzled his mouth with the letter I have written to him."[46]

R. Isaiah Bassan, even while harboring doubts concerning Luzzatto, shared Luzzatto's assessment of Hagiz. He belatedly cautioned Luzzatto, "If you write to him, do so with respect, so as not to cause strife, for he is easily provoked to quarrel and his tongue is like a burning flame."[47] When he defended Luzzatto to the rabbinate of Venice, Bassan did so by discrediting Hagiz. He characterized Hagiz' "scroll of doom" as hearsay, and accused Hagiz of a quick temper and baseless presumption of guilt. He compared Hagiz' response to Luzzatto with his role in the Hayon campaign.[48]

Luzzatto accused the rabbinate of being shallow and greedy, in contrast to pneumatics like himself: "The Sages of Italy are being lured by lucre, very few of them turn to the Lord truly, and they lack wisdom."[49] He openly stated his belief that the pedantic rabbis had become peripheral to the effort of securing the redemption. He presented his own followers as their replacement: "My associates are not people who engage in the Torah as a profession to become rabbis in Italy. They are simple people, but their souls are holy . . . My approach is not that of the other rabbis of our cities, and I must lead this generation according to its needs." What was the difference of approach between Luzzatto and the rabbis? Luzzatto explained: "I leave the straw and the chaff [the exoteric Torah] for the beasts [the rabbis], and I ingest only that which is worthy of human consumption [the esoteric Torah], as R. Simon bar Yohai has advised. Although many of our sages have not accepted this [that their primary pursuit should be the esoteric lore], I can only follow the truth."[50] Luzzatto chided Bassan:

> How could you abandon the innermost good, the brightest light, the choicest portion, to satisfy your soul with fieldgrass, which is the plain, exoteric sense of the Torah . . . The Shekhinah awaits her sons to come and lead her forth from the exile . . . and there is no one. . . . What pleasure can we give our Creator with great Pilpulim and many Codes? . . . True, laws are necessary for Israel . . . and we will set aside time for them because they are indispensable . . . but we will not, Heaven forbid, devote the lion's share of our time to them. Due to our sins, an evil situation exists: Most Sages of Israel have already become distant from the truth to pursue vain dialectics . . . They crave only money and honor.[51]

In a letter to Katzenellenbogen, Luzzatto drew the fateful conclusion from his attitude to the rabbinate: "There may be power among all the Sages of Germany and Poland. . . . But I have the power of the Holy One, Blessed be He, and the *Shekhinah*, and all the members of the Academy on High who illuminate my eyes with a divine light. Please do not disregard my words!" Here, Luzzatto expressed the distinction between institutional rabbinic authority and the redemptive power of direct divine illumination. His remarks were not lost on his rabbinic opponents.[52]

The first circulating open letter against Luzzatto was signed by R. Ezekiel Katzenellenbogen, "Spokesman of the Polish and German rabbinates;" Hagiz appended a postscript. It was addressed to the rabbis of Italy, directed especially at the rabbinate of Padua, Luzzatto's native city. Katzenellenbogen called the rabbis of Italy to arms:

Gather together and annoint your sheaths! . . . Do not hesitate to
nip this growth in the bud. You must be vigilant and investigate
thoroughly. . . . If you find evil, oppress and persecute him and
his entire group of sympathizers, and publicize it to all. If you feel
constrained from doing so [If external conditions did not permit the
mounting of this campaign] please inform us . . . for we have the
power to gather the holy flock, those who wage the war of God. . . .
In the company of the rabbis of Poland and Germany . . . we will
issue a herem.

Hagiz' postscript supported Katzenellenbogen's call for further investigation of Luzzatto. It too was written in a tone which assumed Luzzatto's
guilt. Luzzatto "sowed turmoil among the Jewish congregations with false
prophecies and hallucinations in order to prolong our exile."[53]
    Hagiz expended great effort to secure the support of the Italian rabbis
because the struggle would take place within the Italian Jewish communities. Many potential allies in Italy, reached by Hagiz' epistolary
campaign, were reluctant to join him. R. Jacob Aboab of Venice expressed the feelings of those who refused to condemn Luzzatto: "What
will we achieve by suppressing his fame? . . . So long as he casts no
blemish or doubt on our Torah or the words of our sages . . . and his
goal is straightforward . . .—to implant the fear of the Lord and observance of His commands into the hearts of the masses—what harm is
there in letting him continue?"
    Hagiz responded to Aboab with an emotional argument: "Begging your
pardon . . . I wonder how such words escaped from your pure quill?
Is that how your sainted father [R. Samuel Aboab] reacted when he stood
against Nathan of Gaza with his rabbinical court, and issued decrees and
abolished their words in public? Who will remove the dust from your
eyes?[54] Aboab infuriated Hagiz by providing copies of Hagiz' and Katzenellenbogen's confidential anti-Luzzatto propaganda to Luzzatto himself, so that he and Bassan could formulate responses to it.[55]
    The Italian rabbinate was reluctant to oppose Luzzatto for other rea-
sons as well. Luzzatto was a venerable Italian Jewish family, and R. Isaiah Bassan was one of the most eminent Italian scholars. The circle which
formed around Luzzatto was similar to many societies that had formed
within Italian Jewish communities. By attacking Luzzatto, Hagiz assailed
many pillars of Italian Jewish society, and the rabbinate was resistant to
his call. This did not deter Hagiz, who intensified his efforts to recruit
Italian allies.
    Hagiz especially hoped to enlist R. Joseph Ergas, preeminent Italian

Kabbalist, who had supported him in the Hayon campaign. Unbeknownst to Hagiz, Ergas had already become familiar with the Luzzatto case from another source. After the death of R. Benjamin Kohen, Ergas wrote a letter of condolence to Bassan, adding the following postscript: "Write to me regarding the nature of this man, Moses Hayim Luzzatto of Padua. I have heard that he has a maggid and that holy spirits are revealed to him; that he is writing a work on the Torah dictated by the maggid . . . and that you have seen it and greatly approved. . . . I have seen a letter he sent to the wealthy Cantarini who resides here . . . It is almost certain that all this is impossible."[56]

Bassan's response has not been preserved, but he apparently affirmed Luzzatto's illumination. Ergas investigated Luzzatto's works and found his original skepticism was warranted. In a confidential report to Bassan he wrote that while he had never believed it possible for maggidic revelation to occur to one who did not observe the basic pieties, his critical evaluation of Luzzatto's manuscripts confirmed his doubts:

> One of my informants gave me his "Treatise on Wisdom." I read it from beginning to end. All his words are derived from the works of other kabbalists—there is nothing new in them. Even the *kelalim* [Rules] which he wrote, that you have sent to me, are taken from the *Pardes Rimonim* of Cordovero, revised, and greatly condensed. . . . Even if we were to allow that he has some original material, why must we be convinced that it was taught by a maggid? We can say that he is very clever, with a fertile imagination. . . . As for his demurral that he hasn't yet reached half the level of AR"I . . . this is sheer arrogance. . . . The world is full of charlatans who appear innocent.[57]

Despite this devastating appraisal of Luzzatto, Ergas did not join Hagiz. He intended to travel to Luzzatto to conduct his own investigation, but he died before he could get there. Bassan betrayed Ergas' confidence by showing Ergas' scathing opinion to Luzzatto; perhaps this reflected his own inner doubts. Luzzatto dismissed Ergas' criticism, saying that "Ergas has not grasped the profundity of the *Kelalim*." Nevertheless, he said that he would welcome Ergas if he came to investigate. Two months later, Luzzatto gently chided Bassan for not informing him of the death of Ergas, "who has sustained you and all Israel."[58]

Hagiz also expended great effort to persuade R. Samson Morpurgo to join his campaign. In his first letter to Morpurgo, (mid April, 1730), Hagiz recalled Morpurgo's cooperation in the Hayon campaign. He lamented the loss of their colleagues who had died in the interim (Zebi in

1718, Briel in 1722), leaving the remaining figures to bear a greater share of the burden. He further evoked the bond of solidarity between them with an uncharacteristic and unprecedented diatribe against Polish Jewry. Ostensibly provoked by the poor quality of work produced by his Polish copyist, and the indiscretion of Yekutiel Gordon, a Polish Jew, the vituperative outpouring may have been a reflection of his anger with a failed ally, the Polish Council of Four Lands, which had refused to support him in his previous campaign.

"Just as in an earlier era, Torah emanated from Poland and all good flowed from there, today, in our generation they are thieves, tramps, and pickpockets. . . . One cannot rely on their testimony. Until now I have always covered for them, but I have grown weary of that, and now I must publicize their nature."[59] Hagiz urged Morpurgo to act as his representative in Italy, to enlist other rabbis and set the campaign on its course.

Morpurgo responded immediately to Hagiz, and addressed him as "zealot son of a zealot." He informed Hagiz that he had already known of Luzzatto from other sources, and had taken several steps on his own. He had written to R. Sabbatai Marini in Padua to advise Luzzatto and his circle to conceal news of their illumination, but Marini had rejected this advice on weak grounds: "Who can tell him to conceal when the heavens decreed that he should reveal?" Marini also admitted that even if he were inclined to impose strictures on Luzzatto, he did not have the power to enforce them. Morpurgo had seen Bassan's defense of Luzzatto, and he agreed with Hagiz that Bassan had reacted with improper haste and protectiveness in this grave matter. Morpurgo had found Luzzatto's own testimony regarding his illumination, "strange, almost in the realm of impossibility." Thus, Morpurgo had already been predisposed to join Hagiz in the matter of Luzzatto. Morpurgo wrote that he also undertook several additional actions as a result of Hagiz' letter to him. He distributed copies of the relevant documents to rabbis Abraham Segre in Casale, Joseph Ergas in Livorno, David Finzi in Mantua (shortly to become Luzzatto's fatherin-law), and to Bassan, as Hagiz had suggested. He urged them all to advise Luzzatto that he might continue teaching Torah, but he must say nothing at all of his revelations.

Morpurgo's support of Hagiz' fundamental position notwithstanding, the difference in temperament which had divided them in the past resurfaced in the Luzzatto case. Morpurgo argued that a slight amount of doubt as to Luzzatto's guilt still existed, as God's will was inscrutable. "So long as his writings and teachings remain concealed with him . . .

and I have no evidence of his guilt, . . . and since he has caused many to repent of their sins through his chastisements, I would remain silent, so as not to fan the flames." Morpurgo was emphatic in his insistence that if his own moderate approach would not be successful, Hagiz' method of unbridled controversialism was not an acceptable alternative. "One side declares 'pure', the other side 'impure' and there is no way to decide absolutely between the opinions. . . . If the spirit of persecution were to prevail, . . . it will become a consuming flame . . . until the entire Diaspora will be as a burning torch, with no one, God forbid, to extinguish it."[60]

Upon hearing that Morpurgo was inclined to join Hagiz, Luzzatto wrote to Morpurgo directly. He appealed to Morpurgo's sense of fairness and moderation, emphasizing that he had never taught the secret lore in public. He accused Hagiz of hypocrisy and fomenting quarrels, and he blamed Hagiz for spreading the news of the *maggid:* "Hagiz has arisen today to be my Satan, to arouse fury and great anger. If his silence had been as great as his tumult, the masses would know nothing of this. When his tract to the rabbinate of Venice arrived, the audience grew and the news traveled from there to here, for I had not uttered a word here [in Padua]. But even as R. Hagiz plotted evil, God intended it for good, . . . to revitalize many people." Luzzatto was especially incensed that Hagiz found Sabbatian coloration in the treatise he had sent to Katzenellenbogen. Luzzatto maintained that he had always taught publicly the error of those who believed in Zebi, and Hagiz had conjured a completely false interpretation of his words. Luzzatto urged Morpurgo, and all seekers of truth, to visit him, and promised that they would not return empty handed.[61]

As a result of Luzzatto's communication, Morpurgo strengthened his resolve not to persecute Luzzatto. "My heart tells me, and many agree with me, that if we do not oppose him with provocative words, the matter will fade of its own accord." He argued that rabbinic persecution would intensify Luzzatto's obstinacy, and create heresy and opposition to the rabbinate where none existed before. It had been the opinion of "those who amble in the secret gardens, the greatest Kabbalists" (R. Benjamin Kohen?) who had examined Luzzatto's writings that they were innocent of any deviations. Should he be wiser than the kabbalists and force Luzzatto to suppress his words? Whatever he did in the privacy of his own home was not the responsibility of an international rabbinic coalition. Only if he taught kabbalah in public would the doors be slammed in his face. Morpurgo also suggested a compromise whereby Luzzatto could pursue his revelations: he could emigrate to the Holy Land. There, his illumination could flourish in a pure and godly atmosphere without fear.

Hagiz vehemently rebutted Morpurgo's arguments for restraint. He characterized Kohen's "puzzling" approval of Luzzatto as "idle chatter, which contains no substance, and is contrary to truth and faith." Morpurgo remained unmoved. Once their positions had crystallized, Hagiz and Morpurgo continued to disagree throughout the controversy.[62]

VENICE

Hagiz prodded the rabbinate of Venice at first, and awakened it to its special role in the Luzzatto controversy. He sent a copy of Gordon's letter, with his own cover letter, to Venice, as he had to other cities. When the rabbinate of Padua made it clear that they would not join in the persecution of their native son, Hagiz assigned jurisdiction over Luzzatto to the Venetian rabbinate:

> Luzzatto should come with his staff and his haversack before the High Rabbinical court nearest him . . . the Yeshiva of Venice. It is their responsibility to gather the support of the parnassim and leaders of all the adjacent Italian communities including those of Mantua, Ancona, Rome and others . . . which had participated during the war against the serpent [Hayon] several years ago.[63]

When the rabbis of Venice received the letter of Hagiz by "German post," on November 18 or 19, 1729, they were thrown into turmoil, according to a document recording the day's events. A week later, they called a meeting to discuss Gordon's letter which Hagiz had included. Their debate concerned the fact that while the letter of Gordon contained "neither mention of prophecy nor of Sabbatianism, and only praise of the highest order [for Luzzatto], the note of Hagiz which was appended to it warned of irreparable harm to all Jewry if Luzzatto was not stifled at once. Some of the Venetian rabbis wanted to publicize the "coarse and harsh words" of Hagiz immediately, others wanted to do only what was right."[64] The rabbinate was polarized from the outset, between those who wanted to mount an intensive pursuit of Luzzatto, and those who preferred to proceed with caution. This rift was to divide the Venetian rabbinate throughout the Luzzatto affair. The lack of unity hindered its effectiveness and damaged its reputation.[65]

It was decided to summon the emissary of Safed, then in Venice, R. Raphael Israel Kimhi, to testify concerning Luzzatto. The emissary spoke glowingly in support of Luzzatto who, he testified, had been primed from his youth for a special destiny, as Gordon's letter affirmed. It came as no surprise that he had attained maggidic revelation. Luzzatto himself had never sought publicity. The emissary had been an eyewitness to these revelations on several occasions. He had seen Luzzatto fall on his face and proceed to fill folio upon folio with a swift, automatic writing, a supernatural feat. Since Luzzatto had never published or circulated these writings, but had confined his influence to a small select group, he was innocent of wrongdoing. If the rabbinate of Venice chose to persecute or harm Luzzatto in any way, the guilt would rest on their shoulders.

According to an anonymous source, Kimhi's words left a deep impression on their hearers. They were awed, overwhelmed, and frightened, and the rabbi of the Ashkenazim rose and proclaimed that God had chosen to visit Luzzatto. The session ended with a resolution to take two actions: the rabbinate would write to Gordon to insist that he cease publicizing Luzzatto's revelations and they would also write to Bassan, forwarding a copy of Hagiz' letter. The matter would rest in the hands of Bassan, and they would withdraw.

The inquiry to Bassan betrays no belligerence toward Luzzatto, but rather genuine puzzlement:

> A troubling message has come to us, a scroll of lamentation. It reports that there is a *prophet in our midst*, to whom all the mysteries and secrets [of the Torah] have been revealed. Mystery upon mystery emanate from him, and a maggid tells him all that is above and below. The celestial Host stands to his right side. . . . He knows the root of all things, the sparks of all souls . . . and can tell a person's most hidden secrets by looking at his face. He is viceroy to the King, Simon bar Yohai and he is composing a Zohar . . . and many other wondrous things, as you can see in the letter of his disciple to R. Jaffe of Vienna.
>
> Upon reading two or three paragraphs of that letter, our hearts trembled and we asked one another, "What has God wrought?"

They implored Bassan to undertake a thorough investigation to determine whether his disciple was a holy visionary or a charlatan.[66]

Before Bassan had a chance to respond to the Venetian rabbinate, he received a letter from Luzzatto, written on December 4, 1729. Luzzatto dismissed the Venetian rabbinate with the same arrogance he had displayed toward Hagiz. He informed Bassan that a sympathizer in the

Venetian rabbinate had broken rank, and revealed to him the contents
of their letter to Bassan. He asked Bassan to use his wisdom "to confound
the objections of Aboab, for they are troublemongers . . . They are wise
in their own eyes, but they lack true wisdom, which is why they rattle
about so. The pure of heart, even in Venice, are already acknowledging
the truth."[67] Later, Luzzatto revealed to Bassan that his informant had
been Solomon Zalman of Lvov." Please conceal the letter I sent from
Venice . . . because R. Solomon Zalman and his friends are very concerned lest they be betrayed to the yeshiva. Later, Luzzatto tried to persuade Bassan that the Venetian rabbinate, particularly Jacob Aboab, had
a change of heart and now supported him. He reported that when Katzenellenbogen's condemnation of Luzzatto arrived in Venice, Aboab sent
a copy to Luzzatto instead of to the rabbinate of Padua, so that Luzzatto
could know how to defend himself.[68]

Despite his affected disdain for the opinion of the rabbis of Venice,
Luzzatto was very concerned with their reaction. He confided to Bassan
his belief that Hagiz would not take further steps before hearing from
Venice. After hearing of their negative reaction, Luzzatto addressed the
Venetian rabbinate directly. "My masters, a spirit has come forth from
your anger as mighty as a great torrent of water with no dam. Both
destroy, smash and overturn in their flowing rage, so that the name of
Heaven will be desecrated." Luzzatto urged them to send representatives
to investigate for themselves and not rely on hearsay. When Luzzatto
signed the oath not to share his *maggidic* teachings with anyone, the
Venetian rabbinate withdrew from the controversy.[69]

R. ISAIAH BASSAN

Luzzatto's teacher and mentor, R. Isaiah Bassan, occupied a special position in the controversy. One of the most eminent rabbinic scholars in
eighteenth century Italy, he had occupied the seat of chief rabbi in several Italian cities—Cento, Padua, Ferrara and Reggio-Emilia. Bassan had
been rabbi of Padua, Luzzatto's birthplace, from 1715 to 1722, corresponding to Luzzatto's seventh through fourteenth years of life. When
Bassan left Padua, they continued to correspond. Luzzatto had visited
Bassan and confided to him the news of his maggidic revelations a year
before Gordon's letters were written. Bassan's reaction to his disciple's
momentous announcement: a warning that Luzzatto must maintain ab-

solute secrecy. His restrained response disappointed Luzzatto who had hoped for a more enthusiastic reception.[70]

He did, however, receive an enthusiastic response from Bassan's father-in-law, R. Benjamin Hai [Vitaly] Kohen [RaBa"Kh], one of the foremost Italian Kabbalists, and a secret adherent of Sabbatian kabbalah. When Kohen heard the news of Luzzatto's illumination he accepted it joyfully. Bassan had to steer a difficult course between several antithetical interests. He walked a tightrope between his own instinctive restraint and rabbinic caution, and the unguarded enthusiasm of his illustrious father-in-law and his pupil. He remained true to his fierce, almost paternal protectiveness of his young disciple, yet harbored strong doubts about the nature of Luzzatto's visitations. To the zealots he counseled a path of unswerving moderation, while to Luzzatto he expressed his deep concerns for the possible disastrous consequences of these events. He distributed eloquent words of encouragement or rebuke, as they were warranted, to both sides of the controversy. For his honesty, he earned the stinging condemnation of both.

On December 6, 1729, Bassan wrote the first letter to Luzzatto concerning the tumult unleashed by Gordon. His letter contained the outlines of the stormy conflict to follow. He encouraged Luzzatto to cultivate his revelations, yet his approval was laced with caution and ambivalence. Although he believed that Luzzatto's revelations were well within the realm of probability, he was not yet convinced beyond all shadow of doubt that they were sacred phenomena.

> Regarding the essence of the matter, there is not the slightest doubt in my heart that your words are honorable, . . . for you have been Godfearing since your childhood. . . . But I cannot refrain from stating that the matter is far beyond me . . . for it [your illumination] has reached a degree higher than that of AR"I . . . although he sat in isolation for many years. It is true that nothing is impossible for God, but just as I cannot reject it, I cannot affirm its truth until I have seen, heard, and investigated. . . . I beseech the Lord that you will develope into a mighty cedar, but I have yet to see anything . . . except the smallest amount of your writing.[71]

Bassan suggested that in order to resolve his doubts, he must see Luzzatto again and speak with him: "If you come here with your writings, we would rejoice in our friendship and share our secret with my revered father-in-law, who is, after all, unique in our generation, in our land."

Bassan's invitation would become more urgent as the controversy intensified. Luzzatto refused to see his rabbi without the maggid's approval.
In the end, the noble Bassan journeyed to his disciple.

Bassan's supportive words were tempered by his great dismay over
the publicity Luzzatto had generated. Unable or unwilling to vent his
wrath fully on his vulnerable disciple, Bassan diverted it to the agent
who had spread the news:

> "How did you carelessly reveal yourself to that R. Yekutiel? Don't
> you know that it is the foolish way of Ashkenazic and Polish Jews
> to publicize and confuse everything! They have always been de-
> tractors of the true [Kabbalah] and promoters of confusion, as you
> can see from the book *Emek ha-Melekh*. Others like him have made
> a hodgepodge of the manuscripts of R. Hayim Vital, which they
> stole and printed until the secrets of the Torah were transmitted
> to outsiders in their unclean language. In my opinion, this is one
> of the causes of our prolonged exile. In addition, they were ardent
> supporters of Sabbatai Zebi. Their distortions are still causing harm,
> and the truth is being trampled. This was the reason for Hagiz'
> zealotry in the time of Hayon, for which we must give him credit
> (although he trampled on the heads of our leaders)."

Bassan urged Luzzatto to remain as circumspect as possible in the future.
"For surely you must know that AR"I was punished because of publicity, and his crown was removed from our generation." Luzzatto was aware
of Bassan's protectiveness and fidelity to him. He was confident that
Bassan would defend him to outsiders despite his own misgivings, and
he called upon Bassan to do so several times.[72] For quite some time,
Bassan did so, out of great love for his disciple. He became spokesman
and shield for Luzzatto, especially to the Venetian rabbinate. He described to them his close relationship to Luzzatto:

> It is as though I have given birth to him. . . . He has never wan-
> dered in search of the follies of childhood and youth. . . . The
> Lord blessed him with an ear to hearken and understand, and he
> has been like a son unto me. . . . Because I felt an eternal love
> for him . . . all my treasures were placed in his hands. . . . He
> would shine forth every morning . . . and delve into the words of
> the living God. . . . As he went through all my effects, he stum-
> bled upon some of the chests [of Kabbalistic manuscripts] with which
> God has graced me. He ate of the Tree of Life and entered the
> profundities [of the kabbalah] and indulged in their love. The day

came when he departed from me and pitched his tent, and all those who sought God came to him."

Bassan argued that it was not unusual that so brilliant a receptacle as Luzzatto had received a divine illumination, even at a young age. Bassan bolstered his argument with a long list of distinguished rabbinic and scholarly predecessors who had received revelations, and he exonerated Luzzatto from any suspicion of Sabbatianism: "His writings, free from blemish, are based on those of AR"I. There is no trace of Sabbatianism to be found in him and no deceit like the actions of Hiya [Hayon]. He does not associate with sectarians and has no dealings with those who calculate the End. . . . His conduct and bearing are proof of his worthiness."[73] Bassan beseeched the Venetian rabbinate to investigate thoroughly before pronouncing any harmful verdict against Luzzatto, and his efforts won Luzzatto a brief respite.

As the controversy progressed, the pressure on Bassan grew. The opposition demanded a more definite clarification of the nature of Luzzatto's maggid. Bassan expressed his fear to Luzzatto that the maggid might not be an agent of good at all, but of evil forces trying to ensnare him. Luzzatto tried to calm Bassan reporting to him that their opponents had softened their attacks, when in reality, their voices grew shriller daily. Benjamin Kohen's rapturous acceptance of the maggid undermined Bassan's position further.[74]

Kohen belonged to a school of Italian kabbalists, disciples of R. Moses Zacuto, which had cultivated illuminations similar to the one claimed by Luzzatto. His study hall had become the center for copying manuscripts of Nathan of Gaza and other Sabbatians, from whence they were disseminated throughout Italy. He wrote two Kabbalistic texts, one of which clearly belongs to the Sabbatian school.[75] It is likely that Luzzatto's first exposure to Sabbatian manuscripts came from the Kohen's library, which had been in Bassan's care. In the course of his correspondence, Bassan noted that this library contained two full length works by Nathan of Gaza, *Sefer ha-Beriah* [The Book of Creation] and *Zamir 'Arizim*.[76]

Kohen was not informed by Bassan of Luzzatto's maggid; he heard about it when the news was made public by Gordon. Having spent many years seeking a similar experience, Kohen may have been disappointed that he had been bypassed for the distinction, but he never doubted its authenticity. As soon as he heard the news, he wrote to Luzzatto. His first letter has not been preserved. Luzzatto responded on December 19, 1729, with an apology for having concealed the news until then. He expressed gratitude and joy that Kohen had accepted the matter in "its truth and simplicity."[77] Luzzatto apologized to Kohen that he could not leave his newly penitent adherents to journey to see him. He explained the seminal and redemptive significance of his illumination, and consoled Kohen for his failure to have achieved a similar one. Luzzatto recounted his methods of cultivating appearances of the *maggid*, and the details of his first revelation, apparently all in response to Kohen's queries.

Kohen responded immediately to Luzzatto's letter. Unlike Bassan, he emphasized that he harbored no doubts regarding the exalted source of Luzzatto's revelation. He demanded that Luzzatto journey to see him and Bassan so that "we would understand how the spirit of the Lord began to rise in you, especially in this orphaned generation, in the land of the Gentiles." He begged Luzzatto to provide an explanation from the *maggid* for his personal suffering. Luzzatto replied that Kohen's suffering was not a punishment for personal omissions, but a restorative tikkun for the sins of his generation. Kohen accepted this answer as a balm for his tortured soul, which would enable him to bear the pain as long as God decreed. He expressed his frustration that Luzzatto often ended a profound treatise abruptly, without a satisfactory conclusion by saying, "this is a profound mystery which I cannot reveal in writing."[78]

Kohen died a month after this correspondence, but his unquestioning acceptance of Luzzatto's maggid influenced the course of the controversy. During Kohen's lifetime, Hagiz maintained a respectful silence on the subject of Kohen's Sabbatianism, and even referred to him as "the pietist of our generation" [*Hasid ha-Dor*]. Only when the supporters of Luzzatto repeatedly cited Kohen's support as proof of the maggid's holiness did Hagiz bring up the subject. He declared it a puzzlement and an error that such a luminary had lowered himself to seek advice from Luzzatto. Although his criticism of Kohen's Sabbatianism would have enhanced his polemical position, it remained very moderate. This appears to be another instance in which Hagiz shielded a renowned rabbinical figure from the taint of Sabbatianism.[79]

With the passage of time, Bassan began to lose patience with Luzzatto's continued refusal to visit him and attempts to manipulate him. His doubts and exasperation burst forth for the first time in a letter to Luzzatto of late February 1730. He refused Luzzatto's request that he respond to Hagiz and Katzenellenbogen: "I do not wish to commit anything further to writing until the matter becomes clear as the sun, through *speaking with you, person to person*, to my satisfaction, so that I will be able to affirm everything with a clear conscience." He expressed his anger at Luzzatto by justifying Hagiz:

When Hagiz and his cohorts claimed that your letter was self-contradictory [regarding the claims of Gordon], you should have erased their fears. . . . Hagiz' words at the end of his letter [counselling modesty to Luzzatto] are very apt, and he does not repel you with both hands. . . . Nor is Hagiz' concern over your bachelor status a vain one. . . . My father-in-law and I have taken counsel together . . . about your refusal to grow a beard."

Bassan added that Luzzatto's preoccupation with messianism strengthened his dread suspicion that evil influence may have been the root of the maggid, as Hagiz had cautioned all along. "For the past fifteen days, my heart has been in great turmoil . . . Clear up the matter for me and remove all doubt from my heart. Failing that, I cannot pen another stroke, lest we both be dishonored."[80]

Bassan's tremulous entreaty, which bared his innermost doubts to his disciple, was met with cool disdain. Luzzatto's flip dismissal of all Bassan's concerns must have struck a chill note on Bassan's heart. Disregarding all Bassan's efforts on his behalf, Luzzatto merely chided him for weighing Gordon's letter with such gravity, when it was clearly hyperbole intended only for private scrutiny.

Bassan did not hide the stinging pain which Luzzatto's insouciant reply caused him, but Luzzatto continued to address him in the same tone. Bassan needn't feel obliged to correspond further if it was too onerous. He hoped God would forgive all those who doubted the sacred roots of his revelation, but he was certain that a *maggid* who was privy to all the secrets of the Torah could only be a holy one.[81]

The emotional exchange between master and disciple was punctuated by a scandal. In late April 1730, Luzzatto made amorous advances to a young female relative who was already betrothed to another man. When the news reached Bassan, he attacked Luzzatto for his careless behavior: "I have heard terrible things about you. . . . Do not offer me excuses, for, by the Heavens, I will not accept them; I had faith in you, but the holy spirit cannot reside in impure flesh. . . . If you do not mend your ways, I will come out against you . . . for you are desecrating the Name of Heaven."[82] Bassan warned Luzzatto that, far from diminishing, the number of his detractors was continually multiplying. Moreover, "Hagiz is plotting evil against you every day. He has recently written to instruct Morpurgo to gather convocations against you, and Morpurgo did not defend you to Hagiz. I caused the rabbi of Mantua [David Finzi] to appease Morpurgo." Bassan argued that if he were to continue to support Luzzatto unconditionally, despite Luzzatto's untoward behavior, his own position would become untenable and ineffective. The opposition would dismiss him as a blind supporter, rather than a wise mediator, and he would lose all ability to protect Luzzatto.

Luzzatto's reply to Bassan's remonstrations did not contain the slightest note of contrition or remorse. He invited Bassan to join forces with Hagiz, feigning indifference if this were to happen. One more mortal enemy could not make much difference so long as God was on his side. Luzzatto compared himself to Joseph, who was ultimately proven innocent in the incident with Potiphar's wife. He rejected Bassan's criticism but he did not offer any convincing justification for his undignified behavior.

In an even more impertinent missive, Luzzatto attacked Bassan for behaving inconsistently. He seized upon Bassan's inner vacillation as an opportunity to taunt him, and he cruelly contrasted Bassan's public show of unflagging support to his private criticism: "An evil doer—or beloved by God? The two are mutually exclusive, so I cannot fathom your true opinion. Since you have already decided my absolute guilt, how can you hope that further investigation will exonerate me?" He asked Bassan indignantly: "Am I a hound's head that you tell me . . . I have gone the way of impure flesh and 'by the Heavens, you won't accept an explanation'? Are you succumbing to pressure, running with the crowd?"[83]

After he received these letters, Bassan was ready to renounce all further contact with Luzzatto. Only the intercession of Luzzatto's associates, Isaac Marini and Jacob Kastel-Franco [Ka"F], succeeded in keeping the correspondence—and Bassan's hitherto immutable love for his disciple—alive. Bassan wrote to Luzzatto, "If not for the intercession of Jacob Ka"F I would never have mentioned your name again after receiving your letters. In your consuming wrath, you have overstepped all boundaries, . . . you have likened me to the evil-doers, something you have not done even to Hagiz who plots to annihilate you . . . nor to Morpurgo, who wrote lies about you to Hamburg. . . . To him you write words of praise and flattery, . . . but as for me, I have exhorted you justly, as father to son . . . and you have kicked me with both feet." Bassan was especially stung by the comparison to Hagiz: "What differences there are between us! He is a man of controversy and a quarrelmonger . . . while I am a counselor of peace to you."[84]

Sensing for the first time the gravity of Bassan's anger, Luzzatto tried to conciliate Bassan: "Father, father, had you rebuked me a thousand times more I would have been glad of it, . . . but how could I bear that you passed a verdict against me in your anger? My words, like my soul, churned like the depths of the sea. . . . I beseech you: interpret my words for good and not for evil." Luzzatto invited Bassan to come to him, together with other Kabbalists of Bassan's choosing to examine him in any way they pleased. Bassan made plans to investigate, and selected as his partner R. Nehemiah Kohen of Ferrara, a fateful choice. Thus, at the last minute, the rift between Bassan and Luzzatto was healed, and Bassan made plans to meet his celebrated pupil for the first time since the controversy had erupted.[85]

Just at this moment when Bassan was making overtures to reconcile with Luzzatto, Hagiz intensified his campaign against Luzzatto. He raised his polemic to a new level, comparing Luzzatto to Jesus and to Sabbatai Zebi. Both of the latter had claimed divine affirmation of their missions. Hagiz argued that if Luzzatto's maggid were to be accepted as a legitimate new source of revelation, Jews would have no excuse for rejecting the claims of the Christians and Sabbatians. He urged that Luzzatto must be totally suppressed and massively opposed—regardless of the content of his message, even in the unlikely event that it was pure and holy, simply because its source was inspirational. Hagiz called upon all communities and their rabbis to unite in concerted action against Luzzatto.[86]

Hagiz' call to arms, coming at the time of emotional reconciliation between Bassan and his disciple, sparked a fundamental change in Bassan's role in the controversy. Bassan was stung to hear that Hagiz had not waited for the outcome of his visit to Luzzatto. His anger transformed him from a neutral conciliator who counseled peace to both sides into an aggressive defender of Luzzatto. He became the counterpart of Hagiz on the opposing side, fighting Hagiz both tactically and ideologically.

The subject of the controversy broadened. It was no longer narrowly focused on the merits of Luzzatto, but on the possibility of renewal of divine revelation. Hagiz had urged that Luzzatto's revelations be condemned even if their contents were praiseworthy and their source holy— because they would create a new source of charismatic authority. Bassan defended the possibility that Luzzatto's revelations were direct divine inspirations, and that such a renewal was positive. It was not Luzzatto, but Hagiz who was the false prophet, "who saw a future that had not yet occurred, when he predicted that any renewal in our times is really an obstacle."[87] In a reversal of his earlier position, Bassan accused Hagiz of being opposed to kabbalah. Bassan warned that the purpose of his letter was not to calumniate Hagiz, but to oppose his policies. Thus, Bassan developed an ideological platform directed against Hagiz' justifications for persecution. Bassan decided to marshall support for his side in the same way as Hagiz had—by writing to potential allies and asking them to commit themselves to Luzzatto. He would act preemptively, to reach prospective allies who had not yet been contacted by Hagiz.

Bassan's first letter was sent to R. Gabriel del Rio of Livorno on July 10, 1730. In it, he attacked Hagiz, "who signs his name 'insignificant Moses' but behaves exceedingly important in his own eyes. . . . Like a roaring lion, a seething bear . . . he desires to consume Luzzatto." Bassan appealed to del Rio as a fellow member of the Italian rabbinate, "to stop Hagiz from insinuating controversy into our home [Italy]," by inciting the rabbinate of Venice against that of Padua. He urged del Rio to argue their case against Hagiz to the sages of the city, "lest one who prefers evil to good [Hagiz] precede me." Bassan enclosed the text of Hagiz' letter to Morpurgo, so that could see an example of the way Hagiz fomented controversy. He urged that his letter be concealed because if this (uncharacteristic) attack were to fall into the hands of Hagiz, the controversy would reach new heights of ferocity.

From del Rio's response, it is evident that Bassan had found a true ally, just at the right time. Del Rio reported that just as he was presenting Bassan's case to his fellow rabbis, Hagiz' letter arrived, replete with snares. Hagiz urged that they "write and sign, to destroy and desolate, publicly before the Gentiles." Del Rio, rejecting Hagiz' blind zealotry, pledged that he and his colleagues would not be swayed by inflammatory rhetoric, but would patiently await the outcome of Bassan's investigation.

The exchange with del Rio marked a new phase in Bassan's role in the controversy. His efforts to form a coalition against Hagiz were temporarily halted when he effected a compromise that satisfied all parties, in the form of Luzzatto's oath to desist from publicizing his revelations. When the controversy was to erupt anew several years later, Bassan retained the aggressive stance that developed in reaction to Hagiz' assault. This was the first time in Hagiz' career as polemicist that his opposition was able to develop an open and tenable position against him.[88]

THE OATH

Bassan arranged to go to Padua in the company of R. Jacob Belilios, representing the rabbinate of Venice, R. Nehemiah Kohen of Ferrara, and R. David Finzi of Mantua. In order to silence the critics of Luzzatto's bachelor status, he intended to arrange a marriage for Luzzatto to David

Finzi's daughter. When he arrived, he accomplished his objectives. He succeeded in persuading Luzzatto to sign an agreement which would placate Hagiz and still the controversy. Hagiz had designed the agreement in a letter to the rabbinate of Venice: "He must promise to submit all his works to You, he must swear on pain of herem not to publicize any teaching in the name of maggid orally or in writing." The prohibition against publicizing the maggidic material had been suggested by Morpurgo as well.[89]

Two recensions of Luzzatto's oath have survived. The first, written in Luzzatto's hand, is the more concise. Luzzatto wrote that he agreed to certain strictures on the advice of Bassan, his lifelong teacher and mentor, who had drawn them up together with the Venetian rabbinate:

I will gather and conceal, in accordance with [Bassan's] wishes, all the works I have written until this day which were dictated by the maggid or holy souls; they will not be made public except with his [Bassan's] permission, long may he live, because the sages of our generation do not want new treatises on the true lore of Israel [Kabbalah] to be disseminated, lest harm will befall the masses of Israelites. From this time, I will refrain from composing any work in the language or style of the *Zohar*, or in any language, at the behest of the maggid or holy souls. . . . I have truly chosen this, for it is not my desire to cause strife among the congregation of God. I have accepted willingly everything stipulated in this document, being sound of mind, with no pressure or coercion whatsoever, as the most stringent oath, linked to the severest herem. All these restrictions apply so long as I live in the Diaspora.[90]

Apparently, this text prepared by Bassan was too vague and ambiguous for Luzzatto's foes, and it did not demonstrate sufficient contrition on his part. A second, longer, text was prepared that included several more restrictive provisions than the first. It also differed sharply in tone:

[Bassan] has taught me the gravity of fabricating new works in the true lore [Kabbalah] which had not been envisaged by our forebears, and were not founded by the great sages of Israel, great in wisdom and in numbers, and renowned for piety, humility and sanctity. He commanded me to refrain from writing the various works which I had composed, of the true lore, particularly those which I wrote in the language of the original *Zohar* of RaShB"Y [R. Simeon bar Yohai]. Although I believed I had composed them at the word of the maggid and holy souls which seemed to have

revealed themselves to me, and I wrote as they dictated, my aforementioned master says that I cannot rely on this for harm is likely
and error is nigh. . . . My master also taught me that the prayers
of unity [*yihudim*] to which I had accustomed myself, and through
which, it appeared, I achieved my illumination and strength to
compose these works, are not removed from the ways of the de-
monic side, particularly in the land of the Gentiles.[91]

This second version, in which Luzzatto was forced to write of his
illumination as though it were an evil hallucination, became the official
text of the oath. In it, however, he was able to reserve for himself a right
not specified in the first, discarded version: "To compose original works
in Hebrew only [the language of the Zohar was Aramaic], so long as
they were not in the name of the maggid or holy souls, with the specific
proviso that I will not publicize any work, to any audience in the world
until it has passed the critical eye of my master, or any sages he sees fit
to appoint." In the first version, Luzzatto 'volunteered' to gather and
conceal all the works he had already written under maggidic inspiration.
In the final oath, this was not left to his discretion: "To ensure that I
uphold my oath, I have given my master all the kabbalistic works which
I have composed until now to be concealed as he wishes."

The papers of Luzzatto were gathered under Bassan's supervision, and
placed into a sealed trunk. The trunk was entrusted to Moses Alprun, a
prominent member of the community and an uncle of Luzzatto's, who
remained skeptical of his powers. From another source we learn that as
soon as the oath was signed, Bassan rewarded Luzzatto with a writ of
ordination. Perhaps he had promised it to Luzzatto as an inducement to
accept the compromise.[92] The oath was accepted by both sides in the
controversy on July 17, 1730. Morpurgo informed Hagiz that Luzzatto's
writings had been collected. He praised Luzzatto's contrition and humility in acquiescing to all the conditions imposed upon him. Luzzatto
reported that Hagiz, in turn, had expressed his joy to the rabbinate of
Venice. The issue had been settled peacefully, and this was beneficial
for all Israel.[93]

Did Luzzatto and his circle respect the oath? The evidence is conflicting. Luzzatto maintained to Bassan that he had observed its terms scrupulously. But his enemies accused him of violating the oath on several
occasions and there is ample evidence that Luzzatto's circle regarded the
oath as a coerced confession with absolutely no validity. We shall see
that Luzzatto was able to maintain fidelity to the letter of the oath in
public, while in the privacy of his circle it was disregarded.[94]

THE PERSECUTION IN THE EYES OF LUZZATTO'S CIRCLE

The first rabbinic persecution came as a violent incursion into the orderly and consecrated life of Luzzatto's circle. It left a deep impression on the character and self-perception of the group. A prayer written by Luzzatto and recited by members of the group betrayed the initial sense of despair caused by the harsh persecutions:

> We are downtrodden and rejected in the eyes of all who see us, the leaders of our people, as well as the masses. We are "brambles, evildoers, fools, lunatics, idiots and heretics against the Torah, God-forbid, idolators." . . . There is no Comforter to console us in the darkness that engulfs us. . . . We had hoped for light but there was none. We desired to benefit from Your illumination not for our own pleasure, but because You chose us and desired our service.[95]

Luzzatto wrote to Bassan that he intended to remain silent although there was much he wished to say, "because he did not desire further prosecutions at this time."

With the passage of time, Luzzatto's resolve grew stronger. In a letter to Bassan of October 16, 1730, he belittled his opponents as "mere garlic peels" and expressed his intention to resume his activities "slowly, until the time is ripe." What had at first appeared to be an abrupt end to a sequence of events unfolding according to a predetermined pattern was eventually integrated into that pattern. The elastic paradigm was modified to include flight from persecution. Moses had to flee to Midian before he could return as a redeemer; Bar Yohai had eluded his Roman pursuers by living in a cave for thirteen years. Attempts by evil forces to prevent the restoration of divine illumination prefigured the apocalyptic battle between the forces of good and evil in the messianic era and became a necessary part of the redeemer's biography. Luzzatto ultimately characterized the persecutions as a stimulus to his creativity, just as Moses had received his mandate to redeem Israel while he was in exile, and Bar Yohai had completed the *Zohar* while in the cave.[96]

After the first round of persecution and initial despair, Luzzatto and his circle embarked on a phase of renewed activity in the hope that their efforts would result in an even grander illumination, and an ultimate vindication. Their prayers from this period include a plea that their intensified service of God be accepted so that the truth could be revealed

and the mouths of speakers of falsehoods be stopped.[97] During this period, in January 1731, the members of the circle wrote and signed a new
covenant of unity. It seems certain that the persecutions, culminating in
the oath, were the primary impulse behind this new recension. One pro-
vision encouraged the members to remain steadfast in their undertaking
and never to pay heed to the mockery of others. The new contract also
reflected the renewed commitment of the circle to intensify its efforts
and expand its reach. It made specific provisions for introducing new
members into the circle, although the lines that had separated the inner
circle from other members were not obliterated. The covenant contained,
in an appendix, a special set of obligations for the second rank members
who had not been admitted to the inner circle. Some of these provisions
reveal the degree of messianic intensity that pervaded the circle. The
secondary group, like the inner circle, was cautioned to remain ever alert
to the purpose of the group's activities: cosmic restoration and national
redemption. They must pledge never to accept any form of personal reward or compensation for their studies, as that would deflect them from
the goal. They were to remember always that they were permanently
bound to the unified circle.

The assigned rotations provided for a continuous, uninterrupted flow
of Torah study whose purpose was: "To elevate the Shekhinah so that
it would never descend again . . . to crush the strength of Samael and
his entire evil cohort . . . so that the Bride of Moses [the Shekhinah]
. . . will be united with Moses."[98] The hidden significance of Luzzatto's
newly consecrated circle was described by Luzzatto in *Adir ba-Marom:*

> A covenant is the creation of a bond between those who participate
> in it. *Ze'ir Anpin* (the divine male principle) makes a covenant with
> *Nukba* (the divine female principle). . . . Know, that any place where
> assemblies are gathered for the sake of heaven, an assembly is gath-
> ered above. When associations are forged below, the light of the
> covenant shines among them and unites them. . . . Understand
> well, for in the end of all [time] there will be peace in the world
> and all creatures will form one association to worship the only King.[99]

The covenantal association was an instrument of the redemption, a metaphor for the cosmic union as well as the core from which earthly harmony would radiate. This accounts for Luzzatto's delighted observations
that masses of penitents were flocking toward his circle once its nature
had become known to the public. In the case of Bar Yohai—"Until he
convened the assembly . . . it was a covenant supported by one pillar
[Bar Yohai himself]. When he wished to add a second bond . . . he

gathered the *Idra* . . . These ten members were truly united. With the *Idra*, the covenant was cemented by two pillars, and after that, evil remained powerless."[100] The holy assembly gathered by the central figure was consolidated his redemptive achievements. When the redemption failed to materialize at the anticipated hour after his wedding, Luzzatto blamed the last minute interference by hostile persecutors: "The Bride of Moses [the Shekhinah] descended away from Moses because of the mixed multitude which sowed divisiveness within Israel, may You remove them from the world! . . . The mystical bride returned to the *kelippot*, the dark forces, because of the interference of the "mixed multitude."[101] In the progression of the messianic era outlined by Luzzatto in *Tikkunim Hadashim*, the first stage was the war against the "other side"—the *kelippot*, the "mixed multitude." The "serpent," symbol of the evil forces, would be defeated; the dominion of the Gentile kings would be broken and the darkness would be utterly banished. Only then would the Shekhinah be redeemed, and the messiahs (ben David and ben Joseph) complete their tasks and unite with the Shekhinah. This would be followed by the redemption of Israel from Exile.[102]

In the perception of Luzzatto and his circle, Hagiz and the other persecutors were transfigured into agents of the satanic forces, who had emerged in desperate fury at the last moment to prevent the triumph of good. "The Satan came to stand among us, to put into the heart of a wise man like Hagiz words of anger and rage." Luzzatto said of another opponent in Padua who reported on his activities: "This villain writes exactly what Samael dictates to him."[103] His opponents had become unwitting agents of the evil forces. Luzzatto warned Bassan that he too could fall prey to the clutches of Satan if he remained skeptical of Luzzatto's mission: "Seek the truth before the 'dark side' comes to claim its portion!"[104] Luzzatto, as the vessel which God had chosen for His illumination, must oppose these forces with all his might. He argued that "the objections of Hagiz and his cohorts were not to himself, 'the vessel,' but to God, 'who had chosen him.' " In other instances, Luzzatto identified Hagiz and his allies with Satan himself, as opposed to being merely vessels: "God is with me and He will rebuke the Satan to desist from prosecuting us." "I will pay no heed to any objection of Samael or the Great Satan who foment controversy."[105]

For Luzzatto, Hagiz' error was especially tragic and urgent because he and his allies were arraying themselves on the wrong side just as the Armageddon was about to erupt. Although he professed not to pay any heed to the objections of the satanic forces, Luzzatto mounted a considerable effort to convince his opponents of the error of their convictions.

The writings of Luzzatto were replete with the images of martyrdom and sacrifice even before the persecutions began; the images intensified as the persecutions escalated. To the rabbinate of Venice, Luzzatto portrayed himself as "bound on the altar of God." "Just as Abraham was unafraid at Ur of the Chaldees, and Hananiah, Mishael and Azariah at the fiery furnace, and the martyrs of Lod did not fear death, so I will pay no heed."[106]

By focusing on his role as a martyr, and caricaturing his enemies as satanic forces, Luzzatto kept passions high during the period of relative calm that followed the oath. When the hostilities resumed after several years, they were more intense than ever.

CHAPTER 8

Revival of the Luzzatto Controversy

 WHEN NEWS reached his opponents that Luzzatto planned to publish a kabbalistic book, the debate was reopened. On December 11, 1733, Luzzatto wrote to Bassan of his intention to travel to his brother in Amsterdam. He forwarded to Bassan his manuscript "Polemical Treatise" (*Ma'amar ha-Vikuah*), for which he beseeched Bassan to provide an approbation. The book was to be a defense of Kabbalah against Leone Modena's critique, *Ari Nohem*.[1] After six months of entreaties Bassan responded. He pleaded with Luzzatto not to publish any book since his enemies were bound to attack it, "if not because of its contents, then because of its author." Bassan was greatly concerned that Luzzatto's course would lead to disaster:

> Just as I have never understood your entire affair, I also do not understand your true purpose in publishing this book. . . . To prove to you that my motivations are . . . for your true good, I will not withhold a few lines of permission to publish, and they are herewith enclosed. From what I have seen of your intensity in this matter, I had decided to proceed slowly. I thought: Perhaps, with the passage of time, your natural hotheadedness would subside . . . but I waited in vain. I was sure you would be scorched by the mild [measures taken against you], . . . but nothing deters you. You cannot deny that all your past affairs have been strange, no person knows from what source they come, and you were a byword in the mouths of all. If the Lord had not guided me to find a way to

silence the multitude of voices, who knows what the extent of the damage would have been? And now, you are repaying my kindness with ingratitude by forcing me to affix my name to a work which will surely find disfavor."[2]

The permit (*reshut*) which Bassan included was not an approbation, merely a terse statement of fact: he had seen the work and had found nothing untoward in it.

Luzzatto thanked Bassan and belittled his concerns: "Words of men are worthless to me . . . These people understand nothing, . . . so let them remain silent. If they speak, will I pay the slightest heed? . . . I trust only in God."

The news that Luzzatto was leaving Padua to publish a book in Amsterdam aroused accusations that he had never adhered to his vow. Almost five years after the controversy had been stilled with Luzzatto's oath, it was revived with even greater vigor on the pretext that this publication might violate his oath. This second phase of the controversy differed from the first in several important respects. Sabbatianism receded as the context of the polemical discourse, and other issues dominated. The focal point of the controversy shifted from Italy to central Europe, although the rabbinate of Venice, at Hagiz' prodding, continued to be a most active prosecutor of Luzzatto. Contradictory testimonies and conflicting opinions divided this rabbinate against itself. In this stage of the controversy, Bassan became a victim of persecution alongside his pupil, accused of conspiring with him to break the vow. Hagiz orchestrated this phase of the controversy with characteristic zeal, and Samson Morpurgo continued to provide a sober counterpoint to the passions of zealotry.

CONFRONTATION IN VENICE

The first incident occurred when Luzzatto visited Venice in preparation for the longer journey: "When the agitator Belilios heard of my plans, he assumed that I was going to publish books. . . . He maligned me to the Venetian rabbinate. They sent three agents to me, R. Gabriel Padovani, R. Moses Menahem [Merrari] and Belilios, in the name of the Yeshiva, saying they had heard I intended to publish, in violation of my oath. They accused me of 'teaching my original works to my disciples.'"

Luzzatto told the delegation that he had already received permission from Bassan to publish one book. When they relayed this information to the rabbis at Venice, they reportedly responded: "R. Bassan is not everything. *We* wish to see, *we* must approve the work, the writ of Bassan is insufficient and we must issue our own." They demanded that Luzzatto sign another oath that he would not learn or teach any works of Kabbalah, nor publish anything without their consent. "If he disobeys us . . . we will persecute him to oblivion." Luzzatto dismissed them angrily: "Know, that I am not subservient to them in any respect whatsoever, since I come from Padua and not from Venice." Luzzatto asked Bassan to notify him if the Venetians took any further action.[3] In fact, R. Isaac Pacifico of Venice had already written to Bassan, on behalf of the Venetian rabbinate. They were certain that Luzzatto's only motive for traveling to Amsterdam was publication of his book, "for Amsterdam is a city of publishing without peer." Pacifico intimated that Luzzatto had betrayed Bassan for Sabbatianism. He fulminated against rabbis in positions of power who took no action against Luzzatto, a barb directed at Bassan himself, and urged him to take a stronger stand, "lest this upstart befoul us in the eyes of the Gentiles."[4]

The rabbinate of Venice was very troubled by Luzzatto's curt dismissal of its message, and over the course of several meetings, decided to take vigorous action on their own. In November 1734, they elicited testimonies regarding Luzzatto (*gebiat edut*). Jacob Belilios testified that in 1730 he and Merrari had found Luzzatto's new book of Psalms. He had heard from one of Luzzatto's disciples that Luzzatto had written it to replace the canonical Psalms of David at the time of the Redemption. Belilios claimed that Luzzatto denied authorship of any such volume, and he had blushed and stammered when confronted with the evidence. In addition they had found a book of magical oaths, including one which bound the evil Samael to reveal secrets of the Torah. They also claimed to have found the appurtenances of the occultic practices: a mirror with a black frame, a knife with a black handle, and a candle of black wax.[5]

When the rabbinical court asked Merrari to substantiate Belilios' testimony, they were taken aback by Merrari's reply: "I did not see the book of oaths, nor any paper written by the hand of Luzzatto. I only heard of these things from his master [Bassan] and the two rabbis. I heard from them that he defended himself, saying that the instruments they had found were shaving equipment used to trim his mustache; the candle had become sooty from nightly use." Merrari said that he had not seen the book of Psalms, it was held in Bassan's hand. An anonymous observer commented on the discrepancy between the testimonies of Belilios and Merrari, and the quarrel that ensued: "Harsh and quarrelsome words were exchanged because Belilios wished that Merrari would corroborate his testimony, and he [Merrari] had no intention of doing so, in the interests of truth and justice. Then the rabbis threatened Merrari regarding this. But he replied with the truth as it was known to him . . . and from that day forward, they did not call Merrari again, nor did they show him what they had written. . . . Later . . . Merrari was shocked to see that they had affixed his name to things which he had never said or thought, and he protested loudly."[6]

Even if this document had been written by a partisan of Luzzatto, it is substantiated by Merrari's account. The rabbis of Venice resorted to intimidation of witnesses and distortion of testimony in order to pursue Luzzatto, extreme behavior even in the context of a polemic. Their actions were sufficiently desperate and extreme to warrant an analysis of their motivations. Isaac Pacifico warned Hagiz that he had heard that Luzzatto had planned a sojourn in Frankfurt of several months in order to spread his teachings to the disciples of the study hall there. He urged Hagiz to warn the rabbis of Frankfurt of Luzzatto's impending arrival. Shortly thereafter, he circulated an open letter, addressed to all rabbis. It contained charges based on the hostile testimonies. Luzzatto was accused of declaring himself to be a messiah, a prophet and a poet laureate equal to David. He had challenged the authority of the rabbinate, saying "All the sages of Israel are nothing to me, I am the shepherd of the flock." He claimed that Moses promised that a new Torah would be given through him. The document barely veiled its accusations against Bassan for not using his authority to check his disciple. It boasted of their might and authority to excommunicate Luzzatto and to burn his works.

The distortion and suppression of Merrari's testimony was not the only instance of desperate behavior which ultimately caused as much damage to the rabbinate as it did to Luzzatto. R. Jacob Popers of Frankfurt, an ally of the Venetian Rabbis, was dismayed to discover that they had promoted a testimony against Luzzatto which the alleged witness had repudiated. Popers had received a communication from his disciple, R. Abraham Rakicz who had spoken to R. Hillel Padua, *who denied everything written in his name by the rabbinate of Venice.* Popers himself had recently received four letters from Venice complaining that Luzzatto's papers should have been sent to them rather than to Popers, because Popers might not notice whether any papers had been surreptitiously removed.

Popers complained of their obsessive quest to control every aspect of the Luzzatto affair.[7]

Why were the Venetian rabbis so determined to control the campaign against Luzzatto? One explanation for their zeal might be as compensation for their role in the Hayon controversy. Their "approbation" had appeared on Hayon's first work, *Raza de-Yihuda*, in 1711. They had intended to issue only copyright protection for the author, but not to certify that its contents were free of errors or heresy. When the Sabbatian content was publicized in 1713 during the Hayon controversy, it proved a source of embarrassment because the copyright permission had been interpreted as an approbation of the contents. It is significant that the most violent phase of the controversy against Luzzatto was aroused by the prospect of publication of his work.[8] Memory of their embarrassment during the Hayon controversy contributed to the insistence of the Venetian rabbinate that they must see any work of Luzzatto's before he brought it to print.

Other explanations for the desperate behavior of the Venetian rabbinate can be found in the external pressures facing the Venetian Jewish community. In 1714, as the Hayon controversy raged, Venice was engaged in a debilitating war with the Ottomans, which would not end until 1718, with the Treaty of Passarowitz. An eighteenth century observer, Count Paul Daru, wrote of Venice in that period: "She is reduced to a passive existence. She has no more wars to sustain, peaces to conclude or desires to express. A mere spectator of events, . . . isolated amid her fellow nations."[9] This picture of stagnation was exacerbated within the Jewish community by the exodus of the wealthiest merchants to the free port of Livorno. Many of those who stayed behind lost their ships and property in the struggle against the Ottomans. At the same time as the tax base eroded, more taxes were levied against the Jewish community to help pay for the wars. The Jewish community of Venice, once the most thriving and venerable in Europe, was forced to default on its debts in 1737. The subsidiary communities of Padua and Verona contributed annually toward the reduction of the deficit. A special "Inquisitorate of the Jews" was appointed to Venice.[10]

In light of the disastrous loss of prestige just sustained by Venice, particularly vis-à-vis its subsidiary communities, Luzzatto's frequent taunts that he was only subject to his local rabbinate in Padua take on an additional meaning. As an auxiliary community, the Paduan rabbinate was expected to defer to that of Venice. Hagiz harped on this sensitive subject to goad the Venetian rabbinate into an active role: "You are closest

to the subject . . . . He and his adherents are obligated to submit to you
. . . for you have prior jurisdiction over any other community."[11] Luzzatto's decision to circumvent Venetian authorities by printing in Amsterdam was a further affront to their authority.

In addition, the communities in the Papal states were tormented by
unrelenting persecution and humiliating legislation. In the early eighteenth century every development within the Jewish ghetto was closely
monitored, creating an atmosphere of fear and suspicion. In the Papal
states and in the Venetian Republic alike, the Inquisitors of state and
secret police diminished their presence among the Christian population,
while it was intensified among the Jewish communities. From the outset
of the Luzzatto affair, fear of the Christian reaction to a possible false
messiah dominated the discourse between partisans of both sides. In its
earliest reactions to Gordon's revelations, the Venetian rabbinate articulated this fear: "Let the matter remain concealed from the ignorant masses,
for they are likely to spread the news to the Gentiles within our midst
who will revile us and attack us; it will make us abominable in their
eyes."[12] Some rabbis in Venice protested against joining the campaign
because they feared the adverse publicity. "Remember, we are among
the nations, hatred of our religion is vast, and they devise ways to confound us and harm us." Hagiz addressed their fear: "Do not be concerned
lest this controversy reach the Gentiles, for if he [Luzzatto] refuses [to
appear before the rabbinical court of Venice] . . . they [the Gentiles!]
will bring him to justice when they hear of this strange matter." Hagiz
castigated those who preferred peace to truth, as protectors of false
prophets, "who relinquish their power so other rabbis will take the initiative and they will remain free of danger."[13]

If Jacob Aboab represented those in Venice who wished to act with
restraint, it was Isaac Pacifico who was responsible for the most venomous attacks against Luzzatto. He reported to Hagiz that "the youth"
had written a commentary on the sanctuary in Ezekiel entitled "Supernal
Sanctuary" [*Mishkanei Elyon*]. "And this will play directly into the hands
of the Christians . . . who will say that the prophet was only talking of
the heavenly Temple, and this will put the weapons in their hands to
kill us." (It would give them the polemical weapon of allegorical interpretation.) Pacifico's letter contained venomous ad hominem attacks against
both Luzzatto and Bassan—"first in matters of promiscuity . . . a common scrub bush . . . ." against Morpurgo—"the physician from Ancona
who uncovered impurity and cunning," and against the emissary Kimhi,
"primordial serpent . . . who lived in his home [Luzzatto's] . . . and
copied his book of *Tikkunim* to display its beauty to the world." Pacifico

accused Luzzatto of rank heresy and blasphemy, adding, "What will the representatives of the Gentiles say if Jews scoff at their own Torah and blaspheme against their God?"[14]

The Venetian rabbinate was also afraid that any new book—particularly if it contained elements of Jewish messianism—might ignite another attack against Jewish books. From the mid-sixteenth century, when the Council of Trent instituted the Index to repress books which supported Protestantism, the Church also intensified its surveillance and repression of Jewish books. The forms of repression varied from deletion or blacking out of selected passages, to wholesale confiscation of Jewish libraries, sometimes culminating in book burning. This activity was greatly intensified in eighteenth century Italy, particularly around the time of the Luzzatto controversy, and it left a profound mark on the literature of the controversy. Under Pope Benedict III, Jewish libraries were seized in Ancona. Samson Morpurgo wrote to Hagiz: "Would that the Lord will relieve me of my distress, and proclaim liberty for my impounded study house, my beloved books which have been imprisoned and locked away from me." After the libraries were "purified" of corrupt books, they were later returned to their owners. Pope Clement XII (1730–1740) ordered a confiscation of Hebrew books throughout the ghettos of the Papal states. It was carried out first on May 28, 1731, by a Dominican, Costanzi.[15] Luzzatto wrote to Bassan of the danger of sending manuscripts by conventional routes "because of the danger of the Inquisition."[16]

In a letter of June 24, 1731, Luzzatto announced to Bassan that his circle had anticipated these decrees. The book burning decrees reflected the profound penumbra which would precede Luzzatto's final illumination.[17]

THE APOSTATE

The fear that Luzzatto's works might play into the hands of the enemies of Israel was suddenly realized with the apostasy of a rabbi who had been supporter of Luzzatto, Nehemiah Kohen of Ferrara. The conversion to Christianity of a prominent rabbi and his family sent waves of shock through the Jewish community and for some, it reinforced a desperate and pessimistic view of Jewish prospects. For Hagiz and the Venetian rabbinate, it provided the ultimate proof that support of Luzzatto would lead to disaster. It substantiated the claims of the Venetian rabbis that the Jewish community lived at the edge of a precipice, and the slightest move in the wrong direction would push more individuals over that edge.[18]

Nehemiah Kohen had corresponded with Bassan before the Luzzatto affair. As soon as the news of Luzzatto's maggid was made public, Kohen was avidly interested. On February 5, 1730, he wrote to Bassan: "The affair of Padua concerns me as much as it does you; you are to be commended for your letter to the Yeshiva of Venice . . . I also appreciate the letter which Luzzatto has written to R. Hagiz, in which he nobly and humbly poured forth his soul." Kohen also solicited information from another informant regarding the nature of the maggid, and he rejoiced upon hearing its name, which indicated that it was a servant of God and not of the dark forces. Yet Kohen compared the maggid of Luzzatto to the revelations of the false prophet of Avila centuries earlier, and expressed doubts about the new Psalms of Luzzatto. Kohen volunteered to accompany Bassan to any place, at his own expense, to investigate the maggid first hand. He corresponded with Luzzatto to satisfy his own thirst for knowledge of renewal of the divine inspiration that had visited Luzzatto. Although the correspondence has not been preserved, it is apparent that Luzzatto did not consider Kohen's questions to have been motivated by hostility. He informed Bassan of this correspondence and later remarked that he would welcome an investigation by Kohen because "he will not harm me. I know the man and his ways and he is a gentle person."[19]

In the same letter, Kohen wrote bitterly and resentfully of the bleak conditions of Jewish existence in Ferrara. A new ruler had ascended the throne,

> The embers of his fury have begun to scorch us. Yesterday, it was decreed that Jews must wear green caps, as is the custom in Rome. Even women and children would not be exempt from this ruling, both at home and abroad, to the farthest reaches of his power. Would that his arrows would be spent with this! For due to our many sins there are many and varied opportunities such as this one, to mock and taunt us. . . . We live in a period of distress and darkness, and those who had the ability to defer decrees have passed from among us. Not one of the leaders of the foxes [a derogatory reference to Jewish communal leaders] agreed to appear before him, except through an agent, for he is like unto Pharaoh and all his lackeys are wicked. Alas! . . . our impoverished community has been placed in the hands of such judges . . . May the Lord have mercy on the poor souls who have done no evil.[20]

In this passage, Kohen distanced himself from other Jewish communal leaders, whom he perceived as helpless and spineless. He blamed the vulnerability of Jews to their predators, on Jewish sin. In retrospect, these remarks seem to hint at the momentous break with the Jewish community which Kohen stood poised to make.

Before his apostasy Kohen had manifested a special concern with Christian anti-Jewish polemic. This fact alone would not have indicated that something was amiss—most of his rabbinic contemporaries in Italy were concerned with defending Judaism against the violent polemics generated by the Church. Together with his colleague Isaac Lampronte, Kohen had presented Luzzatto with a Christian polemical treatise against the Kabbalah. Luzzatto was interested in writing a refutation. On June 11, 1730, he wrote to Bassan that he had begun writing a work in defense of the Kabbalah against both its Christian and Sabbatian detractors. The profound influence made on Kohen's soul by Christian polemic would become apparent only in retrospect.[21]

In a strange case of coincidence or prescience, Morpurgo appended a plaintive litany against apostates when reporting to Hagiz that a commission which included Kohen went to induce Luzzatto to sign the oath: "From time to time . . . they rise against us, from amongst our brothers, they frighten and perplex us; they pledge themselves to a new covenant and their actions exceed all limits. . . . [To counteract them] God installs in each generation cedars of Lebanon to shield the generation as in this incident in which all the prophets [rabbis] spoke as one."[22]

Nehemiah Kohen converted to Christianity in May of 1735. The most complete description of the apostasy and the tremors it sent through the Jewish community can be found in a letter of Hagiz and Katzenellenbogen to Bassan:

A short while ago, an item in the news-chronicle stated that one very wealthy scholar of Ferrara apostatized. It appeared they were only exaggerating his station to humiliate and embarrass us. And now, woe! The world has darkened for us! Letters from our own people reported that the idolater had been the sponsor of your disciple [Luzzatto], and one of his earliest supporters. His name was still unknown to us. We discovered it afterwards, from another letter, to be Nehemiah Kohen of Ferrara, and upon hearing this, our hearts were completely shattered. Not because of what he had already done—for in my opinion, what he did had already been accomplished several years earlier—[Hagiz believed that Kohen had already been won over to Christianity long before the actual apostasy.] (It is for this reason, that when many Torah scholars had implored me to write to him and instruct him to desist from heresy, I ignored them, thank the Lord.)—but I grieve for the harm he will inflict on Israel in the future, in all areas of our religion, especially in written polemics which will arouse hostile legislation, for I have just heard of the decrees against the Talmud. I have no doubt that he will expose the esoteric lore of Israel including some of [Luzzatto's] works which we are presently debating. Therefore, his [Luzzatto's] books and letters must be destroyed . . . You should elect to follow our advice . . . the generation and the times demand it. May God save the communities of Italy from the clutches of this villain.[23]

Kohen's impending baptism was a celebrated "gran bela cosa" even before it took place. It was heralded by a celebratory verse, "Nel Solenne Battesimo conferito dal Card. T. Ruffo, al Sign. T. G. Ruffini, gia Graziadio [Nehemiah] Vitta [Hai] q. Jacob Coen Rabbino Ebrea."[24]

Hagiz' remarks, that the apostasy had been completed years earlier, reflected a reality. The apostasy of a prominent rabbi was not accomplished overnight. The Church used all its considerable resources to identify vulnerable prey, and implant seeds of doubt in their souls. Rabbinic colleagues were often aware of this, and they sometimes attempted to reclaim their fellow Jews before a final decision was reached. This explains the considerable number of polemical dialogues recorded between rabbis and other Jews, such as that of Judah Briel in his attempt to salvage the soul of Ezra B. Simon, a Mantuan Jew, and a similar dialogue by Abraham Segre. From Hagiz' remarks it appears that he had been requested to participate in the "deprogramming" of Nehemiah Kohen, but he had refused when he sensed the effort would be in vain.[25]

Hagiz' fear that Kohen would use his knowledge to betray his former co-religionists was not far fetched. Jewish history is replete with instances of apostates who became virulent anti-Jewish polemicists, and eighteenth century Italy was no exception. A rabbi of Ancona, Shabtai Nahamu, was baptized on March 26, 1735, almost the same time as Kohen. Under the Christian name Francisco Maria Ferretti, he published in Venice in 1741 a book entitled, *Revelation of the Truth of the Christian Religion to the Israelites on Basis of Their Own Rabbis.*[26]

Morpurgo responded to news of the apostasy with similar anguish, mourning the defilement of Kohen's priestly pedigree by baptismal waters: "In this confused and decadent generation . . . in these days of anguish . . . the wicked have left the fold, they have prostituted themselves.

Waters from the Holy of Holies were removed to places of filth, in defiance of God. . . . They have exchanged the supernal waters for murky slime."[27]

The apostasy was an opportunity for Hagiz to strengthen his case against Luzzatto. He accused Bassan of "collaborating with the priest of iniquity [Kohen] whose end reflects on their [Kohen and Luzzatto's] original intention. They went as one to deceive the court of Venice." By the same token, members of Luzzatto's circle tried to minimize the role of Kohen's support. The following story, preserved among Italian rabbis, illustrates this:

> A scholar from a priestly family in our city (Nehemiah, who was later called Heremiah, Kohen) became an Ishmaelite [vocalization marks on top of the word suggest that it is being used as a euphemism for "Christian," altered in fear of Christian censorship]. He wanted to accompany [Luzzatto] out of the city to make preparations for the Sabbath. His [Luzzatto's] disciples, R. Jacob Hazak, R. Moses David Valle, and R. Israel Hezekiah Treves said to him: "Master, a scholar is awaiting you outside, a sojourner who wishes to inquire after your welfare and accompany us." [Luzzatto] sighed and replied "Heaven forbid, let him not come, for there is no more hope for his soul." At that time the scholar [Kohen] had been considered untainted by all, and had been studying Torah.[28]

This apocryphal tale attempts to distance Luzzatto from the would-be traitor, and attributed to him the prescient ability to sense Kohen's defection before the others, contrary to fact. After the apostasy, when it was necessary to refer to Kohen's testimony in the Luzzatto controversy, he was not mentioned by name. In the Venetian rabbinic court, he is referred to as "the infamous." In Jacob Emden's anti-Sabbatian polemic, *Torat HaKena'ot*, Kohen's name was completely eliminated from documents he had signed.[29] There was also a sustained effort to trivialize his motives for converting, in the hopes of minimizing the significance of his conversion. Almost a century later, Samuel David Luzzatto heard a tradition that Kohen had been accused of procuring prostitutes and had converted to Christianity to escape the humiliation! A seventeenth-century apostate, Giulio Morosoni, wrote in an introduction to his book *Derekh Emunah* [*Path of Faith*] that he would describe his family's wealth and prominence, to silence Jewish accusations that he had converted to obtain material benefits.[30]

The apostasy of Kohen lifted the Luzzatto controversy above the realm of Sabbatian witch hunting and clashing personalities, and into the larger arena of Jewish-Christian relations in Italy. While the Venetian rabbinate could not openly accuse Luzzatto of contributing to the number of apostates with his false illumination, it was one of the motivations behind their offensive against Luzzatto.

Despite the imprecations of the Venetian rabbinate, Luzzatto left Italy for Amsterdam, stopping first in Frankfurt. Rabbi Jacob Popers, Chief Rabbi of Frankfurt, waited impatiently for Luzzatto's arrival. He pretended to welcome Luzzatto, who had arrived with a letter of introduction from his father-in-law, David Finzi of Mantua, unaware of the planning which had preceded his visit. When Popers suddenly confronted Luzzatto with all the documents that he had collected against him, Luzzatto was stunned. He requested that Popers grant him a fair hearing for his side of the case. Popers "agreed" to have his rabbinical court adjudicate the entire affair provided that Luzzatto would promise to abide by the judgment. A court was promptly convened in Poper's home and a document was drawn up which Luzzatto had already obligated himself to sign. In it, his works were characterized as "erroneous and false" and likely to have stemmed from the forces of darkness. He was made to promise never to print or circulate any work of his in Kabbalah regardless of what it contained. Anyone who would possess, circulate, or print his books would be excommunicated. The agreement reaffirmed his earlier vow of 1730 and forbade him to learn Kabbalah with anyone in the world, especially that which "he Moses the deceiver had invented," until he and his disciple(s) would reach forty years of age.

Luzzatto felt he had been trapped and coerced into signing the agreement.[31]

RENEWAL: THE CORE OF THE CONTROVERSY

While the events at Frankfurt unfolded, Hagiz and Katzenellenbogen issued a decree against Luzzatto. In this decree Hagiz did not even hint that Sabbatianism was the primary reason for opposition to Luzzatto's activities. Luzzatto's ties to Sabbatianism were too nebulous to sustain Hagiz' objections. A more profound issue, which had remained submerged during the early phase of the controversy, now emerged.

Hagiz' first letter in the controversy had expressed only the fear that Luzzatto's "evil sect" would spread its influence to others. Safed emissary Raphael Israel Kimhi was the first to articulate the most important aspect of Luzzatto's maggidic experience, *the renewal of divine illumination:* "God has found him worthy and sent an angel before him . . . This is not a natural phenomenon; its customs and logic lie beyond human comprehension. I saw with my own eyes . . . feats impossible for the human mind and hand . . . because the Lord has visited the Divine Abundance upon him."[32] Why did Kimhi affirm Luzzatto's claim immediately? His writ of appointment as an emissary of Safed was signed by Jacob Vilna and by Moses (son of Raphael Mordechai) Malkhi. Both had ties to the Sabbatians in Erez Israel and it is possible that Kimhi belonged to their circle. Members of those schools of Jewish mysticism, including Sabbatianism, which maintained the revelatory aspect of Kabbalah, took the position that it was certainly possible for contemporary pneumatics to experience legitimate revelation.

When the rabbis of Venice first received a copy of Gordon's letter, they expressed incredulity that renewal of divine revelation could occur in their present circumstances:

Are we to believe that the ancient sublime wisdom that has been hidden from all mankind has been restored through the Lord's illumination and influence? Or are we to assign him to the category of those who hold back the footsteps of the Messiah with their audacity? . . . We will assume that all the actions and ways are misguided and we will deal harshly with him."[33]

The conflicting reactions of Kimhi and of the Venetian rabbinate to the news of Luzzatto's revelation adumbrated the outlines of the controversy that followed. Beyond the question of Luzzatto's personal merit and the content of his particular maggidic revelations, fierce debate raged over the possibility that any person could receive divine revelation of any kind under the circumstances of oppression and exile of Italian Jewry. Those who supported Luzzatto did not necessarily believe that he would play a central role in an imminent messianic drama. They merely affirmed the possibility—even if remote—that his could be an authentic divine revelation. To deny all possibility of such an occurrence would seal the gates of hope and block the true illumination when it finally came.

The most prominent and eloquent advocate for the possibility of renewal was R. Isaiah Bassan, although he refrained from pronouncing a final judgment concerning Luzzatto specifically. Bassan argued that "There is nothing amiss if the Lord appears to him. . . . Although the vessel is new [his training is sufficient] so that nothing untoward would result from his actions. AR"I has taught that all manner of maggidim are possible." Although canonical prophecy usually occurred in the Holy Land, divine illumination often appeared on Diaspora soil, where it was affirmed by tradition.

Daniel was not considered a prophet because he lived in Babylonia, yet his visions were accepted by tradition; Elijah appeared to the Amoraite R. Anan and taught him *Seder Elijah Rabbah* and *Seder Elijah Zuta;* he appeared in the Yeshivot of the Geonim as well. The Hasidim of Provence—R. Abraham ibn David and his disciples—also claimed to have had visitations from Elijah, on alien soil. R. Joseph Karo received his first maggidic revelation in Nicopolis, and R. Menaham Azariah Fano received it in this very city. . . . The author of *Megalleh 'Amukot* [Nathan Nata Shapira] lived in Cracow when the spirit of the Lord appeared to him, and AR"I was in Egypt when he received his calling to the inner sanctum. Thus, the possibility existed in every time and place."[34]

Bassan never pronounced a definite certification of Luzzatto's illumination. He vigorously upheld the *possibility* that it could be authentic until proven otherwise. "All Israel is looking to me [for guidance] in this matter, and I cannot decide whether to ready my spear against the opponents, because I am still pausing on the threshold." Only in his earlier private correspondence to Luzzatto did he express the other alternative— the possibility that Luzzatto was erring, perhaps being misled by the forces of impurity. "It is natural that one who is concerned for you be frightened . . . lest some profane has mingled with the sacred. AR"I, in *Sefer ha-Kavanot* wrote that from the day the Temple was destroyed and the Torah was burned, its secrets and mysteries were given over to outside forces—this is known as the exile of the Torah." Bassan cautioned that leaving doors open to new illuminations allowed false prophecies to gain entry; they were often indistinguishable from the real thing: "At the time of the Zebi, the spirit rested upon many wise-hearted men. They fell on their faces, and they produced mighty treatises with ancient words, a marvel to behold. Above all, R. Nathan [of Gaza] . . . claimed to be following in the footsteps of the AR"I . . . in his books which I have, *Sefer ha-Beriah* and *Zamir Arizim.* He too inspired many to repent and gave *Tikkunim* to thousands of people. . . . Despite this, it all ended in great chaos. So now, pray tell me, what is the difference between one and the other? [Nathan and Luzzatto]. Only that all his work was directed toward Zebi? Who will differentiate?"[35]

Luzzatto argued to Bassan that the content of his revelations was proof of their sanctity: "It is heresy to think that the 'other side' can plumb the greatest secrets and mysteries [of the Torah]. Who has proven that the words of Bar Yohai, and more so, the words of AR"I, are true?" To Bassan's charge that he was too occupied with messianic matters, Luzzatto responded, "All classical Kabbalah must deal with messianism. It begins with the sin of Adam, then looks toward the restoration, Messiah."[36]

Some supporters of Luzzatto did not express any reservations. The yeshiva of Padua glowingly endorsed the attainment of its native son. Even the Chief Rabbi, Sabbatai Marini, who had been a skeptic at first, was convinced that the revelation was legitimate. The Kabbalist Aviad Basilea approved Luzzatto's polemical treatises in defense of Kabbalah, as well as his novellae on Lurianic Kabbalah. Luzzatto had never informed Basilea of his maggid.[37]

While Bassan refused to render a final decision regarding the nature of Luzzatto's revelation until he had personally investigated, Hagiz grew more adamant that a revival of revelation was intrinsically harmful, and should be smothered regardless of its content. Hagiz argued that even the figures cited by Bassan did not write their Torah in the name of the maggid. "Israel cannot, under any circumstances, accept Torah from an angel or seraph or something new which has never existed before." All of Luzzatto's teachings were evil, "but *even if that were not so*, I still say we should not occupy ourselves with *anything novel at all*" [בשום דבר חדש] [בכלל If his books have merit, let them be concealed." [If they contained heresy, they should be burned.] If his books would be printed, they would state how [Moses], Faithful Shepherd; Messiah; and Elijah called him "Our Master! Our Master! A new Torah would emerge from him. This renewal [Hithadshut] can harm, swallow, and destroy the souls of many innocents." Hagiz' stance was most forcefully expressed in the decree against Luzzatto which he and Katzenellenbogen issued in January 1735: "In this orphaned generation, *Israel does not need anything new* [אין] [ישראל . . . נצרכים לשום דבר חדש המתחדש"] which arises from time to time against the truth of one tradition. All Jewish communities and their leaders should agree to this: *that renewal is thoroughly evil—nothing good can ever come of it.*" [כי ההתחדשות אינו אלא דבר רע, ואין דבר טוב יוצא[38] [ממנו.

In March 1735, Hagiz and Katzenellenbogen wrote Bassan a scathing letter meant to demoralize and shame him into total submission. They charged that he had reneged on his obligation to monitor Luzzatto's writings and other activities. They were forced to attribute his lax guardianship to debilitating old age. They demanded that he disqualify himself from any role in the affair, and that he immediately transfer Luzzatto's

papers to the rabbinates of Venice, Frankfurt, or another Ashkenazic
community, which were presumably more objective.

The attacks on Bassan's integrity aroused Samson Morpurgo to defend
him. He wrote letters to Hagiz and his allies, asserting his prior neu-
trality in the controversy: "They are all Torah scholars, beloved and dear
to me—but peace and truth are dearer still." Morpurgo was forced to
write several times before Hagiz deigned to respond. He felt obliged to
remind Hagiz and his allies of his credentials as a bona fide zealot when
he had deemed the cause just. Morpurgo agreed with Hagiz that "In
these dark times, we have nothing to sustain us but the unification of
the hearts and minds of Israel's shepherds." He agreed with Hagiz that
rabbinic unity was crucial; attacking Bassan would defeat this purpose.
Bassan was accomplishing more for the goal of unity by not alienating
Luzzatto's circle, than Hagiz was doing by attacking Bassan.[39]

Morpurgo had a second stratagem to effect peace and compromise.
Hagiz and his supporters had condemned Luzzatto's writings to the pyre,
as false and heretical. Morpurgo urged that the writings be gathered and
buried, rather than burned. This would still achieve the desired effect
of removing them from circulation, but it would leave Luzzatto's supporters with their dignity intact. Burial was appropriate for writings which
were liable to be misunderstood by the masses, but it did not carry the
shameful stigma of burning which was reserved for works of outright
heresy. Morpurgo waged a single-handed, ceaseless campaign for this
simple compromise: "You be the judge! Is it not preferable to arrive at
the desired destination with a tender judgment informed by mercy, and
to cleanse the putrefication with mild waters, slowly, drop by drop . . .
than to inundate it with a mighty torrent of boiling water? Morpurgo's
efforts were not completely in vain. Bassan sent the trunk of Luzzatto's
scripts to Popers at his own expense, where Popers convened an ad hoc
court to decide the fate of the writings. He informed Hagiz that he had
burned a portion of the manuscripts, but the majority had been consigned to burial. "And even this was done in a manner that they will
soon molder and crumble away." Popers also wrote an exoneration of
Bassan from all further culpability in the Luzzatto affair, at Bassan's request.[40]

THE ULIANOV EPISODE

Hagiz' role in the Luzzatto controversy created many new foes. When they discovered that he had committed an error of judgment and fact— in print—they were delighted by the opportunity to reciprocate by defaming Hagiz. In 1728, R. (Solomon) Elijah of Ulianov published his book, *Birkhat Eliyahu* [*Elijah's Blessing*], in Wandsbeck. Hagiz took the opportunity to fill up several remaining blank pages with a brief tract on the subject of Jewish customs and their origin. In the treatise, Hagiz attacked a local printer of a standard prayerbook for what he believed was an error: "As I searched the works of liturgical exegesis I found a stumbling block in the *siddur* printed twice by R. Aaron ben Uri Lippman, z"l, at the press of Sulzbach in 1715." Hagiz had apparently begun a zealous search for deviations from standard texts in the wake of the Hayon campaign, and he had saved this criticism for his treatise on customs.

Lippman had written that it was the custom to say the *Zidkatha* prayers on Sabbath afternoon because King David had passed away on the Sabbath. In this connection, Lippman noted that Moses had died on a Friday. Hagiz cited a tradition that Moses had died on the Sabbath, and he attacked Lippman savagely for this oversight:

> This emendation constitutes blasphemy against heaven and earth. . . . Woe to the generation that sends a sullied hand to tamper with the words of God in our Torah because of doubts and questions which arise under the scrutiny of alien eyes. . . . Who does he think he is, who calls himself an Israelite yet wishes to change even the tiniest pinpoint of our Torah for whatever reason. . . . This leprosy is spreading among the weak of faith . . . as I have seen others supporting his view, . . . I cannot judge him innocent in this detail."[41]

Hagiz' violent condemnation of an insignificant comment aroused a storm of protest in defense of Lippman, a printer of repute. Ulianov, the author, who had kindly consented to allow Hagiz to use the empty space in his book regretted his generosity. Hagiz reported,

> The author of *Birkhat Eliyahu* wrote to me in 18 Tevet and 7 Shevat of this year [December 20, 1728, and January 7, 1729] of all that has passed. When the contemporary scholars read my words against the prayerbook of Sulzbach they are angered. Some demanded that my book should be burned; at the least, banned from Jewish homes

because my words went against *Ba'alei HaTosafot*, *Seder Olam*, and other traditional sources, and they were misdirected.

Rather than apologize, Hagiz appealed to R. Jacob Emden, son of Hakham Zebi, on April 11, 1729, for support against "those who study Torah for ulterior motives." Hagiz asserted to Emden that his opinion, as reflected in the works of like minded others, "is apparent to any scholar . . . simple words, the direct path, to be chosen by those who wish to study Torah for its own sake rather than to provoke contention." Hagiz confided to Emden that he had forwarded his justifications to the printer of the prayerbook, "but I withheld the following information from him because words like these can only be transmitted to the wisest and most modest of scholars, such as yourself." Hagiz' secret: he had disregarded the dates given in *Seder Olam*, for although he did not doubt its authenticity as an early *Beraita*, and its chronology was often cited by the Talmud, he believed that later hands had tampered with it, as was often the case with ancient books.[42]

Jacob Emden disagreed with Hagiz. He apologized profusely, then proceeded to demonstrate that Hagiz had committed a grievous error: the sources Hagiz had cited as support in fact refuted his claim. On July 14, 1729, Hagiz acknowledged that Emden was right in a brief note, a difficult admission for him.

The correspondence with Emden did not put an end to the affair. Luzzatto's partisans used Hagiz' error as proof that Hagiz was susceptible to errors in judgment and could not be relied on. In a letter to Gabriel del Rio, Bassan discredited Hagiz, using this episode as proof: "He does not muzzle his mouth, . . . and he is not careful with his language, condemning the innocent. . . . In the end of *Birkhat Eliyahu* there is a treatise by the mighty agitator [Hagiz], in which he tramples upon the author. . . . From this we learn that he mocks the defenseless, treads upon others, and plots only to do evil." Del Rio agreed with Bassan's assessment: "He exulted and trumpeted forth against R. Aaron Lippman as though R. Aaron had denied the truth of the entire Torah and all its precepts." Five years later, on December 22, 1735, Bassan returned to this incident as a means of discrediting Hagiz. In a letter to R. Barukh Kahana Rapoport of Fuerth he reiterated the entire episode to prove Hagiz' hastiness and unreliability.[43]

Hagiz later came to regret this association for another reason. After the publication of *Birkhat Eliyahu*, Ulianov embarked on another career: "He wandered far and wide, in the West, in Italy and Turkey to learn practical Kabbalah. He collected thousands of documents relating to practical Kabbalah and became an expert in this field." Ulianov became an expert on amulets, a "Ba'al Shem," master of the magical uses to which the names of God could be applied.[44] He also became a supporter of Luzzatto. Like Gordon, he wrote a letter extolling Luzzatto's powers, prompting Hagiz to link both men: "Another one from Poland, R. Elijah, author of *Birkhat Elijah* went out of his mind, due to the trials of poverty (which I know he suffered) and wrote things about the youth [Luzzatto] which are impossible." Hagiz did not specify what claims Ulianov had made for Luzzatto or to whom they were addressed, but Jacob Emden later charged that Ulianov had also written to Mordechai Jaffe of Vienna, and had claimed Luzzatto was the Messiah.[45]

In *Luhot ha-Edut*, R. Jonathan Eybeschutz called upon Ulianov's expertise in practical Kabbalah to defend himself against Emden's charges that the amulets he had written were Sabbatian. In order to uphold Ulianov's credibility, he had to clear Ulianov of Emden's charges of Sabbatianism, as well as the charge that he had acknowledged Luzzatto as a messiah. Eybeschutz wrote to Mordechai Jaffe. Jaffe's response cleared Ulianov of all charges: "You asked whether Elijah, author of *Birkhat Eliyahu* wrote to me in 1730 that R. Moses Hayim Luzzatto *z"l* was the messiah. I was shocked to read this. . . . It is well known that the letter written [about Luzzatto] from Italy by the physician R. Yekutiel [Gordon] was addressed to me, and I sent a copy to the rabbis of Germany to inform them. I have never heard that he was called a messiah . . . Although Gordon exaggerated his praises, he did not attribute the salvation to him at all . . . All this pertains to the letters of R. Yekutiel, but from the aforementioned R. Elijah there have never been any letters at all."[46] Eybeschutz mocked Emden: "Indeed, if he [Ulianov] had believed him [Luzzatto] to be the messiah, this is clear proof that he is not of the Sabbatian sect."[47]

Thus, Bassan and his supporters attempted to discredit Hagiz on ideological and personal grounds, the most formidable rabbinic opposition to any campaign of Hagiz' career. The absence of significant, lay-rabbinic tension in this dispute adumbrated the constellation of forces in the next major rabbinic campaign against Sabbatianism; the Emden-Eybeschutz controversy was a battle of two rabbinic titans.[48]

HAGIZ GATHERED support for the ban against the writings of Luzzatto. On March 31, 1735, he boasted to Bassan that he had already amassed close to forty signatures supporting the decree which also banned any kabbalistic works written during the preceding century, particularly those written after the Sabbatian era.[49]

Hagiz delegated the task of enforcing the bans against Luzzatto's writings—gathering and destroying them—to the Venetian rabbis, under the leadership of Isaac Pacifico. He promised to bolster their authority by collecting additional rabbinic bans. Eleven of these rabbinic bans against Luzzatto's and other Kabbalistic writings have been preserved.[50] Several were addressed directly to Hagiz; almost all indicated that they were writing at Hagiz' request. R. Mordechai Lissa of Berlin wrote that he had been called upon by "the great light, Moses Hagiz." He agreed to the ban against all recent and future Kabbalistic writing, citing Luzzatto only as an example. In contrast, R. Arye Leib of Glogau (son-in-law of Hakham Zebi), writing to "the commander of God's army in this obligatory war, Moses Hagiz," used the most vicious and acerbic language against Luzzatto. While other writs were carefully directed only at Luzzatto's books, R. Arye Leib designated Luzzatto an outright heretic and warned that his "appointment with death will arrive imminently." He warned all cities with printing presses to be especially vigilant lest Luzzatto try to publish any work. R. Jacob Pinchov of Breslau addressed his ban to Moses Hagiz, the zealot, and agreed to Hagiz' request to gather signatures from itinerant Polish rabbis who passed through his town. Pinchov castigated Luzzatto as a wicked villain, Bassan as careless and irresponsible, and the masses of Israel as "stupid, gullible, credulous and weak hearted." Only the Sages of Israel could save the remnants of this poor flock. The only documents which explicitly mention Sabbatianism are those of R. Eliezer of Cracow and the rabbis who relied on his information.[51]

The most interesting text gathered by Hagiz was the one contributed by Jacob Emden. From Emden's introduction it is evident that his relationship with Hagiz and Katzenellenbogen was tense, although he had just moved to Altona. His pride had been hurt when they did not include him as an equal co-signer of the original ban. This is the only public anti-Sabbatian initiative by Emden before his controversy with Eybeschutz, and it provides an important link between the activity of Hagiz, and Emden's later anti-Sabbatianism. In a self-aggrandizing preamble to his ban, Emden wrote of the disappointment of the rabbinate of Venice that he hadn't been asked to sign the original ban, and of their letter to Hagiz, asking that Emden be included. According to Emden, Hagiz blamed the omission on Katzenellenbogen: "My brother, it had been my intention from the start to have you sign as one with us, but the Head of the

Rabbinical Court [Katzenellenbogen] prevented me." Emden's denunciation of Luzzatto was as scathing as that of his brother-in-law R. Arye Leib. Luzzatto was a "plotter of evil against the Lord, a heretic out to entrap souls with his writings, his lies, and his sorcery . . . He wished to propound novel ideas, and gather a study group to separate himself from the Sages of Israel." Emden condemned Luzzatto's books to the flames and recalled the unbridled zealotry of his father, which he hoped to emulate. Emden later included Luzzatto in his anti-Sabbatian tract, *Torat ha-Kena'ot*, as one of the important precursors of Eybeschutz' Sabbatianism.[52]

Empowered by the supporting letters, the rabbinate of Venice issued a Herem against the writings of Luzzatto on October 21, 1735. The ban threatened pain of death, and full excommunication from this world and next to anyone who knew of any of Luzzatto's writings—"books, letters, poems, liturgy and prayers, or any other composition of his"—and did not turn them over to the rabbinate of Venice or to their local rabbinic authority within the next fifteen days. The works would all be burned as works of heresy: none could be spared. The rabbinate of Venice proclaimed the ban in the synagogues of Venice on the Sabbath and sent copies to the rabbis of every city in Italy, exhorting them to read the ban in their congregations.[53]

The extreme position taken in the ban dismayed and shocked Bassan, as it reflected utter disregard for his opinion. He took several steps to combat the Venetian Rabbinate within the rabbinic court system. On November 17, 1735, he arranged a deposition before the rabbinate of Modena, to clear himself and his disciple of the principal charges against them. Bassan sent similar requests to other communities to hold hearings regarding his position in the Luzzatto affair. He wrote to R. Aviad Basilea in Mantua (whose grandson had accepted Bassan's deposition in Modena), to request a statement regarding Luzzatto's books, whether they should be burned as the Venetians had ordered, or buried, as he had suggested. Basilea's reply completely vindicated Luzzatto and Bassan of any ideological errors, and condemned Hagiz for perpetuating the canards against Luzzatto. Bassan sent a similar letter to R. Moses b. Solomon Civita of Mantua. A similar deposition was made to the rabbinical court of Padua, whose decision favored Bassan.[54]

Next, Bassan wrote an emphatic letter to the "small council" of Venice rejecting their ban because it was founded on false and insufficient testimony. He offered an ultimatum: "Let impartial, pious, experts inspect the documents. If they are found to contain even a smattering of heresy, let them be burned; or, if you do not wish to submit the papers to such an inquiry, let them be buried." If they refused both alternatives, Bassan vowed to summon them to an impartial rabbinic court which would hear both sides. In this way he could not be called a "scoffer" against the Venetian ban, at the same time that the Venetian rabbis retained the freedom to weigh the evidence as they saw fit. He issued an "absolute warning" to the Venetian rabbinate: "Whoever shall pronounce any decree to burn the books prior to a proper investigation, . . . the ban shall be null and void."[55] Bassan's tone was terse and free of passion. His emotions erupted in a letter to one of the foremost Jewish pietists in Central Europe, R. Barukh Kahana Rapoport of Fuerth, whose signature had appeared on the ban. He vented his deep anger and frustration with uncharacteristically venomous attacks on individual Venetian rabbis. He accused Pacifico, Belilios, and especially Solomon Zalman of Lvov, for whom he had found a teaching position, of ingratitude. Hagiz and Katzenellenbogen had disregarded him as though he had been "a beast of the field." They had ordered him to hand over Luzzatto's papers, "as though I were dishonest, as though it hadn't been tightly sealed under my guard for the past five years." Worse, Hagiz had likened him to the idolater Nehemiah Kohen, just because Kohen had been a supporter of Luzzatto. He asked Rapoport to deliver words of rebuke against the Venetian rabbinate, and to support him in his battle for truth. He wrote a similar letter to R. Jacob Popers, which has not survived.[56]

Bassan received support from many quarters. R. Hayim Pollack of Lublin derided the Venetian rabbinate, and pledged to campaign for Bassan. He had already contacted Menashe Padovani, R. Barukh Kahana Rapoport, and the Sages of Ashkenaz and the Polish Sages of the Council of the Four Lands to refute the malicious falsehoods spread by the Venetian rabbinate. He defamed R. Solomon Zalman of Lvov, calling him a charlatan who had never set foot in Lvov. Samson Morpurgo lodged protests with the rabbinate of Venice as well as with Hagiz. R. Abraham Rakicz wrote to R. Jacob Popers demanding that Popers respond to Bassan. He discredited another of Bassan's opponents: " R. I. Pacifico, who towers above them, is a scholar to whom one can ask a legal question on any matter—and he will not know the answer. Once, when I praised Talmudic scholarship . . . he mocked me and said there is no purpose in studying the Talmud as all the laws have been arranged in the Codes, so that one does not have to waste time studying Talmud which is like a closed book, replete with enigmas. And . . . he is typical of his cohorts."[57]

In response to Bassan's attempts to defend his honor Hagiz unleashed his rage in an open letter to the rabbinate of Venice:

My anger is not directed against the abominable heretic H.M.L. [Luzzatto], for he has already left *Klal Yisrael,* and has forfeited his share in the world to come, but against his rabbi and other scholars who have come forward to defend him. Whoever does not condemn his work to the flames has enticed the public to sin. . . . The evil has sprung from the distortions of his rabbi, Isaiah Bassan.

Hagiz argued that Benjamin Kohen, a Sabbatian, had never revealed his opinions publicly, and never proclaimed that the bans against Hayon of 1713–1714 were to be taken lightly, while Bassan publicly demeaned the honor of the Sages of Venice by dismissing their ban. He concluded, "I don't know if this rabbi [Bassan] will receive atonement on the day of judgment because he has sinned and caused others to follow suit."

Jacob Popers rejected Bassan's defense with a catalogue of false seers and prophets, all Sabbatians, who had duped his community in the past decades. He did not intend to lower his guard this time, and he urged Bassan to relinquish all Luzzatto's papers either to Hamburg (Katzenellenbogen and Hagiz) or to himself. When Bassan agreed to relinquish the trunk filled with Luzzatto's maggidic writings it was on condition that only Popers would examine the papers. When a rumor reached Bassan "that the rabbis of Venice were boasting that I would return the trunk to them," Popers assured him that he would never violate his promise. When Popers received the trunk, he examined its contents carefully, certifying that they had not been tampered with, and at Bassan's request he issued an apology, exonerating Bassan of all suspicion and notifying Hagiz of this. Popers understood that since there were several copies of some manuscripts in the trunk, there must have been other copies still in circulation, and he concurred with the ban that these outstanding copies must be relinquished to rabbinic authorities.[58]

Popers understood the essence of Luzzatto's writings, correctly analyzing his reenactment of the Zoharic *Idrot.* Popers and his Bet Din pronounced judgment on Luzzatto's writings: a small portion were to be burned, the rest would be buried. That done, he pronounced the controversy closed: "Now is the time to let the matter rest . . . never to be mentioned again, neither in writing nor orally, so that the scholars will cease their quarreling."[59]

Absent from the final stage of the controversy is the voice of Luzzatto. He later boasted to Bassan that he had never accomplished a finer feat than to leave the agitators to stew in their anger while he remained aloof. In 1735, Luzzatto reached Amsterdam where he basked in the warm welcome of the Sephardic community. The Sephardim of Amsterdam did not participate in the controversy, perhaps because of their earlier feuds with Hagiz. From there, Luzzatto tried to direct his circle and encourage his adherents to remain loyal to their covenant.

The first public action taken by the circle without its leader was a defense of its members, and of Luzzatto, written on September 7, 1735, signed by Jacob Hazak, the talmudic scholar of the group. However, neither Hazak, nor anyone else, emerged to fill the vacuum of leadership left by Luzzatto. On November 3, 1735, Luzzatto wrote a letter to his disciples encouraging them to keep their faith during the divinely ordained trial. He warned them not to engage in war with their detractors "because their curses are null and void, and every herem, every excommunication, every imprecation is permitted, forgiven and dissolved for you."

Luzzatto also wrote to Bassan asking him to support his innocent disciples. In fact, Bassan did write to Luzzatto's circle. At Bassan's order, "the page upon which their special rituals had been organized by Luzzatto was torn from the book. The verses are no longer being recited. We study nothing but the text of the *Zohar* and the Halakhah."

The Luzzatto campaign was conducted almost exclusively by correspondence, a fitting response to Gordon's epistolary introduction of Luzzatto. Reliable couriers and competent copyists were essential concerns for both sides. "*Gebiat Edut*," soliciting and validating testimony was also a technique used in the campaign. When Luzzatto's supporters cited the testimony of the Safed emissary, Hagiz countered with testimonies from two Hebron emissaries. Both sides, but especially Hagiz', used dysphemism, unflattering plays upon their opponents' names. As in earlier campaigns, the role of Kabbalah and its appropriateness for the masses was a major issue in the Luzzatto campaign. The hard line adopted by Hagiz and Katzenellenbogen in their ban rendered their position untenable to other rabbis who believed that the good in Kabbalah outweighed the potential for harm.

The novelty in the rabbinic campaign against Luzzatto lies not in its technique, but in its broadened objective. The question of degree of Sabbatian influence on Luzzatto's writing became moot when Hagiz rejected the narrow criteria of Sabbatianism as the test of Luzzatto's acceptability. Sabbatianism remained important only as the original impetus for Hagiz' lifelong crusade, and an oppressive memory to the rabbinate. It colored their judgment of every attempt to revitalize Judaism. The Luzzatto campaign represents the transition from the rabbinic battle against Sabbatianism to an effort to suppress all forms of religious renewal. By firmly positioning rabbinic authority against any renewal of spirit, Hagiz was closing fateful doors for rabbinic Judaism.

CHAPTER 9

Crown of a Career

 SHORTLY AFTER the Luzzatto campaign Hagiz completed the work which he rightly regarded as his magnum opus. The multi-faceted *Mishnat Hakhamim* [*The Lore of the Sages*], is part autobiography, part ethical treatise, and part polemic. It was the summa that brought together the diverse strands of his career. The title essay, (the twenty-third chapter) *"Emunat Hakhamim"* is the cornerstone of the work. It is a term which Hagiz would have translated "faith in the Sages and in the rabbinic tradition."[1]

MISHNAT HAKHAMIM

Hagiz' purpose in *Mishnat Hakhamim* was to address the crisis of faith that beset Jewish society in the early modern period. He located the source of the crisis in two immanent developments in the Jewish world: Sabbatianism, which generated antinomian heresies and weakened the condition of Jewish hope in a post messianic era; and the Marrano complex, which carried with it a tradition of rational skepticism that challenged every source of Jewish authority. The erosion of traditional Jewish beliefs was so pervasive that almost every rabbinic work of that period, in any genre, touched upon it in some fashion.[2] Hagiz had devoted an entire separate treatise to this subject, "the essence of the faith," but it has not survived; the chapter on *Emunat Hakhamim* is a summary of that treatise.

Hagiz declared of this chapter, "It will save multitudes of souls . . . who are crippled in this vital faith, the faith in the Sages, the foundation upon which everything rests. . . . It is the basis of the Torah and *mizvot.*" It represents a more mature stage in the development of Hagiz' response to the anti-rabbinism that had so jolted him when he first encountered it at the beginning of his career.

THE VERY first work that Hagiz had brought to press in 1703 contained a brief essay "On the Benefits of Repentance."[3] At first glance it seems a rather standard piece of hortatory ethical literature which Hagiz inserted "to fill the blank pages." The apparent theme is the uniform obligation of repentance upon all, regardless of whether or not one was the "son of a sinner." Upon closer examination, this is one one of Hagiz' codewords for a former Marrano. In addition to the widely used term '*ba'al teshuba*' [one who has mastered repentance] as a designation for rejudaized Marranos, the terms Abraham ben Terah and *Lo'azim* were also employed by Hagiz.[4] Hagiz devoted one long parable in the essay to the value of circumcision, of refraining from shaving one's sideburns and beard, and of wearing *zizit*, the ritual fringes. It is inconceivable for a list that included circumcision to have been addressed to any Jewish audience other than former Marranos.[5] In the same essay, Hagiz defended the validity of the Oral Law and of rabbinic authority. He intuitively grasped the nexus between these "heretical" ideologies and Marranism; it is to former Marranos that this treatise is addressed.

Hagiz confronted those who denied the authority of rabbinic tradition, the Oral Law. "If the Torah had been given in the form demanded by the 'gluttonous ones,' with everything explicitly stated, including Divine Providence, and reward and punishment . . . there would be scant value to its observance." The unflattering appelation "gluttonous ones," a reference to the Biblical renegades who challenged God's ability to sate them with meat, is indicative of Hagiz' conviction early in his career that hedonistic impulses rather than sincere doubts motivated most of the skeptics.[6] He had attributed the decline of rabbinic authority to the phenomenal wealth of the lay leaders which fueled their greed for communal power, and to their desire to enjoy forbidden fruits: "They overthrow the yoke not because they have found the Sages' Torah harmful to them, but to suit their own purposes. . . . They wish to be free to indulge in promiscuity." Hagiz description of the progress of heresy begins with laxity in observance of the minutiae, and grows to a rejection of the entire traditional faith.

To the heretics who denied that there was a world to come, Hagiz replied: "Who has ever gone there and returned to us to prove all the words of our Sages? . . . They say of the Sages that their words were invented by their imaginations in order to frighten and threaten people, so that they can maintain their authority over them." "If one does not believe the severity [of punishment to be meted out in the world to come] . . . one is a heretic." "Denial of belief in resurrection of the dead, one of the greatest fundamentals . . . has felled many victims . . . in yesteryear and in contemporary times. . . . This fallacy leads to denial of the Creation, for all these principles are inextricably bound to one another." Hagiz included belief in transmigration of souls in his definition of reward and punishment. A generation after Spinoza, Hagiz offered his treatise as "an antidote to the arguments of the secular philosophers who devise malicious and vain questions against our Sages and our Torah."[7]

While this small treatise was only a small addition to the long list of works addressed to Marranos, it is important because it became one of the foundations of Hagiz' thought. In retrospect, this first hesitant expression of rebuke served as exercise for the more forceful formulations that followed. In his first work of social criticism, *Sefat Emet*, written in 1707, his tone was still one of shock and alarm at having found so many Jews openly challenging their traditional faith: "There has never been anything like this! My ears tingle upon hearing it. . . . In their sinfulness they challenge, as though the truth of our faith and its Sages were in doubt."[8]

Hagiz' antidote had been a review of the rabbinic "chain of transmission of the Law" and recommendations of books written in the vernacular to bolster the faith. A bibliography for those seeking guidance, written in 1707, is typical of recommendations offered by spiritual leaders concerned with the same issues as Hagiz:

And if, after all this . . . your heart still doubts, go thee to two or three of the Sephardic Sages who have written a fraction of their wisdom for the "foreigners" in the vernacular, to enlighten the Israelites of our generation who have never known the Torah all their days, for they were as children taken captive among the Gentiles. . . . One book is the *Conciliador* by Menasseh ben Israel, a Sage and great rabbi of your community. It will demonstrate with convincing proofs the necessity to believe and to know the Oral Torah entrusted to the Sages . . .

Learn the book . . . of the Sage Immanuel Aboab . . . who has written on the development of the Oral Torah . . . which in my

opinion is preferable to the former [*Conciliador*] . . . especially
chapters twelve and twenty-two on the testimony of Gentiles . . .
who cannot deny the greatness of our Sages.
"And the third text is decisive" . . . it too elaborates on the chain
of tradition . . . with rational and Divine proofs. . . . The Kuzari
which I have seen translated . . . to the vernacular, Spanish, and
which has given me great pleasure.[9]

In *Mishnat Hakhamim*, the sense of surprise and outrage has given way
to one of determination and purpose. Hagiz addressed his words not only
to the skeptics, but also to the rabbis and teachers who confronted them
daily. He urged them to join him in a massive effort to combat the decline of rabbinic authority. "It is absolutely vital in this day and age, that
all sermons and lessons given by scholars and communal leaders alike,
both to the masses and to other scholars promote only this among the
fundamentals of the faith: the faith in the Sages." Hagiz argued that
the fate of the struggle to reinstate rabbinic authority lay in the hands
of the leaders themselves—the masses could not be held ultimately responsible, "for God did not apportion to them any share of wisdom."[10]
    While Hagiz' analysis of the causes of heresy are more elaborate in
Mishnat Hakhamim, his basic solution did not change: "For this is the rule
of our religion: everything depends on faith in the Sages." His list of
recommended reading in *Mishnat Hakhamim* is similar to the one he had
written decades earlier.[11]
    The central themes and problems in *Mishnat Hakhamim* had already
been articulated by many predecessors and contemporaries of Hagiz. At
the end of his volume of responsa, *Emek Binyamin*, Raphael Dias Brandon
devoted space to the problem of the crisis of rabbinic authority, identical
in tone to *Mishnat Hakhamim:* "I trembled with anger to hear the voices
insulting the angels of heaven, the words of the sages for they are true
and their words are truth . . . They say 'Why must we have faith in
them [the rabbis], they are people just as we are, who know whether
their words are correct?' Accursed be these evil sinners . . . for they
have rejected the yoke of the Almighty who has sanctified us and commanded us to heed the Sages."[12]
    If rabbinic apologetic works of sixteenth- and seventeenth-century
Western Europe, such as Immanuel Aboab's *Nomologia* and Menasseh ben
Israel's *Conciliador*, were often addressed to former Marranos, rabbinic
apologies of the eighteenth century were addressed to a more general
audience. Among such works are David Nieto's *Kuzari ha-Sheni* [*Second
Kuzari*] and Aviad Basilea's *Emunat Hakhamim* [*Faith in the Sages*], a de-

fense of the rabbis primarily as transmitters of Kabbalah. Hagiz' *Mishnat Hakhamim* is an outstanding exemplar of the genre. The published books are only the tip of the iceberg; many similar works were circulated in manuscript. A recent survey of this literature concludes: "The term *emunat hakhamim* assumes a new, almost technical meaning. As distinct from the Christian faith and the Sabbatian "faith," another concept is established—faith in the Sages, the oral law and in the rabbinic tradition down through the ages."[13]

MOSES HAGIZ ON CHRISTIANS AND CHRISTIANITY

If the attitude of Hagiz and his contemporaries to Christians and Christianity appears contradictory, it is the reflection of a paradoxical reality. At the same time as the Catholic church continued to implement its vigorous anti-Jewish policies, to severely oppress Jews living in the Papal States, to burn Marranos at the stake for Judaizing, and to lure converts from Judaism, Protestant countries in the West had begun to admit Jews under favorable conditions. Protestant Hebraist scholars demonstrated a lively and often friendly interest in Jews and their literature. The Hebraists addressed their overtures to many leading rabbinic figures. Thus, the same rabbinic pens that wrote the harshest, most derisive polemics against the Christian religion also maintained close and amicable correspondence with prominent Christian scholars.[14]

Almost every member of Hagiz' circle wrote anti-Christian polemics. Judah Briel wrote "Discorso Apologetico," a defense of Menasseh ben Israel against the priest Vincenzo Ragusa; "Riposta alla *Synagoga Disingannata* dal Padre Pinamonti," and "Animadversiones in Evangelica." He congratulated the physician Isaac Cardoso on his apology, *Las Excelencias de los Hebreos*, and encouraged his pupil, Joshua Segre of Casale, to write anti-Christian polemics as well. David Nieto wrote several polemical works, especially directed against sermons preached at autos da fe; Samson Morpurgo engaged in a polemical dispute with the priest Benetelli. Isaiah Bassan wrote a polemic against the "the writings of the apostles" and recorded his debates with Christian missionaries.[15]

In the seventeenth century, anti-Jewish polemics written by Christians had increasingly begun to turn to recently popularized Kabbalistic works to support their arguments. The failed messianic movement and Sabbatian Kabbalah, especially its messianic and trinitarian elements, became an even sharper sword in the hands of anti-Jewish polemicists. Thus, it is no coincidence that in the eighteenth century, many of the most prominent anti-Sabbatians also engaged in polemics against Christianity.[16]

Hagiz is exceptional among these contemporaries in that he did not write any formal anti-Christian polemics. To the contrary, he seems to have held a very sympathetic attitude to Christians and Christianity.

> If the Torah has commanded us not to spurn the overtures of Egyptians, who enslaved us, . . . and the Edomites, who destroyed our Temple . . . How much more must we open an aperture in this long exile, . . . in which He has shown us kindness before mighty kings. . . . who accept us graciously and grant us spiritual liberty, to observe all that God has commanded us. God has granted that in our own day, the pious kings, father and son, who preceded the present king, and the great kings of Poland and Prussia, may they and their offspring live forever, have granted permission to print the Talmud.

In several places he affirmed that Jews should respect Gentiles who uphold the religious traditions they had inherited from their forebears: "There is neither contempt nor competition in the Jewish heart against people who uphold the faith of their fathers. We say, 'Let them be, for this is their tradition.'"[17] Hagiz believed that direct inter-religious polemics were not effective: "All polemical argument with the masses is a waste of time, it only breeds more hatred and jealousy. We have found that Thomas responded to King Alfonso of Spain that he had never seen a wise person who hated a Jew. They are hated only by the masses . . . And I wish to add to his words, 'There is no hatred like religious hatred.'"[18] Polemic against the benighted masses was hopeless; against enlightened intellectuals, superfluous. "See the difference between the Gentile masses and their Sages. If one presents an argument to a sage, he counters with another, and one can engage in a dialogue. With the masses, there is no decisive argument because their faith is rooted so deeply in their hearts."[19]

Unlike many of his colleagues, Hagiz was born and raised in a most oppressive Muslim society. He had seen ruinous discriminatory taxation and humiliating physical suffering inflicted on Jews. The treatment of Jews in Protestant Western Europe, may have appeared so much improved by contrast, that Hagiz could not summon the same venom as his contemporaries. This does not mean that Hagiz never wrote anti-Christian invective—he did. However, it was invariably embedded in

Hebrew works directed at Jewish audiences, thus demonstrating that he did not desire to engage Christians in direct polemic. His arguments were addressed to Jews who might be tempted to follow in the footsteps of celebrated apostates or unrepentant *conversos*. While it was incumbent upon Jews to seek the welfare of Gentiles, Hagiz singled out apostates as worthy of persecution.[20]

Hagiz cautioned against teaching Torah to Gentiles because of the danger that the Jewish teacher would be influenced by the Christian pupil: "He enters to teach and finds that he has been taught. The falsehoods in their books enter his body like the venom of a viper." Similarly, Hagiz warned against selling Hebrew works to Christians who would not otherwise obtain them, particularly manuscripts, even if the buyer offered to pay more than the actual value, for fear that these materials might be turned into polemical weapons against Jews. However, if a book was already widely available, its sale was permitted.[21]

Years after Hagiz made these hostile pronouncements, he had the occasion to meet with several of the renowned Christian Hebraists of his time, and his attitude changed. The first indication of Hagiz' participation in a correspondence with a Christian Hebraist is indirect, a passing reference in a letter of David Nieto's. Nieto was replying to Christian Theofile Unger, a Christian Hebraist and Hebrew bibliophile. Of their correspondence, only Nieto's reply remains to reveal the tenor of their relationship. Nieto's letter was written in Hebrew, as Unger's had been. Nieto implored Unger in the future, "to write to me in Latin, in Roman letters, because I cannot read Hebrew script of the Ashkenazim; and I will reply to you in Latin." Nieto addressed Unger as, "Wisest of men, greatest of preachers, crown of the Pious . . . Sage in all wisdoms and ethics." The letter is entirely concerned with bibliographic information which Unger had sought, and which Nieto was able to provide only in some instances. Apparently, Unger had asked Nieto to forward a letter of his to Hagiz. Nieto promised to forward Hagiz' reply to Unger as soon as he received it. Unfortunately, Hagiz' reply, if there was one, has not survived.[22]

A similar response to Unger's inquiry was written by Isaac Cantarini. He was asked to provide biographical information on the "seekers of wisdom in Israel" who had lived during the Renaissance from the tombstones of those who were buried in Padua. Cantarini obliged with whatever information he had.[23]

Neither Nieto nor Cantarini ever expressed ambivalence over these exchanges, even though both were authors of anti-Christian polemics. To the contrary, if the purpose of their polemics was to vindicate Judaism against libelous charges, friendly correspondence may have served the same purpose.[24]

In addition to the possible correspondence with Unger, Hagiz made the acquaintance of Johan Christoph Wolf, author of *Bibliotheca Hebraea*. Wolf's research for this monumental Hebrew bibliography led him to the library of David Oppenheim, whose collection formed the basis of the *Bibliotheca*. Hagiz apparently became acquainted with Wolf through Oppenheim, drawn by their mutual interest in Hebrew bibliography. Both Jacob and Moses Hagiz were accorded prominent entries in Wolf's *Bibliotheca*. Hagiz' interests are further reflected in the lengthy section devoted to the Hayon controversy. Hagiz found the many Hebrew manuscript treasures in Wolf's library to be irresistible, and together they pored over the puzzlements of Wolf's priceless ancient Hebrew collection. Hagiz described Wolf in his introduction to *Mishnat Hakhamim*:

> Due to the vagaries of the times, it occurred that I came to the home of the great scholar, praised for his complete mastery of all learning, world renowned for his desire to collect the books of all disciplines and for the books which he has published, the famous preacher of Hamburg, called by the good name, **Professor Doctor Johan Christoph Wolf,** May the Lord in his mercy lengthen his days. In his kindness, he took me up to his attic, a noble place, decorated with thousands of books, of every nation and language. Not only works which have appeared in print, but even the ancient books of our nation in manuscript, he seeks them and expends a fortune to acquire them for his treasure trove . . . because in his eyes the words of the ancients are more dear than any honor or other science. [emphasis in original]

In this passage, Wolf's name is printed in prominent letters that dominated the page. Hagiz made no secret of his pride in his relationship with Wolf.[25]

Only once in *Mishnat Hakhamim* is there a hint that religious polemical tension may have arisen between Hagiz and Wolf. Hagiz wrote that Wolf had shown him an ancient, authentic manuscript of the Hebrew Bible, over one thousand years old, in which the name of God was written as a configuration of three letters *yud* [the tenth letter of the Hebrew alphabet], one above and two below, instead of the usual two letter representation of the divine name. "The wise master [Wolf] professed great wonderment at the significance of the three *yuds.*" Hagiz did not say explicitly whether Wolf indicated that the unusual configuration represented the trinitarian nature of God—in an old Hebrew manuscript. However, Hagiz' lengthy list of possible explanations for this triune representation, and his subsequent affirmation that the Jews were still God's chosen people, seem to indicate that a polemical exchange had taken place.[26]

Hagiz recorded these meetings with Wolf in *Mishnat Hakhamim*, printed in 1733. Their relationship continued over the years; in 1736, Hagiz wrote a warm letter in response to an inquiry from Wolf. The contents of the letter concerned the authorship of an anonymous manuscript in Wolf's possession (Hagiz was unable to determine the author) and variations in Hebrew orthography. Hagiz excused himself as being "very weak, my eyesight is no longer as it was in my youth." In addition, his letter was being written during the High Holy Days, days devoted to introspection and the study of ethical works, so Hagiz could not oblige the request to copy pages of very fine writing. He signed off to Wolf as 'Your dear friend always, and a faithful servant to serve you who blesses your years."[27]

Like the dialogue that took place between learned Jews and Christians in Renaissance Italy, the mutually friendly dialogue between Hagiz' Jewish and Christian contemporaries never broke new ground to become the basis for a substantive change in Jewish-Christian relations.

HAGIZ STUDIED world history and followed current world events with avid interest. His analysis of events was always theological: "They think everything happens to them by coincidence, they do not sense the word of God in this generation." For Hagiz, "It is obvious that the hearts of kings are in the hands of God." He even mentioned that he had written a treatise on the subject, titled "The Intricacies of Divine Providence" ["*Peratei ha-Hashgaha*"], to refute those who claim that there is no divine interest in small affairs of the world. "I have researched and found that this is the opinion of philosophers . . . who have destroyed the world with their false opinions and have confused several wise men among our own people."[28]

Hagiz' conception of history was entirely Judaeo-centric. God manipulated all world events solely for their effect on his chosen people. "Neither evil nor good come to the world except on behalf of Israel."[29] Gentiles served as a convenient foil for Hagiz' admonitions: they donated funds generously to their Holy Land emissaries and treated them royally; Jews would do well to emulate them. Gentile scholars acknowledged the sapience of Jewish sages; Jews should follow their example.

There is clear proof, not only among the sages who follow the Lutheran faith, but even their early scholars who are pillars of the

faith of the Pope in Rome. . . . They not only praise the talmudic
sages as being unparalleled in their competence in matters of law,
but they defend us against our foes who malign the *aggadah* and
the miraculous deeds recounted in it [the talmud] . . . that there
is nothing so alien in them as to subvert their kingdom or their
religion. . . . Surely, all this that the [Gentile] sages have said in
praise of the sages of Israel is only to shame that minority from
among our people who . . . debase and mock the *aggadot.*"

For Hagiz, Jewish suffering was an appropriate punishment for Jewish
sin. He praised the authors of *Megillat Ta'anit* who had recorded the days
of suffering with love because it demonstrated divine justice. He warned
the recently established Jewish communities of Western Europe that they
would share the fate of other Jewish communities, once peaceful and
prosperous, who had abandoned God and spurned his Torah and were
now burdened with sorrows.[30]

HAGIZ' CONTACTS with Christian Hebraists, as well as his interest in
sectarian Jewish history as the basis of comparison for present concerns,
led him to the Karaites, a medieval sectarian group. Founded in eighth-
century Babylonia, the Karaites denied the validity of the oral tradition
and rabbinic authority. "I see that this ancient plague has blossomed anew,
the evil sect *Karaites* . . . It has wafted among the masses and several
individuals have fallen prey out of ignorance, and have doubted the words
of our Sages." While at first it appears that Hagiz' numerous references
to Karaites are merely facile, general appelations for heretics, upon closer
examination, that is not the case. Hagiz addressed several polemical comments to the Karaite sect concerning specific Karaite practices, comments
which would not have been appropriate unless he was referring to authentic contemporary Karaites.[31]

The active Karaite communities in eighteenth-century Crimea and
Lithuania aroused the interest of Christian Hebraists. Among the Christian scholars who wrote treatises about the Karaites in this period was
Hagiz' friend and correspondent, Johann Wolf. His annotation, intro-
duction, and Latin translation of works by and about Karaites, *Notitia
Karaeorum*, was undoubtedly known to Hagiz. Other well known works
by Christian scholars concerning the Karaites such as Gustav Peringer's
Epistola de Karaitarum rebus in Lithuania of 1691 and Jacob Trigland's polemical *Diatribe de Secta Karaeorum* of 1703 may also have been known to
Hagiz.[32]

This attention stimulated the Karaites of this period to write apologia which polemicized against rabbinic Judaism as well as Christianity. Solomon ben Aron Troki wrote the treatise *Appiryon 'Asah Lo*, on Karaism and its difference from Judaism, at the request of Swedish scholars at the turn of the century. Mordecai ben Nisan Kukizow wrote two treatises in defense of Karaism, *Dod Mordecai* and *Lebush Mordecai*, the latter as a reply to questions put to him by King Charles XII of Sweden. While the renewed interest in and activity of the Karaite sect in the eighteenth century cannot be cited as a cause of the decline of the rabbinate, its renaissance in this period gave strength to anti-rabbinic interests and provided an example of an anti-rabbinic form of Judaism that had survived for a millenium. Thus it was appropriate that Hagiz and his rabbinic contemporaries devoted space in their polemical and halakhic works to the Karaites.

APPROBATIONS

One instance in which Hagiz followed his own prescription regarding the reclamation of rabbinic authority was in the area of giving approbations to newly published works. Hagiz deplored the practice of nearly automatic approbation for any book based on misleading sample folios printed for this purpose. He argued that this abandonment of rabbinic prerogative gave wily heretics like Hayon and Luzzatto access to the presses and insured wider dissemination of their ideas. A sample of books published in Amsterdam in 1715, at the height of the Hayon campaign, shows that the careless practices Hagiz decried were rampant. In his approbation to R. Meir Eisenstadt's *Panim Me'irot*, R. David Oppenheim wrote, "I saw only a fraction of the material, several sample pages." Another approbation to the same book admitted that its writer hadn't even seen a sample: "I haven't seen the actual book . . . but since the author is a disciple of Abraham of Broda, it must be holy."[33] Another work published in Amsterdam the same year appeared with no rabbinic approbations at all. The author excused this omission: "Because of their slight value, I did not take an approbation from the Sages." He pronounced his own curses upon those who would infringe on his copyright.[34]

Hagiz was determined to transform the granting of approbations into a medium of power for the rabbinate. Although he had written only two approbations before the Hayon campaign, he wrote fifteen in the two decades between 1718 and 1738, most during or after the Luzzatto controversy. Of course, this acceleration must be attributed to the growth of his renown as well as his resolve. Both Hagiz' approbations and those of other rabbis that appeared in the same books were careful to emphasize that the book—and often the credentials of the author—had been carefully scrutinized before the approbation was given. This tone of caution differed greatly from the laxity prevalent before Hagiz' efforts began. Hagiz' last approbations are also valuable sources of information on his activities, as the date and place of his signature reveal his movements, some of which were otherwise unknown.[35]

In 1718, Hagiz wrote his first approbation after the Hayon campaign, to R. Eliezer b. Joshua of Shebershin's *Damesek Eliezer*. It was a brief compendium of the laws of kosher slaughtering, based on R. Moses Isserles' *Torat ha-Hatat*, itself an abridged form of these laws from the *Shulkhan Arukh*. In addition to his longstanding interests in concisely written books, Hagiz' interest in this book also stemmed from the fact that the author commented on numerous glosses of R. Bezalel Loewe in *Viku'ah Mayim Hayim*, a book to which Hagiz had earlier provided an approbation. In the same year, Hagiz also wrote an approbation to Solomon Zalman Katz' *Sha'arei Torah*. In his approbation Hagiz defended the author against critics of his earlier work.[36]

After these, a long hiatus ensued in which Hagiz did not issue any approbations. He resumed with renewed vigor in 1732, after the first phase of the Luzzatto controversy. In his approbation to Levy ben Solomon of Brody's *Bet Levi*, Hagiz emphasized that he knew the author well, and "had read the book again and again, as one who was studying." The rabbi of the city in which the book was published wrote that he usually refrained from giving any approbations, "but since it is impossible to publish any new work without my permission," he was forced to change his policy. It is likely that the new policy had been adopted at the urging of Hagiz. R. Solomon Zalman b. Judah Leib of Dessau showed his book *Iggeret Shlomo* to Hagiz, who "crouches like a young lion . . . in the community of Altona. For choice has been taken away, and permission to print is not granted to any person to publish any book here in the community of Wandsbeck, whether it be large or small, unless the Rabbi M. [Moses Hagiz] checks it out first."

In 1733, Hagiz wrote an approbation to Ephraim b. Samuel Zanvil Heksher's *Livyat Hen*.[37] The author apologized for not having secured other approbations in addition to the requisite ones of Hagiz and Katzenellenbogen. His reasons are revealing: "Other authors, on their way to publish their books, stop at rabbis' homes to collect haskamot. I have not traveled, and if I would have sent only sample folios, I would have to be concerned lest they say 'who knows if the whole is similar to this part? . . . How can we, who haven't seen, come to testify?' When I applied to two renowned Sages for a haskamah because they knew me, they replied that they could not issue a haskamah for any book, the power had been taken from them and they are no longer in control of this . . . Let my omission not be viewed as a slight to their honor." Heksher's description of a new order in which there was tighter control over the issuance of haskamot, and an atmosphere of reluctance and suspicion to grant haskamot if the book was not presented in its entirety indicated that Hagiz' reforms of the haskamah system were bearing fruit.

Not all the works endorsed by Hagiz were of equal importance. Some haskamot were issued for new editions of halakhic classics, such as the novellae of R. Samuel Eidles (MaHarSh"A), novellae on tractate *Niddah* of R. Solomon ibn Aderet (RaShB"A), and *Pi Shenayim*, novellae of R. Asher (R"ASh) on tractate *Zera'im*. He endorsed Jacob Weil's *Shehitot u-Bedikot* as an indispensable text for ritual slaughterers. He approved a slim volume of exegesis, *Pi Eliyahu* of Elijah Deitz, the responsa of Eliezer ben Solomon Zalman Lipschutz, *Heshib R. Eliezer ve-Si'ah ha-Sadeh*, and David ben Moses of Vilna's *Mezudat David*. Other approbations included R. Dov Ber of Pressburg's *Be'er Tob*, R. Samuel B. Elkanah of Altona's Responsa *Mekom Shemu'el*, R. Solomon Zalman B. Abraham Geiger of Frankfurt's *Kerem Shelomo*, and R. Jacob London of Lissa's *Hishta'arut Melekh ha-Negev im Melekh ha-Zafon*. Hagiz testified that he had personal acquaintance with the author and his family in only one instance, R. Jacob b. Joseph of Seltz' *Zera' Yisrael*. Seltz wrote that Hagiz had extended some financial help to enable him to sustain himself. In all, Hagiz wrote fourteen of the eighteen haskamot he is known to have published between 1732 and 1738, and he left an imprint on the way haskamot were granted during these years.

Most of the books were published in the sister communities of Altona, Hamburg, or Wandsbeck. In some cases, only the approbations of Hagiz and Katzenellenbogen appear. Apparently, no books could be published without passing their scrutiny under the new strict order that prevailed. In his approbation to *Mekom Shemuel*, Katzenellenbogen wrote of having issued the haskamah because the author "had entered my territory to publish his book." In several cases where Hagiz' approbation appears side by side with Katzenellenbogen's, Hagiz' title is *Hakham*. Apparently he filled the role of Sephardic rabbi of the AHW community although he held no official position.

In one instance, Hagiz made his haskamah dependent on the approval of another rabbinic body. After he had already written his approbation to *Kerem Shelomo*, he was informed of an ordinance recently promulgated regarding another form of rabbinic censorship:

> I received a copy of *Mikhtav me-Eliyahu*, and I saw in the intro-duction that the community of Frankfurt had issued an ordinance that no person should publish any book unless it met the criteria specified in the ordinance . . . Therefore, this approbation of mine is completely conditional upon the approval of the rabbinate of Frankfurt, that they should find no trace of antagonism or negation against any custom or behavior of the Gentiles among whom all Israel have found protective shelter.[38]

In addition to his activity as writer and regulator of haskamot, Hagiz was involved in other publication activities. Of the twenty-three books published at the press in Wandsbeck, Hagiz was directly involved as author or editor of eight.[39] Of these there is one case where Hagiz' role has not been amply clarified. Hagiz brought to press in Wandsbeck Abraham ben Samuel Hasdai's *Ben ha-Melekh ve-ha- Nazir* (*The Prince and the Nazirite*). At the end there appears a brief compendium of moral-ethical sayings of no specific Jewish content, "Mi-Sihat Hulin shel Tal-midei Hakhamim" ("From the Profane Conversations of Scholars"). While this work has been attributed to Hagiz, there is no evidence to confirm him as the author. To the contrary, statements in his opus *Mishnat Hak-hamim* imply that Hagiz would not have spent time on a work with no specific Jewish content.[40]

HALAKHAH AND MINHAG IN THE WORKS OF HAGIZ

Viewing his halakhic contribution in retrospect, Hagiz lamented that his life's work lacked cohesiveness and depth. He mourned that his Torah had remained in a state of tatters because of the insecure conditions of his life.[41] Yet Hagiz' halakhic writings are the most numerous in his oeuvre, after his polemical tracts. He continued to publish the series *Leket Ha-KeMa"H*, brief compendia of recent works. In 1714, in Hamburg, Hagiz published the third of a projected four volume series based on the *Shulk-han Arukh*, his *Leket Ha-KeMa"H* to Eben ha-Ezer. The fourth volume was prepared for publication although it was never published. In 1726, he published his *Leket Ha-KeMa"H* on the Mishnah. Hagiz felt that the slim volume did not do his subject justice, and hoped he could print an expanded edition if the opportunity were granted to him.[42]

In the same year, Hagiz also published *Me'orer Zikkaron u-Measaf ha-Mahanot* [*To Arouse the Memory* . . .]. The purpose of the first part of the book, *Me'orer Zikkaron*, was to provide a very concise review of the Talmud for the proficient scholar—with its aid, a scholar could review the entire Talmud in one week! The introduction cautioned that it would be like a "dream without an interpretation" for a reader who was not well versed in the original Talmudic sources. The second part, *Me'asef ha-Mahanot*, was an index to novellae on the Talmud; because of a lack of funds, only part was published. Hagiz published this book anonymously, perhaps because he anticipated criticism that it would provide a shortcut around the original sources, or perhaps, as Katzenellenbogen had written in his approbation, these had originated as private notes and Hagiz may have felt they did not form a substantial enough work to publish in his name.[43]

In addition to his published works, Hagiz wrote many other brief compilations which were never published. He referred to a section of *Leket Ha-KeMa"H* on Maimonides' *Mishneh Torah*, which did not survive. Another work in the same series, attributed to R. Solomon Alghazi, may well have been Hagiz' own.[44] Only a small fraction of another entire series by Hagiz, *Perurei Pat HaKeMa"H*, has survived. It included a commentary to parts of the Hagiographa as well as a treatise on Jewish customs and novellae on the law. Of these, his commentary to *Daniel* has been published in full. Parts of his treatise on customs was published by Ulianov on *Birkhat Elijah*, and other small portions were published in several scattered halakhic compendia.[45]

The emphasis on collecting and organizing material of others does not mean that Hagiz did not write more conventional halakhic literature such as responsa. He published one volume, *Shetei ha-Lehem;* others were prepared for publication, but none have survived.[46] Nevertheless, Hagiz' main distinction and primary self-identification in halakhah is as a *melaket*, a compiler and codifier. Hagiz repeatedly warned that these works were intended only for experienced scholars, as a mnemonic tool—they could never replace analytical study of the sources. Hagiz argued that the revitalization of classics was a worthier enterprise than the composition of original works.[47]

Hagiz's work would support the thesis that works of codification and compilation—as opposed to original novellae—often derived from the impulse to preserve and disseminate material in a period of disorder or crisis. This seems especially true when considering that similar efforts were undertaken at the same time. A son of Samuel Aboab had completed a work similar to that of Hagiz at the same time that Hagiz published the first volume of his *Leket*. Other attempts to collect and disseminate recent halakhic literature were made, and although they differed somewhat from Hagiz' in that they did not compress the material, they sprang from similar motives.

R. Isaac Lampronte of Ferrara, a younger contemporary of Hagiz, was the force behind two notable attempts. In the early eighteenth century, he initiated the first periodical for Jewish Law, *Tosefet Bikkurei Kazir*. Many of Italy's most prominent rabbis participated and offered their wishes for success—half of the space in the first issue was devoted to approbations. The third issue contained a comprehensive outline for the development of the periodical. It would contain the legal decisions of the disciples of the Talmud Torah of Ferrara who had not yet attained rabbinic positions. It would appear bimonthly. Despite Lampronte's well laid plans, the third issue was also the last, apparently because some of the positions he had taken were opposed by other rabbis in Ferrara.[48] Lampronte's example may have been the model for a similar attempt by members of the *Bet Midrash Ez Hayyim* in Amsterdam. Their compendium, *Peri Ez Hayyim*, was also planned as a periodical. It too was not successful beyond the initial issue. The disciples of Abraham Broda of Prague published a compendium of their novellae.[49]

When Lampronte's periodical failed, he did not relinquish his goal of preserving and disseminating scattered rabbinic decisions. He channeled his efforts into a monumental undertaking, an encyclopedia, *Pahad Yizhak*, covering all aspects of contemporary rabbinic literature and organized alphabetically by topic. Lampronte did not live to see his entire work published—that was accomplished in fits and starts over a century. *Pahad Yizhak* remains a source of first importance for the study of the Italian rabbinate in the early modern period.[50]

Hagiz, as champion and advocate of works based on the work of others, had to address a problem invariably faced by even the most careful researcher—occasional faulty attribution of sources, or omission of it. In his Introduction to *Halakhot Ketanot*, Hagiz offered an apology if such lapses were ever found in his books: "Lest I be suspect in the eyes of observers because I forget to mention certain things in the name of their original authors, as though, Heaven forbid, I had an ulterior motive for disseminating them, I apologize. Heaven forfend that the offspring of my father should conceal or obscure. It is known to all that all my words are those of my rabbis, living and departed."

R. Hayim Y. D. Azulai noted a similarity between a passage in Hagiz' *Leket* on the Mishnah and a passage in R. Yair Bachrach's *Havot Ya'ir.* Azulai complained that Hagiz, "has already copied all the 'Rules' from *Havot Ya'ir,* paragraph number ninety-four . . . and printed them in his treatise *Asifat ha-Kellalim.* That entire wondrous treatise is the work of the author of *Havot Ya'ir,* who was only acknowledged in a brief hint in the printer's message."[51]

A section of Hagiz' book, *Zeror ha-Hayim,* appears to have been taken verbatim from an earlier book, *Orekh Yamim,* with no attribution.[52] Given Hagiz' open admission that his works had no claims to originality, these two omissions seem insignificant when measured against the tremendous amount of material diligently collected and correctly attributed by Hagiz.

Another genre of halakhic literature to which Hagiz devoted a portion of his writings was *Sefer Mizvot,* books explicating the 613 precepts. *Sifrei Mizvot* had been an important and popular didactic tool in medieval Jewish literature. In the early modern period, it became a vehicle for educating Jews with little Jewish background, for example, Menasseh ben Israel's *Thesouro des Dinim* and Raphael Dias Brandon's *Orot ha-Mizvot.*[53]

In 1727, Hagiz reprinted his *Sefer Mizvot, Eleh ha-Mizvot,* originally published in 1713. He followed Maimonides' enumeration of the precepts; his purpose was to prove that the accepted rabbinic teaching for each precept was the most appropriate and accurate interpretation of the Biblical text. Torah contained both written and oral (rabbinic) portions, which formed one unit. Any rabbinic teaching was an integral part of that unity, and anyone who rejected any rabbinic teaching, no matter how minute, must be considered a Jewish heretic. For those who challenged the binding authority of rabbinic law, Hagiz responded that all rabbinic teachings were divinely preordained. The term rabbinic "novellae" was really a misnomer—"They are all ancient teachings. . . . They appear now in our times because of the lack of immersion in Torah study in our generation." To encourage constant review, Hagiz divided the book into seven sections, one for each day of the week.

Hagiz also used his expanded edition of *Eleh ha-Mizvot* as a springboard for further social criticism. He maintained that his most important activity since the first printing of the book in 1713—his polemical campaigns—had strengthened Israel, although he did not retreat from his earlier position which maintained that Kabbalah was the core and essence of the Torah, and he retained all references to the *Zohar* and other Kabbalistic works.[54]

In addition to *Eleh ha-Mizvot,* Hagiz wrote other works of the *Sifrei-Mizvot* genre. He wrote a section of *Leket HaKeMa"H* to Isaac Leon's book

Megillat Esther, an arrangement of the precepts, which was never published, and a defense of Maimonides' *Sefer ha-Mizvot* against the criticisms of Nahmanides.[55]

Hagiz devoted one published and several unpublished treatises to the importance of established customs.[56] The mingling of diaspora communities had thrown the fixities of hoary custom into disarray. There were many instances of bitter disputes over customs within communities with recent new arrivals. Influences such as Lurianic Kabbalah and Sabbatianism, affected many Jewish customs, adding to the confusion. R. Moses Zacuto and his disciples had introduced Kabbalah into Italian synagogue ritual, and fierce battles were waged over this. Samson Morpurgo was among the leaders of those who were opposed to allowing Kabbalah to influence synagogue ritual.[57] Isaac, son of Jacob Sasportas, came to Hakham Zevi regarding a quarrel in his congregation between those who wanted to follow the custom based on Kabbalah, and those who opposed the change. The *Meziz u-Meliz* is a record of a similar quarrel in Ferrara.[58]

Hagiz' pronouncements on custom were double pronged. For the most part, they are addressed to those who made light of the sanctity of hallowed customs. Hagiz argued that custom provided a safeguard for the Law and if he could successfully educate the masses to recoil from any changes in custom "they would certainly recoil from any diminution in observance of the Law." "Be heedful and do not mock the customs of Israel which are significant; when we investigate, we realize custom is Torah." He emphasized the Talmudic teaching that certain customs were invested with the stringency of Law, and sometimes must be guarded more vigilantly than Law. Hagiz himself brought examples of erroneous minor customs which should not be corrected "because one does not change from the tradition of one's fathers and teachers. So long as there is the slightest justification for the [erroneous] tradition, we will adhere to it, and silence anyone who attempts to change it. No one may send a hand to tamper with the exact stipulations of the Sages, who are preferable to prophets." Any custom which was followed by the entire Jewish community was perforce sacred, because the Lord would not allow his entire people to stumble in error.[59] Hagiz recorded with great reverence customs of the hesger of Jerusalem in the time of his father and grandfather. Preserving the memory of these customs as his father had done became a way for Hagiz to preserve the memories of Jerusalem of his youth.

Custom ameliorated the pangs of exile by symbolizing the redemption. Hagiz and his rabbinic contemporaries were faced with the sensitive task of reviving the traditional place of messianism within Jewish tradition in the wake of the Sabbatian debacle. The task of rekindling the messianic faith had to be accomplished while subduing and sublimating its activist and heretical aspects. For Hagiz, custom was the most appropriate channel for achieving the delicate balance. An example of this is Hagiz' comment on eating eggs at the Passover Seder. The custom was rooted in the symbolism of eggs as mourner's fare; amidst the festivities, the participants were reminded of the loss of the Temple. Hagiz declared that this custom should be reinstated with an additional level of meaning: "I heard that it symbolized the redemption, *in order to keep the people from despairing*, and it particularly symbolized the birth of the Messiah."[60] The custom contained a message of hope—the true messiah was yet to be born. At the same time, it was expressed in such subtle and muted media as to keep the faith attenuated rather than intense. Charity boxes for redemption of captives would arouse the mercy of the Lord on all Israelites, who are in captivity and exile. The goblet of Elijah at the Seder would remind him to ascend to heaven to commend Israel . . . and hasten the final redemption.[61]

LAST TRACES OF HAGIZ

Hagiz spent his last years in Europe preparing to return to his birthplace. His self-identification as an exiled son of Jerusalem is apparent from almost every instance in which his name appeared in print and he had long expressed the wish to return there before he died. Hagiz' literary career had come full circle. Just as his first major published work, *Sefat Emet*, was concerned with the dignity and centrality of the Holy Land, his last published work, *Eleh Mas'ei*, written as he prepared to leave Europe, was a compendium of laws and customs which could be observed only in Erez Israel. Hagiz taught that the observance of these laws affirmed belief in the sanctity of the land, and as in *Sefat Emet*, Hagiz argued that belief in the sanctity of the land was an extension of the belief in the chosenness of Israel as God's people.[62]

In *Eleh Mas'ei*, Hagiz declared his intention to continue speaking out on behalf of Jerusalem's community. In 1737, the Ashkenazic community of Jerusalem had been dissolved as a corporation, because of its inability to meet its debts. A special "Council of Jerusalem Trustees," was appointed in Constantinople to channel funds that had been donated to the Ashkenazic community of Jerusalem. The council decided to reallocate these funds to the Ashkenazic communities of Safed and Hebron. Hagiz thought that this was unfair, particularly since the Sephardic inhabitants of Jerusalem were often dunned for the debts of their Ashkenazic brethern. He argued that the redirected funds should have gone to Jerusalem's Sephardim, and in *Eleh Mas'ei* he announced his intention to rectify this situation.[63] Hagiz also expressed his intention to continue to criticize the lay leadership in the cities of the Diaspora after he settled in Jerusalem, although there is no evidence that he was able to fulfill this promise.

On May 2, 1737, Hagiz wrote that he was unable to examine R. Dob Ber of Pressburg's book *Be'er Tob* "because of the hardships of travel. I am occupied with preparation for my departure . . . to the Holy City, my birthplace."[64] Hagiz' projected itinerary contained one detour: he was to visit the Jewish communities of France, perhaps at the invitation of the rabbi of Nice. On June 10, 1738, Hagiz wrote that he was passing through the city of Worms, and he praised its rabbis: "I am passing through the community of Worms, famous from ancient times as a place of settlement of many of our great and holy rabbis."[65] The rabbi at the time of Hagiz' visit was Moses, son of Rabbi Abraham Broda. It is unclear how long Hagiz remained in Worms. One year later, on June 13, 1739, Hagiz had travelled to the Provencal city of Nice. There he participated in writing the communal ordinances. His attempt was apparently not too successful, because the community drew up a new set of ordinances to replace the ones Hagiz had written shortly after he left. Rabbis did not usually participate in drawing up communal ordinances, although Ezekiel Katzenellenbogen had been asked to write the ordinances of the Hamburg-Altona-Wandsbeck Jewish community in 1726.[66] Given Hagiz' goal to expand the authority of the rabbinate within the Jewish communities, this was an opportunity he would not decline.

From France Hagiz made his way to Italy, and it is there, in Livorno, that we find the last trace of Hagiz' activities in Europe. In response to a halakhic query, Hagiz wrote: "It is well known that it is quite some time that I am on the road toward the Land of Life, Jerusalem, and I stand today, one foot on land, the other by sea . . . and I do not have my books with me." The question was addressed to Hagiz on June 18, 1739, his response is dated ten days later.[67] Hagiz may have sailed directly from Livorno to the Holy Land—no trace of him has been recorded after this date. R. Hayim Yosef David Azulai recorded that Hagiz "had lived outside the Land [of Israel] for close to fifty years. In 1738 he arrived in Sidon, and after several years he died in Safed, almost a nonagenarian." Whether due to lack of access to a printing press to publicize his activities, or the ill health of which he had recently complained, the remaining years of Hagiz' life were apparently passed in silence.

The year of Hagiz' death, like the year of his birth, cannot yet be fixed with certainty. In 1748, there was a plague in the Holy Land in which many rabbis died. The proofreader of Ezra b. Raphael Mordecai Malkhi's *Malkhi ba-Kodesh*, published in 1749, wrote: "While I was still preoccupied with this sacred work, this great book, . . . news of the passing of MN"H, the great sage Moses, may he rest in peace . . . I saw difficult things in R. Jacob Hagiz' z"l book, *Halakhot Ketanot* . . . and the puzzlement is even greater against the author of *Shebut Ya'akob*, who came to support the author of the *Leket*, z"l." This source had led some scholars to conclude that Hagiz died in 1748.

R. Nehemiah Reischer, then a dayyan in Metz, reported in a letter of February 1751, that witnesses testified to hearing R. Jonathan Eybeschutz saying several times "Blessed is God for killing Hagiz." Since Eybeschutz had left Metz in mid-1750, it would appear from this source that Hagiz had died a short while earlier.

There is a kabbalistic manuscript in the Jewish Theological Seminary Library, in which the copyist thanked Hagiz for allowing him access to the manuscript. The date is 1752, and the copyist referred to Hagiz as though he were still living. It is possible that Hagiz had passed away in 1751, and the news had not yet reached the copyist. Regardless of the exact date of his death, Hagiz lived almost to the eruption of the Emden-Eybeschutz controversy, surely a fitting symmetry.[68]

CONCLUSIONS

Great internal Jewish polemical wars occupy a distinguished place in Jewish history. The premises and goals differ substantially from Jewish polemics directed at other faiths. The Sabbatian controversies of the early eighteenth century provide abundant material from which to draw insight into the dynamics and methodology of internal Jewish conflict. They merit a special place in the pantheon of great Jewish controversies as the bridge from the medieval to the modern world. The canons of controversy which Hagiz established in his eighteenth century campaigns influenced the contours of subsequent internal Jewish controversies, particularly those of the nineteenth century. The rabbinic polemical campaigns against Hasidism and Reform Judaism borrowed freely from the arsenal of polemical techniques and ideological positions which Hagiz had formulated.

Possible historical links between Sabbatianism and Hasidism or Reform Judaism do not concern us here, but rather, the rabbinic campaigns against them, because these illuminate the relationship between organized anti-Sabbatian activity, and rabbinic reaction to movements of religious renewal throughout the modern period. R. David of Makov, lifelong rabbinic zealot against Hasidism, titled his major polemical work *Sheber Posh'im.* Later recensions of his manuscript were entitled *Zot Torat ha-Kena'ot.* Both titles recall the major anti-Sabbatian polemics of Hagiz and Jacob Emden. The titles of polemics are but a triviality; the identical methods used by the opponents of both sects reveal the close parallels. The most common means of calumniating and discrediting the Hasidim was *Gebiat Edut,* the gathering of testimony. The type of testimony solicited, and the rabbinic introduction to each subversive discovery, are remarkably similar to those employed during the anti-Sabbatian campaign of 1725. The bans that were issued against Hasidim cited similar infractions to those issued against Sabbatians in 1725. The reactions of the respective targets were similarly abusive of the rabbinic decrees.[69]

Similarly, parallels can be drawn from Hagiz' campaign against Luzzatto, to R. Moses Sopher's campaign against the Reform movement. They used virtually identical terminology to identify the dangerous core in the movements they opposed: "innovation" (*hadash*). While in the eighteenth century Hagiz attacked claims of renewal of divine revelation— Sopher in the nineteenth opposed human inventions. His attempt to unite the rabbinate and publish their bans against Reform follow the model of Hagiz.

Jacob Katz has suggested a fundamental difference between traditional Judaism as it existed through the medieval period, and "orthodoxy," a defensive reaction to challenges from within Jewish society, or from the larger society beyond it. For Katz, R. Moses Sopher, in his campaign against Reform Judaism, was such an initiator of Jewish orthodoxy. The career of Hagiz has shown that, at least for Sephardic Jews, the foundations of organized rabbinic reaction were laid a century earlier.[70]

Abbreviations

AS	*Alei Sefer*
EJ	*Encyclopedia Judaica*
HUCA	*Hebrew Union College Annual*
JNUL	Jewish National and University Library
JQR	*Jewish Quarterly Review*
KS	*Kiryat Sefer*
MGWJ	*Monatsschrift fur Geschichte und Wissenschaft des Judentums*
PAAJR	*Proceedings of The American Academy for Jewish Research*
REJ	*Revue des Etudes Juives*
RMI	*La Rassegna Mensile di Israel*
SS	Scholem, *Sabbatai Sebi*
TJHSE	*Transactions of The Jewish Historical Society of England*
ZNZ	Jacob Sasportas, *Zizat Nobel Zebi*
SE	*Sefat Emet*
HK	*Halakhot Ketanot*
MH	*Mishnat Hakhamim*
MR	*Moda'a Rabah*
TK	*Torat ha-Kena'ot*
O.H.	Orah Hayim
Y.D.	Yoreh De'ah
E.H.	Eben ha-Ezer
H.M.	Hoshen Mishpat

Notes

INTRODUCTION

Many subjects touched upon in the Introduction are treated more fully in the chapters that follow. I have tried to keep the annotation here to a minimum.

1. On the patronymic Hagiz, see Abraham Laredo, *Les Noms des Juifs du Maroc*, (Madrid, 1978) pp. 505–507, who surmises that the name is derived from the plural of the Judeo-Arabic "hadj"—pilgrim. Yizhak Baer, *Die Juden im Christlichen Spanien* (Berlin, 1936) 2:435, lists the goods of a Don Huda Ajajes, possibly an earlier variant of Hagiz, in an inventory of confiscated Jewish property dated 1499. See also M.D. Gaon, *Yehudei ha-Mizrah be-Erez Yisrael* (Jerusalem, 1935) 2:243, n.1.

2. *Hayyei Moshe*, apparently Hagiz' autogiography, is mentioned in Moses Hagiz, *Leket HaKeMa"H*, Y.D., p. 87v, and see the introduction to *Mishnat Hakhamim*.

3. For Isaac Uziel, see I. Brody, *JQR*, 13:70–73; Cecil Roth, *Menasseh ben Israel . . .* (Philadelphia: Jewish Publication Society, 1934) pp. 22–24, 32–34; Shlomo Simonsohn, Introduction, Leone Modena, *She'elot u-Teshubot Ziknei Yehudah* (Jerusalem: Mossad Harav Kuk, 1955) p. 53. The celebrated poet Miguel de Barrios described Uziel as "tan raro en la Poesia Hebrayca y musica como en la matematica, harpa y doctrina Mosayca." Cited in M. Kayserling, *Biblioteca Espanola-Portugueza-Judaica* (Strasbourg, 1890) p. 107; (repr. N.Y.: Ktav, 1971) p. 129, and s.v. Uziel.

4. Jacob Sasportas: Cecil Roth, *Menasseh*, p. 81, Jacob Sasportas, epilogue to Menasseh ben Israel, *Sefer Nishmat Hayim* (Amsterdam, 1652). Sasportas, *Toledot Ya'akob* (Amsterdam, 1652), Introduction, p. ii. For an example of Sasportas' idealization of his youth in North Africa, see *Ohel Ya'akob*, (Amsterdam, 1737),

#11. Citations from #8, #63. Intro. of Isaiah Tishby to Jacob Sasportaas, *Sefer Zizat Nobel Zebi* (Jerusalem, 1954). Jacob Sasportas, "The Letters of R. Jacob Sasportas . . ." ed. I. Tishby, *Kobez al Yad*, 4, #14, 1946, pp. 143–159. *Edut be-Ya'akob* (n. p., 1672).

5. Azulai: Meir Benayahu, *R. Hayim Yosef David Azulai* (Jerusalem, 1959); idem., ed. *Sefer ha-HID"A*, H. Azulai, *Ma'agal Tob*, ed. A. Freimann (1921–34).

6. On the question of whether Hagiz remained childless, the evidence is conflicting. In his own works he often referred to his desire to merit a child, and he never mentioned the birth of a child. This, to be sure, does not preclude the possibility of a child born to him late in life. R. Israel Moses Hazan, b. 1808, claimed several times in his book *Kerekh shel Romi*, e.g. p. 65r, that his mother was descended from Moses Hagiz. See Jose Faur, *Ha-Rav Yisrael Moshe Hazan: Ha-Ish u-Mishnato*, (Jerusalem: Ha-Ma'arav, 1977).

7. For herem, see the description in Lampronte, *Pahad Yizhak* (Lyck, 1864) s.v. *'niddui'*, p. 10a: "There are many pretentious scholars who impose the ban on good and just people, without the slightest discrimination between good and bad. That is not the method of the true scholar." Several communities forbade their rabbis to impose the ban, reserving the right for the lay leaders. In Hamburg, the ma'amad permitted the rabbi to impose any punishment, "So long as he does not pronounce the ban, for its pronouncement is in the hands of the ma'amad alone." J.C., "Aus dem ältesten Protokollbuch der portugiesisch-judischen Gemeinde in Hamburg," *Jahrbuch der Judisch-Literarischen Gesellschaft*, 11:10. The community of Metz gave R. Abraham Broda free reign, "to compel the people with punishments . . . *but he may not excommunicate without the permission of the Parnassim.*" Simha Assaf, *ha-Onshin Ahar Hatimat ha-Talmud* (Jerusalem, 1922), p. 118, #28.

8. Hebrot: A. Farine, "Charity and Study Societies in Europe of the Sixteenth-Eighteenth Centuries," *JQR* (1973) n.s. 64:6–47; 164–175. David Ruderman, "The Founding of a Gemilut Hasadim Society in Ferrara in 1515," *AJS Review*, (1976) 1: 233–268. Eliot Horowitz, "A Jewish Youth Confraternity in Seventeenth Century Italy," *Italia*, (1985) 5 (1–2):4. Jacob Katz, *Massoret u-Mashber* (Jerusalem, 1958) pp. 184–194. On *'Marbizei Torah'* see Moses Zacuto, *TiftehArukh* (Venice, 1715), The Introduction describes the *hebra Hadashim la-Bekarim* of Mantua, founded by Zacuto, with approbation given by their own *'marbiz Torah.'* p. ii–v. Responsum, Jacob Castro, *Oholei Jacob* (Livorno, 1783), O.H., #102, p. 153r.

9. Barukh Kurzweil, "He'arot le-*Shabtai Zebi* shel Gershom Scholem," *Ba'ma'avak al erchei ha-Yahadut.* Tel Aviv, 1969. David Meyers, "The Scholem-Kurzweil Debate and Modern Jewish Historiography," *Modern Judaism*, (Oct. 1986) 6 (3).

10. Historiographical essay of Gerson Cohen, Introduction to Jacob Mann, *Texts and Studies*, 1, repr. 1971.)

1. ANTECEDENTS

1. Jacob Hagiz, *Halakhot Ketanot*, *(HK)* (Venice, 1704), intro., and similarly, *Ez ha-Hayim*, (Berlin, 1716), Zera'im, Intro. On the impact of the expulsion on descendants of the exiles see H.H. Ben-Sasson, "The Generation of the Spanish Exiles on its Fate," *Zion* (1961), N.S. 26(1):23–64.

2. On Fez in this period, see Jane Gerber, *Jewish Society in Fez, 1450–1700* (Leiden, 1980); H.Z. Hirschberg, *Toledot ha-Yehudim be-Afrika ha-Zefonit*, (Jerusalem, 1965) index s.v. Fez; Haim Beinart,"Fez, A Center of Return to Judaism in the XVIth Century," (Heb.), *Sefunot*, 8, 1964, pp. 319–334.

3. "Index to the Ordinances of the Rabbis of the Maghreb as found in *Kerem Hemer II* by R. Abraham Enkawa," S. Amitay et al., eds. (Ramat Gan, 1975), p. 19. Two of these ordinances, those of 1545 and 1551, bear the signature of Abraham Hagiz, probably a relative.

Georges Vajda, *Un Recueil de Textes historiques Judeo-Marocaines*, (Paris, 1951), Text #XV, XVII. Transl. from Judeo-Arabic, p. 44.

4. Samuel Hagiz, *Debar Shemuel*, Preface (Venice, 1596).

5. The two books were published together in one volume, (Venice, 1596). In 1596, the year in which he published *Debar Shemuel*, he served as proofreader for *Tiferet Israel* of Salomon Duran, in the press of Daniel de Zaniti. B. Friedberg, *History of Hebrew Typography in Italy, Spain, Portugal, and the Orient* (Antwerp, 1934), p. 57.

6. M. Benayahu, *Yehasim she-ben Yehudei Yavan li-Yehudei Italiah* (Tel Aviv, 1980), p. 321, #46. Moses Hagiz, *Mishnat Hakhamim* *(MH)* (Wandsbeck, 1733) #2.

7. Jacob Hagiz, *HK*, 2, p. 51b: "Today, on the 26 of Shevat 5432 [=1572] the Blessed One has brought me to the age of fifty-two." Also Hagiz, *Petil Tekhelet* (Venice, 1652), postscript, and as quoted by Moses Hagiz, *MH*, (Wandsbeck, 1733), p. 9a: "I was a tender and only child to my father."

8. To date the only biographical treatment of Jacob Hagiz consists of entries in works such as Frumkin-Rivlin, *Toledot Hakhmei Yerushalaim* (1928) 2:61–65, and J. M. Toledano's *Ner ha-Ma'arav*. Significant contributions concerning Jacob's years in Italy and his publishing ventures there have been made by Meir Benayahu, "Information on the Printing and Distribution of Hebrew Books in Italy" (Heb.) *Sinai*, 34, pp. 161 ff. Benayahu's pioneering essay on Jacob's achievements in Jerusalem, "Toward a History of Study-Halls in Seventeenth Century Jerusalem" (Heb.), *HUCA* (1948) 21:1-25, has now been superseded by Shlomo Zalman Havelin, "Toward a History of Yeshivot and Sages in Jerusalem in the Late Seventeenth and Early Eighteenth Century" (Heb.), *Shalem* (1976) Vol. 2 esp. pp. 117–130. On Jacob's years during the Sabbatian period, see Gershom Scholem, *Sabbatai Sebi: The Mystical Messiah* (Princeton, 1973), index, s.v. "Jacob Hagiz." A full-scale biography remains a desideratum. A master's essay by Jacob Biton, "The Life and Thought of R. Jacob Hagiz," (Heb.) Bar Ilan, 1983, does not fulfill this need.

9. *MH*, #3, p. 9a; and p. 2. The birthplace of Jacob Hagiz remains obscure. Benayahu, *HUCA*, 1948, p. 2, n.4, rejects the previously held view that Jacob was born in Livorno. He bases this rejection on a postscript by Jacob to Abraham Gediliah, *Berit Abraham*, 1 (Livorno, 1650–52): "When I heard of the fine press that had recently emerged in Livorno, I arrived . . . to publish my work on the Mishnah." Had Jacob been born there, he surely would have mentioned it. Benayahu also rejects the view of Toledano, *Ner ha-Ma'arav*, p. 110, and Y.L. Fishman, *ha-Tor*, 9, #17, who follows Toledano, that Jacob was born in Jerusalem. Benayahu suggests that he was born in Fez, where Samuel Hagiz lived, and Havelin accepts this suggestion, (p. 118, n.2). Nevertheless, Toledano's suggestion should not be rejected out of hand. His source (p. 110, n.79), is a copy of Samuel Hagiz' *Mebakesh Hashem/Debar Shemuel* with holograph annotation. In it, Samuel detailed his itinerary from Fez, through Tripoli, then to Venice in order to publish his books, and thence to Jerusalem, where, he intimated, Jacob was born. Pending other clues, this seems to be the soundest basis for a conclusion.

A close reading of a document found at the end of Moses Hagiz, *Sheber Posh'im* (London, 1714) #4, p. 97, addressed to the rabbinate of Livorno, might lend some support to the opinion that Jacob was born there, but is less likely:

"להשיב את . . . משה . . . לעה"ק ירושלים אם לכבודו ואם לכבוד הרב מר אביו
ז"ל אשר היה ממחניכם קדוש."

The writers of the missive may not have been referring to Jacob's actual birthplace.

10. *Petil Tekhelet*, (Venice, 1652), p. v.

11. *Orah Mishor* (Verona, 1645); *Dinei Birkhat ha-Shahar, Keriat Shema, u-Tefilla* (Verona, 1648). On Jacob's life in Verona, see Benayahu, "Information," *Sinai*, #34, p. 175; Intro. to *Ein Yisrael* of Leone Modena (Verona, 1645); Jacob Hagiz, *Ez ha-Hayim*, I, (Verona, 1645). On the Aboab family in Verona, see Isaiah Sonne, "Cornerstone for a History of Jews in Verona," *Zion* (1938) 3(3):145–150.

On 2 Av, 1664, Samuel Aboab wrote to Jacob Hagiz in Jerusalem: "The notes from your mother to my wife at the end of your letter were dear to me." Benayahu, "Letters of R. Samuel Aboab, Rabbi Moses Zacut and Their Circle Concerning Erez Israel," (Heb.), *Yerushalaim* (1955) 2/5:168.

12. M. Benayahu, "The Hebrew Books Printed in Verona," (Heb.) *Sinai* (1954) 34:174–181. Jacob referred to his stay in Verona in his later works. *HK*, 2, #80.

"וראיתי בק"ק אשכנזים בויירונה יושבים ובק"ק של ספרדים . . . מעומד בחזרה
[של הש"ץ] והיכי משתברא."

In a postscript to Abraham Gediliah, *Berit Avraham*, Jacob Hagiz wrote:

"חבור המשנה אשר זה כמה ימים התחלתי ולא אסתייעא מלתא."

13. Benayahu, "Letters," p. 166. We do not have Jacob's letter, only Aboab's

reply which is dated *Nissan/Sivan* 1659. Jacob Hagiz, *Korban Minhah* (Smyrna, n.d.), p. 12b, #105. On the Karigal family, see Benayahu, *HaRav HID"A* (Jerusalem, 1959), p. 282, and Havelin, p. 121, n.28. On the bequest, see Benayahu, "Letters," p. 146. On the son who died see Jacob Hagiz, *Ez ha-Hayim*, Zera'im, (Livorno, 1654) afterword (in Berlin, ed. 1716, p. 136b).

14. *Azharot* (Venice, 1652), n.p. The original edition differs in several ways from the second edition, reprinted by Moses Hagiz (London, 1714). The 'reshut' in the original edition is placed at the end of the first section with the note: "Belongs at the beginning"; in the second edition, it is in its proper place. The first edition opens with the prolegomenon of Maimonides to his *Minyan ha-Mizvot*, together with dissenting opinions. This is omitted in the second edition. The most important omission from the second edition is a seven-page epilogue by Jacob. On the origin and development of "Azhara" literature, see Adolph Neubauer, "Miscellanea Liturgica: Azharoth on the 613 Precepts," *JQR* (1894) 6:698–709. Jacob Hagiz, *Petil Tekhelet*, T.P., p. iv, p. i.

15. On Duran, see I. Epstein, *The Responsa of R' Simon ben Zemah Duran as a Source of the History of the Jews in North Africa* (New York: 1930). Descendents of Duran were still active in the rabbinate of Algiers at the time of Jacob's youth.

16. On his visit to Livorno, see J. Hagiz, epilogue to Abraham Gediliah, *Berit Avraham*, 1:551b. On Heb. printing in Livorno, see G. Sonino, "Storia della tipografia ebraica in Livorno (1650–1856), 'Turin, 1912 (offprint from *Vessillo Israelitico* (1911–12), vol. 59–60. On Yedidiah Gabbai, see A. Yaari, "Hebrew Printing in Smyrna," (Heb.), *Areshet*, 1:98.

17. The volume on Taharot appeared before that on Kodshim because of unspecified difficulties. In his Introduction to *Almenara de la Luz* (p. ii) Jacob also refers to fulfilling the Divine precepts 'con algunas incomodidades'—perhaps a reference to his poor health or that of his son Samuel who subsequently died. The text of Rashi is printed alongside that of Hagiz' commentary on each page. Where there was no commentary of Rashi, Hagiz used that of R. Samson of Sens. Jacob Hagiz, *Ez ha-Hayim*, Intro.

18. Moses Hagiz, *MH*, #224, quoting from the words of Moses Galante. *Tehillat Hokhma* (Verona, 1647) second edition (Amsterdam, 1709).

19. "Le Voyage de la Terre Sainte fait l'an 1652 par M.I.D.P. Chanoine de L'Eglise Royale," Paris, 1657 (reprint Hirschberg). A. Toaff, "Il Collegio Rabbinico di Livorno," in *Scritti in Onore di Dante Lattes, RMI*, 16, April–June 1939, pp. 184–195, does not mention that Jacob Hagiz filled any official capacity.

20. On the Marranos of Livorno, Cecil Roth: "Notes sur les Marranes de Livourne," *REJ* (1930) 89:1–27; Bernard Cooperman, *Trade and Settlement: The Establishment and Development of the Jewish Communities in Livorno and Pisa* (1591–1626) (Diss. Harvard, 1976).

21. On Isaac Aboab (I) and the structure and sources of the *Menorat ha-Maor*, see "Aboab, Isaac I," *EJ*, 2:90–93; Naphtali Ben-Menahem, ed., *Menorat ha-Maor*, (Jerusalem, 1953) 1, Intro. where no fewer than 76 printed editions are listed. On the pedagogical literature for former Marranos, see Meyer Kayserling, *Bi-*

blioteca Espanola-Portugueza-Judaica (repr. N.Y., 1971) esp. Yosef H. Yerushalmi, Introductory Essay.

Ben-Menahem lists a second edition of Jacob Hagiz' translation, Amsterdam, 1703, cited from J. Zedner, *Catalogue of Hebrew Books in the Library of the British Museum* (1867), p. 381, and a third edition of Amsterdam, 1708. However, this is incorrect. The only subsequent edition listed by Zedner is the 1708 edition, which Kayserling described (51): [I have been unable to locate a copy of this edition.] publ. Amsterdam: J. Alvarez Sotto, Mos. Abenyacar Brandon, y Benjamin de Jongh, 1708.

22. *HK*, 2, #240. On the historical significance of this stance, Yerushalmi, *From Spanish Court*, pp. 22–28; responsa on the Anglican donation, *HK*, #92. Cf. Jacob Sasportas, *Ohel Jacob*, (Amsterdam, 1737) #3. On this issue, see further, David S. Katz, "English Charity and Jewish Qualms: The Rescue of the Ashkenazi Community of Seventeenth-Century Jerusalem," *Jewish History: Essays in Honour of Chimen Abramsky*, A. Rapoport-Albert and S. Zipperstein, eds. (London: Halban, 1988).

23. The correct identification of Jacob's patrons was made by S.Z. Havelin. Moses Hagiz named "*Abraham Israel Vega*, and his brother, the wealthy Jacob Vega," as founding patrons of Jacob Hagiz' Yeshiva Bet Jacob. (*Sefat Emet*, p.26a.) A. Toaff "Cenni storici sulla communita ebraica e sulla sinagoga di Livorno," p. 17, cited a portion of the will of *Abraham Israel Passarigno* (dated Dec. 5, 1677) which stipulated that a portion of the estate of his deceased brother Jacob would go to "the continued support of the Yeshiva in Jerusalem which he had founded and remanded to the care of Jacob Hagiz." Havelin, (addendum to n.31, p. 192) cites a will of *Abraham Israel Passarigno* in the archives of the Jewish community of Livorno dated October 24, 1674, with an identical clause (in paragraph 19) concerning a bequest to Jacob Hagiz' yeshiva. Two documents use *both* names Vega and Passarigno to designate this family. In the Pinkas of Verona, 1653–1706, (JNUL, Ms. Heb. 4° 551), fol. 3r, Abraham Israel *de Vega Passarigno* is listed as a physician of the community. An unpublished responsum of Moses Galante, concerned the will of Raphael Vega who stipulated that his daughters may only marry their *Passarigno-Vega* cousins. Ms. JNUL 8° 2001. The Pinkas of Verona also contains a decade-long drama in which members of the Vega family periodically leave the city to force the Jewish community to lower its tax assessment. See fols. 76v, 94r, 108v, 119v, 121r.

24. Sonne, *Zion*, assessment #46, #50, #74; pp. 158; 166–167.

25. Samuel de Pas was later appointed *dayyan* [judge] in Livorno. He became an active Sabbatian, who engaged Abraham Miguel Cardoso and R. Benjamin Kohen of Reggio in a lengthy and important correspondence concerning the two Sabbatian versions of the "Sod ha-Elohut" ("Mystery of the Godhead"). He rejected radical Sabbatian doctrines that conflicted with Lurianic teachings. In 1709, Samuel de Pas led the dayyanim of Livorno in signing a defamatory notice against Moses Hagiz. (Hayon, "Moda'a Rabah" Amsterdam, 1714, p. 3). Ironically, he mourned the passing of his Sabbatian master, Moses Pinheiro, in 1689 in the

same words that he used to eulogize Jacob Hagiz: "And from my youth he raised me like a son when I took Torah from him." See the approbation of de Pas to *HK*, 1, p. i. See also Benayahu, *Sefunot*, 14, index, s.v. Pas.

26. Raphael Meldola, *Mayim Rabim* (Amsterdam, 1737) O.H. #39, p. 39b. Azariah Figo (1579–1647) became rabbi of Pisa in 1607 and of Venice in 1627. Israel Bettan, "The Sermons of Azariah Figo," *HUCA* (1930) 7:457, n.1.

27. *Sefer ha-Zikhronot* (n.p., n.d.); Benayahu, "Letters," p. 146.

28. M. Benayahu, "Information Concerning the Ties Between the Sages of Erez Israel and The Sages of Italy" (Heb.), *Sinai*, 35, Nisan, 1954, pp. 55–66.

29. *Debar Shemuel* (Venice, 1702), #356. Benayahu, "Letters," p. 148, 140. On Abraham Aboab's yeshiva, see Simha Assaf, *Mekorot le-Toldot ha-Hinukh be-Yisrael*, (Tel Aviv, 1954) 3:30–33. Benayahu, "Information," pp. 56–57. On other Western European Sephardic immigration to the Holy Land, see I.S. Emanuel, "Haham David Lopes Jesurun and his Journey to E.I.," *Minha le-Abraham: Abraham Elmaleh Jubilee Vol.* (Jerusalem, 1959), pp. 90–92. On Hagiz' plans to immigrate, *Ez ha-Hayim*, Kodshim, (Berlin, 1716), p. 150b.

30. *HK*, II, intro. Benayahu, "Letters," #10, 11. On the marriage to ibn Habib, see Moses Hagiz, *MH*, #624, p. 119b; *HK*, I, #105, p. 10: "My son-in-law, Moses ibn Habib." In the same volume, "Kuntres le-Gittin," #21, p. 53b, ibn Habib referred to Hagiz as my "father-in-law." After the death of Hagiz' daughter, ibn Habib married Esther, sister of Moses Galante, becoming an uncle to his former father in law. Benayahu, "Letters," p. 146, n.39. This Moses ibn Habib is not to be confused with his contemporary in Salonika with the same name. Havelin, p. 119, n.22, has found a ms. of sermons in which ibn Habib eulogized Hagiz' wife. The sermons are dated 1669–1672, raising the possibility of another wife for Jacob Hagiz before Miriam Galante. Another daughter of Jacob's married R. Hayim Mordecai Ze'ebi. Mordecai Yosef Meyuhas, *Sha'ar ha-Mayim* (Salonica, 1778), Intro.

31. For a partial list of members of the Jerusalem community, see Joseph Sambari, *Diberei Yosef*, in A. Neubauer, ed. *Medieval Jewish Chronicles*, (Oxford, 1887), 1:152. On Zemah, see G. Scholem, "The Life and Works of R. Jacob Zemah (Heb.)," *KS* (April 1950) 26(2):185–194, and "*Sefer—Mussar*-By R' Jacob Zemah?" (Heb.) *KS* (1946) 22(#3–4):308–310. I. Sonne, "Toward a Biography of R. Jacob Zemah," *KS* (Jan. 1951) 27(1):97–106, followed by the strictures of Scholem, pp. 107–109; Moshe Idel, "Differing Conceptions of the Kabbalah in the Early 17th Century," *Jewish Thought in the Seventeenth Century*, Isadore Twersky and Bernard Septimus, eds. (Cambridge, Mass, Harvard University Press: 1987) esp. pp. 197–198.

32. Moses Hagiz, *MH*, #624. Hananiah is listed in Sambari, *Diberei Yosef*, p. 152, and quoted often by Garmizan, e.g., p. 61, #43. Scholem, *Sabbatai Sebi*, pp. 208–9, regards the legend that Hananiah served as a source of documents for Nathan of Gaza, as apocryphal. See also Benayahu, "R. Abraham ibn Hananiah," *KS* (1944) 21:313–315. Garmizan was born in Salonica, in 1605, and came to Jerusalem with his family as a youth. He had served as rabbi in Malta under

very trying circumstances—the Jews of that island were constantly oppressed and robbed—and returned to Jerusalem in 1660. He occupied an important position in public affairs. He was a disciple of Jacob Zemah's in Kabbalah, and his sermons are collected in "Imrei Noam." Benayahu, p. 8, n.44. See Garmizan's *Sefer Mishpitei Zedek*, with introduction by Benayahu (Jersualem, 1945). On Alghazi, see Benayahu, "Three Sages of Jerusalem," (Heb.) *A.Y. Kook Memorial Volume* (Jerusalem, 1945) pp. 308–313 and Havelin, p. 119, n.23.

33. Moses Hagiz, *Sefat Emet* (Amsterdam, 1707), p. 26. See also Luncz, *Yerushalaim*, 5, p. 192, n.2. On the lower grades, Havelin, pp. 122–126. Comprehensive schools of this sort already existed among Sephardic Jews in the Ottoman Empire in the sixteenth century.

34. I have found only one reference to Lurianic Kabbalah in *HK* of Jacob Hagiz: 2, #79. Jacob Zemah, Introduction to *Kol be-Ramah*, (written Jerusalem, 1645). *Kol be-Ramah* was a commentary to the *Idrah Rabbah* of the *Zohar*. Cited in Scholem, *KS*, 26, p. 194. Moses ibn Habib, *Get Pashut*, in Frumkin-Rivlin, p. 63. "Kuntres le-Gittin," was printed at the end of *HK*. See also *HK*, #21, an exchange between ibn Habib and Jacob Hagiz.

35. Benayahu, "Letters," #9, p. 166; #10, p. 169. On the prize-money, Moses Hagiz, *MH*, #351.

36. Jacob Hagiz, Intro. to *HK*, I. Blessings, HK, #7. See also, *HK*, #131: "It appears to the scholars of the Hesger." 1, #91, is a dissenting opinion against Moses Galante. #105, 107, bring the opinion of Moses ibn Habib. II, #14, 15 cite from Galante's *Korban Hagigah*, #167 and #189 reflect the lively repartee with younger students. There are several weak arguments in *HK*; nevertheless it served as a source for the development of Halakha. In addition to those mentioned by Havelin, another 'slip' is #28:

ש: מהו לכבד אשת האב במקום דאיכא קפידה דאם?
ת: אם אמו נשואה לאביו יניח כבוד אמו ויעסוק בכבוד אשת אביו שהוא כבוד אביו
. . . [והרי אם אמו נשואה לאביו, גם היא אשת אביו!]

In 2, #318, 229, Jacob curtly dismissed questions he thought foolish (yet saw fit to include).

37. *HK*, #54. Some customs are recorded only in order to preserve them, and the formal responsa format is not even adopted. See 2, #143–5, on his custom regarding tithing; #169, 2, on the circumcision rite in Jerusalem; #172, 2, on the Kaddish, #228, 2, on redeeming the first-born, and #255, 2, on carrying the Torah scroll.

38. Moses Hagiz, intro to *HK*, 1, and 2. The Brooklyn 1959 edition adds, "to minimize the expense," although it is not in the earlier printed edition.

39. Havelin, p. 125, n.36, ventures the opinion that an anti-pilpulistic revolution in Talmudic scholarship may have had its inception in Sephardic circles with Jacob Hagiz. That this is incorrect can be demonstrated from the introduction of Abraham Gediliah to his *Berit Abraham*:

"בזמנינו זה . . . אם ישאלו מתורת כהנים נגעים ואהלות . . . לא ידע
אותו על בוריו . . . פלפלת בחכמה . . . מה לו בהבנת דבר מתוך דבר, ואם לא ידע
הפרשה אוי לה לאותה בושה."

This was written by Gediliah by 1650, at least two years before Gediliah met
Hagiz, who added a postscript to the work. Jacob's ideas were developed after
careful comparative analysis of educational systems in various Jewish communities. On the policies he implemented, see Havelin p. 123, and Moses Hagiz,
MH, #1. On the Sephardic approach to study of the Talmud, see Daniel Boy-
arin, "On the Talmudic Method of the Exiles from Spain," *Pe'amim* (Autumn
1979) 3:73–82; H. Z. Dimitrovsky, "The Bet Midrash of R. Jacob Berab in Safed,"
Sefunot, 7:43–102; Hayim Bentov, "Methods of Study of Talmud in the Yeshivot
of Salonica and Turkey after the Expulsion from Spain," *Sefunot*, 13. *Leket*, Y.D.,
p. 32b. *Leket*, Y. D., p. 107a.

"ועיין בס *נשאל דוד*, כ"י, סימן ש"ה דמראה מוסר לחכמים שבודים להם הקדמות
ומדרשים לעשות הרכבות וחילקים, דיחמיר בעונשם."

#123 and p. 110B ff: quoting from Ya'ir Bachrach's *Havot Yair*:

"יבאר סדר ואופן הלימוד לתלמידים באופן שיעמוד להם בחייהם ויצליחו,
והרחקה מהחילוקים הנהוגים באשכנז. ובס' *נשאל דוד מכ"י ס"ה*."

40. On the date of their marriage, see *Korban Hagigah* #33: "I am in exile
with the book *Ez Hayim* which my son-in-law Jacob Hagiz has written." Cf.
Havelin, p. 119, n.22. Although Galante was the same age as Jacob Hagiz, he
greatly admired him. Moses Hagiz, *MH*, #624.

41. M. Hagiz, *HK*, 1, #162.

42. On the title of chief rabbi of Jerusalem, see Jacob Barnai, "The Leadership of the Jewish Community in Jerusalem in the mid-18th Century," (Heb.),
Shalem (1974) 1:297–298, n.134. The *Elef ha-Magen* is a collection of 1, 000 responsa (some still extant in ms.) which may shed additional light on Galante's
intellectual profile. A few of his responsa were included in works of his contemporaries. Ephraim HaKohen, *Sha'ar Ephraim*, (which also contains an approbation
from Galante) #71, 102, and ref. in #101. Mordechai Halevi, *Sefer Darkehei Noam*,
(Venice, 1697), #30–31, and #57 (dated 1677). Moses Hagiz had plans to publish
the responsa, but they never materialized. Moses Hagiz, Intro., *Zebah ha-Shelamim*, p. 1r.

43. *KH*, (Venice, 1704). It was brought to press by Moses Hagiz, who added
an introduction. *ZH*, (Amsterdam, 1708). Intro. to *Zebah ha-Shelamim*.

"נדרתי להיות קובע את יום הששי לכתיבה ממה שיהיה מתחדש אצלי בשאר ימי
השבוע בלמדי ספר עם התלמידים."

44. Moses Hagiz, Intro. to Galante, *Zebah*. Galante's work was published with
the financial backing of a former student of the Yeshiva, Joseph HaKohen, and

Moses Mocatta (*Zebah*, T.P.). HaKohen had been forced to leave Jerusalem in 1689 to earn a living, and was overjoyed when he came upon Moses Hagiz. Each section of the *Zebah* is organized in the following style: 1. excerpt from rabbinic source, 2. difficulty, 3. resolution of the difficulty. Moses Hagiz added interpretations that he had heard orally from Galante, (p. 3a), his own solutions (pp. 3b, 4b, 5a), and his differences with Galante's conclusions, #38.

45. *Korban Hagiga*, #86. Moses Hagiz, Intro. to *Zebah ha-Shelamim*.

46. A eulogy on Galante by his pupil and in law, Moses ibn Habib, (Benayahu,"Lekutot," p. 59) and a poetic dirge by R. Shabtai Urbino of Pesaro (p. 60), attest to Galante's far reaching influence even among the Diaspora communities, and to his unusual personality. For Joseph HaKohen, see his *Diberei Yoseph* (Venice, 1710). See also Yaari, *Sheluhei*, p. 290.

47. There is some evidence that R. Abraham Amigo (and not Jacob Hagiz) was chief rabbi of Jerusalem in 1665, while Hagiz remained head of the hesger. Scholem, *Sabbatai Sebi: The Mystical Messiah* (Princeton, 1973), p. 248, n.140. The psychological drive of sons to expiate for the sins of their fathers as a motive in anti Sabbatianism, has been analyzed by Jacob Schachter, *Rabbi Jacob Emden: Life and Major Works*, (diss. Harvard, 1988) The motive may have been present in Emden; Meir Benayahu has made this point regarding Abraham Yizhaki, and his ardently Sabbatian father, David Yizhaki, (*Baron Jub. Vol.*, pp. 66–67). To this list we can add Joseph Ergas, whose grandfather Moses Pinheiro was one of the first and most faithful followers of Sabbatai.

48. On the excommunication and other activities of the Jerusalem rabbis, Scholem, *SS*, pp. 248–249. Excerpts of Garmizan's sermon, from the ms. of his sermons, *Imrei Noam*, in Scholem, *SS*, p. 361. A. Galante, *Nouveaux Documents sur Sabbatai Sebi* (1935), p. 84, cites the Armenian. Scholem identifies this individual as Jacob Zemah. (*KS*, 26, p. 187).

On Abraham Yizhaki, see Yaari, *Sheluhei*, pp. 353–358; see Yizhaki's Intro. to his *Sefer Zera Abraham* (Smyrna, 1733), I. On his father David Yizhaki, see Scholem,"The Attitude of Rabbis toward Sabbatianism," (Heb.), *Zion: Quarterly* (1948–49) 13–14:47–62, and Benayahu, in *Studies Presented to G. Scholem*, pp. 40–41.

49. Jacob Sasportas, *Zizat Nobel Zebi*, (1954):13, 16, 18, 25. On the fear of reprisals, see the letter of Laniado, *Zion* (1942) 7:192, and Scholem, *SS*, p. 240.: "When news of the preparations reached the rabbis of Jerusalem, they rent their clothes in mourning over the blasphemy *and in fear of the dire consequences for the community* . . ." In Frances "Zebi Mudah," *Kobez al Yad*, O.S., 1, 1885, p. 134, it is clear that opposition of the rabbinate is prompted by warnings from Turkish officials to desist from further seditious activities. For North Africa, see Sasportas, *ZNZ*, p. 152, and for new communities, see Sasportas, *ZNZ*, pp. 17, 98.

50. Benayahu, "Reports from Italy and Holland concerning the Beginning of the Sabbatian Movement," (Heb.), *Erez Yisrael* (1956) 4:200.

51. R. Simon Habib, *Ba'ei-Hayai*, #206, in I.R. Molho, "On Sabbatai Zebi and his Sect," *Ha-Olam*, 26–27, 1947, p. 316. On Aaron Lapapa and the struggle with R. Hayim Benveniste for the rabbinate of Smyrna in the aftermath of the

Sabbatian movement, see Abraham Palache, *Abraham Azkir*, p.35 ff.; Scholem, *SS*, p. 379, n.104; D. Tamar, "A Controversy between R. Hayim Benveniste and R' Aaron Lapapa," (Heb.) *Tarbiz*, 41, 1972, pp. 411–423, and 42, 1973, p. 211; Tamar, "References to the Sabbatian Movement in the Responsa of R. Hayim Benveniste," *Sinai* (1973) 72(1):285–88; and most recently Jacob Barnai, "On the Identity and History of a Responsum Concerning Sabbatai Zebi," (Heb.), *Mehkarei Yerushalaim be-Mahshevet Yisrael* (1982) 2:121, n.115.

52. Scholem, *SS*, p. 202, from the account of Cuenque. See also the testimony of Moses Hagiz, in J. Emden, *Torat ha-Kenaot*, p. 36: "The truth is, he [Nathan] was a disciple of my father's, who ordained him because he was an expert in Talmud."

53. Scholem, *SS*, p. 142, from Sasportas, *Sisat*, p. 4.

54. Scholem, *SS*, pp. 362–3. Barnai, "On the Identity," pp. 118–119. Sadly, the advocates of the "conspiracy of silence" won one small, Pyrrhic victory. Their policy became the justification for retroactive destruction of many valuable records of the trauma left by the movement.

55. *Korban Minhah*, Smyrna, n.d. [1670?].

56. Sasportas, Intro. to Moses Albaz, *Sepher Hekhal ha-Kodesh* (Amsterdam, 1653); and Scholem, *SS*, p. 570. On the competition between the two systems, see I. Tishby, "The Conflict Between the Kabbalah of AR'I and Cordovero" (Heb.), *Zion* (1974), vol. 39 and "The Attitude of R. Abraham Azulai to Cordoveran and Lurianic Kabbalah," (Heb.), *Sefunot* (1980) 16: 191–203.

Similar intellectual grounds formed the basis for the moderate opposition of R. Benjamin Kohen of Reggio, R. Samuel de Pas and others, *within* the ranks of crypto Sabbatians, to the more radical element.

57. For Jacob Frances, see Penina Naveh, Intro., *Kol Shirei Ya'akov Frances* (Jerusalem, 1969). His attitude toward kabbalah, pp. 91, 369 ff., 578; attacks against the rabbis, pp. 100 ff.; anti-Sabbatian satires, pp. 104 ff., 440–572. For Immanuel: Bernstein, pp. 177–192, 285–292, and M. Mortara, ed. *Zebi Mudah*, *Kobez al Yad*. [O.S.], 1, 1855. See also the acerbic "Haggadah le-Tish'a be-Ab," which Habermann attributed to Frances. "Towards a History of Anti-Sabbatian Polemic," *Kobez al Yad*, 3(2):187–215. The anti-Sabbatianism of the Frances brothers has yet to be adequately analyzed.

58. For Isaac Cardoso: Yerushalmi, *From Spanish Court*, pp. 313–343; on Isaac Orobio de Castro, see Joseph Kaplan, *Mi-Nazrut le-Yahadut* (Jerusalem, 1982).

59. Scholem, *SS*, pp. 256–257. Attempts by Benayahu to interpret this letter as referring to another Moses Galante, a native of Aleppo, contradict the information given in Scholem's text, which Galante's itinerary seems to corroborate. Benayahu's denial of Galante's role is part of his earlier effort (in *HUCA*, 1948) to elevate Jerusalem above the fate of all other Jewish communities in this period. To do so, he must prove that its leadership, alone among world Jewry, was unswervingly opposed to Sabbatianism from its inception, a distorted image.

60. Yaari, *Sheluhei*, p. 290.

61. Boton, *Edut be-Ya'akov*, (Salonica, 1720), #11: writes, "Moses Galante passed

through the city in 1667." On Boton's Sabbatianism, Benayahu, *Sefunot*, 14, pp. 20–21, n.5. On Almosnino, Scholem, *SS*, p. 232, and Ephraim HaKohen, *Sha'ar Ephraim*, (Sulzbach, 1688) #64, 65. I am indebted to Jacob J. Schachter for this reference. The proofreader of Galante's *Korban Hagigah*, postscript, mentioned that he saw Galante in Ofen-Buda thirty-six years earlier.

62. Scholem, *SS*, p. 854, argues that Sabbatians remained outside Jerusalem so that they could stay together with other Sabbatians. But Benayahu, *Studies . . . Presented to Scholem*, pp. 43–45, maintains that they could not enter Jerusalem because the ban against Sabbatai was in force.

2. YOUTH IN JERUSALEM

1. Hagiz did not specify the exact year of his birth. In *Mishnat Hakhamim*, #1, he stated that he was three years old at the time of his father's passing; in his introduction to *Korban Hagigah*, he wrote that Galante raised him "From the time my father left me at two years old." In his intro. to *HK* (Venice, *1704*), Hagiz stated, "I . . . am as one of thirty years old." IF the introduction were written in the year of publication, and IF Hagiz meant to indicate that he was exactly thirty, his birthdate would be fixed at 1674, and that of Jacob's death at 1677. Neither of these contingencies can be verified; indeed the indication in a subsequent phrase could be taken to mean that his thirtieth birthday was a while off "הרי אני כבן שלשים שנה" In addition, the phrase, "I am as one of __ years," (cf. Mishnah *Berakhot*, 1, 12b) is used in the sense of looking older than one's actual age; thus he may very well have been 27–28 years of age. A more probable date for Jacob's death is 1674, see Havelin, p. 118, n.20; p. 128, n.53. Thus the most widely accepted date for Moses Hagiz' birth, 1671, is still plausible.

2. The bleak picture painted by the anonymous emissary pamphlet "Hurvot Yerushalaim," (Venice, 1631; repr. Tel Aviv, 1971, with introduction and notes by Minna Rozen) is offset by the more colorful description in Gedalia of Sem-iaticz, *Sha'alu Shelom Yerushalaim* (Berlin, 1716; reprint Z. Rubashov, *Reshumot*, 2, O.S. 1919) for the end of the century.

3. Cited in Cecil Roth, "The Jews of Jerusalem in the Seventeenth Century: An English Account," from an anonymous pamphlet, probably by Henry Jessey. *TJHSE*, Miscellanies, 2, pp. 100–101.

4. Moses Hagiz, Introduction to Jacob Hagiz, *Halakhot Ketanot*, 1; *HK*, 1(78):

"מה שאירע לאבות אירע לבנים, ואני גם כן בגלותי זה פ"א עמדתי בספק זה . . ."

See also *HK*, 2, #318.

5. *HK*, 1, 1. Benayahu (Baron Jub. Vol., p. 57, n.70) cites R. Hayim Yosef David Azulai that there was an agreement that there be no titled chief rabbi of Jerusalem. Azulai's source is Hagiz' *Mishnat Hakhamim*, but there is no such quote in the only known edition (Wandsbeck, 1733).

6. *HK*, 1, 4, and similarly *Sheber Posh'im* (London, 1714), appendix #4:

"ובעוד הרב ז"ל [גלנטי] בחיים, נתגדל כל ימיו בין ברכיו, ובין ברכי החכמים."

7. *HK*, 1, #103, 111, 286.

8. See Abraham Ya'ari, "Yeshivot Pereira in Jerusalem and in Hebron," [Heb.] *Yerushalayim*, 4, 1952, pp. 185–202; and the proposal of Raphael Mordechai Malkhi to build a yeshiva in "Likkutim me-Perush al ha-Torah—Ketav Yad me'et R.M.M.," ed. Rivlin (Jerusalem, 1923) 1, pp. 41–46.

9. Jacob J. Schachter, *Rabbi Jacob Emden: Life and Major Works* (dissertation, Harvard, 1988) ch. 5.

10. Azulai, cited in Meir Benayahu, *Rabbi H.Y.D. Azulai* (Jerusalem, 1959) p. 144. I believe that Benayahu correctly argued that this passage is not necessarily an indication of Sabbatian sympathies:

"מידי עוברי עולם חשך לראות גדולי ישראל נאחזו בסבך ונתפתו וגם כי ידעו מאי דהוה לא שמו לבם. מה אענה ומה אומר, ה' הטוב יכפר בעד. ובמסתרים תבכה נפשי על דור יתום. אוי לנו אהה עלינו."

11. On Malkhi, see Meir Benayahu, *Ma'amarim be-Rephua le-Rabi Raphael Mordecai Malkhi* (Jerusalem: Yad R. Nissim, 1985); Eliezer Rivlin, intro. to Malkhi's "Likkutim." Gedaliah of Semiatycz, "Sha'alu Shelom Yerushalaim," *Reshumot*, p. 466, described Malkhi as "The expert physician that was in Jerusalem, a Sephardi, a great scholar of Torah and the medical sciences, a man of great wealth, Hakham Mordecai Malkhi." See the testimony of his grandson, David da Silva, Intro. to Hezekiah da Silva, *Peri Hadash* (vol. O.H. and E.H., 1706):

"מר זקני מלכי צדק מלך שלם . . . ידיו רב לו בכל התורה ;בנסתר ובנגלה בפילוסופיה ובתכונה ובהויות אביי ורבא."

Hagiz, *HK*, #290.

12. Moses Hagiz, *Sheber Posh'im* (London, 1714; repr. Jerusalem, 1970) p. 80. Gershom Scholem, *Mehkarim u-Mekorot le-Toldot ha-Shabta'ut* (Jerusalem, 1974) p. 276, correctly emphasized that Hagiz did not state that the apostasy had occurred in 1687, but rather, that he had learned of it then. The apostasy took place in 1683.

13. On the great apostasy, see Benayahu, *Sefunot* 14, pp. 79–108. It assumed equal importance in the polemics of Joseph Ergas, *Tokhahat Megulah ve-ha-Zad Nahash*, pp. 19b–20a; and Zebi Ashkenazi, *She'elot u-Teshubot Hakham Zebi*, #13.

14. *Sheber Posh'im*, appendix #4.

15. Moses Hagiz, *HK*, 1, #103. Benayahu, "The Holy Society of R. Yehudah he-Hasid," [Heb.] *Sefunot*, 3–4, p. 156. Responsa of Malkhi in Abraham Ze'evi, *Orim Gedolim*, (Smyrna, 1758) p. 59, #146. Havlin, p. 131, n.160, lists other sources referring to the large number of deaths in 1689.

16. Uriel Heyd, "The Jews," p. 173, ff. *HK*, Intro.

17. Nehemiah Hayon, *Moda'ah Rabah* (London, 1714) p. 3a.

18. Miriam Galante married a prosperous man named Ezra. She became his

second wife in a bigamous marriage. Upon his death, there was a litigious dispute between Miriam and the leadership of Jerusalem. See David Oppenheim, *Nish'al David*, 2 (Jerusalem, 1975) *HM*, #14.

19. Benayahu, *HUCA* (1948) p. 10. The most important source used by Havlin, p. 131, n.60; p. 177, is Hayon's pamphlet, *Moda'a Rabah*, which contained documents concerning the failure of Beth Jacob. Graetz, *Dibrei Yemei Yisrael* (Warsaw, 1913) vol. 8, Appendix 6, p. 599 made use of this document, but his excerpts and interpretations are confusing.

Crypto-Sabbatians often took elaborate precautions to conceal their identities from hostile eyes. See, for example, Benayahu, "Studies . . . presented to G. Scholem," pp. 41–45. This would certainly be the case for Hayon's *Moda'a*. Semiaticz, *Reshumot*, 2:466.

20. The argument we make here is based on Rivlin's published excerpts of Malkhi's commentary to Exodus, p. 64. MS. (Columbia X893 M29) may be Malkhi's commentary to Genesis, contains definite traces of Sabbatian ideology. M. Benayahu, "Information," *Sinai*, #34, pp. 63–64.

21. Malkhi's precise records of the Jewish population of Jerusalem and its finances in this period, are rivalled as primary sources only by Hagiz' *Sefat Emet*, and Gedalia of Semiaticz, *Sha'alu Shelom Yerushalaim* (Berlin, 1716; reprint Z. Rubashov, *Reshumot*, 2, O.S. 1919). Rivlin, pp. 12 ff.

22. Rivlin, p. 46. Some Sabbatian texts were translated into Armenian. Scholem, *SS*, p. 615.

23. Rivlin, pp. 15, 17. [MR, p. 3a.] Malkhi's proposal for a Bet Midrash to be supported by Jews of the Diaspora (p. 42) is modeled on Beth Jacob. Y. Rivlin, "The Proposal of R. Raphael Mordecai Malkhi to establish a Yeshiva in Jerusalem as a center for Jewry" (Heb.) *Yerushalaim: Mehkarei Erez Israel* (1955) 2/ 5:187–194. Malkhi's detailed educational proposals indicate that he harbored aspirations to control the Yeshiva. Hagiz refers to this motive a number of times. *MH*, #352; *SE*, p. 26b.

24. Malkhi's description of friction among factions in Jerusalem: Rivlin 1:51:

"אני מעיד . . . שבזמן י"ח שנים י"ח שנים שאני דר בעיר זו הקודש, לעולם היה קנאה ושנאת חנם בין התל"ח זה לזה ובין היחידים והת"ח ולא ראיתי בזה סדר ותיקון וישוב ביניהם . . . והת"ח ופרט הבחורים היו מעיזים פניהם נגד היחידים הזקנים והיחידים גועלים בת"ח."

Havelin p. 166, concluded that the issue that divided Malkhi and Hagiz was public vs. private ownership. Malkhi's crypto-Sabbatianism and a careful reading of Hayon's account in *Moda'a* support the contention that Sabbatianism was a major factor.

25. On da Silva, see H. Y. D. Azulai, *Shem ha-Gedolim*, s.v. da Silva; Havelin, pp. 140–151, esp. n.s. 72, 73, 99. On Abraham Pereira of Amsterdam see Scholem, *SS* pp. 5, 755, 760; Yaari, "Yeshivot Pereira;" Moses Hagiz, *SE*, p. 21a referred to da Silva as "my brother-in-law." David da Silva, *Sefer Peri Hadass*,

intro., writes about his father Hezekiah da Silva and his grandfather Malkhi. Ms. JNUL, #38766.

3. BEGINNING OF AN ODYSSEY

1. Gedaliah of Semiatycz, *Sha'alu Shelom Yerushalaim* (Berlin, 1716) repr. Zalman Rubashov, *Reshumot*, 2:471. The route described by Gedaliah was probably the same as that of Hagiz: "From Jerusalem to Hebron, and from there through the desert, to Egypt." p. 484. Yaari, *Sheluhei*, p. 307.

2. Benayahu, *HUCA* (1948):19, n.66. The entire episode is summarized in a responsum of David Oppenheim, *Nish'al David* (Jerusalem, 1972–75) 2, H.M., #14, p. 211, with another variation of the merchant's name: Included were 150 Venetian *zecchini* that had been given previously by the judge Moses [Ibn Habib?] to the care of the wealthy *Isaac Kohen Karmina* of Rashid [Rosetta] as an investment on behalf of the widow. After this, within a year, the aforementioned Isaac lost his fortune and the investment was lost, as is widely known; the widow sent her son to endeavor in her behalf. From a letter dated 1694, from the Jerusalem rabbinate to the Egyptian rabbinate, *Sheber Posh'im*, appendix 1, pp. 92–93: "Out of her great desperation and anguish she sent her beloved only son, Moses Hagiz . . . to seek a remedy for her plight."

3. Moses Hagiz, "Leket HaKeMa"H on Nazirite Law," #56, p. 27a, published as appendix to Jacob Hagiz, *Halakhot Ketanot* (Venice, 1704). References to Gershon appear in *HK*, 1(#4); *Kuntres le-Gittin*, p. 53a, appended to *HK*; *Leket HaKeMa"H*, *OH*, p. 44b and 51b; and *Y.D.*, p. 3b. Faraji was author of *Responsa of MaHaRi"f* (Alexandria, 1901). Correspondence with Hagiz, #39, pp. 30–31.

4. Benayahu, *HUCA* (1948), p. 17. Among the works he published were two of R. Hayim Benveniste (Y.D., 1716) and *Sheyarai Knesset ha-Gedolah*, (Y.D., 1717); *Tikkunei Zohar* with Vital's annotation, and two works of Moses Ibn Habib (*Get Pashut*, 1721; *Shemot ba-Arez*, 1727).

5. The text of the consecratory document (Shetar Hekdesh), Benayahu, *HUCA* (1948), Appendix B, pp. 25–26; cf. Havlin, p. 158–159.

6. *Sheber Posh'im*, #10. On the Suleima banking family, see Benayahu, "Correspondence between Abraham Cuenque and Judah Briel," *Sinai* (1953) 32:314, n. 60; Benayahu, *AS*, 5:115. *Sheber Posh'im*, Appendix #7.

7. *Leket HaKemaH*, E.H. (Hamburg, 1719) p. 79a.

8. *Sheber Posh'im*, Appendix #3, 4, and 5. In Venice, Hagiz met two Egyptian Jews, Obadia Fuchs and Sa'adia Kashishi, "who despite their own desperate straits . . . lent Hagiz money toward defraying the costs of publication." Moses Hagiz, Introduction to Moses Galante, *Korban Hagigah* (Venice, 1704). In his responsa, *Shetei ha-Lehem* (Wandsbeck, 1733) #45, p. 46r, Hagiz wrote to Judah Briel of being repeatedly importuned by the rabbinical court of Alexandria while

he resided in Livorno and Venice. *Leket HaKeMa"H*, O.H. (Amsterdam, 1709) p. 6b, is a correspondence from Italy with R. Abraham Halevi of Cairo.

9. See Costa's approbation to Moses Galante, *Korban Hagigah* (Venice, 1704), dated Elul 5462 (Fall 1702): "Moses has come to my hostel six years ago today;" *Sheber Posh'im*, appendix #9, dated 1700: "He has dwelled among us almost five years." Letter of Costa to Gershon, *Sheber Posh'im*, Appendix #8.

Benayahu, *HUCA* (1948), p. 15, assumes that even the earliest obstacles were a result of intervention either by the Sabbatians of Jerusalem, or by Nehemiah Hayon who had sojourned in Rosetta at just about this time. Benayahu assumes that the acquisition of land was done without Nathan's specific approval. Havlin p. 160, argues that the technical delays were sincere, and the purchase was routine. Nevertheless, Havlin agrees (p. 178, n. 229) that the serpent (Nahash) who dissuaded Nathan, referred to in *Mishnat Hakhamim*, #351-2 may be a reference to Hayon.

10. *Moda'a Rabah*, p. 2, col. 4.

"לכן טוב שאפילו דבור דבור לא יתיחדו עמו ולא יגלו לו שום דבר מעסקי עיר קדשינו."

11. The letter focused on Hagiz' youth and inexperience, but elsewhere, Malkhi conceded that Hagiz' qualifications were not at issue. Hagiz was twenty-seven in 1698 and Malkhi admitted "Even if he were worthy, if the public does not accept him [he cannot serve]." Cited in Havlin, p. 163.

12. Hagiz, *HK*, Intro.; on intra-communal tensions related to Sabbatianism, see, in the interim, Ms. Central Archives for the History of the Jewish People, Jerusalem #HM 2803, Escamot e statutos do KK Liorne 1655–1687, Parte III of the 'escamos' punishable by Herem, 4: "ninguna persona qual quier calidad que sea pueda disputar encosas de Sabbatai Zevi ni del Dr. Cardoso ni tena comunicasion o' correspondenzia por escrito soto pena LHMS."; Havlin, pp. 175–176. "The Letters of R. Jacob Sasportas Against the Lay Leaders of Livorno, 1681," (Heb.) ed. I. Tishby, *Kobez al Yad* (1946) 4(14):143–159, and A. Toaff, "The dispute of R. Jacob Sasportas and the Livorno lay leaders" (Heb.) *Isaac ben Zvi Memorial Volume* (1956) 2:167–192.

13. *Leket* (Amsterdam, 1707). Cf. Benayahu, *HUCA*, p. 132.

14. *Sheber Posh'im*, Appendix #6.

15. *Ibid.*, Appendix #8. See also #11, dated 1702; #9.

16. Nehemiah Hayon gained access to the files of the Amsterdam Kehilla in 1714 and published it as "Iggeret Shebukin," together with *Shalhebet Yah*, (Amsterdam, 1714). Not all editions of *Shalhebet Yah* contain it; I have used the copy at JNUL.

17. Four wealthy merchants, David Vecinho, Abraham Penã, Jacob Sarmento, and Daniel Cordovero provided attestations to Hagiz' integrity, in Latin, addressed to Nathan. *Sheber Posh'im* #8.

18. *SE*, 27r. Hagiz printed a three-page appendix concerning the Nathan endowment to Jacob Hagiz' *Orah Mishor* (Amsterdam, 1709) of which only one per-

fect copy is known to exist, in the Bodleian Library. (Cowley, p. 295.) "so that silence will not be taken as an admission [of guilt]."

In *SE*, p. 27r, Hagiz identified the witnesses "the exalted sage, David De'uel, and the wealthy Samuel Ya'avez." Two years later, in the appendix to *Orah Mishor*, he acknowledged that he had erred, and that the second witness was Jacob Revah. Their signatures had been notarized by Nawi and R. Samuel ibn Lahmit. In addition, extra assurances were drawn up to assure the inviolability of the bequest. Hagiz believed one of the witnesses to be his foe.

19. In the Responsa of R. Moses Israel, *Mas'at Moshe*, (Constantinople, 1742) 3, #33, p. 1076 ff., the author, along with rabbis Abraham Monson, Yeshua Natan, and Solomon Alghazi (II), upheld the second will, against the vigorous protest of David Gershon.

20. *Sheber Posh'im*, appendix #11. *Sefat Emet*, p. 27a. The funds of Abraham Nathan were finally used to erect a Yeshiva in Jerusalem in the mid-eighteenth century, after a long and arduous struggle. It survived until the first World War. Havlin, p. 186.

21. (Venice, 1704). This introduction was already referred to in his Introduction to *Or Kadmon*, (Venice, 1703). On the exact date of the writing of this Introduction see Benayahu, *AS*, 2:121, n. 1, who dates it 1702; Havlin, p. 118, n. 20, who dates it 1700; and Shraga Kornbluth, "An Unknown Introduction to a Concealed Edition of Moses Hagiz' *Leket HaKeMaH*," *AS* (1981) 9:115, n. 3., who mediates by suggesting it had been written in 1700 and amended later.

22. Moses Hagiz, Intro. to *HK*.

23. The dynamics underlying these phenomena have been set forth in R. J. Z. Werblowsky, *Joseph Karo: Lawyer and Mystic*, (Philadelphia, 1980), especially pp. 38–83. Cf. *Mishnat Hakhamim* (Wandsbeck, 1733) p. 66, where Moses attributes the structure of the book to "divine inspiration."

24. The italicized words form titles of works by Jacob Hagiz and Moses Galante. The second citation is a reference to this episode in Hagiz' Intro. to *Or Kadmon*.

"הוא דרך עץ החיים הנצחים ותחילת חכמה יהיה לך לאורח מישור כצמיד פתיל תכלת
וקדש עצמך בקדש ישראל . . . הליכותך יהיו הלכות קטנות . . . תמות נפשך מות
ישרים והלכה והיתה בצרור החיים לחיי עולם ותן תודה בזבח תודה,
בקרבן מנחה, וחגיגה . . .

"כרמוז בהקדמתי שם נשאתי עיני למרום בתפילה לעני (תפלה למשה) ישלח עזרו
מקדש ויפתח לי את אוצרו . . . לכל אשר יקראוהו באמת . . . ואחרי ראיתי . . .
כי גמל עלי טובות . . . אמרתי אני אל לבי אף . . . בהיותי בצרה
אעשה מה שמוטל עלי ומי שעוזרני . . . לא ירפני . . . נטפלתי כעת במלאכה האמורה
(דפוס) נכון לבי בטוח בה'."

and in Introduction to *Korban Hagiga* (Venice, 1704).

"לא שקטתי ולא נחתי . . . ונתארך גלותי זה חוץ מארץ מולדתי . . .
השיגוני עונותי במהומה . . . עם כל זה זבדני אלהים זבד טוב ובזכות אבותי השגתי
למעלת הבטחון והזמנתי . . . לב אמיץ ואיני דואג לגזרת הבורא."

A very similar account of a visitation which became an inspiration for publication can be found in _Sefer Bet Levi_ of Levi b. Solomon of Brody (Zolkiew, 1732), Intro., p. ii.

25. Moses Hagiz, Intro. to _HK_.

26. Letters are at the beginning of joint volume _HK_ and Galante's _Korban Hagigah_. Samuel de Pas, a Sabbatian, makes it evident that his letter is not given out of love for Moses, but out of gratitude to Jacob Hagiz who had been his teacher in his youth; Benayahu, _AS_ 2:122, n. 6.

27. Shraga Kornbluth, "An Unknown Introduction to a Concealed Edition of Moses Hagiz' _Leket HaKeMaH_," (Heb.) _AS_ (1981) 9:127–129. On Hagiz' publishing activities in Venice see Benayahu, _AS_ 2:122–128, and Kornbluth, "Unknown Introduction."

28. Unfortunately a sonnet written by Isaac Pacifico in honor of the marriage festivities, which was described by Sonne, Relazione sui tesori bibliografici delle communite Israelitiche d'Italia, ms. JNUL R 2°50B 954, p. 12, #9, was lost during World War II. According to Sonne, the title was "Sonetto Epitalamo di Hagiz Mose ben Jacob e Venturina bat Asher Hafez Gentile a Verona." On the Hefez family, see Cecil Roth, "Stemmi di Famiglie Ebraiche," _Aryeh Leone Carpi Memorial Volume_, (Jerusalem, 1967), p. 177, where the family is listed as Hefez-Ashkenazi. See also Isaac Lampronte, _Pahad Yizhak_ (Lyck, 1874), p. 121a, and Nipi-Gerondi, _Toldot Gedolei Yisrael u-Geonei Italia_ (Trieste, 1853), pp. 167, 238, 70, on other members of this family. Moses Hagiz referred to Jacob Hefez as "the expert scholar," in his responsa, _Shetei ha-Lehem_ (Wandsbeck, 1733), p. 28b. For further details, see Kornbluth, p. 124, n. 38 and 40. On a conflict between Menashe Hefez and a wealthy Venetian layman, see David Oppenheim, _Nish'al David_, (Jerusalem, 1975) H.M., #2, and Hagiz' remarks in _Leket Ha-KeMaH_ (Amsterdam, 1707) Y.D., pp. 110 pertaining to Menashe's refusal to accept the rabbinate of Venice.

29. According to Benayahu, "Rabbi Samson Morpurgo," _Sinai_ (Winter 1979) 84(3–4):142, their first meeting took place in 1702 at the beginning of Hagiz' stay in Venice. Kornbluth, p. 118, n. 11 dates their first meeting shortly before Hagiz' correspondence to Morpurgo, _Shemesh Zedakah_, Y.D., #21, p. 68b, of Fall 1704

"מיום שעמדתי על דעתי והעמידני אוצר החכמה והמדע מורי מהר"ר מנשה גיסו."—

Morpurgo to Hagiz, _Shemesh Zedakah_, Y.D. #20, p. 67b.

30. Benayahu, "Morpurgo," p. 144 and #8, pp. 150–151.

31. On this essay, "Le-Ma'alat hazkarat ha-teshuba," pp. 14–30 in _Or Kadmon_ (Venice, 1703), see infra.

32. Krakovia was the son-in-law of the influential Hayim Friedland of Prague. Approbation of David Oppenheim to _HK_, p. 46. On an uncorrected copy

of the 1704 edition of *HK*, see Benayahu, *AS*, 2, p. 123, n. 9; facsimile of T.P., p. 126.

Havlin, p. 172, n. 208, believes that Hagiz actually traveled to Oppenheim to get his support, but the available documentation, including Oppenheim's letter, dated 4 Kislev 1704, does not support this. Kornbluth, p. 119, n. 15.

33. Benayahu has described pps. 1 and 4 of the Introduction, *AS*, 2:124–128, and Kornbluth has published the missing pages 2–3. If more of the book was published in 1704, it has not yet come to light. In the Amsterdam edition (1707) p. 26, Hagiz cited lack of funds as the reason for interrupting the work, and the help of David Oppenheim during his visit to Eastern Europe in 1706, as the reason for its resumption. Benayahu (*AS*, 2:125–126) suggests that the Venetian rabbinate may have withheld permission to publish after it received complaints from Livorno that Hagiz humiliated them in his introduction to *HK*, when he charged the Livornese leadership with obstructing his efforts to rebuild the Vega/ Nathan yeshivot. Kornbluth, p. 123, n. *32, argues that the harsh words in the Amsterdam edition of the *Leket* were not included in the Venice edition, and thus the argument of preemptive censorship cannot be made here. During the controversy of 1714 Nehemiah Hayon accused Hagiz of having deliberately fled from Venice to Amsterdam because he ran short of funds, leaving the publisher Bragadin with an outstanding debt. This is patently false, as Hagiz was in Venice eight months *after* the work was stopped, and he went to Erez Israel and then Central Europe before proceeding to Amsterdam. Hayon also accused Hagiz of withholding his criticism of Livorno's leadership when he submitted the *HK* for approbations and this may have been true. *Moda'a Rabah* p. 3b.

34. In *Morei De'ah* (Tel Aviv: A. Zioni, 1960): 151–155, Aviezer Burstin tells of a visit of Hagiz to Adrianople where he met R. Judah Rosanes. Burstin does not state his source, and I have been unable to find confirmation of such a visit in the writings of Hagiz or Rosanes. Nevertheless, it is not implausible that such a visit may have taken place on this excursion. Correspondence with Morpurgo, Benayahu, "Morpurgo," p. 153. Oppenheim, *Nish'al David*, 2, H.M., #14. Havlin, p. 211b, has compared the printed edition with Oxford ms. 838 #73, and determined that the parenthetical insertion of Livorno is completely in error, the text elsewhere specifies '*Ir ha-Kodesh*,' Jerusalem, as the locale.

On David Oppenheim, see Koppel Duschinsky, *Toldot R. David Oppenheimer* (Budapest, 1922); Alexander Marx, "Some Notes on the History of David Oppenheimer's Library," *REJ* (1926) 82:451–460.

35. On the *aliya* of R. Judah Hasid, Benayahu, "The Holy Society of R' Judah Hasid and its Aliya to Erez Israel," *Sefunot* (1960) 3–4:133–182; Benayahu, "The Testimony of R. Elijah Ashkenazi of Safed on the Sabbatianism of R. Hayim Malakh and R. Judah Hasid." *Erez Israel*, (1971): 10:67–71. Benayahu, "Correspondence between the Ashkenazic *Kehilla* of Jerusalem and R. David Oppenheim," (Heb.) *Jerusalem Quarterly* (Spring–Fall, 1950), 3(3–4):111 ff.

36. Jacob Emden, *Torat ha-Kena'ot* (Lvov, 1870), pp. 57–62. Another basis for their mutual friendship was bibliophilia. Oppenheim was constantly acquiring

new materials from agents in Erez Israel, and Hagiz had access to many manuscripts, as he often stated.

37. Concerning Hagiz' stay in Prague, see the approbation of R. Abraham
Broda of Prague to *Leket HaKeMaH:* "He has dwelled here in our community
well nigh six months." The approbation is dated Spring 1706, which dates Hagiz'
arrival in Fall 1705. Hagiz mentioned Oppenheim's help in fundraising in his
Introduction to *Leket HaKeMaH* (Amsterdam, 1707), p. 2b.

38. Moses Hagiz, *Sefat Emet* (Amsterdam, 1707), p. 24a. Although the extant
edition was prepared for press in September [Elul], 1707, there is a tantalizing
possibility that an earlier edition had been printed. Azulai cites quotations that
are not in our edition, as Benayahu has pointed out in "The Sabbatian Movement
in Jerusalem," p. 57, n. 70. The ban on this book forbade owning a copy of the
book in *"Hebrew or any other language."* I. S. Emanuel, "The Nehemiah Hiya
Hayon Controversy in Amsterdam," *Sefunot* (1965) 9:223. Since the 1707 edition
is in Hebrew (with a brief introduction in Portuguese) the ban hints at an edition
written solely in Spanish or Portuguese.

39. *SE,* p. 16b. If Hagiz is not exaggerating the powers of the Jerusalem rabbinate here, this would be a unique reference to the use of corporal punishment
by the Jerusalem *Bet Din.*

40. Benayahu, *AS,* 2, pp. 135–136.

41. This anonymous figure may well have been a real individual. In *Leket
HaKeMaH,* (Amsterdam 1707) O.H., p. 38a. In *LeKet HaKeMaH,* O.H., p. 38r,
Hagiz refers to

"הגביר היקר אהובי . . . מרדכי שניאור."

The question attributed to Senior in the *Leket* also concerns *Erez Israel* vs. the
Diaspora, and the discrepancies in the weekly Torah portion read by the respective communities.

42. Benayahu, *AS,* 2, p. 136.

43. Benayahu, *AS,* 2, n. 49, describes a copy that was used for this purpose
as late as 1863. Adam Andreas Cnollenius, *Unschuldige Nachrichten Altes und Neues,*
1713, quoted extensively from *SE* in his depiction of the Holy Land. Johann
Jacob Schudt, *Judische Merckwurdigkeiten,* 4, Bk. 1, ch. 7, pp. 38–39; J. C. Wolf,
Bibliotheca Hebraea, both used Cnollenius as a source. On Cnollenius, see *Allge-
meine Deutsche Biographie,* 4, Leipzig, 1876, s.v. Cnollen, Adam Andreas.

44. The section begins on p. 20v. Other accounts are those of Gedaliah of
Semiaticz, and Raphael Mordechai Malkhi. They tend to corroborate Hagiz' account of the debts of Jerusalem's community.

45. Sonne, "Documents pertaining to Emissaries in Italy," [Heb.] *Kobez al
Yad,* (1951) 15:201, n. 18; David Tamar, *Mehkarim be-Toldot ha-Yehudim,* p. 126;
Gershon Cohen, [Sinai #67(60):73] theorized that the antipathy to emissaries in
Italy may have roots in the controversy over Gentile wine, particularly due to
the activity of Joseph Pardo. Y. Rivkind, "Iggerot Yerushalaim," *Shai le-Yeshaya
Wolfsberg* (Jerusalem, 1955), p. 226. On the subject of unsavory treatment of

emissaries, Salo Baron, *The Jewish Community*, (Philadelphia, 1942) 2:342–343. Responsum of Hagiz in Samson Morpurgo *Shemesh Zedaka* 1, part II (19), dated 1704.

46. Broda letter in approbation to *Leket HaKeMaH* (Amsterdam, 1707). *Sefat Emet*, p. 17a; 19a.

47. A. Yaari, in his massive work *Sheluhei Erez Israel*, covers the entire emissary panorama. He paints a picture of homage and adulation marred only sporadically by internecine emissary squabbling or an occasional imposter. The situation may have been very different in the Ottoman Empire and in Eastern Europe; Hagiz' account is confined to Western Europe, and his experience is limited to Italy and Amsterdam. I. S. Emmanuel, "The Hayon Controversy in Amsterdam," *Sefunot*, 9, p. 211, argued that Hagiz' claims were distorted. He had claimed that the Jews of Amsterdam donated 800–1000 florins a year to the emissaries. Emmanuel brings records that show a figure almost twenty times that amount, excluding special charities, bequests and book subsidies from which Hagiz himself had benefitted. See also his "The Assistance of the Sephardic Community of Amsterdam and Curaçao to the Holy Land and Safed," (Heb.) *Sefer Safed = Sefunot*, 6–7, M. Benayahu, ed. (Jerusalem, 1962).

48. *Ibid.*, p. 22a. A notable exception to this statement is Hagiz' former brother-in-law, Hezekiah da Silva, who traveled to Amsterdam because he had wealthy relatives there; his status would otherwise have dictated that he travel to Turkey, considered the choicest emissary territory.

49. *Sefat Emet*, pp. 17a, 23b.

50. SE, pp. 21a, 25a, 21a, 23b. Hagiz cited the example of the long interval between visits of Hezekiah da Silva and Abraham Karigal.

51. SE, pp. 9b, 24a.

52. SE, Introduction, p. 16b.

53. SE, Introduction.

54. SE, p. 6a.

55. Morris Goodblatt, *Jewish Life in Turkey in the XVIth Century* (New York, 1952), p. 104. See also I. Z. Kahana, "Bequests to Benefit Erez Israel in the Responsa Literature," *Mehkarim be-Sifrut ha-Teshubot* (Jerusalem, 1973), pp. 207–238. Mordecai Halevi, *Responsa Darkhei No'am* (Venice, 1697) H.M., #23, p. 212b.

56. Hagiz' derisive treatment of the emissary Simon Bekhr Jacob in *Leket HaKeMa"H* (Amsterdam, 1707), p. 20b; and SE, p. 3a–b. seems ample proof that emissary status alone did not command his respect in halakhic matters.

57. SE, pp. 7b, 8a, 17a. Yizhak F. Baer, in *Galut* (New York, 1947), pp. 112–113, and Azriel Shohat, *Im Hilufei Tekuphot*, hailed *Sefat Emet* as the first modern work to articulate and denounce the attitudes of Jewish assimilationists.

58. *Leket HaKeMaH*, Y.D., p. 111b.

59. Moses Hagiz, *Leket HaKeMaH* (Amsterdam, 1707) Introduction.

60. HK, (Venice, 1704), pp. 24–28 and p. 52ff. Introduction to edition of Venice, 1704, published by Kornbluth, "An Unknown Introduction," p. 127ff.

61. (Venice, 1651). Despite his intention to write a systematic work, Hagiz

occasionally digressed. E.g., *Leket*, Y.D., p. 51a: "This belongs to the Halakhot of . . . but my pen has spewed it here."

62. *Leket* (Amsterdam, 1707), Introduction, p. i. Only one volume of Aboab's work was printed, years later, by H. Y. D. Azulai, as an appendix to Azulai's *Hayyim Sha'al* (Livorno, 1795/6) on Hoshen Mishpat. Aboab was later to play a role in the polemic against Luzzatto.

63. A classical example is the criticism that attended Maimonides' *Mishneh Torah*. See I. Twersky, "The Beginnings of Mishneh Torah Criticism," *Biblical and Other Studies*, A. Altmann, ed. (Cambridge, 1963), pp. 161–182.

64. *Eleh Ha-Mizvot* (Wandsbeck, 1727) #496. Hagiz used the term "Maskilim" in a pejorative sense, to denote people whose erudition is affected and insincere.

65. The ruling itself is brought in *Leket*, O.H., p. 51b. On the final page of the volume, p. 133b, in a paragraph titled "Omissions of the Typesetter," Hagiz inserted an apology for offending the sensibilities of those who disagreed with the ruling.

66. *Leket*, Y.D. p. 21a. From the end of the paragraph it is clear that the errant student is apologetic fiction. The entire paragraph is worth citing because it shows the attitude Hagiz' work would have taken toward his predecessors.

> "ואף על פי שבפעל ראיתי דברי סותרין מן הקצה אל הקצה אל הקצה דברי מורינו ורבינו
> הגדול הבית יוסף . . . גמרתי בדעתי להודיע לרבים כי כל כי האי מלתא ניחא ליה
> לרבינו הב"י שנסיר המכשלה הזאת מספריו וה' אתנו לא נחדל מלומר שרבים שתו
> ממימיו על רבינו ולבין דברי הכל בו שלא על אמיתותן. ואחר המחילה הראויה מזיו
> כבוד רבונותם . . .
> וחלילה לנו להבין מדעת הקדוש רבנו הב"י שדברים ככתבן עלו לו במחשבה
> ונתעלמה ממנו הלכה אלא שאיזה תלמיד טועה הוסיף על דבריו ונכזב . . . אף אילו
> באמת היה הגדולי ישראל בין החולקין, כי מה בכך? גם אנו, יתמי דיתמי רוח
> אל עשאנו כמוהם ומקום הניחו לנו לדבר."

Hagiz referred to those who opposed him as מתחסרים בעיני הרבים *Leket*, O.H., p. 29b.

67. Moses Hagiz, *Shetei ha-Lehem* (Wandsbeck, 1733), #42, p. 53b.

68. References to the meager sum he netted in I. Sonne, "Correspondence between R. Moses Hagiz and R. Samson Morpurgo over Hayon . . .," *Kobez al Yad*, 2:179. The section of the *Leket* on Hoshen Mishpat has recently been found by Joshua Mondshein, "Leket HaKeMa"H of R. Moses Hagiz—The Section on Hoshen Mishpat," *AS*, 10:92–112 (MS. JNUL #3131). An index was prepared by Shabbetai ben Abraham Ada, an emissary of Hebron. Ms. Jews College #56, pp. 150a–172b.

69. The other selections in *Or Kadmon* are '*Bakasha al ha-Yihud*,' (Entreaty Concerning Unity), "Prayer upon recalling the Day of Death of R. Judah Hasid," a prayer attributed to Bahya Hasid, and Marganita Debei Rab.

"*Keter Malkhut*" acquired a life of its own as an independent genre of liturgical poetry. See *Keter Malkhut* of Solomon Alkabez in R. J. Z. Werblowsky, "A Collection of Prayers and Devotional Compositions by Solomon Alkabetz," (Heb.)

Sefer Safed (Jerusalem, 1962) 1:154–162. Alkabetz' collection also included Ibn Zimra's *Keter*, pp. 165–167.

70. *Mishnat Hakhamim*, #560.

71. *Ibid.*, #148.

72. The text of the ban in I. S. Emanuel, "The Hayon Controversy in Amsterdam," *Sefunot*, 9, 1965, p. 223. Joseph HaKohen had also participated in the publication of a similar, very rare edition of Venice, 1701. Benayahu, *AS*, 2, p. 138. The *Idrot* is bound together with another work, *Seder Keriat Vatikin*, selections from the Bible, Mishnah, and Talmud, to be read on specific occasions. It is unclear whether it was bound together with the *Idrot* on Hagiz' initiative or that of the publisher.

73. Hagiz' description is supplemented by the Introduction to the Venice, 1701 edition, cited by Benayahu, *AS*, 2:138.

74. On Zarfati, see publisher's forward to Abraham Cuenque's *Avak Soferim* (Amsterdam, 1704). Benayahu, *AS*, 2:149. A. Yaari, "The Printers of the Foa Family," *Mahkarei Sefer* (Jerusalem, 1958), pp. 367–374.

75. Foa subsequently reprinted Hagiz' *Index*, with no mention of its provenance, in the back of an edition of the *Zohar* he published in 1748. Benayahu, *AS*, 2:149.

76. Benayahu, *ibid.*, p. 152, n. 82, lists the four known copies of this edition, two of which are in private collections. I have been unable to obtain a copy and have relied on Benayahu's description.

77. David Ibn Zimra, Introduction to *Magen David*.

78. Benayahu, *AS*, 2:159–161 has interpreted the clues. The *Magen David* was printed entirely by the Foa press, except for the first four pages, and the title page states "In the press of Asher Anshel Hazan." Benayahu located a solitary copy of the *Magen David* in which the first four pages were also printed by Foa and the title page bears Foa's imprint. This is Hagiz' personal copy, with his handwritten corrections and marginal notes. Apparently, the Hayon controversy had erupted while the first four pages were captive in Foa's printing shop, and all Hagiz could manage to rescue was one personal copy. Hagiz' statement of his involvement, *Eleh ha-Mizvot*, 1727, p. 161r. Yohanan Helischau was author of the *Ma'aseh Rab* (London, 1707).

79. Hagiz' collection was sought out by Jews and Gentiles alike. The great bibliographer Johann Christoph Wolf consulted Hagiz' collection for his *Bibliotheca Hebraea*. The copyist of one ms. wrote, "This commentary [to the *Idra Zuta*] has been found in the collection of sacred writings of R. Moses Hagiz." JTS, Ms. #2198. 5. The JTS catalogue attributes the work to Hagiz, but from the contents and the copyists' remark, it is clearly just copied from his collection.

80. Moses Hagiz, Introduction to *Or Kadmon*.

81. *Mishnat Hakhamim*, #240.

82. *Leket HaKeMaH*, Y.D., p. 110v. An interesting test of this principle can be found in Zebi Ashkenazi, *Responsa Hakham Zebi* #36 (dated 1706). A query was addressed to Ashkenazi by Isaac, son of Jacob Sasportas. The question: whether

latecomers to public prayer were obligated to join the congregation (halakha), or were permitted to start from the beginning and proceed at their own pace (Kabbalah). Spanish translation of this responsum, Ms. Columbia X893 Sa7. In the response, Ashkenazi cites this ruling of Ibn Zimra's.

83. Moses Hagiz, Introduction to *Eleh ha-Mitzvot*. He published a greatly expanded edition in 1727; *ibid.*, Introduction. *Ibid.*, (1727 ed.), #49, p. 26v; 48r, 51r, 46v., and second introduction. Hagiz loyally adhered to the Maimonidean enumeration of the precepts. On the role of this work in *Sefer Mizvot* literature, see Moise Bloch, "Les 613 Lois," *REJ* (1881) 1:197–211.

84. I. Tishby, "The Controversy over the *Zohar* in 16th Century Italy," *Perakim*, 1 ,(Jerusalem, 1967–8), pp. 131–182; G. Scholem, *Major Trends in Jewish Mysticism* (New York, 1973), pp. 251–258.

85. Hagiz' discussion on whether to promote or suppress Kabbalah in *Leket*, Y.D., pp. 110v–111r.

4. ERUPTION OF THE HAYON CONTROVERSY

1. *LeKet HaKeMaH*, Y.D. (1707) pp. 110b–111a.

2. Perlhefter's remark: I. Sonne, "On the History of Sabbatianism in Italy," (Heb.) *Marx Jubilee Volume* ed. David Frankel, (N.Y., 1943). On Sharaf: G. Scholem, "Cardoso," *Chajes Volume*, p. 331, n.1.

3. On Rovigo's role, see Scholem, "The Dreams of the Sabbatian Mordekhai Ashkenazi," and Benayahu, "Sabbatian Information from the Notebooks of R. Benjamin HaKohen and R. Abraham Rovigo," (Heb.) *Michael* (1972) 1:9–77. Rovigo's statement, Sonne, *ibid.*, p. 92. The letter was signed with only a clue to its author's identity ['Ha-ne'eman be-migo" which rhymed with his name] lest it fall into hostile hands, p. 93, n.10.

4. Jacob Reischer, *Responsa Shebut Jacob* (Halle, 1710), 1, #72.

5. Molkho-Amarillo, "Letters of A. M. Cardoso," (Heb.) *Sefunot* 3–4:204.

6. Cardoso's claim in "Derush ha-Kinuyyim," cited in Scholem, "Cardoso," *Chajes*, p. 331.

7. M. Friedman, "Correspondence of the Hayon Controversy," *Sefunot* letter #30, p. 578. Hayon wrote, "Your eyes witnessed the disputation I had in Smyrna with the disciples of Cardoso, whom I defeated," Hayon, *Moda'a Rabah* (Amsterdam, 1714), p. 2r, col. 1.

8. Benjamin Halevi: Friedman #37. Netanel Halevi, *ibid.*, #31, pp. 589–560.

9. Joseph Ergas, *Tokhahat Megullah*, (London, 1715) p. 32b.

10. *Milhamah la-Shem*, p. 17a.

11. Hagiz, *Sheber Posh'im*, p. 50b.

12. "Our entire goal," Moses Hagiz, Intro. to Joseph Ergas, *Tokhahat Megulla*, p. ii. "Indeed . . .," *Sheber Posh'im*, p. 8. "Not to follow," I. Sonne, "Correspondence of Hagiz-Morpurgo," p. 186. "Our task," Letter of Hagiz to R. Arye

Leib of Amsterdam, in Ms. *Gahalei Esh*, p. 606 cited in M.A. Perlmutter, *R. Jonathan Eybeschutz*, pp. 45–56.

13. "I did not," Jacob Emden, *Torat ha-Kena'ot*, (Lvov), p. 86. "The Rabbinic court," Emden, *Petah Einayim*, pp. 4a–5b.

14. The Christian missionary Callenberg reported a conversation with a rabbi in Halle, in July 1720, "Although *he (Sabbatai) was banned by the rabbis*, believers remain . . .," Scholem, "Information on Sabbatians in the Notebooks of Eighteenth Century Missionaries," *Zion* 9:27.

15. "Many important," H. Graetz, *D.Y.Y.*, 8, appendix vi, p. 590. "haben," Scholem, *Zion*, 9, p. 33, entry dated Aug. 5, 1732. "For the sinners," Ginsburg, *Iggerot RaMHa"L*, p. 333. Letter dated 1735.

16. Letter of Solomon Ayllon to Judah Briel, Friedman, *Sefunot*, letter #19, p. 544.

17. "That there were," Carlo Bernheimer, "Some New Contributions to Abraham Cardoso's Biography," *JQR* (Oct., 1927) p. 125.

"ואכתוב נגד האמונה הרעה . . . לשלוח למלכות פולונייא ולרבני אשכנז כי זה
האיש אשר בא מהם [מלאך] . . . היה מאמין מלא שטות וגם הוא שמע וקבל שש"צ
הוא אלוה ואין צורך עתה לשום חכמת התנאים והאמוראים, ומאז שהוא הגיד לנו,
וקבלתי סוד האלוהות מהח' פרימו . . . הרחקתיו מביתי . . . הגיד לנו חכם אחד
. . ., שבאמונת פרימו היו ויש היום כמה מיני חכמים, ואפי' בירושלים . . ."

"Malakh tried . . .," I. Molho and A. Amarillo, "Autobiographical Letters of Cardoso," *Sefunot* (1960) 3–4:200. "The Ashkenazi Judah Hasid" *ibid.*, p. 190.

18. Elijah Kohen, *Sefer Meribat Kadesh*, Freimann, ed. pp. 18–19. The author of this polemic against Cardoso commented,

"החטאים האלה *חרובי קרתא* מי ירדן ערמתו הוביש בתקנו הישיבה החדשה . . ."

Hagiz' enemies had accused him of being a "*mahrib karta*" in his efforts to establish a non-Sabbatian yeshiva. It appears that R. Benjamin Kohen of Reggio, the prominent Italian kabbalist and rabbinic scholar who was a Sabbatian, also dreamed of a yeshiva in the Holy Land. I. Sonne, ed. "Contributions to the History of Sabbatianism in Italy," *Marx Jubilee Volume*, p. 94: "My spirit moves me to go to the Land of beauty and breadth, where *the Torah shall be my profession*."

19. Emden, *Torat ha-Kena'ot*, (Lublin, 1880 ed.) pp. 62, 66.

20. *Ibid.*, p. 62. The letter was signed by: Abraham Yizhaki, Joseph Cuenque, Samson Gomez Pato, Judah HaKohen.

21. This was known even among Christian missionaries: "It is well known to Jews and Christians of Jerusalem, that his [Sabbatai's] adherents who go forth from there . . . protest bitterly if their faith is not accepted." Scholem, *Zion*, 9, entry for 1720.

22. The ban was printed on a single sheet in Constantinople in 1709; Moses Hagiz, *Lehishat Saraf* (Hanau, 1726), pp. 12–13; Emden, *Torat ha-Kena'ot*, Lvov, pp. 66–67; the ban is signed: Abraham Yizhaki, Isaac HaKohen, and Aryeh Judah HaKohen Leib.

23. For Livorno see Joseph Ergas, *Responsa Diberei Yosef* (Livorno, 1752), #53; for Ferrara, Isaac Lampronti, *Pahad Isaac* s.v. "Kidushei Ed Ehad" pp. 132–140; Verona, Ms. JNUL, 4° 553, p. 124; and for Padua see Samson Morpurgo, *Responsa Shemesh Zedaka* (Venice, 1753) Y.D. #24.

24. "I recalled," "Correspondence of S. Morpurgo—M. Hagiz," I. Sonne, ed. p. 172. The letter is dated 9 Tevet 1708, a misprint for 1712. Hayon's statement in *Moda'a Rabah*, Intro., "An ancient," J. Ghiron, *Mishtah Haramim*, p. 86r, quoted in G. Levi, *Revista Israelitica*, (1912) no. 9, p. 9.

25. Hagiz, Intro. to *Idrot* (Amsterdam, 1708). Yizhaki, like other emissaries brought with him kabbalistic manuscripts from Erez Israel for Hagiz and others to publish. According to Azulai, Yizhaki approved the manuscript of Jacob Zemah's *Naggid u-Mezaveh* which Joseph Eliashar published (Amsterdam, 1712) with the proviso that Eliashar omit all references to 'oblique profundities." Azulai, *Shem ha-Gedolim* s.v. "Naggid u-Mezaveh." Jacob Emden recollected: "When I was small, I saw in Amsterdam the emissary of Zion, Hakham Yizhaki, whom I remember to have been tall, strong and towering above the masses," *Mor u-Keziah*, (Altona, 1778) 2:94.

26. Text of letter in Friedman, #1. The letter sent simultaneously to the ma'amad of Amsterdam is not extant.

27. I.S. Emmanuel, "Documents Related to the Nehemiah Hayon Controversy in Amsterdam," *Sefunot*, (1965) 9(11):242–243.

28. For biographical treatments of Hayon, see Graetz (Heb.) *D.Y.Y.*, 8, no. 2, Appendix VI; Friedman, "Iggerot," *Erez Israel*, 10:486–490, and Scholem, 'Nehemiah Hayon,' *EJ*, 7:1500–1503. On the title page of *Diberei Nehemiah* (Berlin, 1713), Hayon introduced himself as, "From the holy city of Safed," and T.P. of *Raza De-Yihuda* (Venice, 1711), "a native of the north Galilee, the city of Safed." Hayon's semi-autobiographical *Moda'a Rabah* (Amsterdam, 1714) was issued as a self-vindiction at the height of the polemic.

29. *Moda'a*, p. 2r, col. II. Hayon mentioned R. Jacob Se'ias, R. Jonah, R. Jacob Mas'oud, and R. Joseph Biton as his teachers and examiners in the Talmud Torah (elementary school). [Their names are unknown from other sources]. The introduction to Abulafia was arranged by his widowed landlady, a friend of Abulafia's wife.

30. Benayahu, "Sabbatian Information," *Michael*, 1:30; Scholem, "Exchange of Letters," *Behinot*, (1957) 9:80.

31. See the correspondence between Perahia and Hayon in Perahia, *She'elot u-Teshubot Perah Matteh Aaron* (Amsterdam, 1703) 2(80):124.

Hagiz accused Hayon of perpetrating "abominations" while in Uskup, but did not specify, *Sheber Posh'im* p. 37a; Hayon's recension of a letter from the Smyrna rabbinate dated 15 Heshvan 1714, says "he fled from there with the Gentile maid, as everyone knows." Emden, *Torat ha-Kena'ot*, (Lvov) p. 63, gives a recension of the same letter, entitled "Edut le-Israel," in which Hayon purportedly took two horses and kidnapped the Gentile maidservant of a certain Abraham Molina, whose sons pursued Hayon and retrieved the maid. Judah Briel "accepted testimony" which attributed to Hayon "great abominations" and a rep-utation for licentiousness (Friedman, #9, #20).

32. *Moda'a Rabah*, p. 1 col. II.

33. On October 18, 1714, a dispute between Suleima and Nathan's representative, Samuel HaKohen, was adjudicated in Livorno and Suleima was ordered to return certain properties to Nathan. In *Mishnat Hakhamim*, #351–352, Hagiz complained:

"הניחש השיאו להפוך צנורות השפע ולפניו ולתברך גלוי
דכל מה שעשה נחש זה לא היה אלא מחמת קנאה."

Although there are other candidates for the acronym Nahash, which Hagiz used here, Hayon is a favorite. Havelin, p. 178, n. 229 and p. 180, n. 230. Hayon's enemies discredited him in similar words to those used against Hagiz, e.g. the phrase "mahrib arazot," ruining the revival of Erez Israel, was used against both.

34. *Moda'a Rabah*, p. 1b, col. 1.

35. Ronald A. Knox, *Enthusiasm* (Oxford, 1950).

36. Naphtali HaKohen, in Scholem, *Zion*, 3:174, n. 2. Also *Edut le-Israel*, p. 1v, *le-Einei Kol Yisrael*, p. 2r. "Wherever he stayed," cited in Friedman, "Iggerot," p. 490. Fiametta and Mujajon in Friedman, #30.

37. Scholem, *Zion*, 3, p. 174. Scholem had dated the testimony at 1707, but cf. Benayahu, *Sefunot*, 3–4, p. 181–2, who dates it 1702–3. E.g. *Milhamah la-Shem*, p. 28r.

38. Isaac Cantarini, *Et Kez*, p.i.

39. *Sefer Meribat Kadesh*, in Freimann, *Inyanei S.Z.*, p. 37. The statement was attributed to Abraham Cardoso. Isaac Cantarini also worked with a unit of forty years in his calculations: "After the redemption from bondage in Egypt, they had to wait forty years in the desert before entering the Promised Land. . . . So too with the future redemption." *Et Kez*, p. 8v.

40. Zalman Shazar, *The Messianic Hope for the Year 1740* (Heb.) (Jerusalem, 1970), p. 11.

41. "But the strangest," Tobiah Kohen, *Ma'aseh Tobiah Ha-Kohen* (Venice, 1708), p. 27a. Excerpt from Leib b. Ozer's *Beshraibung fun Shabsai Zevi*, cited in Shazar, p. 26. The letter of Pincherle in *Responsa of RB"Kh* (Jerusalem, 1970), p. 14.

42. *Meribat Kadesh*, in Freimann, *Inyanei*, p. 36; Benayahu, "Sabbatian Information," *Michael*, 1, pp. 27–28, n. 76; Scholem, "The Dreams of the Sabbatian, R. Mordekhai Ashkenazi," p. 38, n. 1.

43. Reference to 1714 as a new deadline: "From 1674, when he disappeared, to 1714, is forty years. May he come if God wills it." R. Samuel Feivush Kahana, *Leket Shemuel* (Venice, 1694), cited in Shazar, *Tarbiz*, 5, 1934, p. 354. The cantor Yehuda Leib of Zelichow, also designated the year 1714. *Shirei Yehuda* (Amsterdam, 1697), p. 14.

44. "He has not," Cantarini, *Et Kez*, p. lv; Scholem, 'Missionairies,' part II, pp. 84–85.

45. Luis Landau, "The Attitude of R. Jacob Culi towards Sabbatianism,"

Pe'amim, (1983) 15:58–66; for Abulafia, see Shazar, p. 36. R. Hayim ben Attar, author of the exegetical commentary *Or ba-Hayim* wrote of the hopes for the year 1740, and settled in Erez Israel then. Shazar, p. 29. Isaac Cantarini, whose *Et Kez* is one of the most articulate predictions for 1740, joined several times in the bans against Hayon. See Friedman, #24, pp. 554–563, and *Milhamah la-Shem*.

46. Yehudah Leibes, "The Messianism of R. Jacob Emden and his Attitude to Sabbatianism," *Tarbiz* 49, no. 1–2.

47. *Diberei Nehemiah* (Berlin, 1713) p. 60a. The word messiah appears in one other place, but it does not appear to be invested with special significance. In the description of the lavish farewell tendered in his honor in Smyrna, Hayon described it as so impressive "That the gentiles remarked, 'That must be the messiah, whom they so greatly honor' . . . and among my witnesses is Elijah Tarragon." *Moda'a Rabah*, p. 1, col. ii.

48. *Sheber Posh'im*, p. 58.

49. Although Hayon's unpublished works, including the comprehensive Kabbalistic treatise, *Sefer Ta'azumot*, shed additional light on his system of thought, they did not play any role in the controversy, as they remained unknown to his adversaries. Bibliography of his unpublished works in Friedman, p. 618.

50. "In its merit," Raza de-Yihuda (Venice, 1711), p. 3r. "Verse which is," *ibid.*, p. 45r. The opening lines in Aramaic: [La Bella Margarita . . .]

לא באלהא מרגילאת בפום דכל בר חי"
"כי אם בפום רבינו הוא שמעון בר יוחai.

"Most authors," Hayon, *Ha-Zad Zebi* (Amsterdam, 1714), p. 36r. Judah Briel was the rabbinic adversary who noticed Hayon's ingenuity. See his letter to Ayllon, Friedman, #20, pp. 548–49.

51. "Anyone," *Raza de-Yihuda*, p. 29b; p. 2b. "limsor oto be-yad yehidei am segullah," *ibid.*, p. 2b. The same Venetian rabbis who approved Raza de-Yihuda, also appear in an approbation to *Oz le-Elohim*, which they flatly denied issuing. Judah Perez, copy editor of Hayon's book, was accused of using the approbations he obtained for his *Perah Lebanon* (Berlin, 1712) to help Hayon forge approbations to his work.

52. *Diberei Nehemiah*, p. 1v–2r. On the Sabbatian concept of holiness of sin, see G. Scholem, "Redemption Through Sin," *The Messianic Idea in Judaism* (N.Y., 1971), pp. 78–141.

53. *Diberei Nehemiah*, pp. 81r–81v. Hayon specifically excepted those who converted, but later repented of their conversion. On the radical Sabbatian converts, see Scholem, "The Crypto Jewish Sect of the Donmeh (Sabbatians) in Turkey," *The Messianic Idea*, pp. 142–166.

54. *Ha-Zad Zebi*, p. 31v–32r;

55. A. Freimann, *Inyanei Sabbatai Zebi*, p. 122; Joseph Ergas, *Tokhahat Megullah*, p. 2b; *ha-Zad NaHa"SH*, p. 32a. In Sabbatian circles, the identical manuscript circulated under the title, *Raza de-Mehemnuta le-Amir"a* (an acronym for Sabbatai). Cited in Scholem, *Sabbatai Sebi*, p. 902. Molho-Amarillo, "Cardoso

Letters," *Sefunot*, 3–4, (1960), p. 197. This solution has been suggested, and further expanded upon by Yehudah Leibes, "The Ideological Basis of the Hayon Controversy" (Heb.), *Proceedings of the Eighth World Congress of Jewish Studies* (Jerusalem, 1982), pp. 129–134 and "Michael Cardoso—Author of the book *Raza de-Mehemnuta* which had been attributed to Sabbatai Zebi . . ." (Heb.) *KS*, (July 1980) 55(3):603–616; and "Appendix," *ibid.* (April 1981):373–374.

56. Many other Sabbatian works contained direct references to Sabbatai often as AMIR"A = Adone'nu Morenu Yarum Hodo [Our Lord, Our Master, May he be glorified]; or to other clearly Sabbatian sources e.g., the treatise of Solomon Ayllon, published by Yael Nadav, "R. Solomon Ayllon and his Sabbatian Kabbalistic Tract," *Sefunot* (1960) 3–4:303–347, which contains eight references to writings of Nathan of Gaza. Cf. the treatise ve-Abo ha-Yom El ha-Ayin, in M.A. Perlmutter, *R. Jonathan Eybeschutz and his Attitude toward Sabbatianism* (Tel Aviv, 1947).

57. *Moda'a Rabbah*, p. 1r, col. 1; p. 1v, col. 2. See also p. 2r, col. 1, "You have beheld the great controversy I had in Smyrna with the followers of Abraham Cardoso, until I completely refuted their beliefs."

58. Letter of Fiametta to Ayllon, Friedman, #30, p. 587. *Moda'a*, p. 2v, col. 1.

59. Hayim Wirszubski, "The Sabbatian Theology of Nathan the Prophet" (Heb.), *Knesset*, (1943) 8:210–246; G. Scholem, *be-Ik'vot Mashiah* (Jerusalem, 1944).

60. Wirszubski, "The Sabbatian Ideology of the Apostasy of the Messiah as Stated by Nathan of Gaza and in Iggeret Magen Abraham," (Heb.), *Zion*, (1938) 3:215–245; G. Scholem, "Iggeret Magen Abraham," *Kobez al Yad*, 2, [12]

61. Yizhaki, in Emden, *Torat ha-Kena'ot*, p. 66. Hagiz, *Milhama le-Hashem*, p. 30v–31r.

62. Hayon, *Raza de-Yihuda*, p. 2r.

63. *Oz le-Elohim*, p. i:

"חקור וטרח בכל אורח ואז יזרח אור אפריון
יכיר מהות האלהות בלי שבות ובלי רפיון."

"Those who sit," p. 1r; "Do not pay heed," p. 4r.

64. Tractate *Hagigah*, *BT*, 11b.

65. *Oz le-Elohim*, p. 1v. In this case, as his opponents pointed out, Hayon not only contradicted the accepted interpretation of Rashi, but also of the Talmud itself, (*Hagigah*, p. 16a).

66. "Whether one may study"; "there are false . . ." *Oz le-Elohim*, p. 5r. "Who is wise;" "persons of repute," *ibid.*, p. 5v. "The words of scribes," p. 7a; "the words of the prophet," p. 7v. "I must still insist," from the *Journal* of John Wesley, (entry of 7-6-1746); cited in Knox, p. 454.

67. *Oz le-Elohim*, T.P.

68. "Otherwise we must ask," *Bet Kodesh ha-Kodashim*, ch. 3. "What distinguishes," *Raza de-Yihuda*, p. 10b. "Is the true faith . . .," *Oz le-Elohim*, p. 84b.

69. Letter of Joseph Fiametta to Solomon Ayllon, Friedman, #30, p. 584.

Letter of R. Judah b. Simon of Mainz [Kabbalist, author of *Yad Yehuda*, a commentary to Azariah Fano's *Imrot Tehorot* (Frankfurt, 1698) to Hayon] Friedman,
#17, p. 541. There are several summaries of Hayon's doctrines. See Graetz,
D.Y.Y., 8, appendix 6. Graetz was of the opinion (p. 596) that Hayon identified
the figure of the Sabbatian messiah with his "Malkah Kadisha."
    His one supporting text,"

"נשמות אחרות שיבואו מזיווג מלכא קדישא ושכינתיה בסוד תורה חדשה."

does not necessarily support his conclusion, and the weight of Hayon's work
indicates the contrary; Scholem, "Nehemiah Hayon," EJ, 7:1500–1503; Herling,
"On the Secret Doctrines of N. H. Hayon," *Amanah*. M.A. Perlmutter, *The
Attitude of R. Jonathan Eybeschutz*, pp. 120–122, demonstrated the relationship
between the work of Cardoso and Hayon, as well as the influence of Hayon's
thought over the author of "ve-Abo ha-Yom el ha-'Ayin," the Sabbatian treatise
attributed to Eybeschutz. A contemporary, David Nunez Torres, bookseller and
rabbi in The Hague, wrote a brief essay and catalogue of works related to the
Hayon controversy, *Catologus Librorum . . .* (The Hague, 1728) in which he attributed a belief in a quaternity to Hayon. As Hayon postulated a transcendent
spirit which was not included in his trinity, Nunez Torres did not misunderstand
Hayon.
    70. "Surely you are," Emmanuel, p. 228. 85. "They audaciously," *Milhamah
la-Shem*, p. 41r.

"קהילתם היה [!] בת חורין אינדיפי נדיטו משאר קהילות . . . אינה משועבדת ולא
כפופה לשום קהילה . . . מי אדון לנו? ברוב כוח רבו ומריבים עם כל חכמי ישראל."

    71. I.S. Emmanuel, "The Nehemiah Hiya Hayon Controversy in Amster-
dam," *Sefunot*, 9, underscored the continuity of the hostilities by placing the documents of the earlier controversies between Hagiz and the ma'amad at the beginning of his study of the Hayon material. "Inaccuracies," Emmanuel, p. 223.
"We cannot help," *ibid.*, p. 224–225.
    72. "It is imperative," Friedman, #5, p. 522. "The notables," *Milhamah*, p.
26b. Ghiron, *Mishtah Haramim*, p. 89b, quoted in G. Levi, *Revista Israelitica*,
(1912) 9:14, n. 2; 17, n. 3; *herem* on pp. 27–28.
    73. "After three days," Friedman, #2, p. 515. "is it not," *Milhamah*, p. 28a.
Megillat Sefer, (Warsaw) p. 33. On Ayllon's concealment of the truth, see Friedman, *ibid.*, n. 31. On Hakham Zebi's tenure in Amsterdam, see Judith Bleich,
"Hakham Zebi as Chief Rabbi of the Askhenazic Kehillah of Amsterdam, (1710–
1714)," (M.A. Diss. Yeshiva University, 1965). On his previous clashes with the
lay leaders see Bleich, esp. pp. 124–125, n. 64; Emmanuel, p. 215–216; and
Emden, *Torat ha-Kena'ot*, Lvov p. 33v. "He ordered them," letter of Ayllon to
Briel, Friedman, #19, p. 544.
    74. Emmanuel, pp. 227–228.
    75. *Ibid.*, p. 229–230.
    76. Emmanuel, pp. 236–238, #7. Emmanuel, p. 236, n. 33, noted that the

Spanish translations were provided by Hagiz, although Zebi claimed that they were made by Dr. de Mesa.

77. Response of Zebi, M. Friedman, "New Documents Relating to the Hayon Controversy," *Erez Israel*, 10, #11, pp. 530–32. First ban of the ma'amad, Emmanuel, pp. 238–39. Protest of Ashkenazim, Friedman, #10. Second ban of the *mahamad*, *ibid.*, pp. 240–241. Ban of Mordecai Senior, Emmanuel, pp. 241–242. Letter to Yizhaki, *ibid.*, p. 244.

78. "That their community," *Sheber Posh'im*, p. 22; "Is the community," Sonne, Correspondence Hagiz-Morpurgo, p. 187; Hakham R. Joseph," *ibid.* See also *Milhamah la-Shem*, p. 27a. On Finzi, Friedmann, #8, p. 526.

79. The unnamed source was the father of a member of the Bet Din. Friedman, #4, pp. 520–21; "What shall we," *Ibid.*, p. 523, #6.

80. Emmanuel, p. 221; Nadav, p. 410, n. 43.

81. "Ayllon importuned," Jacob Emden, *Megillat Sefer* (Warsaw, 1897) p. 32.

82. "Solomon Ayllon," Freidman, #10, p. 529. "Ayllon tried," "Hagiz to Morpurgo," Sonne, p. 187; "Whoever," *ibid.*, p. 185; "What impact,"*ibid.*, p. 187. Ashkenazic ban of Hagiz, Friedman, 10:237–239.

83. *Hilkhot Missim*, Amsterdam, 1709. Parts are quoted in Lampronte, *Pahad Yizhak*, 1, s.v. "Bar Mata," pp. 64 ff; and in Moses Hagiz, *Shetei ha-Lehem*, no. 27. See further Benayahu, *AS* (1976) 2:144–147.

84. "Who have always," Friedman, p. 515, #2. "I stand inside," *ibid.*, p. 546, #19. "Ayllon . . .," *Sheber Posh'im*, pp. 71–72. On the interpretation of the thirteen strands, and Ayllon's Sabbatianism, see Yael Nadav, "R. Solomon Ayllon and his treatise in Sabbatian Kabbalah," (Heb.) *Sefunot*, 3–4, 1960.

85. Friedman, p. 542 ff., #18, dated Sept., 1714.

86. "The third," *ibid.*, p. 29. Hagiz accused, *Milhamah,*, p. 29v; Hagiz claimed that the seventh member of the ad hoc commission, David da Silva, was drafted by Ayllon out of turn. "not to camouflage," *Sheber Posh'im*, p. 24; "I swear," *ibid.*, p. 21; The conflict of the sermons, *Milhamah* p. 33v.

87. "Hayon and his cohort," *Sheber Posh'im*, pp. 28–29. "He who can," *ibid.*, p. 24. "demonstrated the fallibility . . .," see letter to Hagiz to Morpurgo, Sonne, p. 186. Ayllon to Briel, Friedman, "New Documents," 237–239. The homily in *Diberei Nehemiah*, pp. 81r–v; "for that is," *Milhamah*, p. 30v.

88. "I pity," Friedman, #9, p. 526.

89. Zebi enclosed personal letters demanding retraction with copies of his denunciations of Hayon. See the letter of Naftali Kohen, Freimann, p. 123, "Your . . . letter has reached me together with a copy of the scroll of doom." Some of the replies are addressed only to Hakham Zebi, others to Hagiz as well.

90. Hayon, *Moda'a Rabah*, p. 3b, col. 4.

91. The first printing of "L'Einei Kol Yisrael" and its Spanish translation have not survived. Texts of the second edition (Amsterdam, 1713) also appear in *Milhamah la-Shem*, pp. 25a–26a; and Freimann, pp. 117–119. The second, untitled, undated proclamation of Zebi can be found in Freimann, pp. 119–122. The reply of Briel, mid Ab (end July) 1713 in *Milhama*, pp. 42v–43v; Freimann,

pps. 126–128. The letter of Jacob Aboab, dated 3 Elul [Aug. 25], 1713, in David Kaufmann, "Correspondence of R. Gabriel Eskeles and R. Jacob Aboab," *ha-Hoker*, (1894) 2(1):14–15; letter of Gabriel Eskeles, *ibid.*, pp. 13–14.

92. The letter of Naphtali Kohen, in Freimann, pp. 122–126; see also D. Kaufmann, "La lutte de R. Naftali Kohen contre Hayyoun," REJ, (1898) 36:256–286; (1899) 37:274–283; M. Hartstein, *Shalshelet Zahav* (Piotrkow, 1931).

93. "Kosh't Imrei Emet," and Hagiz' response did not appear until December 1713 in print, but it had circulated before then in manuscript form. Text of the "Kosh't" in *Milhamah la-Shem*, pp. 26v–42v; another version in Freimann, pp. 128–136. See an earlier version of "Kosh't," entitled "Ma'aseh she-Haya," in Friedman, #3.

94. Correspondence between Naphtali Kohen and Zebi in Kaufmann, "La Lutte," pp. 272–283. From a remark of Morpurgo we learn that Kohen had been assigned to enlist the support of the Great Council in Poland at their next gathering, Sonne, p. 179. Ban of Jacob Popers against Hayon, *Milhamah*, pp. 22r–24v. Letter of Popers, December 21, 1713, Friedman, #13. Letter of Popers to Hagiz, *Milhamah*, p. 50r. Ban of rabbinate of Frankfurt [original Yiddish not extant], in Hebrew translation, Moses Hagiz, *Lehishat Saraf*, (Hanau, 1726), p. iv.

5. EXPANSION OF THE HAYON CONTROVERSY

1. Letter of Eskeles to Zebi, in D. Kaufmann, "Letters of R. Gabriel Eskeles and R. Jacob Aboab," *ha-Hoker*, 1894, pp. 13–14. Letter of David Oppenheim to Leib Hamburger in J. Z. Kahana "The Responsum of R. David Oppenheim," *Sinai* (Aug.–Sept. 1947) 11(11–12):328–334. Especially noteworthy is Oppenheim's accusation concerning Zebi

"הביא אל מזבח הדפוס . . . אפס קצהו . . . ראיה שיש בה פגימה . . . והמותר
בטל בלבו בהעלם דבר."

I am astounded," p. 332. "Reproved him," Emden, *Megillat Sefer* (Warsaw), p. 37. Letter of Aboab to Zebi, Kaufmann, *ha-Hoker*, pp. 13–14. Letter of Pantrimoli, *Milhamah*, pp. 18r–21r.

2. Hagiz to Joel Pincherle, Jan. 30, 1713, Friedman, #29, p. 571.

3. "He advised," Ghiron, *Mishtah Haramim*, p. 86r, cited in G. Levi, *RI* (1912) 9:9. On Benjamin Kohen of Reggio, see Friedman, #25, 26, pp. 564–565. On Mujajon, see Joseph Laras, "The Family of Mujajon in Ancona," 12, pp. 255–270. On Fiametta, see Friedman, #30, p. 576 and pp. 584–590. "Let us not judge," Friedman, #6, p. 523.

4. Friedman, p. 523.

5. On this subject, see Yerushalmi, *From Spanish Court*, p. 348.

6. "A gathering," *Milhamah*, pp. 43v ff. On R. Meir Baki see Friedman, #33, p. 593.

7. "I have," Freimann, pp. 126–128; *Milhamah*, p. 42v–43v. "I hereby affirm," *Milhamah*, p. 43v. "Even if you say," Friedman, #18, pp. 543–44. Letter of October 21, 1713, *ibid.*, #19, pp. 545–58.

8. "I would," *ibid.*, #20, pp. 548–9. "Let it not appear," "Another danger," Friedman, #21, pp. 549–51. Letter of ma'amad of Amsterdam, November 30, 1713, in Emmanuel, pp. 228–229. Letter of Briel to Ma'amad of December 22, 1713, Friedman, #23, pp. 552–3. Letter of Ma'amad, Feb./Mar. 1714, Emmanuel, #5, pp. 229–231. Ayllon's defense of Hayon, Emmanuel, #6, pp. 231–235.

9. Pincherle's herem first appeared on October 26, 1713; *Milhamah*, pp. 20a–21b. "I am certain," Moses Hagiz to Joel Pincherle, Friedman, #29, pp. 572–3, Pincherle was related to Hagiz' wife. Hagiz addressed him as "my kin" and mentioned that the news of Pincherle's good welfare gave his wife great joy. It is the only reference to his wife that I have found in the printed polemical literature. A fragment of the letter of Benjamin Kohen (of August 18, 1713) in Friedman, p. 564, #25. Netanel Halevi of Pesaro, in Friedman, #31, p. 590, dated early Feb., 1714. Letter of Fiametta in *Milhamah* pp. 8r–11v. Fiametta does not mention Briel by name, but "the rabbi of Mantua" is unambiguous. Briel's correspondence with Benjamin Finzi, Friedman, nos. 8–9, pp. 525–528. "I hereby call," *Milhamah*, pp. 44r–v; *Lehishat Saraf*, pp. 10v–11r. Bans of Cantarini, rabbinate of Rome, and Pincherle, in *Milhamah*, pp. 45r–48v. Statement of Olmo, *Milhamah*, pp. 2v–8r; ban signed by entire rabbinate of Ferrara, *ibid.*, p. 47r.

10. Emmanuel, #6, p. 231 ff., repeats Briel's attack on Hayon, together with the refutations of the lay *Bet Din*. Hayon printed it with his own refutations in *Moda'a Rabah*, pp. 4r–v. Versions written by Briel are included in his letter to Benjamin Finzi, Milhamah, p. 44r–v; *Lehishat Saraf*, pp. 10v–11r.

11. "A crisis," Segre, in *Milhamah la-Shem*, p. 13b. "A weakling," *ibid.*, p. 14r. "The Italian rabbis," Hagiz to Morpurgo, Sonne, p. 186. Letter of Baki to Segre, Friedman, #33, p. 593. Letter of Isaac Nizza, addressed to Samuel Walabriga, brother-in-law of Segre, (March 15, 1714) in Friedman, #32, pp. 591–593. "If we must accord," *Milhamah*, p. 48v. Statement of Samson Morpurgo regarding Segre, Sonne, p. 190. On Segre's intention to write a full length work, see *Milhamah*, p. 49v. Letter of Ergas to Segre, Friedman, #36. Ergas mentioned that Hagiz had just sent him a copy of the *Magen David* of Ibn Zimra which he had published, for the same purpose.

12. "Correspondence Between R. Moses Hagiz and R. Samson Morpurgo Regarding Nehemiah Hayon and his Sect," ed. I. Sonne, *Kobez al Yad*, (12) N.S. #2, 1937. "waters of contention," *ibid.*, p. 169, 14 Kislev 1714. "Moses, zealot," *ibid.*, p. 171, "All the rabbis," p. 170. "It is not," p. 171. "Many of us . . .," p. 171. "We have met," p. 172. "This document," pp. 174–175. "They did not consult," p. 178. "Our entire success," "I urge you," p. 179.

13. "but most of them" Sonne, p. 181. "I have disputed," *ibid.*, p. 184. Ban of Hayon, dated March 23, 1714, in *Milhamah la-Shem*, p. 51r. There was one other confirmed Sabbatian on the Bet Din of Ancona, Elijah Mujajon. See Joseph

Laras, "The Family of Mujajon in Ancona," *Sefunot,* 12, pp. 255-270. "I am greatly distressed"; "Since you have," Sonne, p. 190.

14. "Who swear falsely," *Ez ha-Da'at* (Venice, 1704) Intro., p. i. On the burning of *Ashrei ha-Goy,*" See H. Brody, *Metek Sefata'im* (Berlin, 1892), p. 74.

15. "Even the little," *Tokhahat Megulah* (London, 1714), p. 14r. On the ban of Hayon in Livorno, see the statement by Ergas in *Tokhahat,* p. 146,: A group of *ten of the youngest in the flock* had gathered after the morning service to ban Hayon's books. This incident apparently took place without the sanction of the Livornese lay leaders.

"Because they," *ha-Zad NaHaSh,* p. 62r. *Tokhahat Megullah* was printed in 1714, but no copies are extant. It was reprinted together with *ha-Zad NaHaSh* by Hagiz (London, 1715).

Other samples of rejection of Sabbatian Kabbalah in the controversy: Netanel Halevi of Pesaro, Friedman, #31, and Fiametta, *ibid.,* #30.

16. Samuel de Pas had been a student of Jacob Hagiz in Livorno. On the Sabbatian links of de Pas, see Benayahu, "Sabbatian Information . . .," *Michael,* (1972) 1:9-77, passim. De Pas received the "Sod ha-Elohut" from the Sabbatian Jacob Israel Dahan, and was a close correspondent of Abraham Cardoso's, who sent him copies of his Sabbatian treatises. The information on Ergas is taken from Malakhi HaKohen's Introduction to Ergas, *Diberei Yosef* (Livorno, 1742), and resp. #41; Horodetzky, Intro. to Ergas, *Shomer Emunim* (Amsterdam, 1736).

Malakhi HaKohen was one of the rabbis of Livorno who signed a declaration in defense of Eybeschutz [denying his sabbatianism] *Luhot ha-Edut* (Altona, 1755), pp. 22r-v.

17. The account of the confrontation between Hayon and Ergas in *ha-Zad NaHaSh,* p. 32v.

18. Aviad Basilea, *Emunat Hakhamim* (Mantua, 1730). "It would be," J. Ghiron, *Mishtah Haramim,* cited in G. Levi, *RI* (1912) 9:12, n. 2. On Ergas' nonliteral interpretation of Luria, see Roland Goetschel, "La Notion de Simsum dans le *Somer Emunim* de Joseph Ergaz," *Hommage a Georges Vajda* (Louvain, 1980), pp. 385-396. "How Sweet," *ha-Zad NaHaSh,* p. 36r. "You claim to understand," Hayon, *Shalhebet Yah* (Amsterdam, 1714), p. 2r. "But you have," *Tokhahat,* p. 3v. He accused: *Tokhahat,* p. 12v; *ha-Zad,* p. 20r. Responsa R. Levi ibn Habib, end #37 "It is not our way," cited *ha-Zad,* p. 26v.

19. *Sha'ar ha-Shama'im,* in a Hebrew translation, by Isaac Aboab de Fonseca, (Amsterdam, 1655) was the edition used by Ergas. The original Spanish version is extant in several manuscript copies, among them Ms. Columbia University X86/H420. Alexander Altmann, "Lurianic Kabbala in a Platonic Key: Abraham Kohen Herrera's *Puerta del Cielo," Jewish Thought in the Seventeenth Century,* pp. 1-38.

"To prevent others," *Shalhebet Yah,* T.P.; Intro, p. ii; p. 17b. "Hayon has attacked," *ha-Zad NaHaSh,* p. 42r. "It is apparent . . ." "They both claimed," "Edut be-Israel," in *Milhamah,* p. 12v. Note that Morpurgo does not admit to knowledge of the sources, but refers to "heretical philosophers whose memory was preserved in Judah Halevi's *Kuzari*.' "Why do we go," *Milhamah*, p. 21r. Ergas' brief account of the development of Lurianic Kabbalah opens his *Tokhahat Megulah*. See also *ha-Zad NaHaSh*, p. 53r.

20. ״צר לי עליך אילת אהבים ויעלת חן חמדה גנוזה אשר לנגד מרמות ההוא חיויא
ירדה עד דיוטא תחתיה ויחשבוה ההמון לבזויה סורי הגפן נכריה. אורייתא!
אורייתא! נהירו דכל עלמין איכה חשכו מאוריה כארץ מאפליה.״

(*ha-Zad NaHaSH*, p. 15r) Ergas used almost identical language in a letter to Segre, Friedman, #36, p. 598.

21. "They concluded," Friedman, #3, p. 518. "I read the work," *ibid.*, #4, pp. 520–521.

"Even if," Friedman, #20, p. 548. "It is possible," *ibid.*, #21, p. 503. "letter of Fiametta to Ayllon," *ibid.*, #30 pp. 576–577. "lest the Kabbala," *Leket*, Y.D., p. 110v–111r. "Take heed," *Sheber Posh'im*, p. 10. "Kabbala was not given," p. 10. "Even if they should err," *ha-Zad Na-HaSh*, pp. 20–21. *Mabo Petahim*, (Amsterdam, 1736).

Solomon Joseph b. Nathan Karpi's anti-Hayon polemic, *Sefer Raza de-Milta* [*The Secret of the Word*], Ms. London Or. 10223/1 = JNUL #7585, fols. 1r–184, is a response to Hayon's *Oz l'Elohim*. Much of this unpublished polemic is devoted to refuting Hayon's argument for exotericization of Kabbalah.

22. "We knew," *Sheber Posh'im*, p. 22. "We were forced," *ibid*. See also Hagiz' letter to Morpurgo, Sonne, *op. cit.*, p. 185:

״וסוף דבר הביאו הדברים לפני הערכאות כדי
שהם יאמרו אם הספר טוב או מאוס ויכריחו אותנו לקיים גזרתם הטובה להם.״

It seems from another reference that the Parnassim obtained a writ from the magistrate to bar Hagiz from entering the synagogue. "The Parnassim sent the sexton of the synagogue to Moses to bar him from entering their synagogue according to a 'neuva orden.' And he replied that he would comply." *Milhamah*, p. 40r. See the letter of Morpurgo to Hagiz, Sonne, p. 172. One of Hagiz' vilifications of the parnassim—

״הם מוסרים ומהם עכשיו הטילו בעו״ה אימה על הצבור שלא לש״ש.״

is lifted verbatim from Maimonides' description of unfit communal leaders (*Hilkhot Teshuba*, ch. 3, #6).

23. On David Nieto, see Jakob J. Petuchowski, *The Theology of Haham David Nieto: An Eighteenth Century Defense of the Jewish Tradition* (N.J., Ktav Publ. House, 1954; repr., 1970); Cecil Roth, "Haham David Nieto," *Essays and Portraits in Anglo-Jewish History* (Phila. 1962), pp. 113–129 (originally published as an appendix to *Matteh Dan* (Jerusalem, 1958); *Sheber Posh'im* was printed with 'Amsterdam' on the title page. The concluding pages of the text deal almost exclusively with Solomon Ayllon; perhaps they were added later when Hagiz became aware that the book would be completed and distributed in London.

Nieto's controversial sermon, "De la Divina Providencia, o sea Naturaleza universal, o natura naturante: tratado theologico . . ." (London, 1704; repr. London, 1716). The Decision of Zebi, "Decision del Doctissimo y Excellentissimo Senor . . . Zebi Asquenazi con su Betdin sobre el problema si naturaleza, y Dios, y Naturaleza es todo uno . . ." (London, 1705; repr. 1716) and Responsa *Hakham Zebi*, #18.

24. "I have used," *Esh Dat*, Intro., p. viii. "It consists," *ibid.*, Preface, iii–iv. Hayon responded in private notes to some of Nieto's charges. Israel Herling, "Handwritten Notes of Nehemiah Hiya Hayon to *Esh Dat* of R. David Nieto," *KS*, 15:130ff. "In our times," Friedman, #21, p. 550. "If, heaven forfend," Friedman, p. 583, and see *Milhamah la-Shem*, p. 10v. "Ridicule will follow," Ghiron, *Mishtah Haramim*, p. 113r, cited in G. Levy, *RI*. "Let not," *Milhamah*, p. 1r. "The manuscript," Ms. *Gahalei Esh*, cited in Perlmutter, pp. 45–56. See also the apologetic introduction to Tobias Kohen, *Ma'aseh Tobia* (Venice, 1707) which betrays concern that sustained crypto messianism among Jews would be used to their detriment in Jewish-Christian polemics. "I have investigated," *Esh Dat*, p. 15v. "Hayon boasted," *ibid.*, p. 17r. "By denying," *ibid.*, p. 21r.

25. "I could say," *Esh Dat*, Preface, p. xii. "Ah, brothers," *Reflexiones*, sect. #XIII. Full text published by Raphael Loewe, "The Spanish Supplement to Nieto's Esh Dath," *PAAJR*, 48, 1981, pp. 267–296. I have also made use of the English translation graciously provided to me by a colleague, Rabbi Elliot Marrus (unpubl.). In addition to translation of liturgical works to Spanish, Nieto appealed to the interests of the former Marrano community in London with his work on the Inquisition, "Noticias Reconditas . . . de las inquisiciones," (London, 1722) and a response to a conversionary sermon preached at the Auto da Fé in Lisbon, 1705, by Diego Justiniano Alvares de Annunciacao, Archbishop of Cranganor. "That he is," *Reflexiones*, #V. "What will happen," 'what won't they say," *ibid.*, #XI, XII.

26. "The Samaritans," *Sheber*, p. 6. Hayon and Ayllon, *ibid.*, p. 9. "would be inscribed." *ibid.*, T.P., p. 20. "They are more," *ibid.*, p. 53. "They must be," *ibid.*, T.P., p. 53. "Henceforth," *Milhamah*, p. 44v. For the formulation of the concept 'usable dissenting past,' I am indebted to Cecile Zinberg, "The Usable Dissenting Past: John Strype and Elizabethan Puritanism," in R. Cole and M. Moody, eds., *The Dissenting Tradition, Essays for Leland H. Carlson* (Ohio, 1975), pp. 123–139. Ref. to *Hekhal ha-Kodesh*, *Sheber*, p. 25; "deviation which has arisen," *Sheber*, p. 6. "A reminder," *ibid.*

27. Nahamanides' correspondence, cited by Hagiz, *Sheber*, p. 52, 58, had been recently published (Amsterdam, 1712) in *Kobez Teshubot HaRaMBaM*, 3. Samson Morpurgo referred to the Maimonidean controversy, *Milhamah*, p. 12r., "If the great," *Milhamah*, p. 13r.

28. "Send me," Sonne, "Correspondence," p. 19b. David Nunez Torres, *Catalogus Librorum* (The Hague, 1728). Oliver Shaw Rankin, *Jewish Religious Polemic* (Edinburgh, 1956). Jacob Sasportas, *Zizat Nobel Zebi*, ed. I. Tishby (Jerusalem, 1954). Jacob Emden, *Torat ha-Kena'ot*, (Lemberg, 1870). Jacob Frances, "Zebi

Mudah," *Kobez al Yad* (1885), pp. 97–128. The "Haggadah le-Tish'a be'Ab" has been attributed by A. Habermann to the Frances brothers, but he cites no evidence for this attribution. Habermann, "Towards a History of Anti-Sabbatianism," (Heb.) *Kobez al Yad*, 3 N.S. 3(2):187–215. Elijah Kohen, *Sefer Meribat Kadesh*, in Freimann, ed., *Inyanei Shabtai Zebi* (Berlin, 1912). Immanuel Frances, "Sippur Ma'aseh Shabtai Zebi ve-Natan ha-Azati be-Kizur," *KAY*, 1885. A complete bibliography of anti-Sabbatian works remains a desideratum; for the Hayon controversy, Friedman, "New Documents," has appended a bibliography.

29. "Hayon's guilt," *Sheber*, p. 17, and see Emmanuel, p. 234, n. 26. "All my words," *Sheber*, p. 8. "The villains," *ibid.*, p. 9. "Anyone knowledgeable," *ibid.*, pp. 37, 39. "This has caused," *ha-Zad NaHaSh* (London, 1715), p. 19v. Hayon, *Moda'ah Rabah*, p. 3a, col. 2, printed a letter defaming Hagiz which had been originally sent by the lay leaders of Livorno to those of Amsterdam after Hagiz had published the *Leket HaKeMaH* in 1707. "Hayon and Ayllon," *Sheber*, p. 33; Friedman #36, pp. 597–598. "This writ," "If the Smyrna letter," *Moda'a*, p. 1, col. 1, 2.

30. "Triple calamity," *Sheber*, T.P. "Evil triumvirate," Freimann, *Meribat*, p. 7. On Benjamin Halevi, Friedman, #27, p. 566. "Nehemiah . . ." letter of Benjamin Halevy, Friedman, p. 700.

31. References to Cardoso, *Meribat Kadesh*, passim.; "disciples," *Sheber*, p. 43; "books," *ibid.*, p. 48; "Sephardim," *Milhamah*, p. 32b; "Ergas," in *Shalhebet Yah*.

32. "My words," *Sheber*, p. 74. "An abridged," Friedman, #15, p. 539. The Yiddish translation of *ha-Zad Zebi* is no longer extant. "Because they knew," *ibid.* An observer, see Friedman, #5, p. 522. "To vindicate," *Sheber*, p. 63. "Don't allow," *ibid.*, p. 75. "Only to blind," *Milhamah* p. 37v. "And if the spirit," *Sheber*, p. 5, "Regrettably, *ibid.*, p. 8. "I said to myself," *ibid.*, p. 21. "It is not," *Milhamah*, p. 30r. "Pay heed," *Moda'a*, p. 1v, col. 1; see also p. 2r, col. 1, and passim. for other instances where Hayon addresses 'rabbis and scholars,' for instance:

"ועתה רבותי גאוני ארץ העומדים על כסא ההוראה, דינו דיני עם האיש
הלזה [יצחקי]. "

33. "What we have not," Perlmutter, *R. Jonathan Eybeschutz*, pp. 45–46, cited from Ms. *Gahalei Esh*, p. 60v, from a letter of Hagiz to R. Aryeh Leib, brother-in-law of Jacob Emden and later rabbi in Amsterdam, dated Sept., 1725.

Nehemia Kohen of Ferrara, Intro. to Mordekhai Zahalon, *Meziz U'Meliz* (Venice, 1715), p. ii, "Who overrode," Emden, *Torat ha-Kena'ot*, p. 42r.

6. THE CAMPAIGN AGAINST SABBATIAN EMISSARIES

1. This letter was part of a lengthy correspondence with HaKohen which we must reconstruct from the fragments that remain. Hagiz apparently initiated the correspondence with a request that HaKohen help him settle the Nathan

bequest. HaKohen responded on April 8, 1715; the letter quoted is part of Hagiz' response. For the only portion of this correspondence which survived, see *Kerem Shlomo*, (Winter 1982) 5 (3):20.

2. In his eighteenth-century chronicle of Amsterdam's Jewish community, David Franco Mendes described the establishment of a *hesger*, a privately funded yeshiva, in which Ayllon was to assume the position of Rosh [head] and Hakham: "Em 29 Nissan 5478, [April 30, 1718] Fundarao varios devotos todos Jehidim deste ק"ק o Esguer de לקח טוב com contracto firmado por 10 annos, para meditarem nelle os Hahamim com seus discipulos 8 oras por dia . . . os primeiros Administradores que se servirao par pautas distribuidas aos Irmaos par mayoria de votos forao Jacob de Chaves e David Mendes da Silva e par Gabay Thezoureiro Ishac de Fonseca; *Elegerao por Ros ao Haham Rabi Selomoh Ailyon*. [my emphasis] . . ." *Memorias do Estabelecimento* (Amsterdam, 1975) p. 106.

3. *Petil Tekhelet* (London, 1714) Intro., pp. i–ii. (e.p., Venice, 1652). Several of Jacob Hagiz' appendices were not printed in Moses' edition of *Petil Tekhelet*; he reserved them and appended them to *LeKet HaKeMakh* on the *Mishnah* (Wandsbeck, 1726). Benayahu, *AS* (1977) 3:96.

4. There is no mention as to whether Hagiz' wife had accompanied him to London. Hakham Zebi did not bring his family with him to London, but sent for them to join him in Emden. Jacob Emden, *MS* (Warsaw, 1897) p. 34.

5. The documents relating to Hagiz' Mishnah project in ms. Kaufmann 254 have been published by Benayahu, *AS* 5:104–115. Benayahu discovered that Sasportas' project did bear fruit in a 1674 edition of the Pentateuch supported by four hundred subscribers. Hagiz had tried a similar plan unsuccessfully when he tried to publish *Magen Abot*, and successfully for the second edition (1727) of *Eleh ha-Mizvot*.

6. Benayahu, *AS* 5:104–107.

7. On November 14, 1715, Hagiz received the approbation of R. Samuel HaKohen Shattin of Frankfurt, author of *Kos Yeshu'ot* (Frankfurt, 1711).

8. Benayahu, *AS* 5:109, 111.

9. E.g., Y. Meisel, *Pinkas Kehillat Berlin* (Jerusalem, 1962), pp. 6–7, 424, dated 1723. However, some communities did defend the authors. Benayahu, *Haskamot u-Reshut*, p. 45.

10. Mishnah with commentary *Ez Hayim* (Berlin, 1716).

11. Hagiz mentioned his poor health to Briel, *ibid.*, p. 113. Letter of Nieto, *Ozar Tob*, 1878, p. 86. Responsa of Hagiz, *Shetei ha-Lehem* (Wandsbeck, 1733) #44, pp. 54b–55a.

12. I. S. Emmanuel, "The Hayon Controversy in Amsterdam," pp. 244–246. In a manuscript of Jacob Zemah's *Kol be-Ramah* [JNUL 8°5512] the copyist noted under the title: "My colleague from Jerusalem, Moses Hagiz has been liberal with his kindness, and has permitted me to copy this work from the manuscript in his collection which is a copy from the original . . . I have completed the task on 14 Adar, 5477 [Feb. 25, 1717] here in Emden." Benayahu, *AS* 3:96, n. 5.

13. Solomon Zalman Katz, *Sha'arei Torah* (Hamburg, 1718). A. Cassuto, *Ged-*

enkenschrift . . . (Amsterdam, 1927). "It was not," Samson Morpurgo, *Shemesh Zedaka*, #33, 6/7, p. 30v. Benayahu has established that the date of publication of *Leket HaKeMa"H, EH,* is not 1711, as indicated on the T.P., but 1719, a year after Hagiz' arrival at Hamburg, *AS* 3:104–105.

14. Jacob Emden, *Megillat Sefer* (Warsaw, 1897), pp. 107, 110, reported that Hagiz had moved to Altona by 1722. Benayahu, *AS* 3:105, n. 41, suggests that 1722 may be a misprint, perhaps 1732 was intended. Hagiz' *Haskamah* to Eliezer b. Solomon Zalman Lifshiz, *Sefer Heshib R. Eliezer ve-Sia'h ha-Sadeh* (Neuwit, 1749) was written in late February, 1725, in Altona. On convening quorums in private premises, see Jacob Reischer, *Shebut Jacob* (Halle 1710–1719) #9; E. Duckesz, *Iva le-Moshav* (Jaroslav, 1703), p. 23.

15. Graetz, *DYY*, 8:611.

16. "A monstrous bastion," "begged him to uproot," Benayahu, *AS* 3:115.

17. The letter of approbation of Ze'ebi is dated early November, 1715. It was published by Hayon in *ha-Kolot Yehdalun.* Hagiz (*Lehishat Saraf*, pp. 5a–b) impugned the authenticity of the letter and accused Hayon of fabricating it. However, given Ze'ebi's Sabbatian connections (Ze'ebi was also the son-in-law of an ardent Sabbatian, the chronicler Abraham Cuenque) he may indeed have been its author.

18. Joseph Kobo was the author of Responsa *Gib'eot Olam* (Salonika, 1784) and Solomon Amarillo of *Kerem Shlomo* (Salonika, 1719). The text of their letter to Kimhi was given by Hayon in *ha-Kolot Yehdalun* and quoted by Hagiz, *Lehishat Saraf*, 3v. Hagiz cast doubt over their entire letter arguing that Hayon's falsification was evident from a misspelling of one of the signatures. But even if the letter was authentic, Hagiz argued that the two Salonikan rabbis must have written it solely on the basis of Ze'eby's letter, without having read Hayon's book. Hagiz claimed that, "according to reliable witnesses, Hayon, while in Salonika, went to associate with the evil sects of Barukhya and Filosof, the apostates, but they rejected him because they knew that his heresy was of a different sort than their own," *ibid.* There is no evidence to support this charge.

19. Hagiz, *Lehishat Saraf*, p. 4r, acknowledged that Alfandari had supported Hayon "for reasons known to us." Hayon's rendering of his hearing before the rabbinate of Constantinople, *Lehishat*, p. 6v.

20. On Ayllon's refusal to greet Hayon, Jacob Emden, *Edut beYa'akob* (Altona, 1756), p. 23v.

"He began to wander," Hagiz, *Lehishat Saraf* (Hanau, 1725), pp. 3r–v. The incident with the wife and daughter-in-law of Eybeschutz is told in MS. *Gahalei Esh [GE]* Ms. Neubauer #2187. According to Wolf, *Bibliotheca*, 4, p. 929, Hayon travelled to Africa and died in 'Berberia.' According to Jacob Emden, he died in Asia. Hagiz' account of Hayon's son, *Mishnat Hakhamim* (Wandsbeck, 1733), #520–521. My efforts to trace the Christian identity of Hayon's son have not been fruitful.

21. The ban proclaimed in Frankfurt in February 1726, and published by Hagiz *Lehishat Saraf*, p. 1, asserted that regarding Hayon, "חרם הקדמונים לא

הותר [the original Herem had not been lifted] Hagiz repeatedly said of Hayon,
"עדיין הוא בחרם."
22. *Lehishat*, pp. 2r–2v.
23. *Lehishat*, pp. 10v–11r lists *haramot* and correspondence of 1714 along with
a letter of Katzenellenbogen dated August 24, 1725. Ms. *GE*, after several pages
of documents of 1725–26, continues on pp. 85v, 86v, with letters dating back to
1715. "A recurring," *GE*, p. 60v, letter of Hagiz to R. Arye Leib of September
26, 1725.
24. On the development of Sabbatianism in Poland, see the comprehensive
essay of G. Scholem, "The Sabbatian Movement in Poland," *Beit Yisrael be-Polin*,
ed. I. Heilpern (Jerusalem, 1953), pp. 36–76. "Now that," *Lehishat*, p. 2v. "The
root of all," *GE*, p. 82v. "Hayon and his cohorts," *GE*, p. 60v. *Herem* of Lvov
in Emden, *TK*, p. 71. The earliest document of Hagiz' participation in this campaign is his letter to the Council of the Four Lands in July 1725. For further
discussion of this grand gesture, see below. Hagiz' list of villains in the 1725
campaign *Lehishat*, pp. 2v–3r. The Introduction of Hagiz was reprinted by Jacob
Emden in *TK*, p. 80.
25. Emden, *Sefer Hit'abkut*, cited in Perlmutter, p. 27.
26. On Leible, see Yehuda Liebes, "The Author of *Sefer Zadik Yesod Olam*,
The Sabbatian Prophet R. Leible Prosnitz," [Heb.] *Da'at*, 2. A polemical chronicle
of Leible's career as a Sabbatian can be found in *GE*, pp. 39r–46r. See also G.
Scholem, *EJ* 13:1240–1241. "Leible Prostitz," *Lehishat*, pp.2v–3r.
The testimony to rabbinic court of Mannheim, *GE*, p. 71r. *GE*, p. 75r contains
the text of a letter, dated November 24, 1725, from Leible to Isaiah Hasid.
Eybeschutz is the subject of the letter, and Leible's signature was affixed as "Jo-
seph ben Jacob."
"We must arouse," *Lehishat*, ibid.
27. On the movement of Judah Hasid, see Meir Benayahu, "The Holy So-
ciety of R. Judah Hasid," [Heb.] *Sefunot*, 3–4, 1960.
"And did nothing," ibid., p. 153, 157. "He swore," *Edut be-Ya'akob* (Altona,
1756), p. 66, the testimony of R. Isaac of Biale. "When confronted," Emden,
Shebirat Luhot ha-Aben (Zolkiew, 1755), p. 51r. See also Emden's *Sefer Hitabkut*
(Lvov, 1870), p. 1v. "He too," *Lehishat*, pp. 2v–3r.
According to one testimony—that of Nethaniel Weil, disciple of Abraham
Broda, in J. Emden, *Bet Yonatan ha-Sofer* (Altona, 1762), p. 3r. "R. Isaiah gave,"
GE, p. 71r ["Gebiat Edut in Mannheim," 1725], *GE*, p. 60r–v, is correspondence
of Hasid with Leible that fell into rabbinic hands.
28. "Moses Meir," *Lehishat Saraf*, p. 3r. "In Prague," Emden, *Hitabkut*, pp.
1r–v. "When Moses Meir arrived," *Lehishat*, ibid. On the luggage searches, see
also *GE*, p. 68v; "scripts that were found in the bags of M. M.," and p. 83v
"discovered like a thief lying in ambush." Jacob Emden, *Megillat Sefer* (Amsterdam, 1752), pp. 88–89. On Emden's sojourn in Pressburg, see Jacob J. Schacter,
Rabbi Jacob Emden, ch. 4.
29. The most recent review of the literature regarding Eybeschutz' attitude

toward Sabbatianism is Yehudah Leibes, "Sefer Zadiq Yesod Olam: A Sabbatian Myth," *Da'at*, 1, 1978, Appendix II, pp. 115-119. On the confrontation with Oppenheim, see Scholem, *EJ* 6:1074. "The writings discovered," *GE*, p. 67v, also cited by Neubauer, p. 209. "R. Moses Leib," *GE*, p. 74v. "But perhaps," *GE*, p. 63r. "I cannot elaborate," *GE*, p. 67r. "The desert," *Exodus* 14:3.

30. On R. Herschel Zoref, see Scholem, "Sabbatian Movement in Poland," p. 50. "It is already," *GE*, p. 32v. Correspondence of Eybeschutz with Hayon, Hagiz, *Lehishat*, p. 3v. David Friderich Megerlin, *Geheime Zeugnusse vor die Wahrheit der Christlichen Religion, aus vier und zwanzig neuen und seltenen Judischen Amuleten oder Anhang Zetteln gezogen.* (Frankfurt und Leipzig, 1756) writes of a correspondence between Hayon and Eybeschutz from thirty years earlier, 1726: "Wie nun vor 30 Jahren schon der R. Jonathan mit dem gedachten Chajon einen briefwechsel gefuhrt," p. 2r-v, and similarly p. 37.

31. Joseph Dan, *Hebrew Ethical and Homiletic Literature* (Heb.) (Jerusalem, 1975), p. 246, noted that the paradox of Torah scholar/Sabbatian in the case of Eybeschutz was equal to the paradox of the traditionalist preacher/Sabbatian. "There is no clue of this [Sabbatianism] in the hundreds of sermons of R. Jonathan . . . The image of a crypto-Sabbatian of extreme theosophical opinions, stands in sharpest contrast to his image as . . . a strictly orthodox preacher who disseminated Torah and ethics and brought thousands in his audience to fear of God . . . Most of his published sermons, *Ahabat Yonatan, Ya'arot Debash,* and *Diberei Yonatan* were originally delivered orally."

32. "R. Jonathan, head of *Pe'or*," *GE*, p. 66r, letter to R. Judah Leib dated November 2, 1725. "In the previous," Hagiz to R. Aryeh Leib, letter September 26, 1725, *GE* p. 60v. Leipziger's testimony, *GE*, p. 72r. "A great scholar," *GE*, p. 70v. In Moravia, R. Abli testified that the Sabbatian manuscript in his possession had been given to him by a disciple of R. Jonathan, *GE*, p. 60r-v. "R. Feivel," *GE*, p. 70r. "I have written," *GE*, p. 65. "Although at that time," Halperin, p. 477. "Alas, what," *GE*, p. 54. "I was greatly distressed," *GE*, p. 65r. Hagiz was commenting on the book *Or Israel* [Light of Israel], of R. Israel Jaffe [Frankfurt an der Oder, 1702] to R. Michel Hasid of Berlin. "This is a notorious," *Lehishat*, #8. "The unpleasant news," *GE*, p. 63r. "I prophesied," *ibid.* "You should decree," *GE*, p. 60v. The *Pinkas ha-Khruzim* of AHW, 1724–1734, Central Archive, Jerusalem, #AHW/85a. Ordinance #52, fols. 18r-v, and #53, fols. 19r-v are the only ones issued in the name of scholars and laymen alike.

33. "On that night," *GE*, p. 57v. "Sabbatai Zebi," *GE*, p. 32r. "overturned ideas," *ibid.* "The hypocrite," *GE*, p. 60v. "letter . . . dated," *ibid.*, p. 57v. "In this coupling," *Lehishat*, pp. 2v-3r. "showed me," *GE*, p. 72r. The ninth of Ab, a traditional Jewish fast day for the destruction of the Temple was celebrated by Sabbatians as the birthdate of their messiah.

34. "A wicked man," *GE*, p. 62r. "Observed through a crack," *GE*, p. 72r. "R. Nathan," *GE*, p. 69v. "Cursed is he," Deut., 27:21. "But whereas," *GE*, p. 62r-63v. "These are not," *Lehishat*, epilogue.

35. "So that we," *GE*, p. 54r. "A sustained effect," *GE*, p. 60v. "I will send,"

GE, p. 6ov. "Pious man," *ibid.* "I have already notified," *GE*, p. 6ov. "What they have," *GE*, p. 54r. On the circulation of decrees, *GE*, p. 63r.

36. "The time has come," *Lehishat*, epilogue.

37. "The two writs," *GE*, p. 58v. The writs referred to appear on pps. 47–48 and the testimony on p. 49v. The Sabbatian chronicle was that of Abraham Cuenque, printed by Emden, with Hagiz' polemical commentary to Cuenque's account, entitled *Bet ha-Meri* (House of Insurrection) *TK*, p. 16, ff.

38. Correspondence of September 1725, *GE*, pp. 58v, 56. The rabbinic correspondence referred to documents procured in this devious manner without ever questioning the propriety of seizing evidence in this manner, in contravention to the hallowed ordinance of R. Gershom against invading the mail of others. See, e.g., *GE* p. 68v, the letter of R. Jacob Kahane, "In the letters which were found in the satchel of Moshe Meir."

39. "If you are able," *GE*, pp. 66r–v. "An earlier letter," *GE*, p. 67v. "I cannot decipher," *GE*, p. 69v. "Although I had promised," special vigilance, see ban issued by AHW communities on August 8, *GE*, pp. 64r–v, and Hagiz' appendix to this document.

40. "No new works," cited in Scholem, "Ha-Shabta'ut be-Polin," p. 48. "Many of the disciples," *Or Israel* (Frankfurt, 1702), Intro. "I have found," postscript to ban issued by Altona and Hamburg against Sabbatians of August 8, 1725. "as well as," *GE*, p. 54. "Your decree," *GE*, p. 6ov; see p. 67r. "Instruct," *GE*, p. 55.

41. On the existence of a ban from 1670, Scholem, "ha-Shabta'ut be-Polin," p. 46. "To persecute," text of ban in Israel Halperin, ed., *Pinkas Va'ad Arba Arazot* (Jerusalem, 1945), p. 495. "All those who deny," Scholem, *ibid.* p. 48. Ban of 1705, Halperin, pp. 259–261. Halperin mentions that the council issued a ban against Hayon on January 18, 1714. His source is the correspondence between Hagiz and Morpurgo (Sonne, ed.), but his reference is erroneous. On that date there is a letter of Hagiz which mentions that R. Naphtali Katz will try to obtain a condemnation from the Great Council of Poland (Sonne, p. 178). In a letter of July 10, 1714 (Sonne, p. 189) Morpurgo noted that the great Sages of Germany and Poland had condemned the books of Hayon to the flames, but in the same letter (p. 191) he wrote that no further action against Hayon had been taken by the Polish rabbis since the departure of Hakham Zebi.

42. Letter of Hagiz to Council of Four Lands, *GE*, pp. 79v–84r. "All these people," *GE*, p. 8or. On Dr. Portes, see Emden, *Edut be-Ya'akob*, p. 61. "There was a great," Eybeschutz, *Luhot Edut*, p. 9v. cf. Halperin, p. 477. "Hakham R. M. H.," Emden, *TK* (Amsterdam, 1752), p. 36b. Emden's correspondence with the Council, Halperin, pp. 421–424. "At that time," Halperin, p. 496.

43. Jacob Katz, *Massoret u'Mashber* (Jerusalem, 1958), p. 143, n. 14. "For I have not," *Lehishat*, epilogue. On Hagiz' ill health, see e.g., *GE*, p. 63r. "For I am," *GE*, p. 54.

7. THE LUZZATTO CONTROVERSY

1. The first biographer of Luzzatto to draw from archival sources was I. Almanzi, *Kerem Hemed* (1838) 2:112–169. In the same issue, Ghirondi's articles, "Toledot Rabbanei Padua," pp. 89–96, and Vol. 2, "RaMHa"L," pp. 54–67, provide valuable material on Luzzatto's circle. See F. Lachover, *Al Gevul ha-Yashan ve-ha-Hadash* (Jerusalem, 1951) for a criticism of the early biographies. *Leshon Limudim* (Mantua, 1727). See also Nehemia Leibovich, "Mahazot Ra-MHa"L ve-ha-*Zohar*," *Zikhron le-Yehuda* [Blau] (Budapest, 1938) pp. 182–185.

2. Simon Ginzburg, *RaMHa"L u-Benei Doro: Osef Iggerot u-Te'udot*, 1, [Ginzburg, *RaMHa"L*, 1] (Tel Aviv; 1937), 1:39, 69–70. Ginzburg's work is based on ms. JTS #4022 = JNUL mic. #29827.

On the phenomenon of *maggidim* see Moshe Idel, "Studies in the Method of the Author of *Sefer ha-Meshib*," (Heb.) *Sefunot* n.s. #2 (O.S. #17], 1983, pp. 185–266; R.J.Z. Werblowsky, *Joseph Karo: Lawyer and Mystic* (Phila., 1980), pp. 38–83; Laurence Fine, "Maggidic Revelation in the Teachings of Isaac Luria," *Mystics, Philosophers, and Politicians: Essays in Honor of Alexander Altmann* (North Carolina, 1982) Jehuda Reinharz and Daniel Swetschinski, eds., pp. 142–149; Moses Cordovero, "Enquiries Concerning Angels," (Heb.) in Reuben Margolies, *Malakhei Elyon* (Jerusalem, 1945), appendix.

3. Ginzburg, *RaMHa"L*, 1:21, 280; Meir Benayahu, "The Maggid of RaMHa"L," (Heb.) *Sefunot*, 5, 1961, p. 308.

4. Ginzburg, *RaMHa"L*, 1:31, 70.

5. Ginzburg, *RaMHa"L*, 2:292. On the development of similar circles in sixteenth and seventeenth century Italy, see Isaac Barzilay, *Yoseph Shlomo Delmedigo (Yashar of Candia)* (Leiden, 1974), pp. 229–230; "The Life of R. Jacob Daniel Olmo," (Heb.) *ha-Maggid*, no. 49, 1872. Olmo's circle in Ferrara, *Hadashim la-Bekarim*, was modeled after one by the same name in Hebron; A. Farine, "Charity and Study Societies in Europe of the Sixteenth-Eighteenth Centuries," *JQR* (July–Oct. 1973) n.s. 64, pp. 16–47; 164–175.

6. The text of the covenant, Ginzburg, *RaMHa"L*, 1:8–13, and, Ginzburg, *The Life and Works*, appendix pp. 165–168. The reference to an earlier contract, Ginzburg, *RaMHa"L*, 1:12. In a letter to Bassan of June 24, 1731, Ginzburg, *RaMHa"L*, 2:234, Luzzatto referred to an agreement among his friends signed five months earlier to organize a rotation for the uninterrupted study of sacred texts to avert a disastrous sentence which had been decreed against Italian Jews. Thus, there may have been an external reason for the renewal of the contract at that particular time.

7. M. H. Luzzatto, *Sefer ha-Shirim*, J. Zamora, ed. (Jerusalem, 1950), p. 12; Ginzburg, *RaMHa"L*, 1:133. Sabbatai Marini translated Ovid's *Metamorphosis* into Hebrew, in collaboration with Isaiah Bassan.

8. Ginzburg, *RaMHa"L*, 1:143–144.

9. Ginzburg, *RaMHa"L*, 2:222, dated January 22, 1731, "Isaac Marini is in Ferrara today."

10. Isaiah Tishby, "R. Moses David Valle and His Status in the Circle of RaMHa"L," (Heb.) *Zion*, 44 (1979 = Baer Memorial Vol.), pp. 265–302. Valle wrote an anti-Christian polemical treatise and thousands of pages of Kabbalistic manuscript. Tishby has outlined Valle's own messianic odyssey. That Luzzatto was able to incorporate Valle, his senior, into his circle as Messiah ben David, leaving Valle's aspirations intact, yet clearly beneath Luzzatto's position as Moses, was a stroke of genius on Luzzatto's part. After Luzzatto's departure, Valle reverted to leadership of the circle.

11. The messianic interpretation of the *Zohar* in Y. Leibes, "The Messiah of the *Zohar*," (Heb.), *ha-Ra'ayon ha-Meshihi be-Yisrael* (*The Messianic Idea in Israel*) Samuel Ram, ed. (Jerusalem, 1982) pp. 80–236. For further development of this theme within the circle of Luzzatto, see Elisheva Carlebach, "Redemption and Persecution in the Eyes of Moses Hayim Luzzatto and his Circle," *PAAJR* (1987) 54:1–29.

12. *Zohar, Midrash ha-Ne'elam*, 2, p. 15r.

13. *Zohar*, 2, p. 149r.

14. M. H. Luzzatto, *Adir ba-Marom* (Warsaw, 1885), p. 13.

15. *Zohar*, 3, pp. 287v–288r.

16. *Zohar*, selections in I. Tishby, *Mishnat ha-Zohar* (Jerusalem, 1971), pp. 71–75.

17. I am indebted for the messianic interpretation of the *Zohar* to Y. Leibes, "The Messiah of the *Zohar*" (Heb.) *ha-Ra'ayon ha-Meshihi be-Yisrael* (*The Messianic Idea in Israel*) ed. Samuel Ram (Jerusalem, 1982), pp. 80–236.

18. *Tikkunim Hadashim* (Jerusalem, 1958). While the *Tikkunei Zohar* were in the form of commentary to the first verse of Genesis, Luzzatto's *tikkunim* were commentary to the last verse in the Pentateuch, to signify that he would complete the redemption process. Of the *Zohar Tinyana*, no manuscript has survived. Jacob Emden, *Torah ha-Kena'ot* (Amsterdam, 1752), p. 45v, quoted one page from it.

19. *Adir ba-Marom*, p. 5.

"ספר מדרשו של רשב"י . . . כי הוא לגאולה הוכן להצמיח קרן ישועה לבית ישראל."

See also pp. 13, 14, 16, 17.

20. *Toledot AR"I*, ed. M. Benayahu (Jerusalem, 1967), p. 78. Many copies of *Toledot AR"I* circulated in eighteenth century Italy.

21. *Ibid.*, pp. 78, 258.

22. *Ibid.*, pp. 156, 157.

23. Leibes, "The Messiah," p. 136, n. 99 and pp. 109–110, notes that the circle of AR"I modeled itself on that of Bar Yohai, and the similarity between the covenants of unity signed by the AR"I and Luzzatto circles. See G. Scholem, "The Covenant of Unity of Luria's Disciples, (Heb.) *Zion* (1939–40), 5:133–160.

24. *Toledot AR"I*, pp. 179–180; 154.

25. For Luria, *ibid.*, p. 155.

26. Luzzatto, *Tikkunim Hadashim* (Jerusalem, 1958), Tikkun #69, 125. This

passage was cited by Tishby, *Netivei Emunah u-Minut* (Jerusalem, 1964), p. 187, and I. Almanzi, "RaMHa"L," *Kerem Hemed* (1838), 3:138. Tishby's article, "The Messianic Ferment in the Circle of RaMHa"L in the Light of a Marriage Contract . . ." (Heb.) first appeared in *Yitzhak Baer Jubilee Volume* (Heb.) (Jerusalem, 1960), pp. 374–397.

27. Text of "Treatise on the Ketubah," Tishby, *Netivei Emunah u-Minut*, pp. 197–201.

28. "Ma'amar ha-Geulah," p. 55 and similarly pp. 68, 83. *Adir ba-Marom*, p. 26. Other instances abound.

29. On the gradual change in Luzzatto's self-perception from a "channel of Moses" into the actual person of Moses, Tishby, *Netivei*, pp. 190–191. Upon hearing of Luzzatto's death in Acre before he could reach his destination in the heart of the Holy Land. H. Nepi-M. Ghirondi, *Toledot Gedolei Yisrael u-Geonei Italia* (Trieste, 1853), s.v. *Moses Hayim Luzzatto*.

30. "Ma'amar ha-Geulah," p. 56.
31. Ginzburg, *RaMHa"L*, 1:38–39, 142.
32. Ginzburg, *RaMHa"L*, 1:116.
33. "Ma'amar ha-Geulah," p. 53.

"הקלקול הראשון שגרמה הגלות והוא הסתר אור המאורות וגם התורה חסרה מישראל מפני זה."

34. *Ibid.*, p. 93. See similarly *Adir ba-Marom*, p. 11.

"משעה שנסתלקו האותות הנה אין עוד נביא, ואין אתנו יודע עד מה . . . 'אין אתנו'.. . . כי אין ידיעת האחרונים קרויה ידיעה יען הדברים אינם לעיניהם בבירור כראשונים כי רשב"י זלל"ה היו תמיד כל הדברים ברורים לפניו."

35. *Adir ba-Marom*, p. 26.
36. *Ibid.*, p. 12.
37. Ginzburg, *RaMHa"L*, 1:18–20.
38. Ginzburg, *RaMHa"L*, 1:80.
39. Play on 'Jaffe,' see Ginzburg, *RaMHa"L*, 1, p. 18, n. 24. Neither the original text of Gordon's letter, nor that of Hagiz, have been preserved. Gordon's letter was copied, apparently with accuracy, in a letter of the Venetian rabbinate to R. Isaiah Bassan. Hagiz' letter is paraphrased by Almanzi, *Kerem Hemed* 3:149–150. A similar letter was sent to the chief rabbi of Gordon's native city, Vilna, on Aug. 30, 1729, Ginzburg, *RaMHa"L*, 2:407.

40. Ginzburg, *RaMHa"L*, 1:20. See a condensed version, paraphrased by the Venetian rabbinate, on p. 21, and Luzzatto's paraphrase on p. 24: "Arise my lords, prepare your shields, stand in the breach, lest a new sound of tumult grow and issue forth from the land." The variation in the texts suggests that Hagiz sent copies of Gordon's letter with different, brief notes to each recipient. In Ginzburg, *RaMHa"L*, 1:74, Luzzatto remarked that he read that Hagiz had written to Livorno as well.

41. Ginzburg, *RaMHa"L*, 1:98 contains only the opening words of Luzzatto's 'incriminating' treatise. The complete text is in Ms. JTS #4022, pp. 22, 25.

42. Ginzburg, *RaMHa"L*, 1:126. The link between Luzzatto's Kabbalah and Sabbatianism has been the subject of a vituperative scholarly debate. Luzzatto wrote that he was aware of the pervasiveness of Sabbatianism, and readily admitted familiarity with its texts. He vehemently denied that he was a Sabbatian. His *Kin'at Ha-Shem Zeba'ot* in *Ginzei RaMHa"L* (Benei Berak, 1980) is an anti-Christian and anti-Sabbatian polemic. Ginzburg, *RaMHa"L*, 1:153. Isaiah Tishby, *Netivei Emunah u-Minut* argued that Luzzatto accepted overtly Sabbatian elements as part of his polemic. These included the necessity of the Messiah son of Joseph to descend into evil, which according to Luzzatto occurred only in the spiritual realm. The description of the phases that his messiah would pass through are strongly reminiscent of the trials of Sabbatai Zebi, especially coercion into idolatry. Luzzatto maintained that this was not a reference to Sabbatai. (*KHZ*, p. 105). Another Sabbatian notion which appeared in Luzzatto's writing is redemption through sin (*sod aveirah li-shma*). (*KHZ*, p. 95). According to Tishby (*Netivei*, pp. 184–185) Luzzatto was unconscious of these elements in his polemic because he was blinded by the maggidic spell. Benayahu contended that the work was not written under maggidic influence, that he had found many instances in which Luzzatto rejected Sabbatian claims, and that Luzzatto's rebuttals must be accepted at face value. From this dispute it is clear that recognizable elements of Sabbatian Kabbalah had become so detached from their original impulse that their inclusion did not necessarily imply Sabbatian beliefs.

Leibes, "The Messianism of Jacob Emden," has argued that even if Tishby were correct and Luzzatto attributed the status of Messiah ben Joseph to Sabbatai, this did not make him a Sabbatian. Luzzatto believed this Messiah ben Joseph to be the epitome of evil. His only positive value is that his descent into evil was a prerequisite to the final redemption. Leibes showed that Jacob Emden, inveterate opponent of Sabbatianism, attributed a similar negative status in his messianic scheme to a Messiah of the *kelipot*, and he was probably influenced by Luzzatto's writings. Yet it would be absurd to conclude on that basis that Emden was a Sabbatian! How to define Sabbatianism in the post-messianic period remains open to interpretation. It is not our purpose to measure the degree of Luzzatto's Sabbatianism, but to ask to what extent it was known to his persecutors and colored their polemic against him.

43. Ginzburg, *RaMHa"L*, 1:95.

44. There is no date on Luzzatto's letter. As he mentioned it first in a letter to Bassan of Dec. 4, 1729, it was probably written shortly before then. Luzzatto sent a copy of this letter to Jaffe in Vienna. Luzzatto's letter, Ginzburg, *RaMHa"L*, 1:24–25.

45. Hagiz' letter, Ginzburg, *RaMHa"L*, 1:77–79. Hagiz referred to the second edition of his own work, *Eleh ha-Mizvot* (1727) #513 (Jerusalem, 1964 edition, pp. 274–276) where he cautioned against the use of mystical names of God to achieve magical purposes. He also referred to *Sefer Hasidim*, #205, 206, which

cautions, #205: "One who engages in the oaths of angels or evil spirits [*Shedim*] or the practice of witchcraft will come to no good . . . #206: "If you see a person prophesying about the messiah, know that he has engaged in witchcraft or evil spirits as with the Ineffable Name. Angels will tell him [false things] about the messiah so that he should be exposed to the world [as a fraud] . . . it will be to his shame and that of his followers." In a letter to Luzzatto of February 14, 1730, Ginzburg, *RaMHa"L*, 1:86, Bassan urged Luzzatto to be mindful of Hagiz' warning, "for this is the way of the "other side" to confuse the minds with words about the Messiah, to ensnare Israel. And this is what the Hagiz hinted at when he referred to *Sefer Hasidim* #205–206. Study it well."

   46. Ginzburg, *RaMHa"L*, 1:83; Ginzburg, *RaMHa"L*, 1:26, Dec. 4, 1729.
   47. *Ibid.*, p. 30, Dec. 6, 1729.
   48. *Ibid.*, p. 57.
   49. Ginzburg, *RaMHa"L*, 2:237.
   50. Ginzburg, *RaMHa"L*, 2:240, 238.
   51. Ginzburg, *RaMHa"L*, 2:236. In a eulogy for Luzzatto, Moses David Valle expressed a similar sentiment: "We no longer have anyone who can interpret the Talmud in the esoteric way." Cited in Sonne, p. 221. These criticisms of Luzzatto's are very similar to those underlying the Hasidic movement in Poland. See Tishby, *KS* 50 (#3), for specific Hasidic ideas that can be traced directly to Luzzatto.
   52. Luzzatto's letter to Katzenellenbogen, paraphrased by Luzzatto, Ginzburg, *RaMHa"L*, 1:74, 90; by Bassan, Ginzburg, *RaMHa"L*, 2:85.
   53. Katzenellenbogen's letter and Hagiz' postscript, Ginzburg, *RaMHa"L*, 1:80–81. Hagiz and Katzenellenbogen's close collaboration may have been the result of Hagiz' position in the Sephardic community of Hamburg, albeit a de facto one, parallel to that of Katzenellenbogen in the Ashkenazic community. See also, Ginzburg, *RaMHa"L*, 2:289, where Katzenellenbogen's signature was paired with Hagiz': "And as one with him, *Hakham* Hagiz," indicating an equivalent position.
   54. Ginzburg, *RaMHa"L*, 1:160. In rebutting the agnostic approach of Jacob Aboab to Luzzatto by recalling the reaction of his father Samuel Aboab, Hagiz distorted the symmetry of the father-son reaction. In fact, Samuel Aboab at first expressed a similar agnostic reaction to news of the Sabbatian messianic movement. See M. Benayahu, "News from Italy and Holland on the Beginning of Sabbatianism," *Erez Yisrael* (1956) 4:194–205.
   55. Ginzburg, *RaMHa"L*, 1:82. To Katzenellenbogen, Luzzatto wrote: "And if it angers R. Moses Hagiz that his letter has fallen into my hands, know that the Lord is my helper."
   56. Ginzburg, *RaMHa"L*, 1:100.
   57. Ginzburg, *RaMHa"L*, 1:102–103.
   58. Bassan's letter to Luzzatto, Ginzburg, *RaMHa"L*, 1:105. Luzzatto's response, pp. 118, 152. It is ironic that Ergas' *Shomer Emunim* (publ. posthumously in 1731) his own kabbalistic oeuvre against which he measured Luzzatto's *Kelalim*,

never attained the same popularity and classical status as Luzzatto's work. Ergas' book was sometimes published as an appendix to Luzzatto's, as in the (Warsaw, 1888) publication of Luzzatto's *Kin'at Ha-Shem Zeba'ot.*

59. Ginzburg, *RaMHa"L,* 1:124–126.

60. Ginzburg, *RaMHa"L,* 1:133.

61. Ginzburg, *RaMHa"L,* 1:133–134.

62. Letter of Morpurgo to Hagiz, Ginzburg, *RaMHa"L,* 1:135–136. Hagiz' response, p. 166.

63. Letter of Hagiz to Venice, Ginzburg, *RaMHa"L,* 1:160–161.

64. Ginzburg, *RaMHa"L,* 1:21–23. This anonymous document was written by a sympathetic observer or participant who was privy to the proceedings.

65. Bassan, in congratulating the rabbis of Italy for not persecuting Luzzatto at Hagiz' urging, noted this rift: "I extend praise to the rabbis who did not go forth in haste . . . these are the Sages of Italy . . ., except for some rabbis of Venice who envied the wisdom of Luzzatto. But even the two great rabbis of their Yeshiva Kelalit, Simha Kalimani and Jacob Saraval, would not oppose the saintly Luzzatto. Almanzi, *Kerem Hemed,* 2:57.

66. Ginzburg, *RaMHa"L,* 1:16–17.

67. *Ibid.,* p. 27. The signature on the letter to Bassan was illegible; it may have been that of Jacob Aboab.

68. *Ibid.,* pp. 36, 73–74. Solomon Zalman, who betrayed his rabbinic colleagues to support Luzzatto, later betrayed Luzzatto in the second phase of the controversy.

69. *Ibid.,* pp. 67–68, letter of February 14, 1730.

70. On Bassan, see M. Wilensky, "Le-Toldotav shel R. Yeshaya Bassan," *KS* (1951), 27:111–114; M. Benayahu, " A Poem composed by R.I. Bassan for the Wedding of his Disciple, (Heb.), *Dabar,* 1978, 4; Israel Benjamin Bassan, *Todat Shelamim* (Venice; 1741, 1791) esp. vol. 2.

71. Ginzburg, *RaMHa"L,* 1:28–29.

72. Ginzburg, *RaMHa"L,* 1:43, 49.

73. Ginzburg, *RaMHa"L,* 1:59–61.

74. Ginzburg, *RaMHa"L,* 1:74, 77. Luzzatto's letter of February 19, 1730, reports a much milder version of Hagiz' actual letter to Luzzatto.

75. I. Sonne, "Foundation Stones for the History of Italian Jewry: Documents pertaining to the circle of Luzzatto and Lampronte (Heb.), *Horeb* (Nov. 1941), 6:78–79; 79, n. 2.

76. Ginzburg, *RaMHa"L,* 1:105.

77. Ginzburg, *RaMHa"L,* 1:36–39.

78. Ginzburg, *RaMHa"L,* 1:45.

Luzzatto would use the Hebrew letter *samekh* to signify that the topic was closed. Examples, Ginzburg, *RaMHa"L,* 1:53, 56.

79. Ginzburg, *RaMHa"L,* 1:161–166. Tishby, *Netivei,* pp. 230–231, has found a parallel in HID"A's treatment of Kohen. HID"A knew that Kohen was a committed Sabbatian and wrote in a chronicle of 1758 that the Sabbatian emissary

Hayim Malakh had learned the Torah of Nathan of Gaza from Kohen. Yet in a later work, he did not let a hint of blemish fall upon him. To the contrary, he wrote that Kohen had "studied Kabbalah under the holy R. Moses Zacuto, and was renowned for his piety." In Luzzatto's elegy for Kohen, *Sefer ha-Shirim*, ed. Klaar (Jerusalem, 1945) pp. 109–110, he notes the theme of Kohen's vicarious suffering.

80. Ginzburg, *RaMHa"L*, 1:84, ff.

81. Ginzburg, *RaMHa"L*, 1:90, 93.

82. Ginzburg, *RaMHa"L*, 1:138.

83. Ginzburg, *RaMHa"L*, 1:143. Ginzburg, *Life and Works*, p. 39, n. 50, noted that Luzzatto occasionally dropped his customary salutation "my teacher and master" during the angry phase of the correspondence.

84. Ginzburg, *RaMHa"L*, 1:145–147.

85. Ginzburg, *RaMHa"L*, 1:149–151.

86. Ginzburg, *RaMHa"L*, 1:157.

87. Letter of Bassan, Ginzburg, *RaMHa"L*, 1:169–173.

88. Letter of del Rio, Ginzburg, *RaMHa"L*, 1:174–175.

89. Ginzburg, *RaMHa"L*, 1:164, of late June, 1730.

90. Recension [A], Ginzburg, *RaMHa"L*, 1:176. Original manuscript in JNUL Schwadron collection.

91. Recension [B], from Jacob Emden, *TK* (1880) pp. 102–103.

92. This was reported in a letter from Raphael Kimhi, the Safed emissary, to Abraham Segre of Casale. Almanzi, *Kerem Hemed* (1838) 3:152–153. It was confirmed by the complaint of the Venetian rabbis to Hagiz, Ginzburg, *RaMHa"L*, 2:269.

93. Letter of Morpurgo, Ginzburg, *RaMHa"L*, 2:213. Letter of Hagiz (paraphrased by Luzzatto), Ginzburg, *RaMHa"L*, 2:219.

94. See Ginzburg, *RaMHa"L*, 2:219, 235. Benayahu, "RaMHaL's Oath," p. 29, argued that Luzzatto had absolute control over copies of his work in circulation, and so he was able to gather and conceal them all as promised. Benayahu's concern to uphold Luzzatto's integrity conflicts with the evidence produced by Tishby, see below.

95. Tishby, "Prayers of R. Moses Hayim Luzzatto in Manuscipt, (Heb.) *Molad*, 1980, pp. 125–126. Tishby argued that in many prayers, the exiled and persecuted Israel is a metaphor for the persecuted circle, e.g., p. 122, n. 2, and p. 123, n. 2,. Luzzatto did not openly express this identification in the prayers, however, it is explicit in Valle's writings, cited in Tishby, "Moses David Valle," p. 300.

96. Luzzatto, *Adir ba–Marom*, p. 17.

97. Ginzburg, *RaMHa"L*, 2, p. 259. Tishby, "Prayers," *Molad*, 1980, p. 123.

98. Tishby, "Prayers," *Molad*, 1980, p. 124.

99. *Adir ba-Marom*, p. 19.

100. *Adir ba-Marom*, p. 20. See also Tishby, "Moses David Valle," p. 296, n. 98.

101. Tishby, "Prayers," *Molad*, 1980, p. 124, n. 19. The "mixed multitude," *ereb rab*, is parallel to the group by that name who incited the Jews against the Biblical Moses. Tishby notes that Sabbatians consistently used this term to designate those who were unfaithful to their beliefs.

102. Tishby, *Netivei*, pp. 190–192. Luzzatto also outlined the steps by which he would be transfigured into Moses. Ginzburg, *RaMHa"L*, 2:234, 239.

103. Ginzburg, *RaMHa"L*, 1:72, and similarly, p. 74; 2:238.

104. Ginzburg, *RaMHa"L*, 1:69, similarly, p. 147; 2, p. 223: "I am overjoyed that you acknowledge that the Yihudim which gave me strength were uttered in utmost sanctity . . . not as you first suspected of me . . . for *that was the persuasion of Samael*, which God willed, until the appointed time."

105. Ginzburg, *RaMHa"L*, 1:52; p. 40; p. 69; and similarly, p. 75.

106. An anonymous informant who had visited Hagiz in Altona reported that Hagiz had threatened "If the case of Luzzatto will not subside after the Venice Herem was issued (Hagiz) would turn, with the help of influential contacts, to the King and to the Pope that they should mount him on a stake in the center of a plaza because of his audacity . . ." Ginzburg, *RaMHa"L*, 2:414. If these threats reached Luzzatto, they must have contributed to his image as martyr.

8. REVIVAL OF THE LUZZATTO CONTROVERSY

1. This work of Luzzatto's was eventually published under the title *Hoker u-Mekubal* (*The Philosopher and the Kabbalist*), (Shklov, 1784).

2. Luzzatto's requests for an approbation in Ginzburg, *RaMHa"L*, 2, #90 of Dec. 11, 1733; #91 of Jan. 3, 1734; #92 of Jan. 8, 1734; and #93 of June 18, 1734. Bassan's reply, Ginzburg, *RaMHa"L*, 2:245–247. Bassan noted other defenses of *Kabbalah* such as Yasha"r of Candia's, (Crete) *Mazref La-Hokhma* (e.p. Basilea, 1629) on which see Isaac Barzilay, *Yoseph Shlomo Delmedigo* (Leiden, 1974); and Abiad Basilea's *Emunat Hakhamim*, which had recently been published (Mantua, 1730). Bassan's 'reshut,' Ginzburg, *RaMHa"L*, 2:247.

3. Ginzburg, *RaMHa"L*, 2:248–249. Ginzburg has surmised that the anonymous informant to the rabbinate of Venice was Simha Kalimani of Venice, n. 67. For an account of this meeting told by the agents of Venice see Ginzburg, *RaMHa"L*, 2:257–260.

4. Ginzburg, *RaMHa"L*, 2:250–251, Nov. 18, 1734.

5. Belilios' testimony, Ginzburg, *RaMHa"L*, n.s. 105–108, 117, 112.

6. Ginzburg, *RaMHa"L*, 2:266.

7. Ginzburg, *RaMHa"L*, 2:382.

8. Benayahu, *Haskama u-Reshut be-Defusei Venezia* (Ramat Gan, 1971), pp. 135–139. Luzzatto's first printed work, "Hanukat Ha-Aron," poems in honor of the dedication of a new Ark in the Sephardic synagogue of Padua, was published in Venice, 1729 with no authorization of any kind, perhaps because of its small size (Benayahu, p. 136). It contained seven of his Psalms. His disciple, Isaiah Ro-

manin, printed in 1730 a Kabbalistic interpretation of one of the *selihot* prayers *Meliz Yashar*, with only a poem by Luzzatto as authorization. Despite the lack of any official approbation, neither book attracted any attention.

9. Cited in John Julius Norwich, *A History of Venice* (N.Y., 1982) p. 583.

10. The noted emissary R. Hayim Y.D. Azulai, described in detail the difficulties he encountered trying to collect a long-standing debt owed by the Venetian community to the poor relief of Hebron in 1754. *EJ* 16:97–98. Salo Baron, *The Jewish Community*, 3:190, (Philadelphia, 1942).

11. Ginzburg, *RaMHa"L*, 1:165.

12. Ginzburg, *RaMHa"L*, 1:16, and similarly, Ginzburg, *RaMHa"L*, 1:22.

13. Ginzburg, *RaMHa"L*, 1:162, 168, 170.

14. This letter of Pacifico, apparently a response to Hagiz' letter of April 18, 1730 (Ginzburg, *RaMHa"L*, 1, pp. 132–133) was not published. Excerpts from the manuscript, Montefiore #111, pp. 13r–14r, in Tishby, "Kobez . . .," *Kiryat Sefer*, 53 (1):176, 177, n. 58. In the letter Pacifico accused Luzzatto of "interpreting the philosophy of Aristotle . . . in a kabbalistic manner." He also attacked Nehemiah Kohen and Judah Mendola, other supporters of Luzzatto.

15. Ginzburg, *RaMHa"L*, 2:337. On the confiscation see A. Berliner, *Censur and Confiscation Hebraischer Bucher im Kirchenstaate* (Berlin, 1891), p. 13; William Popper, *The Censorship of Hebrew Books* (N.Y., 1969) p. 117.

16. Ginzburg, *RaMHa"L*, 1:37, n.s. 73, 85, letter of Dec. 19, 1729. His reference on p. 32 "I am afraid to carry these works on me . . . but I shall send what I can," might be to Hagiz or the Venetian Inquisitors.

17. Ginzburg, *RaMHa"L*, 2:233.

18. The identity of the apostate rabbi, Nehemia Kohen of Ferrara, becomes complicated. There were three individuals by this name living at the same time in Ferrara, and it is not always clear which one is referred to by the sources. Our apostate was Nehemiah *ben Jacob* Kohen, whose signature appears on Luzzatto's oath of 1730. He was a member of the rabbinical court of Ferrara and a close friend of Isaac Lampronte, who referred to him in *Pahad Yizhak*. "One of the young scholars, *who later apostatized*, wished to prove that it was an old custom in Ferrara." Despite his apostasy, Lampronte did not omit his testimony from the halakhic discourse. 2 (Venice, 1753), p. 86a, s.v. 'Dagim.' In the same entry, p. 86v, Lampronte referred to 'the wealthy Nehemiah *ben Moses* Kohen of Ferrara, the second person by this name. He is apparently the 'gevir' [wealthy] Nehemiah Kohen who attended the wedding of Luzzatto's disciple Moses David Valle and interrogated Luzzatto on that occasion. Ginzburg, *RaMHa"L*, 1:153. A third Nehemiah, *ben Barukh* Kohen was a participant in the controversy in Ferrara which was immortalized in the pamphlet *Meziz u-Meliz*. On the apostate see also Sonne, "Building Blocks . . ." *Horeb*, (Nov. 1941), 6:100; M. Wilensky, "Who was R. Netanel Ha-Levi?" (Heb.) *KS*, (Oct. 1946), 23 (2):139. According to Tishby *KS* 53:177, n. 58, the apostate Nehemiah ordained Luzzatto before the administration of the oath.

19. Ginzburg, *RaMHa"L*, 1:49, 96, 118. In comparing the *maggid* to the prophet of Avila, Kohen referred to the responsa of RaShB"A, #548, cf. Emden, *TK*, p. 99 and Ginzburg, *RaMHa"L*, 2:446, n. 369a.

20. Ginzburg, *RaMHa"L*, 1:64. Ferrara came under the domination of the Church in 1598. Mob attacks on the ghetto and blood libels were not uncommon throughout the seventeenth and eighteenth centuries. Forced attendance at conversionist sermons and an array of legislative restrictions were among the measures against Jews instituted by the Church.

21. Ginzburg, *RaMHa"L*, 1:153. Luzzatto's polemical work was later published in part as *Kin'at ha-Shem Zeba'ot* (Konigsberg, 1862).

22. Ginzburg, *RaMHa"L*, 2:213.

23. Ginzburg, *RaMHa"L*, 2:298. Although Hagiz' letter was written in March, 1735, Cecil Roth, "Forced Baptisms in Italy," *JQR*, (October 1936), 27 (2):117–136, has proved that the actual conversion ceremony did not take place until May, 1735. The impending baptism of Kohen was being celebrated in the Christian press before the ceremony took place.

24. The verse was published in Ferrara, 1735. Roth, "Forced Baptisms," p. 126, n. 15c. A close parallel occured in the Emden-Eybeschutz controversy. When Carl Anton, an apostate, wrote a work in defense of Eybeschutz, Emden used this as proof that Eybeschutz' subversive Sabbatianism had close links to Christianity. See the discussion in *Kerem Hemed*, (1836), 2 (28):169–171; Liebes, "Concerning a Secret Jewish-Christian Sect which originated from Sabbatianism," *Tarbiz* (1988) 57 (3):349–384.

25. See Sonne, "Building Blocks," p. 102, and the response of S. Ginzburg, "Stumbling Blocks: A Luzzatto Controversy," *Bizaron*, (December 1942), 7 (3):206–207.

26. This work was later reprinted in German by an apostate, Alexander Fuerst, *Christen und Juden*, (Strasbourg, 1892).

27. Ginzburg, *RaMHa"L*, 2:332.

28. Ginzburg, *RaMHa"L*, 2:361, 459; Sonne, "Building Blocks," *Horeb*, 6, p. 100

29. Ginzburg, *RaMHa"L*, 2:266, n. 126; Emden, *TK* (Lvov), p. 103.

30. Giulio Morosoni, *Via della fede mostrata a'gli Ebrei* (Rome, 1683), intro.

31. Popers' account in letter to Hagiz, Ginzburg, *RaMHa"L*, 2:287; Writ of Frankfurt rabbinical court, pp. 285–287; 'admission' of Luzzatto, p. 283.

32. Ginzburg, *RaMHa"L*, 1:21. On Kimhi, see Yaari, *Sheluhei*, pp. 849–850.

33. Ginzburg, *RaMHa"L*, 1:16–17.

34. Ginzburg, *RaMHa"L*, 1:60; p. 58.

35. Ginzburg, *RaMHa"L*, 1:104–105. Cf. similar argument of Popers, who listed Sabbatian prophets such as R. Heshel Zoref, R. Daniel [Bonafoux], and R. Leible Prostitz in addition to Sabbatai and Nathan, Ginzburg, *RaMHa"L*, 2:376.

36. Ginzburg, *RaMHa"L*, 1:93–94.

37. Ginzburg, *RaMHa"L*, 1:128; pp. 86–89; 2, pp. 353, 289.
38. Ginzburg, *RaMHa"L*, 1:126, 128; pp.162–163, 2, p. 360; 1, pp. 158–159. Jacob Emden took strong exception to this position of Hagiz. See *TK*, (1752) pp. 48a–b, "An Inquiry into the General Nature of Maggidim" : "Concerning everything said by R.M.H. [Hagiz], may he rest in peace, on this issue, . . . he has raised his voice without wisdom." He argued that if Luzzatto's only sin had been the reception of a maggidic revelation, he would have been blameless.
39. Morpurgo's letters to Hagiz, R. Barukh Rapoport, and Popers: Ginzburg, *RaMHa"L*, 2:332, 335, 346, 362, 384, 388.
40. Ginzburg, *RaMHa"L*, 2:398, 396. Popers wrote this announcement to Hagiz in March 4, 1737, explaining that the deed had been done two months earlier, in Jan. 1737. He wrote after a long period of silence after Hagiz accused him of reneging on his promise to dispose of Luzzatto's writings after he had received them.
41. Elijah Ulianov, *Birkhat Elijah*, (Wandsbeck, 1727) p. 56. Hagiz' treatise begins on p. 55.
42. Emden, *She'ilat Ya'abez*, #33.
43. Ginzburg, *RaMHa"L*, 1:172, 174; 2:354, and no. 348a.
44. Jonathan Eybeschutz, *Luhot ha-Edut*, (Altona, 1755), Intro. pp. iv, xix. Ulianov was a disciple of Abraham Broda of Prague and a son-in-law of Nathan Neta Shapira, author of *Yayin ha-Meshumar* and *Tub ha-Arez*.
45. Emden, *TK*, (Lvov, 1870) pp. 111–117, Jaffe denied this.
46. *Luhot ha-Edut*, p. 14v.
47. *Ibid*. On the prominent role of Ulianov in the defense of Eybeschutz, see *Luhot ha-Edut*, (photo-reproduction Jerusalem, 1966) Index, s.v., Elijah. Ulianov wrote of Eybeschutz: "The portals of Zion are desolate, only one remains open: . . . Your Highness, and even this they wish to close." *Ibid.*, p. 15r.
48. Jacob Emden's implausible attempt to explain Bassan's opposition as the work of Satan is by his own admission "remote." Of the information he received in Amsterdam "that Luzzatto's grandfather had committed a murder against the grandfather of Bassan," I have been unable to find a source. (*TK*, Lvov, p. 112).
Emden believed Luzzatto to be a Sabbatian of the same rank as he believed Hayon and Eybeschutz to be. In his anti-Sabbatian tract *Torat ha-Kena'ot* the documents of the Luzzatto campaign are interwoven into the others.
49. Letter to Bassan, Ginzburg, *RaMHa"L*, 2:295–297. Text of ban, Ginzburg, *RaMHa"L*, 2:290.
50. The eleven bans have been published in Ginzburg, *RaMHa"L*, 2:306–320. Emden's ban was preserved in *TK*, Lvov, p. 113. Hagiz wrote that he intended to publish this collection, "I will leave something inscribed for the [future] generations so they will not sin," (Ginzburg, *RaMHa"L*, 2:306), but apparently, he never got to it. Emden wrote that Hagiz and Katzenellenbagen printed their original ban (Ginzburg, *RaMHa"L*, 2:290), however, he refused to print it because he disagreed with the strictures against the Kabbalistic writings, *TK*, p. 112.

51. Ginzburg, *RaMHa"L*, 2, #'s 9–11. R. Israel Ben David of Brody and Moses Samuel, both emissaries of Safed, wrote that they had relied on R. Eliezer for their information regarding Luzzatto, hence their charges of Sabbatianism.

52. Emden, *TK*, (Lvov) pp. 112–113. His assessment of Luzzatto appears on p. 111: "Although his heresy has not been clearly manifested in his writings . . . nevertheless, there is no doubt that he belonged to the sect of Sabbatai Zebi, may his memory rot, . . . Luzzatto wished to take his place . . . as the letter of his disciple [Gordon] proves." Emden was thoroughly familiar with Luzzatto's works and his pronouncement that Luzzatto had deemed the Sabbatian affair an error, rather than a completely false messianism was the basis of the scholarly dispute over Luzzatto's attitude toward Sabbatianism. cf. Ginzburg, *RaMHa"L*, 1:76, where Luzzatto wrote to Bassan "and the matter of Nathan of Gaza is *completely false* and erroneous." Hagiz did not intend to publish Emden's letter, along with others, because of space limitations. Ginzburg, *RaMHa"L*, 2:320. Emden returned the compliment by omitting Hagiz' writ because "he had arrogantly presumed to decree against the study of Kabbalah' in general." *TK*, p. 112.

53. Text of ban, Ginzburg, *RaMHa"L*, 2:325–328; letter to Italian rabbis, pp. 329–330. The letter was signed by Joseph b. Samuel Aboab, Solomon Mintz, Solomon Altaras, Isaac Pacifico, Solomon Zalman of Lvov, Nissim David ha-Kohen. Jacob Aboab and Menahem Merrari did not sign.

54. Ginzburg, *RaMHa"L*, 2:293–294; 353; 421–422.

55. Ginzburg, *RaMHa"L*, 2:382–383, Dec. 7, 1735; n. 324. Three copies of this text with slight variations indicate that Bassan planned this move carefully, drafting several copies and sending the best one.

56. Ginzburg, *RaMHa"L*, 2:391–396.

57. Ginzburg, *RaMHa"L*, 2:372.

58. Ginzburg, *RaMHa"L*, 2:394, July 6, 1736. Popers did not correspond directly with Bassan but with R. Aaron Rakicz. Rakicz was a brother-in-law of Bassan who acted as an intermediary on Bassan's behalf.

59. Ginzburg, *RaMHa"L*, 2:320–325, 416.

60. Ginzburg, *RaMHa"L*, 2:416.

9. CROWN OF A CAREER

1. Hagiz' alternative definition of the phrase '*emunat hakhamim*' as the faith *of* the Sages was clearly peripheral to his central concern, faith *in* the Sages.

2. Shalom Rosenberg, *"Emunat Hakhamim,"* in Isadore Twersky and Bernard Septimus, eds. *Jewish Thought in the Seventeenth Century,"* (Cambridge: Harvard University Press, 1987), pp. 285–342, is the most comprehensive treatment of the religious turmoil and the rabbinic attempts to deal with it in the Sephardic world. For a description of many relevant unpublished manuscripts of the Amsterdam community, see Richard H. Popkin, "Philosophy and Polemic in the Mss. of Ez Hayim" (Heb.) *Mehkarim al Toledot Yahadut Holland*, 3: 55–63. Other studies, notably, Jacob Katz, *Massoret u-Mashber* (Jerusalem, 1958); Chimen

Abramsky, "The Crisis of Authority within European Jewry in the Eighteenth Century," *Studies in Jewish Religious and Intellectual History Presented to Alexander Altmann* (Alabama: University of Alabama Press, 1979); Ellis Rivkin, *Leon Modena and the Kol Sakhal* (Cincinnati, 1952) chapter 1, do not distinguish between Eastern European Jewish society and Sephardic Western Europe.

3. Moses Hagiz, epilogue, to David ibn Zimra, *Or Kadmon*, (Venice, 1703), pp. 14–30.

4. Cf. the Portuguese introduction to *Sefat Emet* which Hagiz addressed to "*la-lo'azim be-la'az*," a reference to a lack of their facility in Hebrew. In his introduction to *Eleh ha-Mizvot* (1727) Hagiz castigated those who "were circumcized at eight days," who ought to know better.

5. "*Le-Ma'alat*," pp. 15v–16v. Cf. *Eleh ha-Mizvot* (1713) #2, on circumcision. On the reintegration of Marranos, Yosef Hayim Yerushalmi, "The Re-Education of Marranos in the Seventeenth Century," *Feinberg Memorial Lecture*, University of Cincinnati, March 1980.

6. Numbers, 11:34. "*le-Ma'alat*," p. 26r. Alexander Altmann, "Eternality of Punishment: A Theological Controversy within the Amsterdam Rabbinate in the Thirties of the Seventeenth Century," *PAAJR* (1973):1–88.

7. "*Le-Ma'alat*," pp. 16v; 29v; 26v.

8. *Sefat Emet* (Amsterdam, 1707), p. 22V.

9. *Sefat Emet*, p. 5r. Menasseh ben Israel, *Conciliador* (Amsterdam, 1632; 1641–51); Jacob Abendana tr. Judah Halevi, *Cuzary* (Amsterdam, 1663); Immanuel Aboab, *Nomologia o Discursos Legales*, (Amsterdam, 1629). Hagiz wrote a similar recommendation in *Eleh ha-Mizvot*, #613. There he included Menasseh's *Conciliador*, a translation of the work of Isaac Aboab, the *Nomologia* of Immanuel Aboab, and Isaac Cardoso's *Exelencias*. It is surprising that he does not give more prominent notice to his father's translation of Isaac Aboab's *Menorat HaMaor, Almenara de la Luz*. (Livorno, 1656; repr. Amsterdam, 1708.)

10. *Mishnat Hakhamim*, #495, 496.

11. The passage in *Mishnat Hakhamim*, #62, which appeared almost 30 years later, is addressed to Marranos as "loa'azim," and the wise among the Gentiles. The first recommendation is Aboab's *Nomologia*; the second is "a book called *Exelencias de los Hebreos*, written by the physician, healer of souls and bodies . . . Isaac Cardoso." See also *Mishnat*, #61, an extensive analysis of the *Nomologia*. Cf. the list of Samuel Aboab, *Debar Shemuel*, (Venice, 1702) #152.

12. *Emek Binyamin* (Amsterdam, 1753), p. 25b. Brandon's work was written in 1732 and published posthumously.

13. Aviad Basilea, *Emunat Hakhamim* (Mantua, 1730). *Nomologia* (Amsterdam, 1629); *Conciliador* (Amsterdam, 1632); *Matteh Dan ve-Kuzari ha-Sheni* (London, 1714). Rosenberg's "Emunat Hakhamim," describes this material, as well as much new material that is still in manuscript in the *Ez Hayim* library in Amsterdam: Moses Raphael de Aguilar, "Reposta a certas Propostas contra a Tradicao" (1639), Ms. *Ez Hayim* 48All; R. Solomon Judah Leon, "Treatise on the Laws of Moses from Sinai," Ms. *Ez Hayim* 47B4; Elijah Montero, "*Emunat Hakhamim*," Ms. *Ez Hayim*

48D44. Rosenberg, p. 341. In addition, see the work of R. Abraham Hayim Viterbo, *"Emunat Hakhamim,"* in Eliezer Ashkenazi, *Ta'am Zekenim* (Frankfurt, 1854), Isaac Orobio de Castro, "Epistola Invectiva" and ref. "to a manuscript treatise of Simha (Simone) Luzatto . . . in defense of the Oral Torah . . ." *Debar Shemuel* (Venice, 1702), #152.

14. On the Christian Hebraists of England see Herman Gollancz, "Anglo-Judaica, *TJHSE,* (1908–10) 6:56–87, esp. pp. 62ff. On eighteenth century anti-Christian polemics by Jews see Judah David Eisenstein, *Ozar Vikuhim* (N.Y., 1928). A substantial number of the polemics were written in the eighteenth century.

15. Briel's ode to Cardoso, *Ozar Tob* (Berlin, 1878), p. 84. The manuscript of Segre's anti-Christian polemic, *Asham Talui,* includes a treatise by Briel "The Contentions of the Christians Refuted," Mss. Columbia University, X893 J78; JNUL 8° 759; and JNUL 8° 102. Bassan's polemic, ms. JNUL, Yah. Heb. 177, pp. 1r–38r.

Nieto is almost certainly the author of *Noticias Reconditas y Posthumas del Procedimiento delas Inquisiciones de Espana y Portugal con sus Presos* ("Villa Franca," 1722) and (anonymously) Respuesta al Sermon predicado por el Arcobispo de Cranganor enel Auto de Fe . . . Lisboa . . . under the pseudonym. 'Carlos Vero." The place of publication, Villa Franca, may be London (1729?). In his letter to C. T. Unger (see infra.) Nieto admitted to falsifying the title page of his book *Paschalogia* (1693) to appear as though it had been printed in Cologne because the Church would never had permitted it to appear in Italy. On Morpurgo, see Meir Benayahu, "The Polemical Writings of R. Samson Morpurgo against the Priest Benetelli," *AS* (June, 1980) 8:87–94.

16. This confluence has already been demonstrated in Y. H. Yerushalmi, *From Spanish Court to Italian Ghetto* (Columbia University Press: N.Y., 1971), pp. 338–341.

17. *EH,* Wandsbeck, 1727, #564. *MH* #582, and similarly Intro. to *MH.*

18. *MH,* #500. Similar dialogues in *MH,* #s 501–505 closely based on Solomon ibn Verga, *Sefer Shebet Yehuda* (Jerusalem, 1946), pp. 154–155.

19. *MH,* #595.

20. *MH,* #580. Cf. his disparaging remark about Christians, *Sheber Posh'im,* p. 11.

21. *Leket,* Y.D. (Amsterdam, 1707), p. 107r; 96r.

22. "Letter of D.N.," (Heb.) *Ozar Tob* (Berlin, 1878), pp. 85–86.

23. *Ozar Nehmad,* 3, p. 131.

24. Cantarini is probably identical to Isaac Viva [a likely nom de plume for Isaac Vita (Cantarini)] author of *Vindex Sanguinis contra Jacobeens Genusiam* (Amsterdam, 1680; Nuremburg, 1681). See also, "Der Rabbinische Rationalismus: Eine Unterredung des Grafen Gabriel (Tureson) von Oxenstirn mit dem Rabbiner Isac Vita Cantarini aus Padua (1693 orig., repr. Wien, 1899) trans. Samuel Modlinger.

25. *Mishnat Hakhamim* (Wandsbeck, 1733), Intro. p. iv. A caveat to readers

of the (Brooklyn, 1959) edition: the editors have omitted Wolf's name but retained the adulatory praise, leaving the impression that Hagiz was praising some Jewish scholar! 'R. Mosche Chagis' is the source for an anonymous epitaph found on a Jerusalem tombstone in Wolf's collection of poetic inscriptions. *Bibliotheca*, 4, p. 1217.

26. Johan Christoph Wolf, *Bibliotheca Hebraea*, 3 (Hamburg, 1727). *MH*, Intro., p. iv.

27. Letter of Hagiz to Wolf, Ms. Bodleian Library, Cat. Neubauer #1180. This manuscript also contains the letters of Nieto and Cantarini to Unger.

28. *Sefet Emet*, p. 27r; 7v. *Eleh ha-Mizvot* (1727), p. 61r. The treatise has not survived.

29. *SE*, p. 6r. Similar Judaeo-centric views prevailed in most Sephardic historiographic writing of the early modern period, —for a survey of such writing in the sixteenth century, see Yosef Hayim Yerushalmi, *Zakhor: Jewish History and Jewish Memory*, Seattle: University of Washington press, 1982, ch. 3. Hagiz remained untouched by the argument in Solomon ibn Verga's *Shebet Yehudah* that natural laws now controlled Jewish destiny, although he made use of *Shebet Yehudah* for other purposes.

30. *SE*, pp. 17v–18v, and similarly p. 15r; *Sheber Posh'im*, p. 5; *SE*, p. 24r. "There is clear proof," *EH*, (1727).

31. *MH*, #577. Hagiz mocked several Karaite rulings, such as permitting the *shofar* (ram's horn) and *lulab* (palm branch) on the Sabbath, and their calculation of the leap year, as "notorious falsehoods." *MH*, #536. *EH*, (1727) #302, p. 88v; #422, p. 119v. On the entire issue of Karaism and its significance in eighteenth century Sephardic communities, see Yosef Kaplan, "The 'Karaites' in Amsterdam in the early Eighteenth Century," *Zion*, (1987) 52 (3): 279–314.

32. Wolf, *Notitia Karaeorum* (Hamburg, 1714) is mainly a translation of a work by the Karaite Mordechai ben Nisan Kukizow.

33. *Panim Me'irot* (Amsterdam, 1715) approbations at the beginning of the book are not paginated. The second approbation cited is that of R. Leib of Cracow. Oppenheim's son, Joseph, contributed funds to meet the expenses.

34. *Sefer Likutei ha-Pardes*, attributed to Rashi [e.p. Venice, 1519]. The editor of the Amsterdam, 1715 edition, R. Pesah b. Issachar Ber of Slutsk would not have needed an approbation to reprint an older work, but for his own responsa which he appended to his new edition.

35. Before the Hayon campaign, Hagiz wrote approbations to a reprint of the *Responsa of R.M.I.* (R. Moses Isserles) (Amsterdam, 1711) and to *Viku'ah Mayim Hayim* of R. Bezalel Loewe (Amsterdam, 1712). For a list of approbations written by Hagiz, see Leopold Lowenstein, *Mafteah ha-Haskamot* (Frankfurt, 1923) and Benayahu, *AS*, 4:152–154.

36. *Sha'arei Torah* (Hamburg, 1718). The work he defended was Katz' grammatical text, *Binyan Shelomo* (Frankfurt, 1713).

37. *Bet Levi* (Zolkiew, 1732). *Livyat Hen* (Altona, 1733). Zalman b. Judah of Dessau, *Iggeret Shlomo* (Wandsbeck, 1732). Excerpt in Simha Assaf, *Mekorot le-*

Toledot ha-Hinukh be-Yisrael, (Tel Aviv: Dvir, 1947) 4:106. I thank Professor M. Benayahu for this reference.

38. Novellae of Eidles (Altona, 1734); of ibn Aderet (Altona, 1737) and of R. Asher (Altona, 1735). *Shehitot u-Bedikot* (Wandsbeck, 1733); *Pi Eliyahu* (Altona, 1735) and *Heshib R. Eliezer* (Neuwied, 1749) [haskamah of Hagiz to this work is dated 1735; apparently its publication was long delayed]. *Be'er Tob* (Altona, 1737); *Mekom Shemu'el* (Altona, 1738); *Kerem Shelomo* (Hamburg, 1738); *Hishta'arut . . .* (Amsterdam, 1737).

39. Elijah b. Azriel of Vilna's *Mikhtav me-Eliyahu* was a commentary to Menahem di Lonzano's book on the masoretic text of the Bible, *Or Torah*, published together in the edition of (Hamburg, 1738). On *Or Torah*, vide Maria Monasterio, *Texto Hebreo Biblico de Safarad en el Or Torah de Menahem de Lonzano* (Madrid, 1980).

40. For a complete listing see Marx and Margolis, "Bibliographisches Verzeichnis der Hebraischen Drucke in Wandsbeck, 1726–1733," *Festschrift fur Aron Freimann* (Berlin, 1935).

41. Abraham Hasdai's work of the thirteenth century was reprinted many times, the edition under consideration is Wandsbeck, 1727. The attribution to Hagiz of "Mi-Sihat Hulin . . ." was made by A. Habermann, "Mi-Sihat Hulin shel Talmidei Hakhamim of R. Moses Hagiz," *Sinai* (1948) pp. 89–98, where it is reprinted. In *MH*, #69 Hagiz argued against engaging in what the sages call "idle talk."

42. Both Hagiz and his predecessor, Jacob Sasportas, used the same words "Kera'im" (tatters) to describe their halakhic achievement, the price for the unsettled lives they led. Hagiz, Introduction to *HK*, p. 2r; Sasportas, Benayahu, *AS*, 4:137.

43. This section of the *Leket* on *Hoshen Mishpat* was recently found, and portions of interest printed by Joshua Mondshein, "Sefer Leket Ha-KeMa"H le-Rabi Moshe Hagiz—Helek: Hoshen Mishpat," *AS* 10:93–112, from ms. *JNUL* 8° 3131.

Leket on the Mishnah (Wandsbeck, 1726). Hagiz appended his father's treatise *Zikkaron le-Benei Yisrael* which he had omitted from his reprint of *Petil Tekhelet* (London, 1714), where it originally appeared.

44. *Me'orer Zikkaron* (Altona, 1726). It is Katzenellenbogen's approbation which clearly indicates that Hagiz was author.

45. The *Leket* on tractates *Zera'im* and *Mo'ed* were attributed to Alghazi but written by Hagiz' own hand. HID"A (Azulai) believed them to have been written by Hagiz. Benayahu, *HIDA*, p. 85, n. 37.

46. For a complete list of Hagiz' unpublished works see Benayahu, *AS*, 4:137–139, and for fragments which did appear in print, pp. 143–145. *Perurei Pat Ha-KeMaH on Daniel* (Wandsbeck, 1727) was published together with the commentary of R. Moses Alsheikh, *Havazelet ha-Sharon*, Rashi's commentary, and an abridged version of Isaac Abravanel's *Ma'ayanei ha-Yeshu'a*.

47. *Shetei ha-Lehem* (Wandsbeck, 1733) bound together with *Mishnat Hakhamim*.

48. In addition to his introductions, see his defense in *Eleh ha-Mizvot* (Wandsbeck, 1727), #496.

49. On Lampronte's periodical see Isaiah Sonne, "Information on the History of Jews in Italy," (Heb.) *Horeb*, (November 1941) 6:85. This periodical was begun before 1715. In that year R. Mordecai Zahalon published *Meziz u-Meliz* which exoriated Lampronte and the disciples of his yeshiva for one of their decisions concerning cantillation.

50. *Responsa Peri Ez Hayim* (Amsterdam, 1728). Mendel Probst, "On the History of the Development of Hebrew Periodicals, 1667–1920," (Heb.) *KS* 2:212, maintained incorrectly that it was the first attempt at a Hebrew periodical. Max Menko Hirsch, "Frucht vom Baum des Lebens: Ozar Perot Ez Hayim" (Berlin-Antwerp, 1936) is an abridged translation into German. The work of Broda's circle, *Hidushei Halakhot al Gittin* (Wandsbeck, 1731).

51. Only two volumes were published in his lifetime, (Venice, 1750; 1753). The rest were published posthumously, twelve volumes in all. Manuscripts of Lampronte's revised edition were never published. A newly indexed edition (Vol. 1, Jerusalem, 1962) has not been completed. See Boaz Cohen, "A List of Authors of Responsa Printed in the *Pahad Yizhak*," *Festschrift fur Aron Freimann*, ed. Marx & Meyer (Berlin, 1935), pp. 141–143.

52. In *Sefer Keritut* (Amsterdam, 1709). R. Samuel b. Jacob Benveniste, *Orekh Yamim* (ed. pr. Constantinople, n.d.), repr. (Venice, 1600), sections repr. in Moses Roza, *Zikkaron Tob* (Livorno, 1846). Roza noted that Hagiz had not been the only author to cite passages of *Orekh Yamim* without proper attribution. R. Moses Murbezik, in *Sefer Keizad Seder Mishnah* did the same. See S. Assaf, *Mekorot le-Toledot ha-Hinukh be-Yisrael* (Tel Aviv, 1936) 3:16. This is apparently unrelated to his own unpublished treatise entitled *Orekh Yamim* on customs and ethics to which Hagiz referred in Elijah Ulianov, *Birkhat Elijah*, p. 55r.

53. *Thesouro* (Amsterdam, 1645–47). *Orot ha-Mizvot* (Amsterdam, 1753), published posthumously. *Eleh ha-Mizvot* was used in a text for Italian Jewish school children. Gedalya Teikus, *Torat Kattan* (Amsterdam, 1765).

54. *Eleh ha-Mizvot*, intro, n.p.

55. Isaac Leon, *Megillat Esther* (Venice, 1592). The defense of Maimonides is mentioned in *Eleh ha-Mizvot* (1727), p. 156r; it has not survived.

56. The section of *Perurei Pat HaKeMa"H* relating to customs was published in Elijah Ulianov, *Birkhat Elijah*. In it Hagiz referred, p. 56r to "A Treatise on the Observance of Customs" ("*Ma'amar Kiyyum ha-Minhagim*") and pp. 57v, 58r to a "Treatise on Custom," ("*Ma'amar ha-Minhagim*"). Perhaps these names refer to the same work, which has not survived. Hagiz interspersed remarks about custom throughout all his works.

57. Benayahu, "*Sefer Ez Hayim* of Rabbi Samson Morpurgo" (Heb.) *AS*, 6/7:129; Morpurgo, Responsa *Shemesh Zedaka* (Venice, 1743) #4, p. 26r; Lampronte, *Pahad Yizhak*, 2:86, s.v. "*dagim*."

58. The question in *Responsa Hakham Zevi* (Amsterdam, 1710) does not state

who brought the question. I have found a much lengthier version of the dispute in Spanish, ms. Columbia University.

59. Eleh ha-Mizvot (1727), pp. 4r; 9v, 15v; *Orah Mishor* (Amsterdam, 1709); *Birkhat Elijah*, p. 55b; *HK*, 1, #4.

60. Moses Hagiz, *HK*, 2, #139.

61. Eleh ha-Mizvot, 1727, p. 22v; *Birkhat Elijah*, p. 55v. Hagiz occasionally felt compelled to attack those customs which he felt were undignified or rooted in error, e.g., *Birkhat Elijah*, p. 56r. For a case in which Hagiz amended a midrashic text in a work he edited in order to confound the calculators of the end, see Benayahu, *AS* 2:160, n. 110.

62. *Eleh ha-Mizvot* (1727), T.P.; *Eleh Mas'ei* (Altona, 1738), p. 3v.

63. Jacob Barnai, "Government of the Jewish Community of Jerusalem in the Mid-Eighteenth Century" (Heb.), *Shalem*, (1974) 1:271–315.

64. *Be'er Tob* (Altona, 1737).

65. Hagiz' approbation to Solomon Geiger, *Kerem Shelomo* (Hamburg, 1738).

66. On the Jewish communities of France in the eighteenth century, see Zebi Loker, "From Converso Congregation to Holy Community—the Bordeaux Jewish Community in the Eighteenth Century." (Heb.) *Zion* (1977) 62 (1–2) :49–94. On the writing of communal ordinances by rabbis see Salo Baron, *The Jewish Community*, (Phila., 1938), 2:30.

67. Isaac Lampronte, *Pahad Yizhak*. Vol. 5. (Livorno, 1839), p. 109v, s.v. "Mekhira al menat le-hahzir." Jacques Decourcelle, *La Condition des Juifs de Nice aux 17e et 18e siecles*, (Paris, 1923), pp. 229ff.

68. Azulai, *Shem ha-Gedolim*, s.v. Moses Hagiz. The proofreader's words are ambiguous, and it is unclear from the Hebrew text whether the scholar Moses who passed away was in fact Hagiz. The discussion within that paragraph of Hagiz' halakhic position is not sufficient basis for this identification. The reference to "HaRab ha-*Leket* z"l (= zikhrono li-berakha, may his memory be a blessing) seems more certain. Abraham Joshua Heschel, "R. Gershon Kutover: His Life and his Emigration to the Land of Israel," (Heb.) *HUCA* (1950–52) 23 (2):49, n. 121 was the first to refer to *Malkhi ba-Kodesh* (Salonika, 1749) as a source for Hagiz' date. [The reference given, to p. 127 is a misprint; the correct page is 157.] Nevertheless, the other evidence does not sustain this date conclusively.

Letter of Reischer in Jacob Emden *Sefat Emet*, (Jerusalem, 1971, repr. of Altona, 1751) p. 41; (Lvov, 1877) p. 12b. I thank Professor Leiman for bringing this source to my attention. JTS Ms. #2198, Commentary to *Idrah Zuta*, p. 254. The copyist, R. Sabbatai b. Zebi Hirsch, thanked Moses Hagiz for providing him with the original. Dated Rashkov, 1752.

ברוך נותן ליעף כח ולאין אונים עצמה ירבה אנס"ו נשלם בזה הפירוש בע"ה
אשר נמצא פירוש זה בגנזי כתבי קודש של הרב החכם הכולל המפורסם מוהרר
משה חאגיז נר"ו וזיכה הרבים ונתן להעתיקו כמ"ש הון ועושר בביתו וכו'
זה הכותב ספרים ומשאילן לאחרים והועתק זה הספר ע"י המעתיק . . . לסדר
ולפרט וידבר משה אל ראש"י [1752] המטות לפ"פה קק ראשקוב.

69. Jacob Katz, "The Possible Connection of Sabbatianism, *Haskalah* and Reform Judaism," *Studies . . . Presented to Alexander Altmann* (Heb.) (Alabama, 1979), pp. 83–100.

70. Azriel Shohet, *Im Hilufei Tekuphot* (Jerusalem, 1960), is the only account of the early nineteenth century to cite the precedent of Hagiz, although in a somewhat different context. See esp. ch. 5, "The Attitude toward Torah Scholars and Communal Leadership."

Glossary

[Some of these terms have other meanings in different contexts. I have given only those definitions relevant to the present work.]

Bet din: court of Jewish law
Bet midrash: house of study
Dayyan: rabbinic judge
Hakham: sage; rabbi
Halakhah: Jewish law
Haskamah, pl. haskamot: approbation
Hebrah, pl. hebrot: a voluntary society, fraternity, or study circle
Herem: ban of excommunication
Hesger: a small institution devoted to advanced Torah study
Kehillah pl. kehillot: the Jewish community
Ma'amad: lay council
Maggid: a mentor angel
Parnassim: lay leaders of the Jewish community
Semikhah: rabbinic ordination
Shekhinah: the presence of God; in Kabbalah, the feminine principle within the Godhead
Takkanah: ordinance
Tikkun: restoration; a prayer to bring about the cosmic restoration
Yihud: a brief prayer recited to effect the union of the divine elements

Bibliography

1. MANUSCRIPTS

Oxford, Bodleian Library. Cat. Neubauer #1900. Nehemiah Hayon, *Nahash Ne-hoshet*.

Oxford, Bodleian Library. Cat. Neubauer #1180. Letter of Hagiz to Wolf; Nieto and Cantarini to Unger.

Oxford, Bodleian Library. Cat. Neubauer #2187. Joseph Prager, ed. *Gahalei Esh*.

Jerusalem, Central Archives for the History of the Jewish People, #AHW/85a. Pinkas ha-Kheruzim, AHW, 1724–1734.

N.Y., Columbia University Library. X893 M29. Commentary to *Genesis*, perhaps by Raphael Mordekhai Malkhi.

N.Y., Columbia University Library. X893 J78. Judah Briel, The Contentions of the Christians, Refuted.

N.Y., Columbia University Library. X893 SA7. Query of Isaac Sasportas to Zebi Ashkenazi.

Jerusalem, Jewish National and University Library [JNUL]. Ms. Heb. 4 551. Pinkas Verona (1653–1706).

Jerusalem, JNUL. MS 8° 1500. Sermons of Moses ibn Habib, 1669–1672.

Jerusalem, JNUL. MS 8° 3131. Moses Hagiz, *Leket HaKeMaH*, H.M.

Jerusalem, JNUL. MS 8° 5512. Jacob Zemah. Kol be-Ramah.

N.Y. Jewish Theological Seminary [JTS]. MS 4022, Luzzatto Letters.

N.Y., JTS. MS 2198, #5. Commentary to *Idrah Zuta*, copied from a manuscript belonging to Moses Hagiz. Rashkov, 1752.

Budapest. Kaufmann Collection, #254. Documents pertaining to Hayon Controversy.

Jerusalem, JNUL #8° 2001, fol. 19r–26v. Responsum of Moses Galante.

Jerusalem, JNUL #38766. David da Silva, *Sefer Peri Hadass.*
Jerusalem, Central Archives, Ms. #HM 2803, Escamot e Statutos do KK Liorne 1655–1687.

2. PRINTED WORKS OF MOSES HAGIZ

Ed., Intro., David ibn Zimra, *Or Kadmon.* Venice, 1703.
Epilogue: "le-Ma'alat Hazkarat ha-Teshuba."
Intro., Moses Galante, *Korban Hagigah.* Venice, 1704.
Ed., Intro. Jacob Hagiz *Halakhot Ketanot.* Venice, 1704.
Sefat Emet. Amsterdam, 1707.
Ed., Intro., *ha-Idrot ha-Kedoshot.* Amsterdam, 1708.
Preface, Moses Galante, *Zebah ha-Shelamim.* Amsterdam, 1708.
Epilogue, Jacob Hagiz, *Orah Mishor.* Amsterdam, 1709. [In Bodleian copy only.]
"Hilkhot Missim." Amsterdam, 1709.
Ed., *Mafteah ha-Zohar.* Amsterdam, 1710.
LeKet HaKeMa"H. On Nazirite Law. Venice, 1704. Appendix to *HK.*
—— Y.D. Amsterdam, 1707.
—— O.H. Amsterdam, 1709.
—— E.H. Hamburg, 1719. T.P. = 1711.
—— Mishnah, Wandsbeck, 1726.
Intro., David ibn Zimra. *Magen David.* Amsterdam, 1713.
Sheber Posh'im. London, 1714. (T.P. reads: Amsterdam).
Milhama la-Shem ve-Hereb la-Shem. Amsterdam, 1714.
Preface, Jacob Hagiz, *Petil Tekhelet.* London, 1714.
Eleh ha-Mizvot. Amsterdam, 1713; repr. Wandsbeck, 1727.
Me'orer Zikkaron u-Measef ha-Mahanot. Altona, 1726.
Lehishat Saraf. Hanau, 1726.
Perurei Pat HaKeMaH, Daniel. Wandsbeck, 1727.
Perurei Pat HaKeMaH, appendix to Elijah Ulianov, *Birkhat Elijah,* Wandsbeck, 1727.
Zeror ha-Hayim. Wandsbeck, 1728–1731.
Mishnat Hakhamim. Wandsbeck, 1733.
Shetei ha-Lehem. Wandsbeck, 1733.
Parshat Eileh Mas'ei. Altona, 1738.

3. OTHER WORKS CITED

Aboab, Immanuel. *Nomologia, o discursos legales.* Amsterdam, 1629.
Aboab, Samuel. *Sefer ha-Zikhronot.* N.P., N.D.
Almanzi, I. "RaMHa"L." *Kerem Hemed* (1838) 3:112–169.
Amarillo, Solomon. *Kerem Shelomo.* Salonika, 1719.
Ashkenazi, Zebi. *She'elot u-Teshubot Hakham Zebi.* Amsterdam, 1710.

Assaf, Simha. *Mekorot le-Toledot ha-Hinukh be-Yisrael.* Tel Aviv: Dvir, 1936; 1954.

Azulai, Abraham. *Zohorei Hamah.* Venice, 1655.

Azulai, Hayim Yosef David. *Shem ha-Gedolim.* Livorno, 1798.

—— *Ma'agal Tob.* ed. A. Freimann. Berlin, Mekize Nirdamim, 1921–34.

Barnai, Jacob. "The Leadership of the Jewish Community in Jerusalem in the mid-18th Century." (Hebrew) *Shalem* (1974) 1:271–315.

—— "On the History of Sabbatianism and its Role in Jewish Life in the Ottoman Empire." (Hebrew) *Pe'amim,* (1980), vol. 3.

Baron, Salo. "A Controversy in the Kehillot of Verona according to a Responsum of Mordekhai Bassan in the late 17th Century." (Hebrew) *Samuel Krausz Jubilee Volume.* Jerusalem (1936), pp. 222–225.

—— *The Jewish Community.* 3 Vol., Phila., Jewish Publication Society, 1942.

Barzilay, Isaac. *Yoseph Shlomo Delmedigo.* Leiden, Brill, 1974.

Basilea, Abiad Sar-Shalom. *Emunat Hakhamim.* Mantua, 1730.

Bassan, Israel Benjamin. *Todat Shelamim.* Venice, 1741; 1791.

Ben-Zebi, Yizhak. *Erez Yisrael ve-Yishuva be-Yemei hashilton ha-Ottomani.* Jerusalem, Mossad Bialik, 1955.

Benayahu, Meir. "Letters of R. Samuel Aboab, R. Moses Zacut and Their Circle Concerning Erez Israel." (Hebrew) *Yerushalaim* (1955), vol. 2/5.

—— "Correspondence between Abraham Cuenque and Judah Briel." (Hebrew) *Sinai* (1953), vol. 32.

—— "Correspondence between the Ashkenazic Kehilla of Jerusalem and R. David Oppenheim." (Hebrew) *Jerusalem Quarterly* (1950), vol. 3.

—— "The Great Apostasy." (Hebrew) *Sefunot* 14:103–104.

—— "The Hebrew Books Printed in Verona." (Hebrew) *Sinai* (1954) 34:174–181.

—— "Hidusha shel ha-Semikha be-Zefat." *Baer Jubilee Volume.* Jerusalem, 1961, pp. 248–269.

—— "The Holy Society of R. Judah Hasid." (Hebrew) *Sefunot* (1960) 3–4:131–182.

—— *Ha-Rav HID"A.* Jerusalem, Mossad HaRav Kook, 1959.

—— *Haskamah u-Reshut be-Defusei Venezia.* Ramat Gan, Ben-Zvi Institute and Mossad HaRav Kook, 1971.

—— "Information Concerning the Ties Between Sages of Erez Israel and the Sages of Italy." (Hebrew) *Sinai* (Nisan 1954) 35:55–66.

—— "Information on the Printing and Distribution of Hebrew Books in Italy." (Hebrew) *Sinai,* vol. 34.

—— "Italian Documents Relating to the Destruction of the Safed Kehilla." (Hebrew) *Erez Yisrael* (1954), vol. 3.

—— "The Key to Understanding Documents on the Sabbatian Movement in Jerusalem." (Hebrew) *Studies in Mysticism and Religion Presented to Gershom Scholem.* Jerusalem, 1967.

—— *Kitbei ha-Kabbalah shel RaMHa"L.* Jerusalem: Menahem Press, 1979.

—— "The Maggid of RaMHa"L." (Hebrew) *Sefunot* (1961), vol. 5.

—— "A Poem Composed by R. I. Bassan for the Wedding of his Disciple." (Hebrew) *Dabar* (1978), vol. 4.

—— "The Polemical Writings of R. Samson Morpurgo Against the Priest Benetelli." (Hebrew) *aS* (June 1980) 8:87–94.

—— "R. Abraham ibn Hananiah." (Hebrew) *KS* (1944) 21:313–315.

—— "Reports from Italy and Holland concerning the Beginning of the Sabbatian Movement." (Hebrew) *Erez Israel* (1956) 4:194–205.

—— "R.Samson Morpurgo." (Hebrew) *Sinai* (1979) 84 (3–4).

—— "Sabbatian Information from the Notebooks of R. Benjamin HaKohen and R. Abraham Rovigo." (Hebrew) *Michael* (1972), vol. 1.

—— "Safed Ordinances to Exempt Scholars from Taxes." (Hebrew) *Sefunot* (1963), vol. 8.

—— "Shebu'at RaMHa"L Lahdol mi-Lehaber Sefarim Al-Pi 'Maggid,' Mahuta ve-Toza'oteha." *Zion* (1977) 42 (1–2).

—— "The Status of the Sabbatian Movement in Jerusalem." (Hebrew) *Salo Baron Jubilee Volume*, Jerusalem, AAJR, 1974, Vol. 3, pp. 41–70.

—— "The Testimony of R. Elijah Ashkenazi of Safed on the Sabbatianism of R. Hayim Malakh and R. Judah Hasid." *Erez Israel* (1971) 10:67–71. ——

"Three Sages of Jerusalem." (Hebrew) *A.Y. Kook Memorial Volume*. Jerusalem, 1945.

—— "Toward a History of Study Halls in Seventeenth Century Jerusalem." (Hebrew) *HUCA* (1948) 21:1–25.

—— "Works written and Works Published by R. Moses Hagiz." *AS* (1976–1979) vols. 2–5.

—— *Yehasim she-ben Yehudai Yavan le-Yehudei Italiah.* Tel Aviv, HaMachon Le-Heker ha-Tefuzot, 1980.

Ben-Menahem, Naphtali, ed. Isaac Aboab, *Menorat ha-Maor.* Jerusalem, Mossad HaRav Kook, 1953.

Ben-Sasson, Hayim H. "The Generation of the Spanish Exiles on its Fate." *Zion* (1961) N.S. 26:23–64.

Beinart, Hayim. "Fez, A Center of Return to Judaism in the XVIth Century." (Hebrew) *Sefunot* (1964) 8:319–334.

Berliner, A. *Censure und Confiscation Hebraischer Bucher im Kirchenstaate.* Berlin, 1891.

Bernheimer, Carlo. "Some New Contributions to Abraham Cardoso's Biography." *JQR*, (Oct. 1927).

Bettan, Israel. "The Sermons of Azariah Figo." *HUCA* (1930), vol. 7.

Bleich, Judith. "Hakham Zebi as Chief Rabbi of the Ashkenazic Community of Amsterdam, 1710–1714." M.A., Yeshiva University, 1965.

Boton, Abraham. *Edut be-Ya'akob.* Salonika, 1720.

Brody, H. *Metek Sefata'im.* Berlin, 1892.

Cantarini, Isaac. "Der Rabbinische Rationalismus: Eine Unterredung des Grafen Gabriel (Tureson) von Oxenstirn mit dem Rabbiner Isac Vita Cantarini aus Padua." Transl. Samuel Modlinger. Wien, 1899.

—— *Et Kez.* Amsterdam, 1710.

Castro, Jacob. *Oholei Jacob.* Livorno, 1783.

Cohen, Boaz. "A List of Authors of Responsa Printed in the Pahad Yizhak." *Festschrift fur Aron Freimann.* Marx and Meyer, ed. Berlin, 1935. 141–143.

Cooperman, Bernard. *Trade and Settlement: The Establishment and Development of the Jewish Communities in Livorno and Pisa (1591–1626).* Dissertation, Harvard, 1976.

Cordovero, Moses. "Enquiries Concerning Angels." *Malakhei Elyon* ed. Reuben Margolies. Jerusalem, Mossad HaRav Kook, 1964.

Dan, Joseph. *Sifrut ha-Musar ve-ha-Derush.* Jerusalem, Keter, 1975.

Dias Brandon, Raphael. *Orot ha-Mizvot.* Amsterdam, 1753.

—— *Emek Binyamin.* Amsterdam, 1753.

Dob Ber of Pressburg. *Be'er Tob.* Altona, 1737.

Duckesz, E. *Iva le-Moshav.* Jaroslav, 1903.

Duschinsky, Koppel. *Toledot R. David Oppenheimer.* Budapest, 1922.

Eisenstadt, Meir. *Panim Meirot.* Amsterdam, 1715.

Eisenstein, Judah David. *Ozar Vikuhim* N.Y., 1928.

Emmanuel, I.S. "Hakam David Lopes Jesurun and his Journey to E.I." *Minha le-Abraham (Elmaleh).* Jerusalem (1959) pp. 90–92.

—— "Documents Related to the Nehemia Hayon Controversy in Amsterdam." *Sefunot* (1965) 9:211–246.

Emden, Jacob. *Beit Yonatan ha-Sofer.* Altona, 1762.

—— *Edut be-Ya'akob.* Altona, 1756.

—— *Megillat Sefer.* Warsaw, 1897.

—— *Mor u-Keziah.* Altona, 1761.

—— *Sefer Hitabkut.* Lvov, 1870.

—— *Shebirat Luhot ha-Aben.* Zolkiew, 1755.

—— *She'ilat Ya'abez.* Altona, 1737.

—— *Torat ha-Kena'ot.* Amsterdam, 1752; Lvov-Lemberg, 1870.

Enriques Ribera, F. *Viage de Jerusalem.* Abad, 1733.

Epstein, Isidore. *The Responsa of R. Simon ben Zemah Duran as a Source of the History of the Jews in North Africa.* New York, 1930.

Ergas, Joseph. *Tokhahat Megulah ve-ha-Zad Nahash.* London, 1715.

—— *Shomer Emunim.* Amsterdam, 1736.

—— *She'elot u-Teshubot Diberei Yosef.* Livorno, 1742.

Eybeschutz, Jonathan. *Luhot ha-Edut.* Altona, 1755.

Faraji, Jacob. *Responsa of MaHaRi"F.* Alexandria, 1901.

Farine, A. "Charity and Study Societies in Europe of the Sixteenth-Eighteenth Centuries." *JQR* (1973) 16–47:164–175.

Fine, Laurence. "Maggidic Revelation in the Teachings of Isaac Luria." *Mystics,*

Philosophers and Politicians: Essays in Honor of Alexander Altmann, ed. Jehuda Reinharz and Daniel Swetschinski. North Carolina, 1982.

Frances, Immanuel. *Diwan le-R. Immanuel ben David Frances*. (Tel Aviv, 1932).

—— "Chronicle of Sabbatai Zebi and Nathan Ashkenazi." *Kobez al Yad*. (1885) O.S., 1.

Frances, Jacob. *Kol Shirei Ya'acob Frances*. Jerusalem, 1969. ed. Penina Naveh.

—— "Zebi Mudah." ed. M. Mortara *Kobez al Yad*. (1885) O.S. 1:97–128.

Franco Mendes, David. *Memorias do Estabelecimento*. Amsterdam, 1975.

Freimann, A. ed. *Inyanei Shabtai Zebi: Sammelband Kleiner Schriften uber Sabbatai Zebi und dessen Anhänger*. Berlin, Hebrah Mekizei Nirdamim, 1912.

Friedberg, B. *History of Hebrew Typography in Italy, Spain, Portugal and the Orient*. Antwerp, 1934.

Friedman, Menahem. "New Documents Relating to the Hayon Controversy." *Erez Israel*, 1971, 10, pp. 237–239.

Galante, Abraham. *Nouveax Documents sur Sabbetai Sevi*. Istanbul, 1935.

Galante, Moses. *Tehillat Hokhma*. Verona, 1647. repr. Amsterdam, 1709.

—— *Kehillat Ya'akob*. Safed, 1578. repr. Jerusalem, 1977.

—— *Mafteah ha-Zohar*. Venice, 1566.

Galante, Moses of Damascus. *Sefer Berakh Moshe*. Livorno, 1809.

Galante, Yedidiah. *Hidushei Galante*. Sdilkov, 1836.

Gaon, Moses David. *Yehudei ha-Mizrah be-Erez Israel*. Jerusalem, 1935.

Garmizan, Samuel. *Sefer Mishpitei Zedek*. Jerusalem, 1945.

Gedaliah of Semiaticz. *Sha'alu Shelom Yerushalaim*. Berlin, 1716. repr. *Reshumot* (1919) 2, O.S.

Gediliah, Abraham. *Berit Abraham*. Livorno, 1650–52.

Gerber, Haim. "Jews and Money Lending in the Ottoman Empire." *JQR* (1981) 72(2):100–118.

Gerber, Jane. *Jewish Society in Fez, 1450–1700*. Leiden, Brill, 1980.

Ghirondi, M.S. "Toledot Rabbanei Padua." *Kerem Hemed* (1838) 3:89–96.

—— "RaMHa"L." *Kerem Hemed* (1836) 2:54–67.

Ginzburg, Simon. *The Life and Works of Moses Hayim Luzatto*. Phila., 1931; repr. Conn. 1975.

—— *RaMHa"L u-Benei Doro: Osef Iggerot u-Te'udot*. Tel Aviv, 1937.

—— "Stumbling Blocks: On Nehemiah HaKohen of Ferrara who Apostatized." (Hebrew) *Bizaron* (1942) 7(3):205–212.

Goetschel, Roland. "La Notion de Simsum dans le *Somer Emunim* de Joseph Ergaz." *Hommage a Georges Vajda*. Louvain, 1980. 385–396.

Goldstein, David. "A Possible Autograph of R. Moses b. Mordechai Galante." *Studies in Bibliography and Booklore* (1980) 3:17–19.

Gollancz, Herman. "Anglo-Judaica." *Transactions of the Jewish Historical Society of England* (1908–10) 6:56–87.

Graetz, Heinrich. *Diberei Yemei Yisrael*. Warsaw, Ahiassaf, 1913.

Grajewski, Pinhas. "Two Historical Documents Pertaining to the Jewish Settlement in Safed, 1612 and 1778." *mi-Ginzei he-'Avar*. Jerusalem, 1929.

Haberman, Abraham. "'mi-Sihat Hulin shel Talmidei Hakhamim' of R. Moses Hagiz." *Sinai*, (1948) 12(8–10):89–98.

—— "Towards a History of Anti-Sabbatian Polemic." *Kobez al Yad*, 3 (N.S.) (1940) 187–215.

ibn Habib, Moses. *Get Pashut*. Constantinople, 1719.

HaKohen, Ephraim. *Sha'ar Ephraim*. Sulzbach, 1688.

HaKohen, Joseph. *Diberei Yosef*. Venice, 1710.

Hagiz, Jacob. transl. Isaac Aboab. *Almenara de la Luz*. Livorno, 1656; Amsterdam, 1708.

—— *Dinei Birkhot ha-Shahar, Keriat Shema, u-Tefillah ve-Dinei Tefillot Shabat u-Tefillot Mo'ed, ve-Hilchot Birkhat Kohanim*. Verona, 1647.

—— *Ein Yisrael*, ed. Jacob ibn Habib, Verona, 1645.

—— *Ez ha-Hayim*. Verona, 1645; Berlin, 1716.

—— *Halakhot Ketanot*. Venice, 1704.

—— *Korban Minhah*. Venice, 1704.

—— *Orah Mishor*. Verona, 1645; Amsterdam, 1709.

—— *Petil Tekhelet*, Venice, 1652.

—— *Sefer Keritut*. Amsterdam, 1709.

—— *Sefer Zebed Tob; be-Shem Zikhron le-Benei Yisrael Yekhone*. Vilna, 1837.

—— *Zikaron le-Benei Yisrael*. Epilogue to *Petil Tekhelet*, Venice, 1652; London 1714.

Hagiz, Samuel. *Debar Shemuel*. Venice, 1596.

Halevi Judah. *Kuzari*. transl. Jacob Abendana. Amsterdam, 1663.

Halevi, Mordechai. *Sefer Darkhei Noam*. Venice, 1697.

Halperin, Israel. ed. *Pinkas Va'ad Arba Arazot*. Jerusalem, Mossad Bialik, 1945.

Hartstein, M. *Shalshelet Zahav*. Piotrkow, 1931.

Havlin, Shlomo Zalman. "Toward a History of Yeshivot and Sages in Jerusalem in the Late Seventeenth and Early Eighteenth Centuries." (Hebrew) *Shalem* (1976) 2:117–130.

Hayon, Nehemiah Hiya. *Diberei Nehemiah*. Berlin, 1713.

—— "Iggeret Shebukin." Amsterdam, 1714.

—— *Moda'a Rabah*. London, 1714.

—— *Oz le-Elohim u-Bet Kodesh ha-Kodashim*. Amsterdam, 1714.

—— *Raza de-Yihuda*. Venice, 1711.

—— *Shalhebet Yah*. Amsterdam, 1714.

Heksher, Samuel Zanvil. *Livyat Hen*. Altona, 1733.

Herling, Israel. "On the Secret Doctrines of N.H. Hayon." *Amanah*, (1939) 1:259–274.

—— "Handwritten Notes of Nehemiah Hiya Hayon to Esh Dat of R. David Nieto." *KS* (1948–49) 15:130–135.

Heyd, Uriel. "The Jews of Erez-Israel in the late Seventeenth Century." (Hebrew) *Yerushahaim*, Peress Volume (1953) 173–184.

Hidushei Halakhot al Gittin. Wandsbeck, 1731.

Hirsch, Max Menko. *Frucht vom Baum des Lebens: Ozar Perot Ez Hayim.* Berlin-Antwerp, 1936.

Hirschberg, H.Z. *Toledot ha-Yehudim be-Afrika ha-Zefonit.* Jerusalem, Mossad Bialik, 1965.

Horebot Yerushalaim. Venice, 1637, repr. Jerusalem, 1927.

Horowitz, Eliot. "A Jewish Youth Confraternity in Seventeenth Century Italy." *Italia*, 5, 1–2, (1985).

Idel, Moshe. "Iyunim be-Shitato shel Ba'al Sefer ha-Meshib." *Sefunot* (1983) 2, n.s.:185–266.

Israel, Moses. *Mas'at Moshe.* Constantinople, 1742.

Isserles, Moses. *She'elot u-Teshubot.* Amsterdam, 1711.

Jaffe, Israel. *Ohr Israel.* Frankfurt, 1702.

Jeshurun, Isaac. *Panim Hadashot.* Venice, 1651.

Kahana, David. *Toledot ha-Mekuballim ha-Shabta'im ve-ha-Hasidim.* Odessa, Moriah, 1913. Repr. Jerusalem, Makor, 1970.

Kahana, Samuel Fievush. *Leket Shemuel.* Venice, 1694.

Kaplan, Yoseph. *Mi-Nazrut le-Yahadut.* Jerusalem, Magnes Press, 1984.

Katz, Jacob. "The Semikha Controversy in Safed." *Zion* (1951) 16(3–4):28–45.

—— *Masoret u-Mashber.* Jerusalem, Mossad Bialik, 1958.

—— "On the Question of the Relationship between Haskalah and Reform." *Studies in Jewish Religious and Intellectual History: Presented to Alexander Altmann,* Siegfried Stein and Raphael Loewe, ed. Alabama: University of Alabama Press, 1979.

Katz, Solomon Zalman. *Binyan Shelomo.* Frankfurt, 1713.

—— *Sha'arei Torah.* Hamburg, 1718.

Kaufmann, David. "Contributions a la Biographie de Mose Hayim Luzatto, Yekutiel Gordon et Moses Hages." *REJ* (1891) 23:256–264.

—— "Correspondence of R. Gabriel Eskeles and R. Jacob Aboab," *ha-Hoker.* (1894) 2:13–15.

—— "La Lutte de R. Naftali Cohen Contre Hayyoun." *REJ* (1898) 36:256–286; (1899) 37:274–283.

Kobo, Joseph. *She'elot u-Teshubot Gib'eot Olam.* Salonika, 1784.

Kohen, Benjamin. *Responsa RaBa"Kh.* Jerusalem, 1970.

Kohen, Tobias. *Ma'asei Tobiah.* Venice, 1707; Jessnitz, 1721.

Kornbluth, Shraga. "An Unknown Introduction to a Concealed Edition of Moses Hagiz' Leket HaKeMaH." (Heb.) *Alei Sefer* (1981) 9:115–129.

Knox, Ronald A. *Enthusiasm: A Chapter in the History of Religion with Special Reference to the XVII and XVIII Centuries,* N.Y., Oxford University Press, 1950.

Kurzweil, Barukh. *Ha-Ma'avak al Erkhei ha-Yahadut.* Jerusalem, 1969.

Lampronte, Isaac. *Pahad Yizhak.* Lyck, 1840.

Lachover, F. *Al Gevul ha-Yashan ve-ha-Hadash.* Jerusalem, 1951.

Land-Sofer, Jonah. *Responsa Me'il Zedakah.* Prague, 1756.

Landau, Luis. "The Attitude of R. Jacob Culi towards Sabbatianism." (Hebrew) *Pe'amim* (1983) 15:58–66.

Laras, Joseph. "The Family of Mujajon in Ancona." (Hebrew) *Sefunot*, 12:255–270.

Leibovich, Nehemiah. "Mahazot RaMHa"L ve-ha-Zohar." *Zikhron le-Yehuda* [*Blau*]. Budapest, 1938, pp. 182–185.

Levi b. Solomon of Brody. *Bet Levi.* Zolkiew, 1732.

Liebes, Yehudah. "The Ideological Basis of the Hayon Controversy." (Heb.) *Proceedings of the Eighth World Congress.* Jerusalem, 1982, pp. 129–134.

—— "The Messiah of the Zohar." (Hebrew) *ha-Ra'ayon ha-Meshihi be-Yisrael*, ed. Samuel Ram, Jerusalem, 1982, pp. 80–236.

—— "The Messianism of Jacob Emden and his Attitude to Sabbatianism." *Tarbiz.* 49:1–2.

—— "Michael Cardoso—Author of Raza de-Mehemnuta attributed to Sabbatai Zebi, and the Erroneous Attribution of 'Iggeret Magen Abraham' to Cardoso." (Hebrew) *KS* (1980) 55(3):603–616. "Appendix." *KS* (April 1981) 56(2):373–374.

—— "Sefer Zaddik Yesod 'Olam—A Sabbatian Myth." *Da'at* (1978) 1(1).

Loewe, Bezalel. *Viku'ah Mayim Hayim.* Amsterdam, 1712.

Loewe, Raphael. "The Spanish Supplement to Nieto's Esh Dath." *PAAJR* (1981) 48:267–296.

Loker, Zebi. "From Converso Congregation to Holy Community the Bordeaux Jewish Community in Eighteenth Century." (Hebrew) *Zion* (1977) 62(1–2):49–94.

Lowenstein, Leopold. "Die Familie Aboab." *MGWJ* (1904) 68(11–12):661–701.

—— *Mafteah ha-Haskamot.* Frankfurt, 1923.

Luzzato, Moses Hayim. *Hoker u-Mekubal.* Shklov, 1784.

—— *Kin'at Ha-Shem Zeba'ot.* Konigsberg, 1862.

—— *Leshon Limudim.* Mantua, 1727.

—— *Letters.* ed. S. Ginzberg, *RaMHa"L u-Benei Doro.* (See Ginzberg.)

—— *Sefer ha-Shirim.* ed. J. Zamora. Jerusalem, 1950.

—— *Sefer ha-Shirim.* ed. Klaar. Jerusalem, 1945.

—— "Shir Hanukat he-Aron." Venice, 1729.

Malkhi, Raphael Mordekhai. "Likkutim me-Peirush al ha-Torah Ketav Yad meet R.M.M." Rivlin, ed. Jerusalem, 1923.

Marx, Alexander. "Some Notes on the History of David Oppenheimer's Library." *REJ* (1926) 82:451–460.

Marx, Alexander and Margolis, eds. "Bibliographisches Verzeichnis Hebraischen Drucke in Wandsbeck, 1726–1733." *Festschrift fur Aron Freimann.* Berlin, 1935.

Maundrell, Henry. *A Journey from Aleppo to Jerusalem at Easter.* A.D. 1697. Oxford, 1714.

Meisel, Y. *Pinkas Kehillot Berlin.* Jerusalem, 1962.

Meldola, Raphael. *Mayim Rabim.* Amsterdam, 1737.

Menasseh ben Israel. *Conciliador.* Amsterdam, 1632.

—— *Sefer Nishmat Hayim.* Amsterdam, 1652.

—— *Thesouro des Dinim.* Amsterdam, 1645–47.

Modena, Leone. *Ein Yisrael*. Verona, 1645.

—— *She'elot u-Teshubot Ziknei Yehuda*. ed. S. Simonsohn. Jerusalem, 1954.

Molkho, I. and Amarillo, A. "Autobiographical Letters of Cardoso." (Hebrew) *Sefunot* (1960) (3–4).

Mondshein, Joshua. "Sefer Leket HaKeMa"H of R. Moses Hagiz—The Section on Hoshen Mishpat." (Hebrew) *AS*, 10:93–112.

Morpurgo, Samson. *Shemesh Zedaka*. Venice, 1753.

—— *Ez ha-Da'at*. Venice, 1704.

Nadav, Yael. "R. Solomon Ayllon and his Sabbatian Kabbalist Tract." *Sefunot*, (1960) 3–4:303–347.

Neubauer, Adolph. "Miscellanea Liturgica: Azharoth on the 613 Precepts." *JQR*, (1894) 6:698–709.

Nieto, David. "Letter of D.N." (Hebrew) *Ozar Tob*. Berlin, 1878, 85–86.

Nipi, Hananel, and Gerondi, M. *Toledot Gedolei Yisrael u-Geonei Italia*. Trieste, 1853.

Norwich, John Julius. *A History of Venice*. N.Y., 1982.

Nunez Torres, David. *Catalogus Librorum, quibus Usus est*. Hague, 1728.

Oppenheim, David. *She'elot u-Teshubot Nish'al David*. Jerusalem, Machon Hatam Sofer, 1972–1975.

Perahia, Aron. *Perah Matteh Aaron*. Amsterdam, 1703.

Perlmutter, M.A. *R. Jonathan Eybeschutz ve-Yahaso el ha-Shabta'ut*. Tel Aviv, 1947.

Pinkus, Ben Zion. "The Portuguese Community of Hamburg and its Leadership in the Seventeenth Century." M.A. Thesis, Bar Ilan University, (1983).

Popper, William. *The Censorship of Hebrew Books*. N.Y., 1969.

Probst, Mendel. "On the History of the Development of Hebrew Periodicals, 1667–1920." (Hebrew) *KS*, 2:212–214.

Rankin, Oliver Shaw. *Jewish Religious Polemic*. Edinburg, 1956.

Reischer, Jacob. *She'elot u-Teshubot Shebut Jacob*. Halle, 1710.

Responsa Peri Ez Hayim. Amsterdam, 1728.

Rivlin, Y. "The Proposal of R. Raphael Mordekhai Malkhi to Establish a Yeshiva in Jerusalem as a center for Jewry." (Hebrew) *Yerushalaim: Mehkarei Erez Israel*, (1955) 2/5:187–194.

Roth, Cecil. "Forced Baptisms in Italy." *JQR*, (1936) 27: 117–131.

—— "Haham David Nieto." *Essays and Portraits in Anglo-Jewish History*, Phila., 1962, pp. 113–129.

—— "The Jews of Jerusalem in the Seventeenth Century: An English Account." *TJHSE*, 2.

—— *Menasseh ben Israel*. Philadelphia, 1934.

—— "Notes sur les Marranes de Livourne." *REJ* (1930) 89:1–27.

—— "Stemmi di *famiglie Ebraiche*." *Aryeh Leone Carpi Memorial Volume*. Jerusalem, 1967.

Ruderman, David. "The Founding of a Gemilut Hasadim Society in Ferrara in 1515." *AJS Review*, (1976) 1:233–268.

Sasportas, Jacob. *Edut be-Ya'akob.* N.P., 1672.
—— *Epilogue to Menasseh ben Israel, Sefer Nishmat Hayim.* Amsterdam, 1652.
—— The "Letters of R. Jacob Sasportas against the Lay Leaders of Livorno, 1681." (Hebrew) I. Tishby, ed. *Kobez al Yad,* (1946) 4(4):143–159.
—— *Ohel Jacob.* Amsterdam, 1737.
—— *Toledot Jacob.* Amsterdam, 1652.
—— *Zizat Nobel Zebi.* ed. I. Tishby. Jerusalem, Mossad Bialik, 1954.
Schechter, Solomon. *Studies in Judaism.* 2nd Series, 1908.
Scholem, Gershom. "The Attitude of the Rabbis toward Sabbatianism." (Hebrew) *Zion: Quarterly,* (1948–49) 47–62.
—— *be-Ikvot Mashiah.* Jerusalem: Schoken, 1944.
—— "The Covenant of Unity among AR"I's Disciples." (Hebrew) *Zion,* (1940) 5:133–160.
—— "Iggeret Magen Abraham." *Kobez al Yad,* 2,
—— "Information on Sabbatians in the Notebooks of Eighteenth Century Missionaries." (Hebrew) *Zion,* 9.
—— *Kabbalah.* N.Y., 1974.
—— "The Life and Works of R. Jacob Zemah." (Hebrew) *KS,* (1950) 26(2):185–194.
—— *Mehkarim u-Mekorot le-Toledot ha-Shabta'ut ve-Gilguleha.* Jerusalem, Mossad Bialik, 1974.
—— *Sabbatai Sebi: The Mystical Messiah.* Princeton, 1973.
—— "The Sabbatian Movement in Poland." *Beit Yisrael be-Polin.* I. Heilpern, ed. Jerusalem, 1953, pp. 36–76.
—— "Sefer-Mussar—By R. Jacob Zemah?" (Hebrew) *KS,* (1946) 22(3–4):308–310.
Schwartz, Zechariah. "A letter of Jacob Sasportas to the Yeshiva of Hamburg." *Alim,* (1935) 2.
Sefer Kol Bokhim. Venice, 1589.
Sefer Likutei ha-Pardes. Venice, 1519, repr. Amsterdam, 1715.
Shazar, Zalman. *The Messianic Hope for the Year 1740.* (Hebrew) Jerusalem, 1970.
Shohat, Azriel. *Im Hilufei Tekuphot.* Jerusalem, 1960.
da Silva, Hezekiah. *Peri Hadash.* Amsterdam, 1692.
Sonino, G. "Storia della tipographia ebraica in Livorno, 1650–1856." Turin, 1912.
Sonne, Isaiah. "Building Blocks: Documents Pertaining to RaMHa"L and his Circle." *Sefer ha-Shanah le-Yehudei America.* (Hebrew) (1935): 218–224.
—— "Building Blocks: RaMHa"L's Opponents in Venice." (Hebrew) *Sefer ha-Shanah le-Yehudei America,* (1938):154–162.
—— "Building Blocks toward a History of Jews in Italy: Documents and Research Pertaining to the Circles of RaMHa"L and R.I. Lampronte." (Hebrew) *Horeb,* (Nov. 1941) 6:76–114.
—— "Cornerstone for a History of the Jews in Verona." (Hebrew) *Zion,* 3, 3, (1938) 145–150.

—— "On the History of Sabbatianism in Italy." (Hebrew) *Marx Jubilee Volume.* N.Y., 1943.

—— "The Role of Kabbalah in the Church's Proselytization in the Seventeenth Century." (Hebrew) *Bizaron,* (1957) 36:7–12; 57–66.

—— "Toward a Biography of R. Jacob Zemah." (Hebrew) *KS,* 27, #1 (Jan. 1951) 97–106.

Sonne, Isaiah ed. "Correspondence Between R. Moses Hagiz and R. Samson Morpurgo Regarding Nehemiah Hayon and his Sect." *Kobez al Yad,* (1937) 12(2):159–196.

—— "Information on the History of the Jews in Italy." (Hebrew) *Horeb,* (Nov., 1941) 6.

Tamar, David. "History of Safed." (Hebrew) *Tarbiz,* (1957) 27:111–115.

—— "A Controversy between R. Hayim Benveniste and R. Aaron Lapapa." (Hebrew) *Tarbiz,* (1972) 61:411–423.

—— "References to the Sabbatian Movement in the Responsa of R. Hayim Benveniste." *Sinai,* (1973) 72:285–288.

Tishby, Isaiah. "A Collection of Kabbalistic Writings of RaMHa"L." (Hebrew) *KS,* (1978) 53(1):167–198.

—— "Poems and Piyyutim from RaMHa"L: From Ms. Ginzburg 745." *Molad,* (1976) 7.

—— "Prayers from R. Moses Hayim Luzatto." (Hebrew) *Molad,* (1980):122–132.

—— *Netivei Emunah u-Minut.* Jerusalem: Magnes Press, 1964.

—— "The Spread of RaMHa"L's Kabbalistic Writings in Poland and Lithuania." (Hebrew) *KS,* (Dec., 1969) 65:127–155.

Toaff, Alfredo S. *Cenni Storici Sulla Communita Ebraica e Sulla Sinagoga de Livorno.* Rome, 1955.

—— "Il Collegio Rabbinico di Livorno." Scritti in Onore de Dante Lattes, *RMI,* (April–June, 1939) 16:184–195.

—— "The Dispute of R. Jacob Sasportas and the Livorno Lay Leaders." (Hebrew) *Isaac ben Zvi Memorial Volume,* (1956) 2:167–192.

Toledano, J.M. *Ner ha-Ma'arav.* Jerusalem, 1911.

Ulianov, Elijah. *Birkhat Elijah.* Wandsbeck, 1727.

Vajda, Georges. *Un Recueil de Textes Historiques Judeo-Marocaines.* Paris, 1951.

ibn Verga, Solomon. *Sefer Shebet Yehuda.* Y. Baer, ed. Jerusalem: Mossad Bialik, 1946.

Wilhelm, Y.D., and G. Scholem. "Rabbinic Bans against Sabbatians." *KS,* (1954) 30(1):99–104.

Wilenski, Michael. *Hasidim u-Mitnaggedim.* Jerusalem, 1970.

—— "Testimony Against the Hasidim in the Polemic Literature of the Mitnaggedim." (Hebrew) *Yizhak Baer Jubilee Volume,* Jerusalem, 1960, pp. 398–408.

—— "Towards a Biography of Isaiah Bassan." (Hebrew) *KS,* (1951) 27:111–114.

—— "Who Is R. Netanel Halevi?" (Hebrew) *KS,* (Oct., 1946) 23(2):131–136.

Wirszubski, Hayim. "The Sabbatian Ideology of the Apostasy of the Messiah as stated by Nathan of Gaza and in Iggeret Magen Abraham." (Hebrew) *Zion*, (1938) 3:215–245.

—— "The Sabbatian Theology of Nathan the Prophet." (Hebrew) *Knesset*, (1943) 8:210–246.

Wolf, Johann Christoph. *Bibliotheca Hebraea.* 3, Hamburg, 1727.

—— *Notitia Karaeorum.* Hamburg, 1714.

Ya'ari, Abraham. "Hebrew Printing in Smyrna." (Hebrew) *Areshet*, 1.

—— *Masa'ot Erez Yisrael.* Tel Aviv, 1946.

—— *Sheluhehei Erez Yisrael.* Jerusalem, 1951.

—— "Yeshivot Pereira in Jerusalem and in Hebron." *Yerushalaim*, (1952) 4:185–202.

Yerushalmi, Yosef Hayim. *From Spanish Court to Italian Ghetto: Isaac Cardoso, A Study in Seventeenth Century Marranism and Jewish Apologetics.* New York, Columbia University Press, 1971.

—— Intr. Meyer Kayserling, *Biblioteca Espanola-Portugueza-Judaica.* New York: Ktav, 1971.

Yizhaki, Abraham. *Zera' Abraham.* Constantinople, 1733.

Zacuto, Moses. *Tifteh Arukh.* Venice, 1715.

Zahalon, Mordechai. *Meziz u-Meliz.* Venice, 1715.

Ze'evi, Abraham Israel. *Orim Gedolim.* Smyrna, 1758.

Zinberg, Cecile. "The Usable Dissenting Past: John Strype and Elizabethan Puritanism." *The Dissenting Tradition, Essays for Leland H. Carlson.* Athens, Ohio University Press, 1975, pp. 123–139.

Index